European Constitutionalism

European Constitutionalism redraws the perimeters in the debate on the nature of the European constitution. Offering a fresh approach to both doctrinal and theoretical issues, this book discusses general characteristics of the European constitution under the headings of relationality, perspectivism and discursiveness, and contains forays to sectoral constitutionalization in the micro- and macroeconomic, social and security dimensions. European constitutionalism must be examined in its interaction with Member State constitutionalism, which plays an essential role in channelling democratic legitimacy to the EU. Written by a leading expert in the field, this book will be of great interest to students and scholars alike.

Kaarlo Tuori is Professor of Jurisprudence and Academy Professor at the University of Helsinki. He was formerly Vice President of the Venice Commission of the Council of Europe and serves as a consulting expert on the Constitutional Law Committee at the Finnish Parliament.

Cambridge Studies in European Law and Policy

This series aims to produce original works which contain a critical analysis of the state of the law in particular areas of European law and set out different perspectives and suggestions for its future development. It also aims to encourage a range of work on law, legal institutions and legal phenomena in Europe, including 'law in context' approaches. The titles in the series will be of interest to academics; policy-makers; policy formers who are interested in European legal, commercial and political affairs; practising lawyers, including the judiciary; and advanced law students and researchers.

Books in the series

EU Enlargement and the Constitutions of Central and Eastern Europe
Anneli Albi

The European Civil Code: The Way Forward
Hugh Collins

The Limits of Legal Reasoning and the European Court of Justice
Gerard Conway

New Governance and the Transformation of European Law: Coordinating EU Social Law and Policy
Mark Dawson

Social Rights and Market Freedom in the European Constitution: A Labour Law Perspective
Stefano Giubboni

The European Convention on Human Rights: Achievements, Problems and Prospects
Steven Greer

European Broadcasting Law and Policy
Jackie Harrison and Lorna Woods

Ethical Dimensions of the Foreign Policy of the European Union: A Legal Appraisal
Urfan Khaliq

Services Liberalization in the EU and the WTO
Marcus Klamert

The Evolving European Union: Migration Law and Policy
Dora Kostakopoulou

Implementing EU Pollution Control: Law and Integration
Bettina Lange

Referendums and the European Union: A Comparative Enquiry
Fernando Mendez, Mario Mendez, Vasiliki Triga

The Constitution for Europe: A Legal Analysis
Jean-Claude Piris

The Lisbon Treaty: A Legal and Political Analysis
Jean-Claude Piris

State and Market in European Union Law
Wolf Sauter and Harm Schepel

The Transformation of Citizenship in the European Union: Electoral Rights and the Restructuring of Political Space
Jo Shaw

The European Union's Fight Against Corruption: The Evolving Policy Towards Member States and Candidate Countries
Patrycja Szarek-Mason

International Trade Disputes and EU Liability
Anne Thies

European Constitutionalism
Kaarlo Tuori

The Eurozone Crisis: A Constitutional Analysis
Kaarlo Tuori and Klaus Tuori

Brokering Europe
Antoine Vauchez

The Allocation of Regulatory Competence in the EU Emissions Trading Scheme
Josephine van Zeben

The Ethos of Europe: Values, Law and Justice in the EU
Andrew Williams

European Constitutionalism

Kaarlo Tuori

CAMBRIDGE
UNIVERSITY PRESS

CAMBRIDGE
UNIVERSITY PRESS

University Printing House, Cambridge CB2 8BS, United Kingdom

Cambridge University Press is part of the University of Cambridge.

It furthers the University's mission by disseminating knowledge in the pursuit of education, learning and research at the highest international levels of excellence.

www.cambridge.org
Information on this title: www.cambridge.org/9781107087095

First published 2015

A catalogue record for this publication is available from the British Library

Library of Congress Cataloguing in Publication data
Tuori, Kaarlo, author.
European constitutionalism / Kaarlo Tuori.
pages cm
Includes bibliographical references and index.
ISBN 978-1-107-08709-5 (hardback)
1. Constitutional law – European Union countries. 2. European Union – Constitution. 3. Constitutions – European Union countries. I. Title.
KJE4445.T86 2015
342.24 – dc23 2014046187

ISBN 978-1-107-08709-5 Hardback

Contents

Series editors' preface *page* xi
Preface xiii

Prologue 1
Examining European constitutionalism 1
A relational concept of constitution 9
Constitutional law as higher law 10
Constitutional culture and constitutional theories 15
An outline of the book 17

Part I: General characteristics

1 **Relationality** 21
Constitutional dimensions 21
Constitutional functions 28
Transnational and national constitutionalism 37

2 **Interlude: the framing juridical constitution** 45
Constituting the European legal system 45
Claiming the autonomy of European law 53
Positioning European law 59
Pre-emption as a sub-principle of supremacy 72
General principles 74

3 **Perspectivism** 78
Perspectives on legal perspectivism 78
Legal diversity 81
Legal pluralism 86
European fundamental rights pluralism 88
Conflict or dialogue? 102

4 **Discursiveness** 108
Revolutionary and evolutionary constitutionalism 108
European constitutional discourse 112
Perspectives on constitutional discourse 120

Part II: Sectoral constitutionalization

5 **The triumph of the microeconomic constitution** 127
Origins of a concept 127
The process of economic constitutionalization 136
Underlying controversies 150
The European economic constitution and national constitutions 164
Implications for the political dimension 169

6 **Mutation of the macroeconomic constitution** 174
From Rome to Maastricht 174
The Maastricht principles 178
Underlying economic assumptions 183
From crisis prevention to crisis management 187
Strengthening European economic governance 192
The new roles of the ECB 195
The constitutional basis of the Eurozone regime 199
Still a Union based on the rule of law? 209
Legitimacy concerns 217

7 **The European social constitution: between solidarity and access justice** 227
Is there a European social constitution? 227
Why does the national welfare state have primacy? 232
Restrictions on free movement 234
Extension of internal market law to welfare services 237
Welfare services for mobile workers and citizens 243
Denationalization and deterritorialization of welfare services 248
Consequences of macroeconomic constitutionalization 251
Regulatory private law 257
Two notions of justice: complementary or conflicting? 265

8 **The insecure security constitution** 269
The paradox-ridden relationship between the constitution and security 269
From Trevi to Maastricht 273
The significance of Amsterdam 278
Lisbon and after 284
From state of emergency to security 289
Freedom, security and justice 296
Security and fundamental rights 301
Constitution or anti-constitution? 312

Epilogue 319
Towards a general theory of the European constitution 319
Perspectivism of legal disciplines 340
Final comment 358

Bibliography 359
Index 373

Series editors' preface

We are delighted to welcome this important book by the Finnish jurist Kaarlo Tuori to the series *Cambridge Studies in European Law and Policy*. Tuori is one of a number of legal theorists and jurists who have turned their attention in recent years to the study of the European Union. They have acknowledged that it is a unique polity which is underpinned by a significant body of transnational law which deserves study in its own terms, as well as in comparison to other polities. The work of these jurists has enriched the field of EU legal studies considerably – just as they themselves acknowledge that their own work as legal theorists has required some rethinking in response to the challenges posed by EU law and the EU legal order. In that vein, this book is a must-read summation of Tuori's previous work within the framework of the Helsinki University Centre of Excellence in the Foundations of European Law and Polity which he directed for many years until 2013, and his own work as an Academy of Finland Professor at Helsinki University Faculty of Law.

The book has at its heart two important confrontations which frame the 'many constitutions' of Europe. The first is the more commonly written about confrontation between national constitutionalism and an emergent constitutionalization process at the European Union level. The properties of transnational law in this context represent a significant challenge to conventional legal theories concerning how multiple legal orders can and should coexist. In Part I of his book, Tuori shows how adopting a constitutional perspective which views the constitution as a relational concept (i.e. it has to be understood in terms of its relations with other legal phenomena) helps us to capture the most important features of the EU legal order in a manner which navigates between a discursive approach (describing what is) and a normative approach (postulating what ought to be). In the second part of the book, he engages with a different confrontation, and that concerns the process of sectoral constitutionalization, acknowledging that the lenses of economics, social policy and security policy could lead to the construction of very different – and competing – visions of 'Europe'.

It is the intersection of those two confrontations that Tuori handles with such dexterity. He recognizes the two simultaneous truths: that the EU is nothing unless it is understood as a transnational legal order which makes certain normative claims, but equally it is nothing unless that order is invested with certain sectoral principles, that do not always coincide effectively, as witness the conflicts between notions of freedom and solidarity which he highlights in the chapters of Part II. Navigating these choppy waters with such a deft hand, Tuori has succeeded in producing what we hope will be a significant contribution not only to the field of EU legal studies, but also to the emergent field of 'transnational law' more generally.

Jo Shaw
Laurence Gormley
October 2014

Preface

To write about European constitutionalism, aspiring to an overall portrayal, is not an easy task. There are many constitutions in Europe, and in at least two senses. First, we have the diversity and pluralism of the transnational European constitution and the national Member State constitutions. Transnational constitutionalism must always be seen in its interaction with national constitutionalism. But, as is another central premise of this book, we should speak of the transnational European constitution too in the plural. The European constitution consists of distinct constitutional dimensions; of the framing juridical and political constitutions, and of the sectoral economic, social and security constitutions. Indeed, multidimensionality is one of the distinctive features of the European constitution that set it apart from the state constitution template.

Sectoral constitutionalization lies at the very heart of European constitutionalism. Comprehensive constitutional analysis must make forays into substantive fields where constitutional scholars do not usually venture and where they may not feel particularly at home either. At the European level, policy issues are constitutionalized which in the state setting are usually left to majoritarian democracy. Even constitutional scholars must familiarize themselves with the doctrine and theory of, say, free movement and competition law. My academic background lies in legal and constitutional theory but not in EU law. I am not interested in internal market law or the social or security dimension of the EU for its own sake. I am interested in EU law and the EU constitution as a legal and constitutional theorist, my starting point being that today relevant legal or constitutional theory cannot be pursued if transnational law in general or European law in particular are not taken seriously. But satisfying my primary research interest has required detours through sectorally differentiated EU law doctrines and theories.

The fundamental policy orientation of the EU has left its mark on European constitutionalism too. A comprehensive discussion of European constitutionalism must move at different levels, which may baffle the reader. Part II of this book examines sectoral constitutionalization and its dimension-specific theoretical foundations. In contrast, the focus in Part I and the Epilogue is on the general theory of the European constitution or general constitutional theory. Readers whose principal interest lies in 'hard-core' European law might feel tempted to skip the discussions in Part I and progress directly to the forays into sectoral constitutions, while more theoretically oriented readers might be inclined to leave Part II for only cursory perusal. I can but hope that my analysis will also be taken as a whole. Although my major ambitions lie at the level of a general theory of the European constitution, it must be constructed on the basis of a preceding scrutiny of sectoral constitutionalization and must also resort to concepts whose domicile lies in general constitutional theory.

The Eurozone Crisis: A Constitutional Analysis (Cambridge University Press, 2014), written together with Klaus Tuori, already tested the relational, multidimensional approach which this book sets out in more detail. In the previous book we also introduced the distinction in the economic dimension between microeconomic and macroeconomic constitutions. The original idea probably was Klaus's. In Chapter 6 of this book, dealing with the mutation of the macroeconomic constitution, I have been able to draw on our common work on the Eurozone crisis.

This book summarizes what I have learned during my adventures in European law, which began in earnest with the launch of the Centre of Excellence in the Foundations of European Law and Polity at the Helsinki Law Faculty in 2008. At the Centre we were able to gather together committed researchers at diverse stages of their academic careers, create an atmosphere of intellectual curiosity and mutual learning, and establish an international network of similarly committed and intellectually curious partners, who have entered European law scholarship through diverse gateways. My greatest gratitude is to the Centre and its partners as a collective who made my research possible and contributed decisively to whatever might be of value in this book. I started the final phase of composing the book in spring 2014 in Florence at the European University Institute. This gave me a unique opportunity to avail myself of the excellent research infrastructure of the EUI and, above all, the intellectual resources of the Law Faculty. Before Florence, I did not know much about, say, internal market law. Now I do; at least I hope so. My stay in Florence was facilitated by my friend Hans-W. Micklitz, Dean of the Faculty and also a Member of our Centre. Hans has also been an invaluable source of ideas, as the reader may notice from my discussion of the notion of access justice in Chapter 7.

As a novice in European law, I have been dependent on commentators and interlocutors perhaps even more than is usual. I would especially like to express my gratitude to the following colleagues who have had the patience to read and comment on drafts at varying levels of finalization: Loic Azoulaï, Gareth Davies, Sabine Frerichs, Samuli Hurri, Niilo Jääskinen, Claire Kilpatrick, Jan Klabbers, Jan Komárek, Emilia Korkea-aho, Petri Kuoppamäki, Mel Marquis, Hans-W. Micklitz, Tuomas Ojanen, Jiri Priban, Suvi Sankari, Martin Scheinin and Heike Schweitzer. Once again, my trusted colleagues Christopher Goddard and Anna-Maria Rehbinder have offered me precious assistance at the very last stage of the project: Christopher in checking the language, and Anna-Maria in checking references and notes and in other editorial work. The Academy of Finland has kindly borne the financial burden, funding both the Centre and my Academy professorship and enabling my focus on research.

Loppi
August 2014

Prologue

Examining European constitutionalism

This is a book about the theoretical bases of the European constitution. The book adopts a constitutional perspective and employs constitutional vocabulary. These are not innocent choices but predetermine how the EU and its law will be portrayed. In another conceptual framework, the issues raised and their interrelations would be conceived of differently. This is a token of the inevitable perspectivism which imbues all law but is particularly pronounced in EU law.

By my choice I do not negate the possibility of alternative portrayals, produced from other perspectives and relying on other conceptual frameworks. Thus, I will not ignore the international law connections of European law,[1] but I will subordinate them to my constitutional point of view. Adopting an international law framework, the order would be reversed: constitutional features would be inserted in an international law setting. Two main perspectives and four main conceptual frameworks are available for a legal scholar who aims at a comprehensive, theoretically oriented depiction of European law and polity: the perspectives of Member State and European law, and the conceptual frameworks of international, federal, administrative and transnational law. My perspective will be that of European law. International law and administrative law accounts may include a constitutional aspect, but they both tend to

[1] I shall use 'European law' as a generic concept which covers pre-Maastricht law of the European communities with the emphasis on the Treaty on the European Economic Community (TEEC); post-Maastricht Community and third-pillar law; post-Lisbon EU law; as well as various international law complements to primary and secondary Community and Union legislation. Correspondingly, 'European constitution' and such derivatives as 'European constitutionalization' and 'European constitutionalism' will cover all the diverse stages of European law.

reject the autonomous constitutional claims of European law and reduce constitutionalism to state constitutionalism. Due to the juridical constitutionalization driven by the European Court of Justice (ECJ) and the constitutional self-understanding its case law reflects, such a rejection is difficult to defend from the perspective of European law. After adopting this perspective, the remaining alternatives are the federal and transnational. I shall opt for the latter, because I think it best captures the particularities of the EU as a polity and a legal system. However, opting for one conceptual framework should not entail blindness to contributions employing another approach. Discursiveness is not only a descriptive characteristic of European law (see Chapter 4) but also a normative guideline which should govern scholarly efforts to catch the specificity of European law. Availability of diverse conceptual frameworks manifests the controversial nature of the theoretical foundations of the European constitution. This is one of the peculiarities of European constitutionalism with which we shall become familiar in the course of this book. But scholarly confrontations involving diverse disciplinary premises should not be seen merely as hegemonic contests; they also contain potential for mutual learning.

Modern constitutional theory has been elaborated in the context of modern states and their national legal systems. In order to speak of 'constitutionalism beyond the state',[2] we should be able to demonstrate that, for instance, the EU as a polity and a legal system displays sufficient similarities with its state counterparts to warrant a common constitutional approach and vocabulary. We cannot perceive the object of our study but through a particular conceptual framework. However, we are of course not free to adopt any framework whatsoever; if our concepts restrict how we see the object, the object sets restrictions on our conceptual and methodological freedom. It would not make much sense to apply to European law, say, the conceptual apparatus of quantum mechanics. In this Prologue, I will point to some central features which European constitutionalism shares with its state equivalents and which justify employing constitutional language in the first place: such as the idea of constitutional law as a higher law. But I will also briefly evoke some of the particularities of European constitutionalism that complicate transferring constitutional concepts from state to European level. These include the multidimensionality and still emergent and process-like nature of the European constitution.

[2] Cf. J. H. H. Weiler and M. Wind (2003).

The term 'constitutionalism', appearing in the very title of this book, is in need of explication. 'Constitutionalism' is often used, especially by American authors, in a thick normative sense, referring to vital elements of the American notion of a constitutional democracy and the European notion of a democratic *Rechtsstaat*, such as democracy and fundamental rights. In this conceptual setting, 'constitutionalism' is intimately linked to legitimacy: 'constitutionalism' implies that the legitimacy of a polity and its law should be achieved through democratic procedures and fundamental rights.[3] Another related reading connects 'constitutionalism' to constitutional culture. Joseph Weiler has claimed that a characteristic of the European Union is a 'constitution without constitutionalism'.[4] Here 'constitutionalism' alludes to the general political culture among the citizenry which supports a polity and a legal system based on the principles of a constitutional democracy or a democratic *Rechtsstaat* and secures their legitimacy.

A thick concept of constitutionalism is implicit both in the debate on constitutional pluralism and the administrative law depiction of the EU and its law, most forcefully propounded in recent years by Peter Lindseth. Its problem is that it reflects the persistent dominance of the state template of constitutions and hence risks blocking the view to the specificity of European constitutionalism. It focuses on the juridical and political constitutions, and tends to neglect sectoral constitutionalization, a distinct feature of European constitutionalism which corresponds to the basic teleological, policy orientation of European law. I shall use 'constitutionalism' in a normatively more neutral sense. By 'European constitutionalism' I simply refer to the particularities of the European constitution and its theoretical foundations. I do not deny the relevance for European constitutionalism of the normative ideas of a constitutional democracy (a democratic *Rechtsstaat*) or the conception of legitimacy they imply. Where there is power it must be legitimated and restricted, and where there is law – which always implies power too – it must also be legitimated and restricted. But I stress that efforts to secure what Lindseth calls democratic and constitutional legitimacy should be examined through the interaction between the transnational and national levels of constitutionalism. In some crucial respects, European constitutionalism

[3] D. Halberstam (2009, 2010 and 2012) identifies constitutionalism with limited self-governance. In turn, P. Lindseth (2010) connects constitutionalism to democratic and constitutional legitimacy.

[4] J. H. H. Weiler (1999), p. 298.

has been, and still is, parasitic on national constitutionalism, and this also holds for constitutional and democratic legitimacy.[5] In order to be able to catch the specificity of European constitutionalism, we should not burden our basic concepts with normative assumptions that are too demanding. This goes for the very concept of a constitution too. To justify the use of constitutional vocabulary, European constitutionalism must be shown to display, not only divergences from, but also similarities to national constitutionalism. European constitutionalism and state constitutionalism in its diverse national variants express different conceptions of a shared concept of a constitution.

An obvious objection exists to resorting to constitutional vocabulary in the European context: namely, the fate of the Constitutional Treaty. Can we any longer talk of a European constitution after the failure of the Constitutional Treaty, following the debacle of the referenda in France and the Netherlands? Has not European citizenry rejected the idea of European constitutionalism?

The failure of the Constitutional Treaty attests to a wide discrepancy between the legal and political culture of the European elites and of the general public. In constitutional scholarship, much energy has been spent to detach the concept of a constitution from its state template and to demonstrate its viability in a transnational law – and even in an international law – context too. However, constitutional vocabulary seems to meet resistance among European citizenry. In their constitutional enthusiasm, the elites easily think that constitutional rhetoric will contribute to the general legitimacy of the EU as it does to the legitimacy of the national political and legal system. This seems to have been a misjudgement. European citizens often enough experience European constitutionalization more as a threat than a promise. In general legal and political culture, the constitution appears to remain inseparably linked to the state. Thus, the constitutionalization of the EU was commonly seen to lead to the EU acquiring state-like, federal attributes. And this is not what the general public, which still invests its main political allegiance in the state, was willing to accept. As Neil Walker has suggested, at the cultural level a constitution can be analysed as a condensed symbol, as a symbolic frame of reference.[6] But at least for the general public, it refers not only to

[5] As P. Lindseth (2010) refuses to examine putative European constitutionalism in its interaction with national constitutionalism, he ends up by denying the justification for a constitutional depiction of the Union and its law.

[6] N. Walker (2003), pp. 33–4.

human rights, democracy and the rule of law; it also refers to state and sovereignty.[7]

The European political and legal elites learned the lesson and deleted from the text of the Lisbon Treaty direct allusions to state-like attributes and constitutional vocabulary evoking federalist connotations. Was not this the final deathblow to the idea of European constitutionalism; a deathblow which even makes it questionable for scholars to employ constitutional language at all?

This question points to the general methodological issue of *double hermeneutics*, typical of human and social sciences. Through their concepts, scholars try to make sense of a piece of social reality which is moulded by the way the social actors themselves conceptualize and try to make sense of their social world. Due to inescapable double hermeneutics, the *meta-language* of scholars cannot drift very far from the *object language* of social actors whose ideas, behaviour or artefacts they are studying. Scholars share the culture they are examining; their meta-language draws from the same cultural reservoir as the object language under examination. A theorist may strive for and even attain a reflexive distance to surrounding culture, but reflexivity too is subject to cultural constraints.[8]

How should the relevant object language be defined for a study of the constitutional theory of the EU? As will be explained in Chapter 4, a constitution is brought about through constitutional speech acts, issued by relevant constitutional actors and linked together to make up a constitutional discourse. European constitutionalization cannot be separated from the constitutionalization of the discourse on European law and polity. Constitutional theorists are engaged in a *second-order*, meta-level discourse about the first-order discourse among constitutional elites. The meta-language of theorists should be attentive to the object language of first-order constitutional discourse; otherwise it would not do justice to

[7] Of course many reasons may exist for rejection of the constitutional project by the general public and the failure of the referendums in France and the Netherlands, some of these perhaps connected more to national politics than the development of the EU. I do not claim that the links which in general constitutional culture are seen between constitution and state were the only or even the main factor; I only claim that these links played a non-negligible role. Here we should also be wary of sweeping generalizations: there certainly are differences in the political and legal cultures of different Member States with regard to the connection between constitution and state. Thus in federal states the idea of multilevel constitutionalism is perhaps easier to accept than in unitary states.

[8] For a discussion on the object and meta-language of constitutional theory, see also N. Walker (2006a), pp. 10–14.

its object. Constitutional concepts have made their entry into the vocabulary with which legal and political actors express their descriptive and normative views of the past, present and future of European law and polity. Constitutional vocabulary has become part of the object language of the discourse which provides the source material for a constitutional theorist. But it is not the only vocabulary used, and other second-order conceptualizations can be defended as well. Yet what is important now is that the first-order discourse provides enough anchorage for second-order constitutional theory. The 'de-constitutionalization' in Lisbon does not alter this judgment. In a sense, the Lisbon Treaty was an insincere speech act, intended to pacify and even delude European citizenry: the main normative contents remained the same as in the abortive Constitutional Treaty.

The second-order point of view distinguishes legal and constitutional *theory* from *doctrinal* research. Together with contributions by the constitutional legislator and the ECJ as the constitutional court, doctrinal research is one of the main participants in the ongoing first-order discourse which drives forward the process of European constitutionalization. Next to the ECJ, legal scholarship has borne the main responsibility for elaborating the doctrine through which Treaty law is interpreted and, in some instances, even complemented. Here the dual citizenship of legal scholarship is evident: legal scholarship, in particular doctrinal research, is not only an academic but also a legal practice, fulfilling important functions in the legal system and contributing to the production and reproduction of law; that is, its own object of research.[9] Doctrinal research forms part of the discursive normative material in the focus of second-order theoretical studies. However, the distinction between first- and second-order discourse is far from watertight; theoretical accounts of the European constitution also possess normative implications to which first-order constitutional speech acts may relate.

In my examination of the theoretical bases of the European constitution, I am engaged in a second-order discourse in relation to the ongoing first-order discourse among European constitutional actors. But in a sense, my reconstruction represents a second-order discourse with regard to theoretically oriented constitutional debates as well. The European constitution possesses multiple dimensions, and in each of these dimensions discourse is conducted at both doctrinal and theoretical levels; consequently,

[9] See my discussion of legal scholarship's dual citizenship in K. Tuori (2002), pp. 285 ff.

constitutional theory is also differentiated along constitutional dimensions. My approach to *dimension-specific constitutional theories* is reconstructive. In each of the constitutional dimensions, I try to excavate the basic theoretical disagreements but, mostly, I refrain from taking a position on rival views. My ultimate purpose is to contribute to a *general theory of the European constitution*, rather than to participate in dimension-specific debates which are an object for my reconstructive enterprise. Indeed, a general theory of the European constitution should address the contested nature which labels the theory underpinning both the sectoral constitutions and the framing juridical and political constitutions.

A general theory of the European constitution transcends the restricted perspectives of the diverse constitutional dimensions. Yet no bird's-eye view is available in constitutional theory either. A scholar elaborating a general theory of the European constitution necessarily proceeds from a particular point of view which directs the gaze and limits its view. A general theory of the European constitution, such as this book seeks to contribute to, adopts the perspective of European law. It must recognize the existence of the Member State perspective too, and attend to the pluralism of transnational European and national Member State law. But it approaches perspectivism and pluralism from the perspective of European law.

Exponents of constitutional pluralism have argued that their theorizing takes off from ground rising above the potentially clashing perspectives of European and national law.[10] In effect, this would mean that theirs is a second-order theoretical discourse in relation to European and national discourses on the theories underlying the respective constitutions, including the general theory of the European constitution. Now at issue would no longer be the theory of a particular constitution but *general constitutional theory*. The pretension of constitutional pluralism of neutrality with regard to European and national perspectives has been contested from both sides. Those privileging the point of view of European law claim that constitutional pluralism implies acknowledging the reservations of national constitutional courts[11] in respect of European law's claim to supremacy and, consequently, favours the perspective of national law.[12] By contrast, those adopting the point of view of national law argue that as

[10] See, e.g., N. Walker (2006a), p. 18.

[11] Not all Member States possess a constitutional court. When referring to national constitutional courts I also include supreme courts with constitutional jurisdiction.

[12] J. Baquero Cruz (2008), p. 414.

constitutional pluralism (unjustifiably) accepts the existence of European constitutionalism, it favours the perspective of European law.[13] Thus, divergent notions of the perspectival commitments of constitutional pluralism provide yet another example of the impact of perspectivism on scholarship of European law.

A central task for general constitutional theory is to elaborate concepts which pin down general characteristics of constitutions and facilitate examining particular constitutions, including their theoretical foundations. In our present constitutional situation, 'constitutional pluralism' and other, more specific concepts pertaining to a pluralist constellation of overlapping constitutional claims of authority certainly belong to the conceptual reservoir of general constitutional theory. Although the main objective of this book is to reconstruct the theoretical bases of the European constitution(s), this requires forays into general constitutional theory as well. Both in this Prologue and in Part I, I discuss concepts with their domicile in general constitutional theory: such as 'constitutional relation', 'constitutional function' and, indeed, 'constitutional pluralism'. In these discussions, my perspective surpasses that of European law. Yet general constitutional theory too is always conducted from a distinct legal cultural framework, which theorists of constitutional pluralism cannot dispense with either. This framework results only partly from conscious choice; to a large extent, it is a matter of unconsciously functioning legal *Vorverständnis*, impregnated by what I shall call the perspectivism of legal orders, roles and disciplines.

Although legal and constitutional theory distances itself from the ongoing first-order discourse which determines the ever-changing contents of the law in force, it shares the internal perspective on law. The ultimate impetus for European constitutionalization lies in extra-legal factors. Reconstructive constitutional theory should not ignore the external social influences – of, say, a political, economic or ideological character – which govern legal development. Yet its cognitive ambitions do not focus on causal, social-scientific explanations. Reconstructive constitutional theory nurtures explanatory aspirations merely in the sense of making constitutionalization processes intelligible and discovering their internal logic, if such a logic there be! The internal perspective of legal scholarship only captures external causal factors after these have been translated into the language of law and filtered through the internal workings of the legal system. Despite its cognitive and explanatory

13 P. Lindseth (2010), p. 266.

pretensions, legal and constitutional theory shares the normativity of first-order discourse. This is obvious with regard to dimension-specific constitutional theories, which have direct normative implications for the doctrinal level. However, these theories also imply a view of the societal object of constitutional law – an implicit social theory, as I shall call it – which adds to sectoral constitutional theories a descriptive and even explanatory flavour but does not negate their normative thrust. But nor can reconstructive constitutional theory avoid normative implications. Reconstructions always involve choices and are never normatively innocent.

A relational concept of constitution

Constitutional concepts are contested concepts of which rival conceptions exist. This holds for the very concept of a constitution too. A central premise of this book is that 'constitution' is a relational concept which refers to the *constitutional relation* between *constitutional law* and its object of regulation: that is, a *constitutional object*. In a state context, Niklas Luhmann, for instance, has proposed examining the constitution as belonging to both the legal and political sub-system of society and establishing a structural coupling between the two.[14] Translated to my conceptual apparatus, Luhmann distinguishes between a juridical and a political constitution and points to their intertwinement; law-making, for example, is an operation in both the legal and political subsystems and regulated by both the juridical and the political constitution.

The European constitution also possesses a juridical and a political dimension. In the juridical constitution, constitutional law relates to the EU legal system and in the political constitution to the EU as a polity. In a typical state setting, political and juridical constitutions frame sectoral policies and legislation which, however, are usually left to the province of ordinary politics and law-making. By contrast, in a functionally oriented transnational polity, such as the EU, with a substantively limited claim to political and juridical authority, even central sectoral policies are constitutionally anchored. Hence, in addition to the two *framing constitutions* – the *juridical* and the *political* ones – I propose that we distinguish between three *sectoral constitutions*, all of them possessing a distinct constitutional object to which constitutional law relates: the *economic*, *social* and *security* constitutions. Furthermore, economic constitutionalization

[14] N. Luhmann (2004), pp. 404 ff.

has proceeded in two sub-dimensions which merit separate analysis: a *microeconomic* and a *macroeconomic* one. The process-like character of the European constitution also enhances the need to distinguish between constitutional dimensions and the inclusion of sectoral constitutions among them. The constitutional dimensions have emerged at different times and developed each at their own pace. This calls for a differentiated analysis of the European constitution as a *process of constitutionalization*.

Thus, unlike a standard state constitution, the European juridical and political constitutions do not frame merely ordinary policy- and law-making but its constitutional foundations as well; that is, sectoral constitutions. The framing function of the juridical and political constitutions points to another aspect of the relationality of the European constitution complementing the constitutional relation between constitutional law and its object: an *inter-dimensional* relationality.

So the European constitution actually consists of many constitutions. But there are many constitutions in Europe in another and perhaps more familiar sense as well. European constitutional space is a crowded space, inhabited by both Member State national constitutions and the European transnational constitution and, consequently, characterized by constitutional diversity and pluralism. The European constitution must always be examined in its interaction with its national counterparts. This interaction is also an important aspect of the relationality of the European constitution.

Constitutional law as higher law

The constitution occupies a particular position in modern law: it represents a higher law, the law of laws. The idea of a higher law can be linked to the conceptual distinction between the formal and material constitution, familiar from the writings of, above all, Hans Kelsen. The concept of *formal constitution* refers to the legal form and status of constitutional norms: to their codification into a single legal act and their position in the hierarchical order of legal norms. In turn, the concept of *material constitution* evokes the typical contents or functions of constitutional norms and is thus specified in accordance with what these are held to be. For Kelsen the main function of a constitution is to regulate the production of new legal norms, and this view, then, shaped his conception of 'material constitution'.[15] The norms making up the constitution in the material sense may, but need not, be codified in a single statute (a constitution

[15] H. Kelsen (1989), p. 222.

in the formal sense). So, as every undergraduate student in comparative constitutional law well knows, the United Kingdom has a constitution in the material but not in the formal sense.

The idea of a higher law, which assigns the constitution a privileged position with respect to other law, can be given either a formal or a substantive reading. The *formal* reading is epitomized by Kelsen's hierarchical structure – *Stufenbau* – of legal norms, where the constitution occupies the highest level next to the *Grundnorm*. A constitution as a higher law provides the authorization for the issuance of lower-level norms and, in cases of conflict, defeats these. The requirement of a qualified procedure for amending the (formal) constitution or for issuing a new constitution is related to the formal reading as well. Because the constitution stands higher than, and constitutes the legal foundation for, other law, it should enjoy exceptional stability and legitimacy; hence such requirements for constitutional amendments as qualified majority, approval by more than one parliamentary composition or acceptance in a referendum. Some (formal) constitutions – the German Basic Law, for instance – have declared certain constitutional provisions unamendable, thus introducing an internal formal hierarchy within constitutional law.[16] The formal status of the constitution as higher law also implies or at least makes intelligible the need of particular institutional arrangements for guaranteeing its observance. These range from a constitutional court to bureaucratic or parliamentary forms of *ex ante* constitutional review.

One of the contributions that examining the European constitution may have for general constitutional theory may lie in enhanced analytical rigour. European constitutional peculiarities may compel us to sharpen our analytical precision, to unravel 'lump concepts'. Constitutional features which at state level go together and whose intertwinement we therefore tend to take for granted may at the European level be disconnected. Hence either–or questions are often misguided with regard to the European constitution. This goes for the applicability of the notion of a formal constitution too: it may turn out that some features customarily attached to this notion are relevant in the European setting, while others are not.

Some observers claim that the EU does not possess a formal constitution, although it may well have a material one. Yet, ever since the *Les Verts* ruling in 1986,[17] the ECJ has characterized the Founding Treaties as the constitutional charter of the EC (the EU), implying that these amount to a formal constitution. The ECJ's claim of the Treaties as a constitutional

16 Art. 79(3) of the Basic Law. See also the Venice Commission Report (2010).

17 Case C-294/83 *Les Verts v Parliament* [1986] ECR 1339.

charter obviously involves the idea of higher or superior law. But superior to what law? One of the constitutional particularities of the EU is that superiority works in two directions: with regard to other EU law and with regard to the national law of the Member States. In the internal relations of EU law, the Treaties both enjoy primacy in norm conflicts and provide the competence basis for lower-level normative acts, such as regulations and directives. With regard to Member State law, the superiority of EU law is reflected by the principle of *supremacy* of which the *primacy* of EU law in norm conflicts before national courts is a sub-principle. However, only directly effective Treaty norms enjoy primacy over conflicting national norms, but, to further complicate matters, so do even other directly effective European norms, regardless of their position in the internal hierarchy of EU law. Moreover, the other Kelsenian characteristic of superiority is wholly missing in relations between European and national law: EU law is not the basis of national law's validity. In sum, EU law and national law do not constitute a unitary hierarchical structure or *Stufenbau* as the application of Kelsenian ideas of constitutional superiority would require.

As regards a qualified amendment procedure as a formal criterion of the superiority of constitutional law, the Treaties clearly stand out from other EU law. The Treaty on the European Union sets a particular drafting and decision-making procedure for Treaty revisions. Moreover, amendments to international treaties have to be ratified by every Member State in accordance with the national constitution. Those defending an international law portrayal of the EU are prone to emphasize that the Member States remain Masters of the Treaties, while the Treaties form part of international law. According to the tenets of an either–or logic, the Treaties cannot possess both an international law and a constitutional character. Again, dichotomous thinking may be misleading. Why could the Treaties not both obey international law in their amendment procedures and function as constitutional law with respect to other EU law and Member State national law? Kelsen, for one, did not see any difficulty in an international treaty functioning as the constitution of a legal order.[18]

What further complicates labelling the Treaties as a formal constitution is the role of *general principles* in EU constitutional law. Some of the most pertinent constitutional principles are not enshrined in the Treaties but have been articulated in the case law of the ECJ; these include supremacy and direct effect, as well as efficacy (*effet utile*) and uniformity as meta-level justificatory principles. Initially, fundamental rights were also introduced

[18] H. Kelsen (1920), p. 194. See also the discussion in R. Schütze (2009), pp. 37–9.

into EU law as general principles through judicial legislation. The ECJ has expressly granted general principles constitutional status.[19] Thus, even if the Treaties as a constitutional charter were characterized as a formal constitution, it is crucial to remember that not all constitutional norms enjoy institutional support in explicit Treaty provisions.

The ECJ is a hybrid court with many functions, reflecting the hybrid character of the EU legal system and polity.[20] It is not a mere constitutional court, but among its many tasks it does exercise functions which equal those of state constitutional courts: through judicial review, it guards the EU constitution as a higher law with regard to both lower-level EU law and the municipal law of Member States; it engages in protection of fundamental rights; it resolves conflicts of competence between the EU and the Member States in a way reminiscent of the role of a constitutional court in a federal state; and it settles disputes among the main EU institutions, such as the European Parliament, the Council and the Commission. Indeed, these functions of the ECJ are a major argument for applying constitutional concepts to the European level.

The substantive sense of higher law relates to the normative contents of constitutional law. In this sense 'higher' equals 'basic' or 'fundamental': a constitution is supposed to give expression to the basic normative principles of the polity and its law, even society in general. Here the modern constitution has taken over the legacy of pre-modern *lois fondamentales*.[21] What the basics are that a constitution should affirm is of course open to contestation. Equally controversial is the extent to which the political legislator, armed with a democratic mandate, is and should be bound by constitutional provisions. In many states, including Germany, debates have focused on the role of fundamental rights as general principles unfolding their effects throughout the legal order and imposing restrictions even on the legislator.

In recent years, the international Carl Schmitt renaissance has influenced European constitutional discourse too. Schmitt replaces the concepts of material and formal constitution with those of a 'constitution

[19] Case C-101/08 *Audiolux and Others v Groupe Bruxelles Lambert and Others* [2009] ECR I-9823, Para. 63.

[20] R. Dehousse (1998) analyses the ECJ as an international, constitutional and administrative court.

[21] In a terminological respect, it might be considered instructive that the German constitution is called Basic Law (*Grundgesetz*) or the Finnish constitution *Perustuslaki* (in Swedish *Grundlag*). See on *lois fondamentales* Q. Skinner (1978), pp. 259 ff.

as a decision' or a 'constitution in the positive sense' and 'constitutional laws', and gives the idea of substantively higher law a decisionist twist. In his *Verfassungslehre*, Schmitt defines a constitution in the positive sense as a decision by the people, i.e. the political unit, of its specific form of existence.[22] The notion of a constitution in the positive sense as distinct from constitutional law bestowed on Schmitt's theory a vagueness which facilitated its application to the rapidly changing political situation under the Weimar Republic. The content of the constitution in the positive sense was very much a matter of interpretation, as is evinced by the divergent views Schmitt himself advocated in the different stages of Weimar's tragic history.

Where Schmitt did not change his views was the absolute primacy of the constitutional decision over constitutional laws. The constitutional decision is an existential decision, taken by the people as a *pouvoir constituant* and unbound by pre-established rules: if constitutional substance and form clash, substance should prevail! Schmitt's theoretical discursive moves are undoubtedly linked to his political objective as a leading ideologue of the so-called conservative revolution: the destabilization of the Weimar constitutional settlement and its replacement with an authoritarian regime. But even if we do not accept the Schmittian disconnection of the substantive and formal aspects – as, to my mind, we should not – we should still grant the justificatory primacy of substance over form. It is the substance of the constitution, its status as the Basic Law or *loi fondamentale*, which warrants its formal position as a higher law: prevalence in norm conflicts, qualified procedure for amendment and institutionalized constitutional review. The formal reading of the superiority of a constitution is only intelligible against a substantive backdrop: a constitution is accorded formally superior status because of the substantive pertinence of its normative contents.

We have already observed a typical vagueness in the formal contours of the EU constitution. A similar ambiguity affects the substance of this constitution in all its diverse dimensions. The premise, however, should be clear enough: time and again, we are dealing with a *loi fondamentale*, a law of the basics, whether the juridical, political, economic, social or security constitution is at issue. These basics can be identified only through reconstructing the cultural or theoretical layers underlying 'surface-level' Treaty law and doctrine.

22 C. Schmitt (2008), pp. 75–9.

Constitutional culture and constitutional theories

The law possesses two aspects. It can be approached both as a normative *legal order* and as particular social practices – *legal practices* – specialized in producing and re-producing this legal order and localized in particular institutional settings: law-making in the legislature, adjudication in the courts and legal scholarship in law faculties and other academic institutions, to list the main legal practices of modern law. Together, these two aspects, the legal order and institutionally framed legal practices, make up what I call the *legal system*. We can – and, to my mind, should – make a corresponding distinction between constitutional law in the symbolic-normative sense – the constitutional order – and constitutional practices upholding and revising it.

In a 'mature' modern legal system, law as a legal order consists of multiple layers. It is not exhausted by the surface of explicit, discursively formulated normative material, such as individual statutes and other regulations, together with court decisions and positions taken by doctrinal legal scholars. A mature legal order also involves 'sub-surface' cultural layers, which both constitute the possibility for and impose restrictions on what can appear on the law's surface as the result of the speech acts of legislators, judges and legal scholars. The cultural layers do not fall from heaven but are products of a process of sedimentation starting from the law's surface.[23] Constitutional law – the constitutional order – should also be approached through the interrelations connecting explicit surface-level speech acts – such as formal constitutions, constitutional case law and contributions of constitutional law scholarship – with constitutional culture.

How does the conceptual framework elaborated with a view to a mature state legal system mesh with European law? The analysis of the two aspects of law – law as a legal order and as institutionally framed legal practices – is certainly applicable, and European constitutionalization can be examined as the interplay between constitutional order and constitutional practices. By contrast, transferring insights on the layeredness of the legal order is more complicated. Largely due to the pronouncedly teleological character of European law, its sub-surface life differs from that of ideal-typical modern state law. In the state setting, legal cultural principles, which also produce the substantive coherence of the legal order, are

23 I have presented my view on the two-dimensional and multilayered nature of modern law in K. Tuori (2002 and 2011).

typically closer to Ronald Dworkin's morally laden principles – principles *sensu stricto* – than policies related to goals and programmes concerning the desired state of society.[24] What has detached European law from an ideal-typical state legal order is its fundamental *policy orientation* which has left its impact on constitutional law too. The policy orientation is most conspicuous in sectoral constitutions, but it has affected juridical constitutionalization as well. Such key principles of the juridical constitution as direct effect and supremacy were also motivated by policy considerations; by the effective and uniform application of European law which aimed at the establishment and functioning of the common market. In the course of European constitutionalization, other objectives have been added, but this has not deprived European law of the policy emphasis.

Accordingly, the substantive coherence which European law has achieved has been a result of policies rather than principles. But building up sub-surface foundations for policy-oriented law, including constitutional law, has been an arduous process. Sectoral constitutions address policy issues which fall outside the typical *materia constitutionis* of state constitutions, and here Member State constitutional traditions can offer but meagre support for the development of a particular EU constitutional culture. In central fields, EU law, comprising constitutional law too, has started cultural sedimentation from scratch: no national free-movement law exists, and even national competition law is a relative newcomer. Hence, in my discussion of the diverse dimensions of the European constitution I shall drop the too-demanding term 'constitutional culture' and, instead, employ a distinction between constitutional *doctrine* and constitutional *theory*.

In their sub-surface foundations, the juridical and political dimensions partly differ from the general picture. General policy orientation affects the European framing constitutions too, as is shown by the backdrop to direct effect and supremacy, and the justificatory principles of efficacy and uniformity. But an important sub-field of the juridical and political constitutions exists which EU constitutional law shares with its national counterparts, where national constitutional traditions have been an important source and where morally laden principles temper the policy emphasis; namely, fundamental rights law. Maastricht enshrined in Treaty law the contribution of national constitutional traditions to fundamental rights as general principles of European law.[25] In respect of fundamental rights

[24] R. Dworkin (1978).

[25] Present Art. 6(3) TEU provides that 'fundamental rights, as guaranteed by the European Convention for the Protection of Human Rights and Fundamental Freedoms and as they

law, it is also evident that EU and national legal systems share the same 'deep culture' where the universalist values now listed in Art. 2 TEU also find their place.[26]

An outline of the book

I have divided my examination of European constitutionalism into two parts. Part I explores general characteristics of European constitutionalism under the catchwords of *relationality* (Chapter 1), *perspectivism* (Chapter 3) and *discursiveness* (Chapter 4). The catchwords connote features which can be discerned in national legal systems and state constitutions too, but which are especially pronounced in the transnational European context. Relationality, perspectivism and discursiveness are general characteristics of the European constitution, which also set it apart from standard state constitutions.

Under 'relationality', I discuss the constitutional relation between European constitutional law and its dimension-specific constitutional objects, as well as the interaction among constitutional dimensions. I also introduce discussion on the interrelations between the transnational European constitution and national constitutions. After an interlude where I present an overview of the juridical constitution (Chapter 2), I continue this discussion in Chapter 3 under 'perspectivism'. I defend a cultural understanding of legal perspectivism. I distinguish between three sub-species of legal cultural perspectivism: perspectivism of legal orders, legal roles and legal disciplines. I concentrate on the perspectivism of legal orders, which I examine in terms of legal diversity and legal pluralism. This conceptual framework enables me to comment on European constitutional pluralism, which I approach through the central issue of fundamental rights pluralism.

In Chapter 4, under 'discursiveness', I argue that the European constitution should be seen as a multidimensional process of constitutionalization. I propose examining this process as an ongoing constitutional discourse composed of interlinked constitutional speech acts by relevant

result from the constitutional traditions common to the Member States, shall constitute general principles of the Union's law'. In the Preamble to the TEU, the Member States confirm 'their attachment to the principles of liberty, democracy and respect for human rights and fundamental freedoms and of the rule of law'.

26 'The Union is founded on the values of respect for human dignity, freedom, democracy, equality, the rule of law and respect for human rights, including the rights of persons belonging to minorities. These values are common to the Member States in a society in which pluralism, non-discrimination, tolerance, justice, solidarity and equality between women and men prevail.'

constitutional actors. I also demonstrate how speech-act theory facilitates an understanding of two divergent approaches to European constitutionalism: a conflict-oriented and a dialogical one. These approaches are already alluded to in Chapter 3, in discussing European constitutional pluralism.

Part II scrutinizes sectoral constitutionalization in three dimensions: economic, social and security. Depicting the economic constitution involves adopting a distinction between micro- and macroeconomic layers. Sectoral constitutions are analysed as processes of constitutionalization which possess both a formal and a substantive aspect. The formal aspect reflects the intertwinement of juridical and sectoral constitutionalization. The substantive aspect is discussed applying the distinction between constitutional doctrine and theory. In all sectoral constitutions, the underlying theory is a matter of controversy. Reconstructing the major theoretical controversies is one of the objectives of Part II.

In the Epilogue, I attempt to summarize the conclusions to be drawn at the level of a general theory of the European constitution. The general theory must account for sectoral constitutionalization, with its backdrop in the policy orientation of the European polity and law. Yet the general theory must largely focus on the juridical and political constitutions. These constitutional dimensions not only frame sectoral constitutionalization but also respond to its consequences in terms of, say, legitimacy needs and gather together its juridical and political implications. In this sense, they are not only framing but also summarizing constitutions. The juridical and political emphasis of the general constitutional theory of the EU offers me an opportunity to complement the overview of the juridical constitution presented in Chapter 2 and the scattered observations on the political constitution in both Part I and Part II. In the Epilogue, I also resume discussion of the alternative disciplinary frameworks for an overall portrayal of the EU and its legal system, and defend opting for transnational law through a criticism of the international, administrative and federal law approaches.

PART I

General characteristics

1 Relationality

Constitutional dimensions

As the 'constitutional charter' of the EU, the Founding Treaties are bewildering reading for someone familiar merely with typical state constitutions. Indeed, the general embarrassment among the citizenry confronted with the substance of the Constitutional Treaty has been identified as one of the reasons for its rejection. The Treaties contain an abundance of provisions which do not pertain to typical *materia constitutionis*, as this is commonly understood in the setting of state constitutions: most conspicuously provisions on diverse policy fields. The European constitution is not only about European law and polity; it is also about European economy, European social welfare and European security. In brief, the European constitution possesses multiple dimensions; the constitutions of Europe are many.

To examine constitutional multidimensionality, 'constitution' must be understood in relational terms. I treat 'constitution' as a legal concept, referring to a legal, normative, entity. But this normative entity is not shut in a self-contained realm of the Ought; a province in a Popperian World 3. Through a constitution, the law relates to something else (or, in case of the juridical constitution, to itself), to a *constitutional object*, and, thus, establishes a *constitutional relation*. This is a two-way relation: constitutional law is expected to influence the constitutional object – its object of regulation – but the constitutional object also impacts constitutional law. The expected impact of constitutional law on its constitutional object can be discussed in terms of *constitutional functions*, while the *implicit social theory* inherent in constitutional law plays a key role in the reverse influence.

In defining 'constitution' through the constitutional relation between constitutional law and constitutional object, I have been inspired by two – at first glance – widely diverse theoretical directions: Niklas Luhmann's systems-theoretically oriented understanding of the constitution and institutional theory of law, instigated by Friedrich Carl von Savigny and in recent decades expounded by, first of all, Neil MacCormick and Ota Weinberger.[1] What unites these seemingly disparate approaches to the constitution and law in general is a relational emphasis. The institutional theory of law has taught us that all law can – and should! – be examined in its relation to its object of regulation: the law generates legal-institutional facts where the social or psychological factual side and the legal normative side are intertwined, and this, arguably, is the very point of law. In turn, Luhmann argues that the constitution possesses a dual domicile among the sub-systems of modern society: it belongs to both legal and political systems. Moreover, and what is especially relevant for our present discussion, the constitution establishes an interrelation – a *structural coupling* – between these differentiated, autopoietically functioning social sub-systems: it channels the influences of the legal into the political system and vice versa.[2]

Luhmann's ideas are valuable, especially in the context of the state constitution, but they provide inspiration for examining the European constitution too. State constitutions usually limit themselves to regulating the polity and the legal system or – expressed with Luhmann's concepts – the political and legal sub-systems. These two dimensions exist in the European constitution as well. In the political dimension, constitutional law regulates the EU as a polity and in the juridical dimension the EU legal system. But as is manifested by the bafflingly wide *materia constitutionis* of the Treaties, EU constitutional law constitutionalizes sectoral fields which at state level are usually the province of ordinary policy- and law-making. In state constitutions, the basic premise is the universality of the political and legal claim to authority; hence, no sector-specific constitutional authorizations are needed. The assumption of comprehensive powers is not valid for the European transnational polity and legal system. In accordance with the basic policy orientation of the EU, its juridical and political claim to authority is substantially (functionally) limited; the *principle of conferral* substitutes for that of comprehensive powers. Not only must the European constitution provide the general juridical and political framework for sectoral policies; it must also

[1] F. C. von Savigny (1981); D. N. MacCormick and O. Weinberger (1986); D. N. MacCormick (2008).

[2] N. Luhmann (2004), pp. 404 ff.

set sectoral objectives and create sectoral competences. The two *framing constitutions* – the *political* and the *juridical* – are complemented by three *sectoral constitutions*: the *economic*, *social* and *security* constitutions. Furthermore, economic constitutionalization has led to a differentiation of two subfields: a *microeconomic* constitution, based on the Treaty of Rome but in crucial respects elaborated by the ECJ, and a *macroeconomic* one, based on the Maastricht provisions on Economic and Monetary Union (EMU). The microeconomic constitution is centred around free movement and competition law and focuses on the economic activity of individual economic actors, while the macroeconomic constitution addresses macroeconomic objectives and policies.

Distinguishing sectoral constitutions presupposes differentiation at both poles of the constitutional relation: in respect of both constitutional law and its societal object of regulation. The sectoral constitutions possess distinct constitutional objects: European economy, social well-being and security. A corresponding differentiation is noticeable in Treaty law, as well as constitutional doctrine and theory. The exact contours of the sectoral constitutions can, though, be debatable. Should education be included in the constitutional object of the social constitution? Does the constitutional object of the security constitution cover both internal and external security? It might also be asked why I have not included, say, an environmental dimension in the sectoral constitutions. The answer lies in the criterion of differentiation: primary environmental law or the accompanying constitutional doctrine and theory have not reached the required level of differentiation.

Luhmann's concept of a constitution focuses on state constitutions. By contrast, Gunther Teubner's societal constitutionalism tries to catch the specificities of transnational constitutionalization; constitutionalism beyond the state. Teubner's view of societal constitutions shares the relationality of Luhmann's approach but extends it beyond the interrelations of the legal and political systems. Teubner discusses societal constitutions in the context of global functional social systems, such as economy, health, science and religion. He suggests that societal constitutions be examined in terms of lasting structural couplings which connect the specific reflexive mechanism of the global functional social system with constitutional law as the reflexive instance of law. Teubner's account is inspiring but problematic. He has difficulty in identifying the constitutional subject which at the transnational level would substitute for the state, nor does he manage to explain where the constitutional law which complements the auto-constitutionalization of the functional social system emanates from and how this constitutional law is related to transnational politics. Teubner clearly assigns the juridical and political constitutions a framing function but is not able to localize these constitutions at the transnational level, or to specify the framing function or the way it is accomplished.[3] The systems-theoretical ballast of Luhmann's and Teubner's constitutional vocabulary accounts for both its strength and its weakness. In some specific issues, the notion of structural coupling may prove fruitful for analysis of the constitutional relation or the interaction of diverse constitutional dimensions. Yet the wealth of these relations cannot be compressed to the conceptual Procrustean bed of structural coupling. So let us not burden our constitutional conceptual apparatus with too wide-reaching systems-theoretical assumptions, whilst not categorically rejecting the cognitive potential of the Luhmannian approach either.

The term 'juridical constitution' may cause some confusion. All the constitutional dimensions possess a legal character in the sense that constitutional law always occupies one of the two poles of the constitutional relation; all the constitutional dimensions are about the constitutional relation between constitutional law and its constitutional object. What distinguishes the juridical constitution from other constitutional dimensions is the fact that here both poles of the constitutional relation are legal in nature. In the juridical constitution, the law establishes a reflexive relation to itself. The political constitution possesses a legal character too; here the object of constitutional law is the EU as a polity. Thus, the concept of a political constitution as used in this book should not be confused with the political constitutionalism which Richard Bellamy, for instance, has advocated as an alternative to the legal constitutionalism of judicial fundamental rights review.[4]

So, distinct dimensions can be discerned in the European constitution. Yet their distinctness is not absolute, but they enter into specific relations with each other. The very term – 'framing constitutions' – I propose for the political and juridical constitutions implies a claim of such interrelationality. How, exactly, do the political and juridical constitutions frame the sectoral ones? Put briefly, the political constitution provides the institutional framework for sectoral constitutionalization, while the juridical constitution offers the legal instruments. The political constitution

[3] G. Teubner (2012). See the perceptive criticism by J. Priban (2012).
[4] R. Bellamy (2007).

regulates the EU institutions to which sectoral competences are granted: such as the European Council, the European Parliament, the Council of Ministers, the Commission and the ECJ. At the individual pole of the polity relationship, the political constitution establishes and defines European citizenship, with potential implications in all sectoral dimensions. Correspondingly, sectoral constitutional dimensions rely on the legislative and judicial instruments, institutions and procedures provided by the juridical constitution. Moreover, the general principles developed in the course of juridical constitutionalization, such as direct effect, supremacy, the rule of law and fundamental rights, are pertinent in all sectoral dimensions. Thus, the framing constitutions exercise both a constitutive and a restrictive function with regard to the sectoral constitutions.

All the sectoral constitutions possess distinct political and juridical features as well: they have their characteristic institutional structures and legal particularities. The economic constitution cannot be examined without including the role of the Commission as the European Competition Authority or – after Maastricht – the European Central Bank (ECB) as the executor of European monetary policy. Correspondingly, in addition to general EU legal instruments, sectoral constitutions have resorted to particular means too, such as the Maastricht Social Policy Protocol and Agreement in the social dimension or framework decisions in the security constitution. Institutional or juridical particularities should be discussed in the context of sectoral constitutionalization. But they should also be conceived of as elements in the overall European political and juridical constitutions. The political and juridical constitutions do not merely facilitate sectoral constitutionalization. They also react to and summarize its implications and consequences.

In an important sense, the EU reverses the relationship between the political and juridical constitutions and the sectoral policy fields to which we are accustomed at the state level. A state constitution is usually equated with the political and juridical dimensions which, according to the traditional understanding, establish the political and legislative sovereignty of the state. In turn, sectoral policies result from the exercise of this sovereignty. The political and juridical constitutions are primary in relation to sectoral policy fields which, as a rule, do not enjoy constitutional dignity. In a policy-oriented transnational polity and legal system, such as the EU, the claim to authority is substantively (functionally) limited. Juridical and political constitutionalization are not ends in themselves but largely respond to the needs and implications of sectoral constitutionalization. Economic constitutionalization would not have been possible without simultaneous juridical constitutionalization, which, for instance, produced the crucial principles of direct effect and primacy. Sectoral constitutionalization displays both formal and substantive aspects; by and large, the formal aspect of sectoral constitutionalization coincides with juridical constitutionalization. In turn, the Maastricht Treaty, which, for instance, reinforced the position of the European Parliament and introduced European citizenship, signified a leap in political constitutionalization. An important backdrop to this leap was the legitimacy deficit which was perceived to have ensued from the preceding economic constitutionalization driven by the ECJ. In the European constitution too, the framing political and juridical dimensions enjoy *constitutive primacy*. But they are subjected to the *functional primacy* of sectoral constitutions. The relationship between framing and sectoral constitutions is recursive: through their functional primacy sectoral constitutions trigger juridical and political constitutionalization, the results of which will then be available for subsequent framing purposes.

Arguably, because of the functional primacy of sectoral constitutionalization, it is here that the very crux of European constitutionalism lies. As theorists of constitutional pluralism tend to identify the European constitution with its juridical and political dimensions, their version of constitutionalism beyond the state remains crucially attached to the state perspective. A similar reductionism which does not see beyond the juridical and political constitutions labels the administrative law portrayal of the EU, employing a thick normative concept of constitutionalism and ending up with denying the very existence of European transnational constitutionalism.

European integration has primarily been an economic project, and in spite of the expansion of EU activities into new policy domains, economic integration retains a dominant position. This has left its imprint on inter-dimensional relations within the European constitution. The economic constitution has benefited from a functional primacy with regard not only to the framing constitutions but to other sectoral constitutions as well. The functional primacy of the economic constitution can be observed not only in juridical constitutionalization but in the emergence and further development of non-economic sectoral constitutions too. The social policy provisions of the Treaty of Rome had an economic rationale: they served free movement of workers or securing a level playing field for the industries of different Member States. In turn, the origins of the security dimension lie in the consequences of opening internal Community borders in order to implement free movement of workers, which is an essential element of the economic constitution. The functional primacy of the economic constitution has also limited the developmental options of the non-economic constitutions, as can be seen in the subjection of healthcare and social security to free movement and competition law. The functional primacy of the economic constitution may also manifest itself in *relations of limitation*.

Still, the functional primacy of the European economic constitution should not be understood in absolute terms. Although owing their initial momentum to the economic constitution, in their further development non-economic constitutional dimensions may have obtained at least partial independence from economic considerations. The original institutional organization of the Community – the nascent institutional pole of the European polity – was largely tailored to the needs of the economic constitution, but subsequently, in and since Maastricht, specific political values, such as democracy and transparency, have gained in importance in political constitutionalization. In the security dimension, the scope of the risks to which the security constitution responds has expanded and transcends those deriving from the opening of internal borders. Similar signs of independence – or at least striving for independence – are detectable in the social constitution too. A model example of growing autonomy is offered by the way the Treaty provision on equal pay was progressively detached from its economic rationale and turned into a nucleus of EU anti-discrimination law. The gradual development of constitutional social rights also reflects an aspiration for independence, although cross-border social rights in particular owe much of their initial dynamics to the implications of the economic constitution. Free movement of workers has provided the impetus to the right to cross-border social security and free movement of services to the right to cross-border healthcare.

The at least partial independence of the social constitution points to yet another type of relations between constitutional dimensions: *relations of conflict*. Increasing autonomy may lead to normative results which contradict the requirements of the economic constitution. The normative implications of the economic constitution may clash with those of, say, the political or social one. Before the ECJ, such constitutional conflicts often assume the guise of a contestation between different types of rights. Economic rights derived from free movement law may clash with social rights, or civil or political fundamental rights. In a standard constellation before the ECJ, the issue is whether protection of other types of rights justifies derogating from economic rights; reference can be made to such celebrated rulings of the ECJ as *Omega*, *Schmidberger*, *Viking* and *Laval*.[5] The functional primacy of the economic constitution is obvious in the very posing of the issue: in conflicts of rights, what needs justification is restricting not a fundamental right but an economic right. Yet, as *Omega* and *Schmidberger* demonstrate, functional primacy does not necessarily dictate the result of the balancing exercise.

Economic rights possess an instrumental character; they serve the basic policy objective of establishing and securing the functioning of the common (internal) market. The conflictual relations between the economic and the political or social constitutions can often be conceptualized as a tension between policy-oriented economic rights and principle-based fundamental rights. The above-mentioned landmark cases also point to an aspect of conflict resolution in the framing function of the juridical constitution. The juridical constitution may be called upon to resolve inter-dimensional constitutional conflicts.

Constitutional functions

'Constitutional function' refers to the effects that constitutional law is expected to produce in the constitutional object; it specifies the constitutional relation from the point of view of constitutional law. Constitutional functions can be discussed at the level of both state and transnational constitutions; indeed, analogous constitutional functions for their part warrant transposition to a transnational level of constitutional vocabulary elaborated in the state setting. Constitutional functions or their respective importance may vary in the diverse dimensions of the European constitution: the functions of, say, the economic constitution are not necessarily identical to those of, say, the juridical constitution. Separate chapters are devoted to the sectoral constitutions in Part II. Here I am mainly interested in the two framing constitutions. In this section examples are mostly taken from the political constitution, while the way the juridical constitution exerts its functions will be discussed in the following chapter. Through the framing relation, accomplishment of the functions of the political and juridical constitutions impacts sectoral constitutions as well. Thus, if the political constitution succeeds in its

[5] Case C-36/02 *Omega Spielhallen* [2004] ECR I-9609; Case C-112/00 *Schmidberger* [2003] ECR I-5659; Case C-438/05 *International Transport Workers' Federation and Finnish Seamen's Union* [2007] ECR I-10779; Case C-341/05 *Laval un Partneri* [2007] ECR I-11767.

legitimacy function, the sectoral constitutions benefit from this success too.

I propose to distinguish between the following interrelated and partly overlapping functions:

- a constitutive function: bringing about the constitutional object;
- a positioning function: defining the position of the constitutional object in relation to other entities of the same kind;
- an organizing function: bringing order and stability into the constitutional object;
- a restrictive function: preventing the constitutional object from exceeding its limits;
- a legitimizing function: promoting the acceptance of the constitutional object among relevant addressees.

Let us start with the *constitutive function*. The constitutional object of a political constitution is a polity which possesses both an institutional and an individual pole. The institutional part of the political constitution defines the basic organizational structure of political power: the main institutions of the polity, as well as their competences and mutual relationships. This has been a major function of the European political constitution too. The constitution is also supposed to render the institutional organization the order and stability necessary for its effective and frictionless functioning. In a polity aspiring to meet the criteria of a democratic *Rechtsstaat*, the constitutive and organizing functions are accompanied by a *restrictive* one. Through fundamental rights, the constitution restricts the power that the institutions of the polity are allowed to wield with regard to individuals. In the European polity, constituting and organizing the institutional pole has been accompanied, although with a certain delay, by developing fundamental rights law which restricts the power that European institutions – including Member State authorities acting in the scope of European law – are allowed to exert in respect of European individuals. But fundamental rights are not the only constitutional limitation on the powers of European institutions. As a transnational, policy-oriented polity and differing from states, the EU does not possess a universal scope of activity, but its competences are limited to the substantive fields defined in the Treaties. The principle of conferral is an essential restrictive principle of the EU political constitution, distinguishing it from its Member States where the principle of comprehensive powers reflects the universality of a sovereign state's claim to political authority.

A political constitution defines the individual pole of the polity as *citizens*, endowed with citizenship rights, among which fundamental rights possess a privileged position. From the perspective of individuals, fundamental rights protect them against abuse of power by the institutional pole of the polity and guarantee them spheres of private and public autonomy. The exercise by citizens of their public autonomy renders a polity its democratic character.

In a nascent polity, such as the European one, the constitutive function should be examined in even broader, foundational terms. The political constitution is expected to contribute to the emergence of the polity itself; this expectation can be articulated as a *polity-building* function. For polity building, establishing and stabilizing the institutional organization and relating it to the individual pole of citizens does not suffice. Individual citizens should be interlinked as a citizenry: a demos capable of engendering the communicative power without which democracy would remain an empty promise of the formal constitution. Here the constitutional practices where European citizens jointly, across national borders, exercise their political autonomy are of crucial importance; it is only through these practices that European belongingness and solidarity or a European civil society and public sphere can develop. In polity building, the emergence of a constitutional culture shared by European legal or political elites does not suffice. What is needed is a civic constitutional culture forging individual citizens into a European citizenry; a source of communicative power controlling European political institutions and infusing them with democratic input legitimacy.

The constitutive function, so important for the political constitution of an emergent European polity, is accompanied by an equally important *positioning function*: defining the relations of the polity to other polities. This is a function of state constitutions too, but it is particularly pertinent in a transnational polity, such as the EU.

The basic positioning relates to the *claim to autonomy* that a constitution typically involves. With regard to their *occasio constitutionis*, state constitutions can be roughly divided into three groups. Firstly, revolutionary constitutions signal the beginning of a new political regime and perhaps even a new social order. The classic examples are the American and French constitutions of the late eighteenth century. Secondly, there are constitutions which amount to declarations of independence. Drafting a constitution is the first thing a newly independent state engages in, and in adopting a constitution it reinforces its claim to autonomous existence. Let me take two Nordic examples: the Norwegian Constitution of 1814, the oldest constitution still in force in Europe, and the Constitution of Finland of 1919, adopted after Finland had seceded from the Russian Empire. But not all constitutions herald the beginning of a new political or social era, or reaffirm newly won independence. A third type of codificatory constitution exists as well. Such constitutions by and large merely codify and sanctify social, legal and political developments that have already occurred. Again, the Nordic countries offer two examples: the 1975 Swedish Constitution, which replaced the Constitution dating back to 1809, and the Finnish Constitution of 2000, which replaced the first constitution of independent Finland. The claim to autonomy is, of course, most conspicuous in constitutions amounting to a declaration of independence, but it is relevant for constitutions falling in the other groups too. State constitutions typically involve explicit provisions on independence or sovereignty (or both).

Because of the process-like nature of European constitution(alization), it cannot be compressed into any of the three categories of state constitution. Furthermore, the character of the Treaties has evolved on the long road from Rome to Lisbon, under the impact of constitutional speech acts by both the constitutional legislator and other constitutional actors as well, most importantly the ECJ as the constitutional court. Discussing the relevance of the claim to autonomy takes us back to the overall characterization of the EU and its law. Opting for the transnational alternative and adopting constitutional language to depict the EU polity and legal system entails attaching to the European constitution a claim to autonomy as well. Through this claim, the European political constitution distinguishes the EU polity from Member States and international organizations under public international law.

The positioning function is not exhausted by the claim to autonomy but usually includes further specification of the external relations of the polity at issue. State constitutions involve provisions on participation in international cooperation and, especially in Europe, authorize transfer of sovereignty rights to international or transnational organizations, such as the EU. In federal constitutions, the relations of the central level and the federated entities are pivotal constitutional topics. A transnational constitution, such as the European one, may also attempt to position the polity in a global setting. Still, what is particularly important are the interrelations with the Member States. Consequently, principles pertaining to the division of competences between the EU and the Member States, as well as provisions concerning the participation of Member State political bodies – mainly governments and parliaments – in decision-making in the EU, are essential elements of the European political constitution.

In a polity aspiring to be a democratic *Rechtsstaat*, the organizational and restrictive functions are inseparable from the *legitimizing* one. For individuals, the political constitution of a democratic *Rechtsstaat* promises autonomy, citizenship and democracy. These promises are intimately linked to the claim to legitimacy, so intimately associated with constitutionalism in its thick normative sense and constitutional vocabulary. Constitutional law is expected to bestow legitimacy on the constitutional object, such as the polity as the object of the political constitution. But it can only accomplish this if it is considered legitimate in itself.

From where does a constitution draw its legitimacy? Here the particularities of constitutional history are, of course, highly relevant. Clearly, different types of constitution – revolutionary constitutions, declarations of independence and codificatory constitutions – differ with regard to their characteristic conditions of legitimacy too. In general terms, two principal explanations can be suggested for constitutional legitimacy: origin-based and content-based. *Origin-based legitimacy* derives from the circumstances in which a formal constitution has been enacted or the procedure which was thereby adhered to: the constitutional moment which gave birth to the constitution. Characteristically, the constitutional moment giving rise to a revolutionary constitution is marked by wide political mobilization and intensive discourses within civil society and among the citizenry as the demos – the ultimate subject of the constituent power – perhaps culminating in a referendum.[6] In addition, the constitutional moment may come to symbolize a turning point in the existential history of the nation, such as gaining political independence or autonomy; here we could speak of a *symbolic legitimacy*. For instance, the Norwegian constitution of 1814 evokes the memory of Norway's detachment from Denmark and entry into a personal union with Sweden as an autonomous entity. Origin-based legitimacy is typical of revolutionary constitutions and constitutions as declarations of independence.

In turn, *substantive* or *content-based legitimacy* flows from the substance of the constitution; from its accordance with the basic ethical values and moral principles of society. Constitutional provisions on

[6] The international revival of the concept of the constitutional moment, together with related concepts of the revolutionary constitutional tradition, owed much to B. Ackerman (1993).

fundamental rights endow the basic moral principles of modern society with legal form and consequences. Origin-based and content-based legitimacy can be, and often are, mutually supportive and complementary. The US or Norwegian constitutions could only have retained their origin-based legitimacy as complemented by content-based legitimacy. But the two types of legitimacy may also be detached from each other. So it seems that the legitimacy that the German Basic Law has gained over the years is mainly content-based: the circumstances in which the Basic Law was adopted were not very conducive to its legitimacy. On the other hand, it may happen that origin-based legitimacy loses its edge because of an increasing discrepancy between constitutional provisions – for example, an outdated Bill of Rights – and social values and moral principles.

How should we assess the legitimacy of the European constitution in the light of the above alternatives? Arguably, the legitimacy of the Founding Treaties has primarily been origin-based. No constitutional moment exists in the European process of constitutionalization, nor can legitimacy be based on direct participation of European citizenry as a European demos. The Treaties owe their origin-based constitutional legitimacy to their international law aspect, to the fact that they have been ratified by national parliaments or in referendums, in accordance with the provisions of the national constitution. As is typical of the *two-stage European legitimating mechanism*, national democratic procedures are crucial for the origin-based legitimacy of the transnational European constitution. If this observation holds, the veritable legitimacy problem concerns constitution-making by the ECJ. Especially in the fields of (micro)economic and juridical constitutions, the role of the Court has been vital, not only in implementing and further specifying Treaty-based constitutional law but also in introducing central constitutional principles with only scarce or no support in explicit Treaty provisions. Well-known and widely debated examples include, in the juridical constitution, direct effect and primacy and, in the (micro)economic constitution, the *Dassonville*, *Cassis de Dijon* and *Keck* formulas, as well as the principle of mutual recognition introduced by *Cassis de Dijon*.[7] Constitution-making exceeds the ordinary judicial role of interpretation and application, and cannot draw on the output legitimacy of independent juridical expertise. But nor can the ECJ rely on the two-stage legitimating mechanism functioning through the intermediary of national democratic procedures. The legitimating effect which

7 Case C-8/74 *Dassonville* [1974] ECR 837; Case C-120/78 *Cassis de Dijon* [1979] ECR 649; Joined cases C-267/91 and C-268/91 *Keck* [1993] ECR I-6097.

flows from granting private litigants access to national courts in issues related to European law and, by the same token, making them stakeholders in judicial legislation must also be deemed quite restricted.[8] The judicial citizenship established by the gradually widening scope of direct effect has benefited but a minor proportion of European citizens; for the most part, actual litigants have been companies instead of individual citizens.

What about, then, the content-based legitimacy of judicial constitution-making, especially in its pre-Maastricht heyday? Juridical constitutionalization through ECJ case law was closely intertwined with the development of the economic constitution in a microeconomic direction, by and large corresponding to a market-liberal reading of the Treaty of Rome. German ordoliberals have always argued for the substantive legitimacy of their version of the microeconomic constitution and, indeed, after Lisbon too, have presented it as a panacea for the legitimacy problems of the Union.[9] The argument is simple: an open market economy with free competition is grounded in the values of freedom and equality, lying in the very ethical foundation of modern societies. However, in a European economy where the main economic actors are big, and increasingly multinational, companies, such an individual-related claim to substantive legitimacy is hardly convincing.

Substantive legitimacy presupposes principle-oriented constitutionalism. *Pace* ordoliberal claims, the dominance of economic constitutionalism reflects the basic policy orientation of European integration. Still, elaboration of the fundamental rights dimension and references to universalist values in EU primary law have added a principle aspect to European constitutional law. This can be seen as an attempt to insert substantive legitimacy into the European constitution.

The legitimacy of constitutional law itself is a necessary condition, though not a sufficient one, for accomplishing the legitimacy function in relation to the constitutional object, such as the EU as a polity or its individual institutions and policies. The initial legitimacy which the EU may enjoy because of the status of the Member States as Masters of the Treaties does not suffice, but the claim to legitimacy must be constantly re-redeemed. This concerns both *system legitimacy* – the overall legitimacy of the EU – and the *policy legitimacy* of individual policies and institutions responsible for these; the question can be raised as to where, say, economic or monetary policy or adjudication by an independent judiciary

[8] Cf. M. Poiares Maduro (1998). [9] J.-M. Luczak (2009).

derives its legitimacy. Here Fritz Scharpf's distinction between *democratic input legitimacy* and *result-based output legitimacy* is important.[10] In state constitutions, provisions on legislative and budgetary procedures, as well as participatory citizenship rights, aim to produce democratic input legitimacy at both system and policy level. In turn, provisions on independent expert bodies, such as courts or central banks, seek to facilitate output legitimacy in terms of, say, impartial and reasoned adjudication or monetary policy objectives, such as monetary stability.

At the European level, the distinction between system and policy legitimacy has not always been very sharp. Especially in the early, pre-Maastricht decades, the functional definition of competences made it possible to understand European integration as a whole as a cluster of specific policies[11] and to assess integration in terms of output legitimacy. Bracketing the second-order objective of maintaining peace in Europe, what was decisive was whether the promise of increased economic prosperity (re)distributed through national mechanisms was kept or not. Enlargement of European competences through ECJ case law and the prominent role of the ECJ in European law- and constitution-making in general raised concerns about the need for democratic input legitimacy. The boost to political constitutionalization in Maastricht has, and I think rightly, been seen as a response to these concerns. In addition to balancing policy orientation with principle-related provisions, the Maastricht Treaty tried to enhance direct democratic input legitimacy by strengthening the position of the European Parliament in law-making and by introducing explicit provisions on European citizenship. Yet, as will be discussed in the next section, Member State constitutionalism has retained a crucial role in providing system and policy legitimacy for the EU. The legitimacy function of the European political constitution should always be examined in the setting of the interaction between transnational European and national Member State constitutionalism.

The typology of constitutional legitimacy is still in need of a vital addition. It is also possible that the proponents of constitutionalization put their faith in the sheer legitimating force of constitutional rhetoric – which, in turn, is only explicable against the background of what can be called constitutional normalcy, i.e. origin- or contents-based legitimacy.

10 F. Scharpf (1999), pp. 6–8.

11 Such an understanding was implicit in Hans Peter Ipsen's often-cited characterization of the European Communities as *Zweckverbände funktioneller Integration*. See H. P. Ipsen (1972).

At issue is *parasitic legitimacy*. When a military junta has a facade 'constitution' adopted by a puppet parliament or in a rigged referendum, it aims at parasitic legitimacy, drawing upon the positive connotations that constitutional vocabulary evokes or at least is expected to evoke. Attempts to attain parasitic legitimacy can be detected in European constitutional discourse as well. Critical observers may condemn recourse to constitutional language *per se* as parasitic legitimacy seeking. Some constitutional dimensions may be more vulnerable than others to such criticism. For instance, in the security dimension expressions such as 'right to security' might be seen as an abuse of constitutional language for legitimizing purposes. However, the fate of the Constitutional Treaty shows that constitutional talk does not necessarily produce expected results, at least not among the general public. Instead of promoting the legitimacy of the European project, it may deepen the distrust of the citizenry.

The constitutional relation is not a one-way route: not only does European constitutional law affect the constitutional object, but the constitutional object also affects constitutional law. A major channel for the influence of the constitutional object on constitutional law is the implicit social – or in the reflexive juridical constitution, legal – theory of constitutional law.

How external society can impact law is one of the intractable problems which the assumption of autopoeitically closed social sub-systems creates for Luhmann's disciples. They must, however, be credited for the insight that external society does not have direct access to law. External influences are channelled and transformed in the interplay of the legal order and institutionally framed legal practices. Legal actors with their legal *connaissance* and *savoir*[12] constitute the connecting link between the two aspects of law. Law as a legal order always implies a particular conception of the object of legal regulation; law would remain ineffective if it did not heed the characteristics of the social field subjected to legal regulation. *Travaux préparatoires* may contain social scientifically informed accounts of the present and desired state of affairs, and even courts may engage in overt teleological, policy reasoning. However, of special importance in reconstructing the social theory of national law is the legal cultural layer

[12] Foucault's notions *connaissance* and *savoir* correspond to Anthony Giddens's distinction between discursive and practical knowledge. A. Giddens (1979), pp. 24–5. Legal actors' *Vorverständnis* is a province of legal *savoir* or practical knowledge. See also K. Tuori (2002), p. 149.

underpinning the surface of explicit regulations or court decisions. The doctrines of diverse fields of law – private law, criminal law, administrative law and so on – reflect a particular view of the respective social field. Even in scholarly doctrinal expositions, this view is often left unarticulated; this warrants the term 'implicit social theory of law'.[13] A vital task for theoretically oriented legal scholarship is to unearth this implicit social theory.

All this holds, *mutatis mutandis*, for European constitutional law as well. The constitutional theory underpinning constitutional doctrine in diverse constitutional dimensions is normatively oriented. Still, it also includes a particular view of the constitutional object: an implicit social theory; or, when talking of the juridical constitution, an implicit legal theory. However, because European sectoral constitutions constitutionalize controversial policy issues, the implicit social (or legal) theory must be expected to be a matter of contestation as well.

It may turn out that the implicit social theory does not stand the test of social reality. As we shall see in Chapter 6, the Eurozone crisis invalidated many of the central economic assumptions of the Maastricht provisions on Economic and Monetary Union. And, as we shall also see, this was the primary impetus to the constitutional mutation which the crisis launched. But developments in the social field under regulation have no direct way of imposing changes on the legal order. This can only occur through legal practices and through knowledge of the social object of regulation that relevant legal actors rely on. Constitutional law too can only change through constitutional practices.

Transnational and national constitutionalism

Transnationalization and *individualization* – granting rights to private subjects and establishing direct relationships between them and European institutions – are central criteria for European constitutionalization. Still, despite such individualization, manifested by the progressive enrichment of European citizenship, the transnational constitution also retains its interaction with the national constitutions of the Member States. Even the concept of European citizenship, such as it is defined in Treaty law, reflects an intertwinement of the transnational, national and individual levels: individuals obtain European citizenship as a consequence of their Member State citizenship (Art. 20(1) TFEU). In what follows I shall discuss

13 K. Tuori (2011), pp. 197–8.

the interplay between the transnational and the national under three topics: mutual positioning, complementarity and the two-stage mechanism of democratic legitimation.

Let us start with *mutual positioning*. During the last twenty years, constitutional pluralism has dominated scholarly discussion on the relations between the European constitution and its national counterparts. The *Maastricht* decision of the German Constitutional Court[14] was the crucial catalyst which brought the issue into the focus of academic constitutional discourse too. In scholarly debates, Neil MacCormick's seminal articles played a major initiating role.[15] The debate on constitutional pluralism addresses an important aspect in the relations that the European transnational constitution entertains with Member State national constitutions: the fact that these constitutions raise rival claims of authority in European constitutional space. Positioning is a central function not only for the EU political and juridical constitutions but for national constitutions as well. Yet no *a priori* guarantee exists that the positioning of the European legal system with regard to national legal systems is in harmony with the positioning of national legal systems with regard to the European one. As has been repeatedly observed in recent debate, the pluralist constellation is conflict-sensitive. However, as I will argue in Chapter 3, mutual positioning should be analysed not only in terms of actual or latent conflicts but also as a dialogical and cooperative relationship between legal orders; reminders of the ever-present possibility of *constitutional conflicts* should be complemented by references to normative and institutional *interlegality*.

In addition to its one-sided conflict focus, the debate on constitutional pluralism has addressed the consequences of mutual positioning merely in the juridical dimension. In the positioning exercised by state constitutions, 'sovereignty' is a key concept.[16] Member States' defence of their political and legislative sovereignty – the universality of their political and legal claims to authority – has implications for European sectoral constitutions too. Member States have raised sovereignty concerns with regard to fiscal and other economic policy; welfare policy and the choice of welfare regimes; and use of the coercive power of the state, its 'monopoly

[14] BVerfGE 89, 155, 2 October 1993.

[15] These articles are collected in his *Questioning Sovereignty*, D. N. MacCormick (1999).

[16] Constitutional theorists have increasingly expressed doubts about the fruitfulness of the very concept of sovereignty. See, e.g., the contributions in N. Walker (2006b). Yet 'sovereignty' still belongs to the object language of both European and national constitutional legislators and judges which constitutional theorists cannot totally ignore in elaborating their meta-language.

of legitimate use of violence'. The influence of these concerns confirms the reciprocity of constitutional positioning: not only does European positioning affect national constitutions, but Member State positioning narrows the leeway for European constitutionalization.

Examples of normative interlegality and intertwinement show that the respective positioning of transnational and national constitutions need not be interpreted in the spirit of a black box model. Normative interlegality is complemented and facilitated by *institutional interlocking*. Within the juridical constitution the major manifestation of this intertwinement is the dual role of national courts: their belonging to both the national and the European legal systems. In turn, somewhat paradoxically, intergovernmental institutions such as the European Council or the Council of Ministers in its different compositions play a vital role in the institutional organization that the political constitution has established for the transnational Union polity. Heads of state and government in the European Council and government representatives in the Council of Ministers appear in a dual role: they are expected to express and convey the interests and normative standpoints of their national polities but, simultaneously, as members of a Union institution they explain and defend Union decisions to national parliaments and constituencies. Members of the Council may even have an obligation under national constitutional law to defer to the instructions of national constitutional bodies, such as the parliament, and convey information on decisions taken. Even the head of state or government as the national representative in the European Council may have a constitutional duty to brief their national parliament on decisions the Council has taken.

From the very beginning, national parliaments too have occupied a place in the institutional structure of the transnational European polity. Until 1979, Members of the European Parliament were elected by national parliaments. After that the contribution of national parliaments was channelled in unofficial forms outside the Treaty framework, such as the Conference of European Community Affairs Committees (COSAC), which was created in 1989 to maintain contact between national parliaments and their European counterpart. Subsequently, COSAC's position has been constitutionalized through the Protocol on the role of national parliaments in the European Union.[17] The Protocol on the application

[17] COSAC 'may submit any contribution it deems appropriate for the attention of the European Parliament, the Council and the Commission'. It should also 'promote the exchange of information and best practice between national Parliaments and the European Parliament, including their special committees' (Art. 10).

of the principles of subsidiarity and proportionality, also attached to the Lisbon Treaty, entrusts national parliaments with the task of supervising adherence to the principle of subsidiarity.[18] Both protocols include provisions on the obligation of Union institutions to provide national parliaments with information on draft legislative acts.

The European and national levels are intertwined even at the individual pole of the polity relationship. Individuals are citizens of both the national and the European polity. And if the European political constitution ever succeeds in its polity-building function, this will undoubtedly require a networking of national demoi and the transnational European demos.

In addition to mutual positioning, the relations between the European transnational constitution and Member State national constitutions can be examined from the point of view of *complementarity*. For instance, the positioning function of the political constitution implies division of competences, while division of competences, in turn, can express division of labour. But this is not necessarily so: division of competences may free the Union and Member States to pursue their distinct objectives and policies within their fields of competence. It is misleading to assume that the Union and its Member States constitute in every relevant respect a multilevel *Verfassungsbund* where relations between the transnational and the national are primarily characterized by intertwinement and complementarity.[19] Complementarity in the sense of division of labour presupposes common objectives; only with regard to common objectives can an expedient division of labour and corresponding allocation of competences be adopted. In the field of shared competences, the principle of subsidiarity, as formulated in Art. 5(3) TEU, does presuppose the existence of common objectives; the Union will step in only if the objective at issue cannot be better achieved by lower-level action. A presumption of common objectives, grounded in a common value basis whose existence

[18] National parliaments are entitled to issue reasoned opinions on the non-compliance of a draft legislative act with the principle of subsidiarity. If these reasoned opinions represent the required proportion of votes allocated to national parliaments the Union institution at issue must review the draft. The institution may amend or withdraw the draft but it can also maintain it. It must, though, give reasons for its decision (Arts. 6–7).

[19] The idea of a multilevel *Verfassungsverbund* was propounded, first of all, by Ingolf Pernice. See, e.g., I. Pernice (2009).

Art. 2 TEU postulates, also facilitates an understanding of the demarcation between national and Union fundamental rights review in terms of complementarity (see Chapter 3).

All the sectoral constitutions imply relations of complementarity. EU constitutional law does not comprise all the constitutional guarantees which must be in place to enable a European internal market, based on undistorted competition. The fundamental rights that a market economy requires are mainly ensured by national constitutions: by provisions on the right to property, freedom of contract and freedom of trade. Hence, the European microeconomic constitution is premised on the complementary contribution of Member State constitutions. In turn, the European macroeconomic constitution has presupposed Member State budgetary autonomy, although its use has been subjected to European constraints. In the social dimension, the European economic and social constitutions have relied on the existence of national redistributive welfare regimes. In the security dimension too, core security functions and their judicial supervision have been retained under Member State sovereignty.

A relation of complementarity labels the participatory rights of European citizens as well. In their EU constitutional practices, EU citizens rely on the public autonomy guaranteed to them as Member State citizens, such as the freedoms of assembly, association and the press. The tripartite polity relation connecting political institutions, citizenry and individual citizens could not work without the support of Member State constitutions either. As this example shows, complementarity may also be conceptualized as a supportive relation.

The initial technocratic policy orientation of European integration, prominent in, for instance, Jean Monnet's functionalism, left its mark not only on the Paris Treaty on the European Coal and Steel Community (ECSC) but on the Rome Treaty on the European Economic Community as well. It largely ignored the issue of *democratic legitimacy*. The Member States had ratified the Treaties according to their constitutional requirements, and the democratic legitimacy this produced was considered sufficient. However, embryos of democratic legitimation of European policy-making were inserted in the Treaty of Rome through the Council and the Assembly (European Parliament) too. These embryos manifested the two-stage mechanism of democratic legitimacy which is such a distinct feature of European constitutionalism and the significance of which has grown in line with the widening of European competences. The contribution of national democratic procedures to the legitimacy of European policies is a vital epitome of the complementary relation between national and European constitutionalism. The administrative law portrayal of the EU not only ignores sectoral constitutionalization; from its exclusive Member State perspective, it also refuses to examine putative European constitutionalism through interaction between the transnational and national levels. It declines to place national democratic procedures of control, oversight and implementation in the context of European constitutionalism.

In the course of political constitutionalization, efforts have been made to create direct legitimating relations between European citizenry and European institutions, most notably through direct election of the European Parliament and the introduction of European citizenship. However, as the low turnout in European elections has most dramatically proved, the cultural and social prerequisites for the formation of a European civil society and public sphere, capable of sustaining a Europe-wide democracy, are still largely lacking. On their own, European constitutional practices, culminating institutionally in the election of the European Parliament and its legislative and supervisory powers, can hardly live up to the high expectations of the thick normative concept of constitutionalism. This has only accentuated the importance of the contribution of national constitutionalism to the democratic legitimacy of the EU.

Intergovernmental EU institutions work under the guidance of national democratically legitimated bodies, and national parliaments even participate directly in Union law-making. Furthermore, the major part of Union legislative and other measures is implemented and enforced by national authorities. EU directives are transposed into the municipal legal order by the national legislator, thereby receiving an injection of democratic input legitimacy. But nationally applicable EU law is integrated into the whole of the national legal order and, as it were, scrounges off the general legitimacy of the latter. In Jürgen Habermas's distinction between regulatory law (law as a medium) and law as an institution,[20] EU law has mainly fallen into the former category. Law as an institution is intimately related to the moral and value texture of society; hence, this department of law is vital to the overall substantive legitimacy of the legal order. In so far as EU law enjoys substantive legitimacy, it is at least partly parasitic on the substantive legitimacy of national legal orders. In sum, the fact that the general public has primarily confronted EU measures, not directly,

[20] J. Habermas (1989), p. 365.

but indirectly, through the political and administrative institutions and the legal system of the respective Member State, has been crucial for the legitimacy that the Union and its individual policies have enjoyed among European citizenry.[21]

As Peter Lindseth has shown, Member State parliamentary oversight of European policies has intensified during recent decades.[22] Yet, contrary to what Lindseth contends, this is not an argument for rejecting the existence of European constitutionalism. Along with the importance of sectoral constitutionalization, the interaction between the transnational and national levels belongs to the features which distinguish European from state constitutionalism. This interaction is vital for providing European institutions and policies with democratic legitimacy. The Treaty of Lisbon explicitly recognizes the role of Member State constitutionalism in realizing the democratic principle. Art. 10 TEU proclaims that the functioning of the Union is founded on representative democracy. Not only are citizens directly represented at Union level in the European Parliament; in addition, Member States are represented in the European Council by their heads of state or government and in the Council by their governments. In turn, these representatives are themselves democratically accountable either to national parliaments or citizens. Art. 10 TEU expressly confirms the complementarity of direct European democracy and the two-level mechanism which harnesses national procedures to the service of European-level democratic legitimacy.

The relation between transnational and national constitutionalism is of a reciprocal character. Not only does national constitutionalism complement and support its transnational counterpart; European constitutionalization has also impacted in important ways on Member State constitutions. This impact is most conspicuous in express constitutional provisions on, for instance, transfer of powers to the European level or deliberation of European issues in the national parliament. Furthermore, European integration has had repercussions for the respective power positions of national parliaments and governments. European intergovernmentalist mechanisms have often been assumed to have reinforced national executives at the expense of parliaments. For many Member States this conclusion is probably too straightforward and hasty. Parliamentary oversight mechanisms in European affairs may actually have put the brakes on, and even reversed, a development which in the post-Second

[21] F. W. Scharpf (2012), p. 19. [22] P. Lindseth (2010).

World War era has strengthened the executive in Western democracies. As regards the judiciary, the dual domicile of ordinary courts in both national and European legal systems has enhanced their position vis-à-vis the national legislature. As guardians of European law they have attained the power of judicial review over national legislation even in countries where the national constitution does not allow for such review.

2 Interlude: the framing juridical constitution

The juridical and political constitutions frame not only substantive constitutional dimensions but each other too: the juridical constitution the political one and vice versa. The juridical and political constitutions are closely intertwined. Luhmann argues that the (state) constitution establishes a structural coupling between the legal and political sub-systems. Diverging from Luhmann, my focus is on the interaction between, not two social sub-systems, but two constitutional dimensions. The constitutional object of the juridical and political constitutions is different: respectively, the European legal system and the European polity. But these two framing constitutions are interlocked through common elements: such as principles concerning the division of competences between the European and Member State level, provisions on law-making procedure, or fundamental rights as restrictions on both political power and legal regulation.

As is the case with the European constitution in general, the juridical constitution should be approached as an ongoing process of constitutionalization. This process amounts to an increasing detachment, under the functional primacy of economic constitutionalization, from an international law background. It would, however, be fruitless to try to define the exact moment when European law crossed the borderline between international and transnational law to accomplish juridical constitutionalization. Not only is this borderline fluid; even more importantly, no end exists to juridical constitutionalization.

Constituting the European legal system

The constitutional object of the European juridical constitution is the EU legal system, understood as a combination of the two aspects of law, that is, EU law as a symbolic-normative entity – a legal order – and as institutionally framed legal practices. For a new legal system, such as EU law, the constitutive and positioning functions of the juridical constitution are central. The juridical constitution constitutes EU law as a distinct legal system and positions it in relation to other legal systems.

Corresponding to the Kelsenian understanding of material constitution, the European juridical constitution enables the EU legal order through Treaty provisions on legislative and judicial competences. What the European juridical constitution has not been able to achieve is Kelsenian clarity in the internal organization of this legal order; EU law can hardly be presented as a hierarchical *Stufenbau* where higher level norms provide the validity basis for lower level ones and prevail over them in norm conflicts. A degree of uncertainty has always permeated the relations among Treaty-based legal instruments. The Lisbon Treaty, though, sought to add clarity by introducing categories of legislative, delegated and implementing acts (Arts 289–91 TFEU). Still, to the puzzlement of an observer searching for Kelsenian unambiguity, no internal hierarchy prevails between regulations, directives and decisions, and they may all be issued either as legislative, delegated or implementing acts.[1] Furthermore, the Treaties as the 'constitutional charter' do not manifest the importance of the law-making power of the ECJ or the constitutional role of the general principles the Court has established. The Court has interpreted very liberally its Treaty-based task to 'ensure that in the interpretation and application of the Treaties the law is observed' (now Art. 19(1) TEU). On the ECJ's interpretation, general principles, which the Court has itself articulated, have a constitutional status and, hence, form part of primary law.[2]

Kelsen conceived of the order of a legal order in formal, hierarchical terms; in Kelsen's pure theory of law the contents of the legal order did not play any role. But *pace* Kelsen, the order of a legal order can be examined in substantive terms too. Substantive order, *coherence*, is produced through legal principles (*sensu lato*) permeating the norm material. Employing the vocabulary of Ronald Dworkin, coherence can be due either to policies or to principles *sensu stricto*, such as fundamental rights. The fact that the Treaty of Rome bypassed the formal relations among acts of secondary legislation can be explained by the prevalence of a substantive order,

[1] See on the interrelations between EU secondary law instruments K. Lenaerts and M. Desomer (2005); H. Hofmann (2009); A. Rosas and L. Armati (2012), pp. 61–5; P. Craig (2013), pp. 247 ff.

[2] Case C-101/08 *Audiolux and Others v Groupe Bruxelles Lambert and Others* [2009] ECR I-9823, Para. 63.

brought about by the policy orientation of the Treaty and the secondary legislation it authorized. All the legislative acts were expected to promote establishment of the common market as the main objective of the Treaty. The order of European law was conceived of as a policy-based coherence. Subsequent developments have complicated the situation. Fundamental rights and reference to universalist values (Art. 2 TEU) have complemented policy-based coherence with principle-related elements.

In state legal orders too, substantive coherence has complemented and partly even replaced formal principles of order. The increasing openness of national legal orders to norms of international or transnational origin has made it more and more difficult to stick to a Kelsenian hierarchical conception. For its part, policy-oriented European law, claiming direct effect, supremacy and integration, has induced confusion in the hierarchical structure of the national legal order. Substantive coherence, produced by morally laden general legal principles, such as those related to fundamental rights, has become ever more vital for the order of the national legal order.[3] In clashes of authority between European and national law, often enough two different principles of order confront each other: the policy orientation of European law and the principle orientation of national law. This is one way of depicting the reservations that national constitutional courts have made to the supremacy of European law: constitutional courts defend the principle-based foundations of national law against the policy-motivated claims of European law.

In a democratic *Rechtsstaat*, the hierarchy of legal norms is intimately linked to legitimacy considerations: a link on which Kelsen's pure theory of law remains silent. Hierarchy of norms corresponds to different degrees of democratic legitimacy: constitutional law issued by the constitutional legislature, ordinary laws issued by the parliament and by-laws or regulations issued by the executive branch. At the time of drafting the Treaty of Rome, secondary legislation was still understood to be of a mainly regulatory character and not in need of direct democratic input legitimacy. Accordingly, the Assembly (the European Parliament) was reserved merely a consultative role. If democratic input legitimacy was expected at all, it was channelled through the representatives of the national executives in the Council. The distinction between regulations, directives and decisions was grounded, not in considerations of legitimacy, but in their different legal effects and different tasks in promoting the policy objectives enshrined in the Treaty.

[3] See the interesting discussion in G. Itzcovich (2012).

Kelsen's formalistic conception emphasizes the constitutive function but ignores another, equally important constitutional function: namely, the *restrictive* one.[4] In the constitution of a democratic *Rechtsstaat*, the restrictive function falls to fundamental rights, positivized by constitutional provisions and constitutional jurisprudence, and supervised by constitutional review. Differing from a state legal order, claiming universal jurisidiction, EU law's claim to authority is substantively (functionally) delineated. The *principle of conferral* requires that Union legislative competences be grounded in express Treaty authorizations, whereas use of these competences is supposed to be governed by the principles of *subsidiarity* and *proportionality* (Art. 5 TFEU).

Because of the foundational policy orientation and the functional delineation of European competences, the framers of the Treaty of Rome did not perceive any need for additional fundamental rights guarantees. The subsequent introduction and gradual elaboration of fundamental rights law is related to two developments. The restrictive power of what is now called the principle of conferral was weakened by the way the Commission and the Court interpreted Treaty competences: in particular, the general competence to issue harmonizing directives for the purpose of promoting the establishment and functioning of the common (internal) market (Art. 100 TEEC; now Art. 114 TFEU), and the so-called flexibility clause which allowed for European measures deemed necessary for attaining Treaty objectives even where no express Treaty authorization existed (Art. 235 TEEC; now Art. 352 TFEU). Further leeway was created by the doctrine of *implied powers*, which the ECJ introduced in its *ERTA* ruling.[5] Explicitly granted legislative competences too were greatly enlarged through successive Treaty revisions, starting with the Single European Act (SEA) in 1986. Moreover, the restrictive effect of the principle of conferral presupposes efficient *ultra vires* review. Quashing by the ECJ of European legislative acts on the grounds of missing competence has been rare, with the *Tobacco Advertising* case in 2000 as a lonely exception.[6] However, the Maastricht Treaty and the subsequent *Maastricht* ruling by the German Constitutional Court seem to have brought about an adjustment in the Court's approach. The Treaty widened explicit competences, which

[4] See my discussion of the post-natural law dilemma in K. Tuori (2002), pp. 217 ff., and K. Tuori (2011), pp. 237–9.

[5] Case C-22/70 *Commission v Council (ERTA)* [1971] ECR 263.

[6] Case C-376/98 *Germany v Parliament and Council (Tobacco Advertisement)* [2000] ECR I-8419. See on the significance of *Tobacco Advertisement*, S. Weatherill (2011) and J. Snell (2014), pp. 316–19.

reduced the need to resort to implied powers or the flexibility clause. For its part, the German Constitutional Court recalled that the flexibility clause should not be employed to circumvent the procedure for Treaty revision.[7] Opinion 2/94,[8] where the ECJ rejected recourse to the flexibility clause as a competence basis for Union accession to the European Convention on Human Rights, has often been understood as a reaction to the *Maastricht* ruling of the German Court. The ECJ emphasized that 'Article 235 cannot be used as a basis for the adoption of provisions whose effect would, in substance, be to amend the Treaty without following the procedure which it provides for that purpose.'[9]

Widening of European competences made it evident that the principle of conferral did not suffice to accomplish the restrictive constitutional function. Particularly important was the incorporation of the security dimension – the Area of Freedom, Security and Justice (AFSJ), as the Treaty of Amsterdam called it – because it brought under Union competences fields which are highly sensitive to fundamental right issues. National implementation of policy-oriented Community measures had also shown that these too could collide with fundamental rights. In order to ward off national review, the ECJ reacted by introducing fundamental rights as general principles of Community law. Fundamental rights complemented the principle of conferral as a restrictive ground in the European juridical and political constitutions. By the same token, the original policy orientation of European law has been mitigated by the principle orientation of fundamental rights. However, just as the impact of the principle of conferral presupposes efficient *ultra vires* review, the restrictive effect of fundamental rights depends on an attentive review mechanism. In general, the ECJ has been more vigilant in reviewing national measures falling within the scope of EU law than Union legislative measures. This also holds for fundamental rights review. Yet a change may be in the air. In the intricate balancing between security and fundamental rights considerations the Court has assumed a more active role and has not spared EU legislative acts from quashing, as has been shown by, for instance, *Kadi* and the more recent *Digital Rights Ireland* (2014). In the latter ruling, the Court declared the Data Retention Directive invalid on the grounds of 'a wide-ranging and particularly serious interference with those fundamental rights in the legal order of the EU, without such an interference being precisely circumscribed by provisions to ensure that it is actually

[7] BVerfGE 89, 155, 2 October 1993. [8] Opinion 2/94 [1996] ECR I-1759.
[9] See on the use and interpretation of the flexibility clause T. Konstadinides (2012).

limited to what is strictly necessary'.[10] Coinciding with the Court's novel activism, *ex ante* constitutional review by the Commission, sometimes involving consultation of the Union Fundamental Rights Agency, has also gained in significance.[11]

The juridical constitution not only constitutes EU law as a legal order; it also establishes the institutional framework for developing and enforcing that legal order. The Treaties include provisions on the composition, competences and procedures of both constitutional and ordinary legislatures. The provisions manifest the simultaneously juridical and political character of legislative practices; the institutional and procedural provisions belong to both the juridical and the political constitution.

Furthermore, the Treaties regulate the Union Courts, their competences and the procedures for instigating legal proceedings, including *locus standi* before them. Provisions on the Courts' jurisdiction over Union institutions, bodies, offices and agencies, as well as measures that these adopt, are relatively unambiguous. The Treaties also indicate some but not all of the tasks which justify labelling the ECJ a constitutional court. The Court has been expressly granted jurisdiction to assess the legality of Union acts; here it can exercise both *ultra vires* and fundamental rights review.[12] According to present Art. 263 TFEU, action can be brought both by (other) Union institutions and a Member State. This entails ECJ jurisdiction in both inter-institutional and Union/Member State conflicts of competence; jurisdiction which corresponds to essential functions of a typical (federal) state constitutional court. By contrast, private subjects have but a limited standing before the Court. European constitutional law has not adopted any correspondence to individual constitutional complaints (*Verfassungsbeschwerde*), which would instigate, say, fundamental rights review by the ECJ. Private subjects can only 'institute proceedings against an act

[10] Joined Cases C-293/12 and C-594/12 *Digital Rights Ireland and Others*, judgment of 8 April 2014 (not yet reported), Para. 65.

[11] The Commission routinely includes in its legislative proposals an assessment of impacts on fundamental rights. See Commission Staff Working Paper, Operational Guidance on taking account of Fundamental Rights in Commission Impact Assessments, SEC(2011) 567 final.

[12] Art. 263 TFEU expressly mentions lack of competence as a ground for assessing the legality of Union measures. Fundamental rights review is not explicitly indicated but falls under the general title of 'infringement of the Treaties or of any rule of law relating to their application'. In total, the grounds for review comprise 'lack of competence, infringement of an essential procedural requirement, infringement of the Treaties or of any rule of law relating to their application, or misuse of powers'.

addressed to that person or which is of direct and individual concern to them, and against a regulatory act which is of direct concern to them and does not entail implementing measures'. However, the preliminary ruling procedure enables private subjects to influence initiation of European judicial review in a case pending before a national court. Referrals for preliminary ruling can also concern 'the validity and interpretation of acts of the institutions, bodies, offices or agencies of the Union' (Art. 267 TFEU).

Where the Treaty basis for ECJ jurisdiction is more unclear is judicial review of Member State legislation, where the ECJ monitors the supremacy of EU law and seeks to guarantee its effectiveness and uniform implementation. The procedural basis consists of provisions on preliminary rulings (now Art. 267 TFEU). These provisions, which have formed an essential part of Treaty law ever since Paris and Rome, have proved to be crucial for the interaction between European and Member State law. In addition to 'the validity and interpretation of acts of the institutions, bodies, offices or agencies of the Union', referral for preliminary rulings can focus on interpretation of the Treaties as well. After introducing the doctrines of direct effect and supremacy, the Court has interpreted its jurisdiction to cover assessment of Member State legislation in the light of European law. By the same token, it has established itself as a constitutional court in respect of Member State legislation too. Thus, the constitutional basis for judicial review of national measures through the preliminary ruling procedure is largely the ECJ's own creation. Diverging from its jurisdiction over Union measures, the ECJ cannot declare contradictory Member State measures void. Yet the principle of supremacy may entail an obligation for the Member State concerned to revise its legislation.[13]

Enforcement of European law falls mainly on national courts, which are an integral part of the European legal system; in the words of the ECJ, national courts are '"ordinary" courts within the European Union legal order'.[14] However, the role of national courts in the European legal system has never been explicitly defined in Treaty law but only hinted at. Art. 189 TEEC (now Art. 288 TFEU) confirmed the direct applicability of Community regulations, which implied applicability in national courts as well.

13 See J. Komárek (2007b).

14 Opinion 1/09 *European and Community Patent Court* [2011] ECR I-1137, Para. 80. The term 'ordinary courts' perhaps hints at the ECJ's self-understanding of itself as the constitutional court 'within the European Union legal order'.

Moreover, Art. 177 TEEC provided for the preliminary ruling procedure, which was destined to become the main procedural channel between European and national courts. Provisions on the preliminary ruling procedure would have been meaningless without the applicability of European law in national courts. The principles of direct effect and supremacy have further specified the role of national courts and their interplay with the ECJ. Moreover, as a central pronounced rationale for direct effect was to engage private litigants in securing effective implementation of European law, doctrinal development has also contributed to clarifying the standing of private parties before national courts.[15] The role of the national judiciary in the European legal system is also evoked by the new provision that the Lisbon Treaty added to Art. 19(1) TEU. The provision obliges Member States to 'provide remedies sufficient to ensure effective legal protection in the fields covered by Union law'. In Opinion 1/09, the ECJ grounded in this very provision its claim that the EU judicial system comprises Member State courts and tribunals too (Para. 67). In this Opinion, the Court also extended to national courts the constitutional duty to ensure that the law is observed in the interpretation and application of the Treaties (Para. 69).[16]

When calling national courts ordinary courts within the European Union legal order, the ECJ adopts the perspective of European law and confines its claim to the scope of European law. When national courts act beyond the scope of European law, they remain courts of the national legal system even from the Union point of view. Moreover, national law may consider them courts of the national legal system even when they

[15] In *Van Gend en Loos*, the Court argued that the fact that Arts. 169 and 170 TEEC 'enable the Commission and the Member States to bring before the Court a state which has not fulfilled its obligations does not mean that individuals cannot plead these obligations, should the occasion arise, before a national court, any more than the fact that the Treaty places at the disposal of the Commission ways of ensuring that obligation imposed upon those subject to the Treaty are observed, precludes the possibility, in actions between individuals before a national court, of pleading infringements of these obligations. A restriction of the guarantees against an infringement of Article 12 by Member States to the procedures under Articles 169 and 170 would remove all direct legal protection of the individual rights of their nationals. There is the risk that recourse to the procedure under these Articles would be ineffective if it were to occur after the implementation of national decisions taken contrary to the provisions of the Treaty. The vigilance of individuals concerned to protect their rights amounts to an effective supervision in addition to the supervision entrusted by Articles 169 and 170 to the diligence of the Commission and of the Member States.' Case C-26/62 *Van Gend en Loos* [1963] ECR 3. See also P. Craig (1992) on the enforcement function of direct effect.

[16] Opinion 1/09 *European and Community Patent Court* [2011] ECR I-1137.

are implementing EU law.[17] National courts occupy a pivotal hinge position in relations between European and national law. Their referrals for preliminary rulings contribute to the judicial development of European law, and through their rulings they are expected to channel into national law the impact of European law, including ECJ interpretations. Without national courts performing their expected intermediary role, ECJ efforts to guarantee the effective and uniform implementation of European law would have come to nothing. But the hinge position of national courts also points to the limits that legal cultural perspectivism imposes on the allegiance of national courts. National courts remain bound to the national legal culture, which judges have internalized during their university studies and professional career and which mainly unravels its impact through their legal *Vorverständnis*.

Claiming the autonomy of European law

Corresponding to the two dimensions of law, establishing a distinct legal system implies a double claim to autonomy: to both *normative and institutional autonomy*. European law's claim to autonomy is addressed in two directions: international law and Member State national law. However, in neither direction does the claim to autonomy exhaust the positioning function of the European constitution. Autonomy is not identical to closedness, and principles which further specify European law's relation to international law and Member State law are vital elements of the juridical constitution.

Van Gend en Loos and *Costa v Enel* are primarily celebrated for introducing the principles of direct effect and supremacy which define the impact of European law on national law.[18] However, these landmark rulings also imply a declaration of autonomy by European law in respect of both (general) international law and Member State law. *Van Gend en Loos*, issued in 1963, pointed to features which distinguished the EEC Treaty from ordinary international law. It especially emphasized that the Treaty reached out beyond the contracting states to private parties. The Court argued that the objective of establishing a common market was of 'direct concern to interested parties in the Community' and that, hence, the Treaty was 'more than an agreement which merely creates mutual

[17] B. de Witte (2011a), p. 351, argues that this is the case in all Member States, with the possible exception of the Netherlands.

[18] Case C-26/62 *Van Gend en Loos* [1963] ECR 3; Case C-6/64 *Flaminio Costa v Enel* [1964] ECR 585.

obligations between the contracting states'. The Court found more support for its view in the Preamble to the Treaty of Rome, which referred not only to governments but to peoples as well and, more specifically, to 'the establishment of institutions endowed with sovereign rights, the exercise of which affects Member States and also their citizens'. The Court also contended that through the Treaty provisions on the preliminary ruling procedure the Member States had acknowledged that the authority of Community law can be invoked by their nationals before national courts and tribunals. The Court concluded that 'the Community constitutes a new legal order of international law for the benefit of which the states have limited their sovereign rights, albeit within limited fields, and the subjects of which comprise not only Member States but also their nationals'.

With the expression 'a new legal order of international law' *Van Gend en Loos* still located Community law under the international law umbrella. The following year, 1964, *Costa v Enel* took a step forward, dropped the reference to international law and explicitly endowed the EEC Treaty with constitutive effects exceeding those of ordinary international treaties: 'by contrast with ordinary international treaties, the EEC Treaty has created its own legal system'. Through the Treaty, the Member States had limited their sovereign rights, 'albeit in limited fields', and transferred corresponding powers to the Community, creating 'a body of law which binds both their nationals and themselves'.

Through the claim to normative autonomy, a legal order asserts exclusive power to identify the norms it comprises, and to determine their legal effects and relations to other normative orders. These are claims of a constitutional nature, so that normative autonomy implies that the putatively autonomous legal order possesses a constitution in the material sense of the term. Up to this point, it is warranted to follow the Kelsenian view. By contrast, it is unnecessary to burden the idea of an autonomous legal order with the assumption of a transcendent *Grundnorm* founding the normativity of the (historically) first constitution. It is equally unwarranted to attach, in the vein of Theodor Schilling, normative autonomy to the very un-Kelsenian presupposition of a popular constituent power as the source of the constitution.[19] Instead, normative autonomy is intimately linked to institutional, especially judicial, autonomy. Normative

[19] See T. Schilling (1996).

autonomy cannot be defended without judicial and concomitant *interpretive autonomy*: ultimately, the composition and effects of the legal order, as well as its relations to other normative orders, are decided in individual legal proceedings.

Neither *Van Gend en Loos* nor *Costa v Enel* employed the term 'constitution'; only *Les Verts* in 1986 labelled the Treaty a constitutional charter.[20] Yet by severing the international law moorings and claiming that the Member States had given birth to a new legal order, *Van Gend en Loos* and *Costa v Enel* clearly approached the Treaty as a material constitution. Autonomy from international law, achieved through the constitutional effect of the Treaty, was a central justification for the assertion of direct effect and supremacy, which broke with the established doctrine on the relation of international law to state law.

In its subsequent case law, the ECJ has jealously guarded the normative and interpretive autonomy of European law with regard to both international and Member State law. In its Opinion 1/91, it explicitly linked autonomy to the constitutional character of the TEEC. The Court pointed to the fundamental distinction between the TEEC and the draft Agreement on the European Economic Area. The Agreement was 'an international treaty which merely creates rights and obligations as between the Contracting Parties and provides for no transfer of sovereign rights to the inter-governmental institutions which it sets up'. By contrast, the TEEC, albeit concluded in the form of an international agreement, amounts to the constitutional charter of the Community based on the rule of law. The Court repeated the claim of *Van Gend en Loos* and *Costa v Enel* that 'the Community treaties established a new legal order for the benefit of which the States have limited their sovereign rights and the subjects of which comprise not only Member States but also their nationals'. The Court also elevated direct effect and primacy to essential characteristics of the Community legal order.[21] Moreover, the Court linked normative to interpretive autonomy. It stated that to confer on the Court of the European Economic Area jurisdiction over the respective competences of the Community and the Member States would be 'incompatible with Community law, since it is likely adversely to affect the allocation of responsibilities

20 Case C-294/83 *Les Verts v Parliament* [1986] ECR 1339.

21 Opinion 1/91 *Draft Agreement* [1991] ECR I-6079. The Court has repeated this characterization of European law as new in legal order in, e.g., Opinion 1/09 *European and Community Patent Court* [2011] ECR I-1137, Para. 5.

defined in the Treaties and the autonomy of the Community legal order'. The Court claimed exclusive responsibility for assuring this autonomy. Here it invoked the Treaty provision (now Art. 19(1) TEU), which set outs that 'the Court of Justice shall ensure that in the interpretation and application of this Treaty the law is observed' and which has provided the standard justification for the ECJ's claim to interpretive autonomy. The Court also buttressed this claim by reference to the Treaty provision where the Member States had undertaken 'not to submit a dispute concerning the interpretation or application of the Treaty to any method of settlement other than those provided for therein' (now Art. 344 TFEU). The Court found in the draft Agreement a further conflict with its interpretive autonomy. With a view to ensuring legal uniformity throughout the Economic Area, the draft Agreement would have conferred on the Court of the European Economic Area jurisdiction to interpret not only the provisions of the Agreement but the corresponding provisions of the Community legal order too.

In its Opinions 1/00 and 1/09, the ECJ has shown similar concern for its interpretive autonomy, threatened by courts established under international law. In Opinion 1/00 on the draft Agreement on the European Common Aviation Area (ECAA), the Court stressed that mechanisms must exist which prevent the Community being bound by 'a particular interpretation of the rules of Community law referred to in the agreement'. Otherwise uniform interpretation of Community law and the function of the Court to review the legality of acts of Community institutions would be undermined. The autonomy of the Community legal order requires that 'the essential character of the powers of the Community and its institutions as conceived in the Treaty remain unaltered'.[22] In Opinion 1/09 on the draft Agreement on the European and Community Patents Court, the ECJ reaffirmed its task of securing respect for the autonomy of the EU legal order. It also emphasized the role of national courts in the Union legal system and stressed that to ensure that in the interpretation and application of the Treaties the law is observed is a duty of national courts too (Para. 66). The draft Agreement would have conferred on an international court exclusive jurisdiction to interpret and apply Union law in its field. This would have deprived national courts of their power to interpret and apply Union law. In turn, the ECJ would have lost its power to reply

[22] Opinion 1/00 *Proposed Agreement between the European Community and non-Member States on the establishment of a European Common Aviation Area* [2002] ECR I-3493, Paras. 11–13.

by preliminary ruling to questions posed by national courts. This would have altered 'the essential character of the powers which the Treaties confer on the institutions of the European Union and on the Member States and which are indispensable to the preservation of the very nature of European Union law' (Para. 89).

Kadi from 2008 is the most widely discussed ruling since *Van Gend en Loos* and *Costa v Enel* which asserts the autonomy of European law from international law. In *Kadi*, the Court recalled its position that 'an international agreement cannot affect the allocation of powers fixed by the Treaties or, consequently, the autonomy of the Community legal system, observance of which is ensured by the Court by virtue of the exclusive jurisdiction conferred on it by Article 220 EC'. The Court also referred to its view of the foundational character of this jurisdiction.[23] In turn, in his Opinion AG Poiares Maduro argued for normative and interpretive autonomy by stating that 'in the final analysis, the Community Courts determine the effect of international obligations within the Community legal order by reference to conditions set by Community law'.[24]

The ECJ has very resolutely defended European law's normative autonomy with regard to Member State law as well. The legality of European measures, including legislative acts, can only be assessed by the ECJ and against criteria established by European law. Thus, in a string of cases, starting from *Internationale Handelsgesellschaft* in 1970, the Court has emphasized that a possible infringement of a fundamental right by a European measure can only be judged in the light of European law. The Court has warranted the normative autonomy of European law by reference to the principles of uniformity and efficiency, the second-order principles which were invoked in *Van Gend en Loos* and *Costa v Enel* to support direct effect and primacy, and related to the establishment of a common market as the primary Treaty objective. In *Internationale Handelsgesellschaft*, the Court stated that judging the validity of Community measures by the legal rules or concepts of national law would adversely affect Community law's uniformity and efficacy, and that validity judgments can only

23 Joined Cases C-402/05 P and C-415/05 P *Kadi and Al Barakaat* [2008] ECR I-6351, Para. 282. See also *Kadi II*, where the Court reconfirmed its position (Joined Cases C-584/10 P, C-593/10 P and C-595/10 P *Commission and Others v Kadi*, judgment of 18 July 2013 (not yet reported)).

24 Opinion AG Poiares Maduro, Joined Cases C-402/05 P and C-415/05 P *Kadi and Al Barakaat* [2008] ECR I-6351, Para. 23.

be made in the light of Community law.[25] If Community law could be overridden by national rules of national law, it would lose its normative autonomy, based on the Treaty as an independent source of law: 'In fact, the law stemming from the Treaty, an independent source of law, cannot because of its very nature be overridden by rules of national law, however framed, without being deprived of its character as Community law and without the legal basis of the Community itself being called in question.' This entails that 'the validity of a Community measure or its effect within a Member State cannot be affected by allegations that it runs counter to either fundamental rights as formulated by the constitutions or the principles of a national constitutional structure'.[26] Preserving normative and interpretive autonomy was a central rationale behind the introduction by the ECJ of fundamental rights as general principles of Community law. In turn, autonomy was justified in teleological terms, with reference to the uniformity and efficiency of European law required by the common market objective. The principle orientation brought about by fundamental rights was motivated by policy considerations!

With respect to Member State law, the ECJ has left no doubts as to its view that it alone possesses the competence to determine the reach of Union competences: the famous *Kompetenz-Kompetenz*. It has based its assertion of European law's interpretive autonomy and its own exclusive constitutional jurisdiction on explicit Treaty provisions, such as its tasks to ensure that the law is observed in the interpretation and application of Treaties, and to review the legality of legislative acts and other acts of Union institutions. In legality review, the Court also decides actions brought by Member States on the ground of lack of competence. In 1987 in *Foto-Frost*, the Court confirmed that national courts do not have the power to declare Community acts invalid but the Court's jurisdiction under Art. 173 TEEC (now Art. 263 TFEU) is exclusive. If doubts about validity arise, national courts must refer the issue to the Court under the preliminary ruling procedure, the main purpose of which is to ensure the uniform application of Community law. The Court argued that uniformity

25 In *Hauer*, the Court expressly related the principles of uniformity and efficacy to the common market objective. According to the Court, 'the introduction of special criteria for assessment stemming from the legislation or constitutional law of a particular Member State would, by damaging the substantive unity and efficacy of Community law, lead inevitably to the destruction of the unity of the common market and the jeopardizing of the cohesion of the Community'. Case C-44/79 *Hauer v Land Rheinland-Pfalz* [1979] ECR 3727, Para. 14.

26 Case C-11/70 *Internationale Handelsgesellschaft* [1970] ECR 1125, Para. 4.

is particularly imperative when the validity of a Community act is in question, as 'divergence between courts in the Member States as to the validity of Community acts would be liable to place in jeopardy the very unity of the Community legal order and detract from the fundamental requirement of legal certainty'. Thus 'the coherence of the system requires that where the validity of a community act is challenged before a national court the power to declare the act invalid must also be reserved to the Court of Justice'.[27] National courts are ordinary courts of EU law, and they also serve its correct application and uniform interpretation. Yet the ultimate interpretive autonomy falls to the ECJ.

Positioning European law

The claim to autonomy is a step in positioning EU law with regard to international law and Member State law. But it is only the first step. In relation to international law, the European juridical constitution has adopted the standpoint of *qualified monism*. The ECJ has regarded the provisions of international agreements concluded by the EU as an integral part of European law and has held the Union institutions to be bound by customary international law too. However, the ECJ has defined threshold criteria which provisions of international agreements have to meet before they can have direct effect in European law and give rise to individual rights or serve as a basis for legality review. Most famously, it has denied WTO law direct effect in Union and Member State law.[28]

The ECJ has also specified the position of international law in the internal hierarchy of European law. Allan Rosas and Lorna Armati locate international law higher than secondary but lower than primary EU law. International law can be invoked in reviewing the legality of secondary legislation but not primary law.[29] However, *Kadi* – arguably the most important ruling for positioning European law with regard to international law – is somewhat ambiguous as to whether all primary law enjoys primacy over international law. The ruling expressly declares the primacy of international law over secondary European law, but is more equivocal about its relation to primary law. The Court states that international law's 'primacy at the level of Community law would not, however, extend to

[27] Case C-314/85 *Foto-Frost v Hauptzollamt Lübeck-Ost* [1987] ECR 4199, Paras. 15–17.

[28] See on the direct effect of international agreements A. Rosas and L. Armati (2012), pp. 82–5, and F. Martines (2014).

[29] A. Rosas and L. Armati (2012), p. 59.

primary law, in particular to the general principles of which fundamental rights form part'. The Court supports its view by the Treaty provision (now Art. 218(11) TFEU) which lays down that an international agreement may not enter into force if the Court has delivered an adverse opinion on its compatibility with the Treaties (Paras. 307–9). This reference would appear to imply that all primary law enjoys primacy over conflicting international law. On the other hand, in preceding paragraphs of the ruling, the Court formulates its reservation to the primacy of international law in terms of 'principles that form part of the very foundations of the Community legal order'. It argues that 'the obligations imposed by an international agreement cannot have the effect of prejudicing the constitutional principles of the EC Treaty, which include the principle that all Community acts must respect fundamental rights'. An explicit Treaty provision ensures the validity of international agreements which states concluded before their membership (now Art. 351 TFEU). Yet this provision 'may in no circumstances permit any challenge to the principles that form part of the very foundations of the Community legal order, one of which is the protection of fundamental rights, including the review by the Community judicature of the lawfulness of Community measures as regards their consistency with those fundamental rights' (Para. 304). Allusion to foundational constitutional principles has led some observers to perceive an analogy between the ECJ reservation to the primacy of international law and reservations of national constitutional courts to the primacy of European law. However, *Kadi* is ambiguous in its formulations and it is possible that the ECJ claims wider exemption than national constitutional courts, which have been explicit in not claiming primacy for all national constitutional law.[30]

In *Van Gend en Loos* and *Costa v Enel*, the assertion of autonomy from international law was a prelude to the claim of European law's direct effect in, and primacy over, Member State law. The assertion of autonomy cleared the way for the European juridical constitution to claim jurisdiction over issues which international law leaves to the province of national constitutions. International law may enjoy both direct effect and internal primacy in national law but only on the basis of the national constitution. By contrast, the European juridical constitution claims the power to impose

[30] See on the possible analogy between *Kadi* and national constitutional courts' reservations as to the primacy of European law, e.g., N. T. Isiksel (2010), D. Halberstam (2010) and M. Kumm (2012).

these principles on national law. Thus, it ignores Member State constitutional choices (their opting for the dualist or monist alternative) in respect of international law's internal effects.

Van Gend en Loos defined direct effect in terms of rights which individuals can invoke before national courts. The question posed by the referring court was 'whether Article 12 of the Treaty has direct application in national law in the sense that nationals of Member States may on the basis of this article lay claim to rights which the national court must protect'. The ECJ replied in the affirmative: independently of Member State legislation, the Treaty confers rights on individuals 'not only where they are expressly granted by the Treaty, but also by reason of obligations which the Treaty imposes in a clearly defined way upon individuals as well as upon the Member States and upon the institutions of the Community'. The Court emphasized that the fact that under Art. 12 TEEC 'it is the Member States who are made the subject of the negative obligation does not imply that their nationals cannot benefit from this obligation'. The assertion of direct effect was a bold move by the ECJ. The Court rejected Member State international law objections and refused to apply the right of a sovereign state under international law to choose between the monist and the dualist alternative. As Bruno de Witte has pointed out, what distinguished *Van Gend en Loos* from international law doctrine was not direct effect as such but the fact that the decision in favour of the monist model was taken at the European level and not left to the Member States as signatories of the Treaty.[31] The immediate reaction by the budding European law community and the comments by ECJ actors show that the significance of the ruling was generally recognized.[32] Still, the Court was very cautious in its words. It refrained from formulating direct effect as a comprehensive principle covering European law in general but restricted the argument to Treaty provisions. Moreover, in explaining why Art. 12 TEEC was a suitable candidate for direct effect the Court raised the threshold quite high. It emphasized that the prohibition in Art. 12 is clear and unconditional and imposes not a positive but a negative obligation, implementation of which requires no national legislative intervention.

The subsequent (hi)story of direct effect is about the gradual expansion of its scope through ECJ case law, without intervention by the constitutional legislator. *Van Gend en Loos* dealt with a particular instance

[31] B. de Witte (2011a), p. 327.
[32] See on the contemporary discussion M. Rasmussen (2012); A. Vauchet (2010).

of Treaty law. In its subsequent jurisprudence, the Court has step by step enlarged the scope of Treaty provisions possessing direct effect and extended the principle to secondary legislation, such as regulations and directives. Moreover, the Court has granted direct effect to general legal principles and to international treaty law, integrated into European law in accordance with its monist choice.[33] In addition, the Court has transferred direct effect from vertical relations between the state and individuals to horizontal relations between private parties.[34] Here, however, directives constitute an exception.

Regulations appear to be natural candidates for direct effect, because of the explicit Treaty provision according them direct applicability in Member States (now Art. 288 TFEU). Direct applicability, though, does not necessarily imply direct effect: not all regulations confer rights on private parties or can otherwise be invoked by these, nor do all regulations meet the threshold criteria, initially borrowed from the international law doctrine of self-executing treaty rules.[35] Yet directives are the legal instrument which has most occupied doctrinal construction by the ECJ and European law scholars. If the Treaty definition of regulations can be read to entail direct effect for regulations which meet the threshold criteria, the Treaty provision on directives, by contrast, appears rather to exclude it. After all, directives are declared to be binding on Member States merely as to the result to be achieved, and the national authorities are left with the choice of form and methods. Indeed, conferring direct effect on unimplemented directives has required plenty of doctrinal creativity and considerable loosening of the threshold criteria. In *Van Duyn* in 1974, the Court pointed out that the Treaty declared regulations to be directly applicable and that, consequently, regulations may 'by their very nature have direct effects'. According to the Court, this does not, however, entail that other acts of secondary legislation mentioned in the Treaty article could never have similar effects. The Court argued that it would be incompatible with the binding effect that the Treaty attributed to a directive to exclude, as a principle, the possibility that private parties may invoke the obligation that the directive imposes. Again the Court alluded to the principle of effectiveness and declared that the 'useful

[33] See P. Craig (1992) and B. de Witte (2011a), pp. 338–9.

[34] With regard to Treaty law, the landmark case was Case C-43/75 *Defrenne v SABENA* [1976] ECR 455, which dealt with the provision on equal pay in Art. 119 TEEC (now Art. 157 TFEU). On the horizontal effect of free movement law, see below, Chapter 7.

[35] See, e.g., A. Hinarejos (2008), pp. 622–3.

effect' of a directive 'would be weakened if individuals were prevented from relying on it before their national courts and if the latter were prevented from taking it into consideration as an element of Community law'. As an additional argument the Court invoked the Treaty provision on the preliminary ruling procedure, which empowers national courts to refer to the Court questions concerning the validity and interpretation of all Community acts. For the Court, this implied that all acts of secondary legislation, and not merely regulations, may be invoked by individuals in national courts. In conclusion the Court stated that 'it is necessary to examine, in every case, whether the nature, general scheme and wording of the provision in question are capable of having direct effects on the relations between Member States and individuals'.[36]

By contrast, the Court has consequently denied directives horizontal direct effect on relations between private parties. As a justification it has invoked the principle of legal certainty and the wording of the Treaty provision on directives which accords directives binding effect merely in respect of Member States.[37] These arguments have not convinced critics, who have pointed out that the Court has granted direct effect to Treaty provisions which, according to their wording, are addressed only to Member States; that directives often enough are formulated as precisely as regulations; and that the threshold criteria for direct effect can ward off legal certainty concerns. Indeed, denying horizontal direct effect for directives may be a reaction to misgivings that national courts had expressed about ECJ judicial activism.[38]

Lack of direct horizontal effect has been counterbalanced by what has sometimes been called *indirect horizontal effect*; namely, the duty of national

[36] Case C-41/74 *Van Duyn v Home Office* [1974] ECR 1337, Para. 12.

[37] In *Marshall*, the Court emphasized that 'according to Article 189 of the EEC Treaty the binding nature of a directive, which constitutes the basis for the possibility of relying on the directive before a national court, exists only in relation to "each Member State to which it is addressed"'. This entails that 'a directive may not of itself impose obligations on an individual and that a provision of a directive may not be relied upon as such against such a person'. Case C-152/84 *Marshall v Southampton and South-West Hampshire Area Health Authority* [1986] ECR 723, Para. 48.

[38] In its *Cohn-Bendit* judgment in 1978 (*Ministre de l'intérieur c Cohn-Bendt* Rec. CE 1978, 524), the French Conseil d'État had ruled that individuals may not invoke a directive as a ground for the annulment of an individual administrative act. De Witte surmises that 'the misgivings expressed by national courts may well have led the European Court of Justice to exercise moderation in its later rulings on the direct effect of directives' and that 'its refusal to recognize the horizontal direct effect of directives might be explained in this way'. B. de Witte (2011a), p. 348.

courts to employ even unimplemented directives as standards for interpreting national legislation. In *Von Colson* (1984) and *Marleasing* (1990), the Court argued that national courts are also bound by the Treaty obligation to contribute to achieving the result envisaged by a directive. In addition, the duty of *sincere cooperation* (now Art. 4(3) TEU) concerned national courts too.[39] Subsequently, the Court has derived from the duty of sincere cooperation a comprehensive principle of *consistent interpretation* which entails the obligation to interpret all national legislation in conformity with European law.[40] Now the indirect horizontal effect of directives is a sub-category of this larger principle. The *Frankovich* doctrine, which entitles private parties to damages from a Member State which has failed to implement a directive, was also adopted to compensate for the missing horizontal direct effect of directives. In *Frankovich* (1991), the duty of sincere cooperation, alongside the principle of effectiveness, was again a central justification. Although introduced in the context of an unimplemented directive, *Frankovich* established state liability for breaches of Member State obligations under European law as a general principle.[41] As liability only comes into consideration where direct effect or consistent interpretation is excluded, it is clearly a supplementary doctrinal

[39] Case C-14/82 *Von Colson and Kamann v Land Nordrhein-Westfalen* [1984] ECR 1891, Para. 26; Case C-106/89 *Marleasing v Commercial International de Alimentación* [1990] ECR I-4135, Para. 8.

[40] See A. Rosas and L. Armati (2012), pp. 72–4, and the cases referred to there.

[41] The Court argued that 'the full effectiveness of Community rules would be impaired and the protection of the rights which they grant would be weakened if individuals were unable to obtain redress when their rights are infringed by a breach of Community law for which a Member State can be held responsible' and that, consequently, 'the principle whereby a State must be liable for loss and damage caused to individuals as a result of breaches of Community law for which the State can be held responsible is inherent in the system of the Treaty'. According to the Court, 'a further basis for the obligation of Member States to make good such loss and damage is to be found in Article 5 of the Treaty, under which the Member States are required to take all appropriate measures, whether general or particular, to ensure fulfilment of their obligations under Community law'; 'among these is the obligation to nullify the unlawful consequences of a breach of Community law'. In *Francovich*, the Court also formulated the three conditions for state liability which it has applied in its subsequent case law: 'The first of those conditions is that the result prescribed by the directive should entail the grant of rights to individuals. The second condition is that it should be possible to identify the content of those rights on the basis of the provisions of the directive. Finally, the third condition is the existence of a causal link between the breach of the State's obligation and the loss and damage suffered by the injured parties.' Joined Cases C-6/90 and C-9/90 *Francovich and Bonifaci v Italy* [1991] ECR I-5357, Paras. 32, 34–5, 40. K. Lenaerts and T. Corthaut (2006), at 312, identify for state liability, in addition to the duty of sincere cooperation, even international law roots.

instrument.[42] Finally, in 2005 *Mangold* showed that although a directive cannot achieve horizontal direct effect between the parties, the general principle of European law it expresses – in *Mangold*, prohibition of age discrimination – can.[43]

The extension of direct effect would not have been possible without considerably stretching the threshold criteria from their first formulation in *Van Gend en Loos* and abandoning the fairly strict preconditions for self-executing treaty rules under international law doctrine. In the Court's account in *Van Gend en Loos*, Art. 12 TEEC was suited to direct effect as it created a merely negative state obligation and did not need implementing by European or national legislation. Soon enough the Court discarded these standards and granted direct effect to Treaty provisions which established positive state obligations and expressly presupposed implementing legislation. In its express formulations, the ECJ still sticks to the criteria of clarity, precision and unconditionality. Yet it is evident that the Court has significantly weakened the limiting force of these yardsticks to allow for the direct effect of a steadily increasing number of Treaty provisions and secondary law instruments.

While *Van Gend en Loos* introduced the principle of direct effect, the other central positioning principle of primacy had to wait its turn until *Costa v Enel*. Primacy was not an issue in the monist Netherlands where *Van Gend en Loos* had its origin and where the constitution accorded international law internal primacy over conflicting national law. But it was an issue in dualist Italy where *Costa v Enel* originated and where primacy of international over national law was not part of the constitution. Again the Court diverged from international law doctrine and asserted the competence of European law itself to decide on its internal primacy in Member State legal orders; in contrast to the rule under international law, the issue was not left to the province of national constitutional law. In its rather opaque reasoning, the Court took recourse to two principles which are not easily reconcilable: *independence* and *integration*. European law is declared to be both independent from and integrated into the national law of the Member States:

The integration into the laws of each Member State of provisions which derive from the Community and more generally the terms and the spirit of the Treaty,

42 S. Prechal (2006), pp. 301–2.

43 Case C-144/04 *Mangold* [2005] ECR I-9981. See also Case C-555/07 *Kücükdeveci* [2010] ECR I-365.

make it impossible for the states, as a corollary, to accord precedence to a unilateral and subsequent measure over a legal system accepted by them on a basis of reciprocity. Such a measure cannot therefore be inconsistent with that legal system . . . The law stemming from the Treaty, an independent source of law, could not, because of its special and original nature, be overridden by domestic legal provisions, however framed, without being deprived of its character as Community law and without the legal basis of the Community itself being called into question.

In *Costa v Enel*, the ECJ already made clear that even secondary Community legislation enjoys primacy over municipal law. Here the Court invoked the Treaty definition of the legal effects of regulations. The Court argued that 'the precedence of Community law is confirmed by Article 189, whereby a regulation "shall be binding" and "directly applicable in all Member States"'. According to the Court, 'this provision, which is subject to no reservation, would be quite meaningless if a state could unilaterally nullify its effects by means of a legislative measure which could prevail over community law'. In its initial formulation in *Costa v Enel*, primacy superseded merely the municipal *lex posteriori* principle: later municipal law could not override earlier European law. In its subsequent jurisprudence, the Court elevated the supremacy of European law above all the standard principles which address the internal relations among norms of a particular legal order. Thus, the Court asserted primacy for European law even over conflicting national constitutional law.[44]

The European constitutional legislator has never expressly confirmed the principle of primacy either. However, interestingly enough, the abortive Constitutional Treaty included a provision on primacy, which was dropped from the Lisbon Treaty, undoubtedly for fear of its possible federalist connotations: 'The Constitution and law adopted by the institutions of the Union in exercising competences conferred on it shall have primacy over the law of the Member States' (Art. I-6). The provision never entered into force, but it still conveys an important, albeit legally speaking self-evident, message: *ultra vires* legislative acts cannot attain either primacy or direct effect.[45]

[44] The landmark ruling is *Internationale Handelsgesellschaft*, where the Court argued that 'the validity of a Community measure or its effect within a Member State cannot be affected by allegations that it runs counter to either fundamental rights as formulated by the constitution of that state or the principles of a national constitutional structure'. Case C-11/70 *Internationale Handelsgesellschaft* [1970] ECR 1125, Para. 3.

[45] Deletion of the provision was part of the effort to obliterate conspicuous constitutional implications from the text of the Lisbon Treaty. However, a Declaration of the Intergovernmental Conference was attached to the Treaty. In the declaration, the

For decades, scholars of European law have been puzzled by the exact definition and legal consequences of direct effect and primacy, as well as the mutual relationship between these pivotal principles. The debates reflect the doctrinal and theoretical instability which still, half a century after *Van Gend en Loos* and *Costa v Enel*, labels European constitutional law even in its core areas and which accumulation of ECJ jurisprudence over decades has not been able to eradicate. Divergent scholarly positions can all find support in case law. Doctrinal volatility reflects the unsettledness of the legal theory underpinning the juridical constitution: the uneasy relation between the principles of *independence* and *integratedness*. Should EU law and national law be treated as distinct legal orders or as one integrated order? The question is posed from the perspective of European law but actually relates to how the European juridical constitution expects national courts to approach European law: as a separate legal order or as integrated into national law. By contrast, European law has not raised the federalist-smacking pretension that Member State law should be treated as integrated into European law.[46]

On their face, direct effect and primacy seem to point to diverging answers. Direct effect appears to presuppose two different legal orders of which one – the European – imposes specific effects on the other – the national. In turn, primacy seems to imply the integrated model: European law implants itself on top of the internal hierarchy of national law. Indeed,

Conference recalled 'that, in accordance with well settled case law of the Court of Justice of the European Union, the Treaties and the law adopted by the Union on the basis of the Treaties have primacy over the law of Member States, under the conditions laid down by the said case law'. The Conference also decided 'to attach as an Annex to this Final Act the Opinion of the Council Legal Service on the primacy of EC law as set out in 11197/07 (JUR 260): Opinion of the Council Legal Service of 22 June 2007'. The Opinion states the following: 'It results from the case-law of the Court of Justice that primacy of EC law is a cornerstone principle of Community law. According to the Court, this principle is inherent to the specific nature of the European Community. At the time of the first judgement of this established case-law (Costa/ENEL, 15 July 1964, Case 6/64) there was no mention of primacy in the treaty. It is still the case today. The fact that the principle of primacy will not be included in the future treaty shall not in any way change the existence of the principle and the existing case-law of the Court of Justice.' See also B. de Witte (2011a), p. 345.

46 In her discussion of the relations between European and Member State law, J. Dickson (2011) has distinguished between three models: the Distinct but Interacting Legal Systems model, the Part of Member States' Legal Systems model and the 'One Big Legal System' model where Member State legal systems are treated as subordinate sub-systems of the EU legal system. However, as noted above, European law has not raised claims amounting to Dickson's One Big Legal System model. Dickson's conclusion is that the way directives operate in national law points to the Distinct but Interacting Legal Systems model. See also J. Dickson (2012).

in the light of the integrated model the doctrine of direct effect may appear wholly superfluous; an infant disease of European law, as Pierre Pescatore, a former judge of the ECJ, famously put it in 1983.[47] By contrast, adherents to the model of two distinct legal orders cling to the necessity of the doctrine of direct effect: only directly effective norms can possess primacy over conflicting national norms. This is the *trigger* account of the relations between direct effect and primacy. According to Michael Dougan, ECJ case law provides support for both the trigger model and the alternative primacy model, which points to the integrated view.[48] Furthermore, as instruments of European secondary law, directives and regulations arguably reflect different legal theories. Directives lie closer to the idea of two distinct legal orders: as a rule a European directive is effective only after it has been transposed into the national legal order through an explicit national act. By contrast, the direct applicability of regulations matches the integrated model.

Two conceptions exist of the concept of direct effect: one narrow, the other broad. The narrow conception corresponds to the meaning expounded in *Van Gend en Loos*: directly effective European law gives rise to individual rights which individuals can claim before national courts. The broad conception has borrowed the French legal term *invocabilité*: European law is directly effective, if private parties can invoke it before national courts, not only in support of individual rights but also as, say, criteria for legal review of national measures or standards of interpretation, in accordance with the duty of consistent interpretation. However, such a definition evidently overlaps with the doctrine of primacy. Indeed, authors such as Sacha Prechel have proposed retaining the narrow definition which reduces direct effect to individual rights justiciable in national courts. Yet the difficulty in reconciling the two principles is apparent in Prechel's account as well. She advocates the integrated model even though direct effect in its narrow sense too clearly hints at the 'distinct legal orders' model.[49]

[47] P. Pescatore (1983). [48] M. Dougan (2007).

[49] S. Prechal (2007). K. Lenaerts and T. Corthaut (2006) also embrace a narrow definition of direct effect. They argue that for judicial review of national legislation, the duty of consistent interpretation or state liability it is not necessary to establish that the threshold criteria for direct effect are met. The authors seem to adhere to the integrated model, when they allude to a hierarchy of norms in the context of primacy and consistent interpretation. Thus, they state that 'the duty of consistent interpretation is inherent in any hierarchy of norms and thus a simple corollary of the principle of primacy is that it is the easiest way to ensure that no inconsistent national laws are applied over EU law'. By contrast, their account of direct effect clearly implies the

Much ink has been spilled over the terminological issue whether one should speak of the primacy or supremacy of European law.[50] Proponents of 'primacy' evoke the distinction between disapplication and invalidation or – to use German legal terms – *Anwendungsvorrang* and *Geltungsvorrang*. A conflict between a European and a national norm does not lead to the invalidation but merely the disapplication of the latter.[51] The precedence of European law is a conflict-of-laws rule addressed to national courts and hence should be called primacy and not supremacy. However, even with regard to national courts, European law's claim to precedence is wider than a mere conflict-of-laws rule intimates. Thus, the duty of consistent interpretation can be linked to precedence rather than direct effect, in spite of its origin as a substitute for the missing horizontal direct effect of directives.[52] This supports opting for 'supremacy' and understanding primacy as a sub-principle of supremacy. 'Supremacy' would then cover the consequences of European law for the national legislator as well. The national legislator has the negative obligation to refrain from legislating, not only within exclusive Union competence, but also in areas of shared competence and covered by European law's *pre-emptive* effects. Furthermore, the legislator may even have a positive obligation to amend national legislation in order to remove a discrepancy with European law. In its case law, the ECJ has held a state liable for damages that the breach of European obligations by the legislator has caused to private parties. All in all, opting for 'supremacy' instead of 'primacy' does not necessarily imply a Kelsenian – and undoubtedly erroneous – view of European law as possessing not only *Anwendungsvorrang* but *Geltungsvorrang* as well.

The ambiguity of the relations between the two positioning principles is also manifested by the debate on the exact implications of the primacy

'distinct legal orders' model. They define direct effect as 'the technique which allows individuals to enforce a subjective right, which is only available in the internal legal order in an instrument that comes from outside that order, against another (state or private) actor'.

50 For an overview of the discussion, see M. Avbelj (2011).

51 The standard formulation of national courts' duty of disapplication stems from *Simmenthal*: 'a national court which is called upon, within the limits of its jurisdiction, to apply provisions of Community law is under a duty to give full effect to those provisions, if necessary refusing of its own motion to apply any conflicting provision of national legislation, even if adopted subsequently, and it is not necessary for the court to request or await the prior setting aside of such provision by legislative or other constitutional means'. Case C-106/77 *Amministrazione delle Finanze dello Stato v Simmenthal*, Para. 24.

52 See the argument presented by K. Lenaerts and T. Corthaut (2006). A similar position is embraced by, e.g., A. Rosas and L. Armati (2012), p. 72.

of European law. These implications have been discussed in terms of *exclusion* and *substitution*, concepts borrowed from French administrative law doctrine. The question is whether primacy of a European norm can entail not only the non-application of a conflicting national norm and its replacement by another norm of national law, but the substitution of the national norm by the European norm as well. Evidently, the substitutionary consequence of primacy would bring us to the field of direct effect and blur the distinction between the two principles.[53]

Costa v Enel is sometimes portrayed as making explicit an implicit normative consequence deriving from *Van Gend en Loos*. However, no logical connection exists between direct effect and primacy. It is entirely plausible to think that in dualist states in particular, internal conflict-of-norms standards would restrict the range of direct effect.[54] But neither needs the exclusionary consequence of primacy to be restricted merely to directly effective European norms. By contrast, *legal certainty*, which the Court has evoked as a counter-principle to direct effect and primacy, would certainly favour recognizing a substitutionary consequence only for directly effective norms. Indeed, what has been termed the substitutionary consequence appears to come close to direct effect. The threshold criteria for norms capable of achieving direct effect aim, among other things, to guarantee legal certainty. Arguably, their circumvention with recourse to a substitutionary consequence of primacy should not be made possible. Legal certainty would require that substitutionary effect be accorded only to norms the cognizability of which meets certain minimum conditions. In turn, these could not but resemble the threshold criteria of direct effect.[55] Again, the overlap between direct effect and the substitutionary consequence of primacy is obvious.

European law's claim to supremacy requires that Member State law retreat from Kelsenian formal precision in its internal relations. In Kelsen's hierarchical *Stufenbau*, the supremacy of higher-order norms is not reduced to *Anwendungsvorrang*, which presupposes setting aside contradictory lower-order norms in concrete cases, but also covers

[53] See on the discussion of the exclusionary and substitutionary aspect of direct effect M. Dougan (2007), where the discussion is related to the alternative underpinning theoretical models: the 'trigger' model and the 'primacy' model.

[54] Here, though, regulations are a tricky case because of the lack of a domestic norm of incorporation. Thus, it is no wonder that in *Costa v Enel*, the ECJ invoked the Treaty provision on regulations in defence of the principle of primacy.

[55] M. Dougan (2007), p. 941, raises a similar point.

Geltungsvorrang, which entails their invalidation as well. In addition, higher-order norms not only invalidate but *validate* too: they establish the competence to issue lower-order norms. Neither of the two models for conceiving of the relation between European and national law claims a validating or even a directly invalidating function for European law. Even in the integrated view, the supremacy of European law only signifies *Anwendungsvorrang*. European law's assertion of supremacy dissects the three effects – *Anwendungsvorrang*, *Geltungsvorrang* and validation – which in Kelsen's *Stufenbau* go together. A further messing up of Kelsenian hierarchy ensues from the transposition of directives. European law endows the national legal instrument effectuating the transposition – say, a parliamentary statute – with legal consequences which set it apart from 'purely' national instruments. Both the integrated and the distinct legal orders model require that the national legal instrument at issue – whatever its hierarchical level in municipal law – participates in the supremacy of European law. Thus, validation and *Geltungsvorrang* follow the hierarchy of municipal law, while *Anwendungsvorrang* is determined by European criteria. By the same token, standards which in municipal law govern the relations between norms of one and the same hierarchical level – such as *lex posteriori* and *lex specialis* – are ignored. The positioning principles of European law, grown out of policy considerations, pose a threat to both the formal unambiguity and principle-based substantive coherence of national law.

The perspective of a national legal order presumably favours the two distinct legal orders model. However, the friction between the two models cannot be reduced to a tension between the European and national perspectives. Despite a perceivable movement in the direction of the integrated view, no unequivocal position can be attributed to the European juridical constitution. Quite simply, some of the features of the European juridical constitution point to the integrated model and some others to the distinct legal orders model. Thus, directives or the preliminary ruling procedure can but awkwardly be accounted for within the integrated model. Hence, the tension is destined to remain inherent in the legal theory of the European juridical constitution. And due to the intractable tension in the theoretical foundation, doctrinal debates will most probably continue on the definition and interrelation of direct effect and primacy; the location of the auxiliary doctrines of consistent interpretation and state liability in respect of the two foundational positioning principles; as well as the justification for a distinct principle of direct effect.

Pre-emption as a sub-principle of supremacy

Primacy as a sub-principle of supremacy addresses Member State courts. In turn, pre-emption specifies the supremacy of European law in relation to Member State legislatures. The doctrine of pre-emption is an import from federal states, primarily the United States.[56] In the European law context, it has mainly been elaborated in the literature. By contrast, the ECJ has not explicitly employed it or clarified its normative contents in general terms.[57] The doctrine prohibits action by federated entities if the federation has through its own action pre-empted the issue. The doctrine only finds use where both the federation and the federated entities are competent to act; exclusive competence of either level is omitted from the scope of the doctrine. The general provisions of the TEU and TFEU on the division of competences between the Union and the Member States, complemented by the Protocol on shared competences attached to the Lisbon Treaty, set out the terms for discussing the relevance of the pre-emption doctrine for EU law.

In the area of exclusive competence of the Union, the starting point is Member State non-competence, and no recourse to the doctrine of pre-emption is needed. Art. 2(1) TFEU lays down that 'when the Treaties confer on the Union exclusive competence in a specific area, only the Union may legislate and adopt legally binding acts, the Member States being able to do so themselves only if so empowered by the Union or for the implementation of Union acts'. If in a particular area no competence at all has been conferred upon the EU, the law is equally clear. As is expressly stated in Arts. 4(1) and 5(2) TEU, competences remain with the Member States, and no pre-emptive EU legislation can exist. In EU law too, problems can only arise in areas of shared competences. Here the Lisbon Treaty introduced an explicit provision (Art. 2(2) TFEU):

> When the Treaties confer on the Union a competence shared with the Member States in a specific area, the Union and the Member States may legislate and adopt legally binding acts in that area. The Member States shall exercise their competence to the extent that the Union has not exercised its competence. The

[56] R. Schütze (2006), p. 1034: 'The doctrine of pre-emption is a federal theory of normative conflict.'

[57] In specific fields, relevant ECJ case law exists, even if the term 'pre-emption' is not employed. This goes especially for foreign relations, where the *ERTA* ruling is the early landmark case. Case C-22/70 *Commission v Council* (*ERTA*) [1971] ECR 263. On the relevance of *ERTA* for the pre-emption discussion see J. H. H. Weiler (1999), pp. 169–74, and R. Schütze (2009), pp. 329–40.

Member States shall again exercise their competence to the extent that the Union has decided to cease exercising its competence.

In US doctrine, a distinction is made between field, rule and obstacle pre-emption.[58] In field pre-emption, simply by taking action the federation has occupied the policy field as a whole; in rule pre-emption, federated entities are precluded from adopting rules which contradict existing federal legislation; whereas in obstacle pre-emption federated entities may not adopt legislation which would hamper realizing the objectives of federal legislation.[59] On its face, Art. 2(2) TFEU does not take any clear position on alternative understandings of pre-emption. Yet the general tone of the provisions on the division of legislative competences between the Union and the Member States points to rejection of the widest reading, that is, field pre-emption. Subsidiarity, as defined in Art. 5(3) TEU, establishes a presumption of Member State action in areas of shared competence: 'the Union shall act only if and in so far as the objectives of the proposed action cannot be sufficiently achieved by the Member States, either at central level or at regional and local level, but can rather, by reason of the scale or effects of the proposed action, be better achieved at Union level'. Field pre-emption would clearly militate against the constitutional presumption favouring Member State action.

Excluding the widest sense of pre-emption finds confirmation in the Protocol on shared competences, attached to the Lisbon Treaty. With reference to the Treaty provision on shared competence, the Protocol lays down that 'when the Union has taken action in a certain area, the scope of this exercise of competence only covers those elements governed by the Union act in question and therefore does not cover the whole area'.[60] 'Area' obviously refers to the areas of shared competence enumerated in Art. 4 TFEU. Yet it would also be erroneous to restrict pre-emption merely to rule pre-emption which would only restrain Member States from adopting legislation which stands in conflict with EU law. Actually, such an effect would coincide with the principle of supremacy of EU law, now

[58] For different accounts of pre-emption, see R. Schütze (2006).

[59] For a succinct discussion, see *ibid.*, p. 1038.

[60] ECJ case law preceding the Lisbon Treaty also seems to have rejected field pre-emption. In its *Bangladesh* ruling on development aid, the Court confirmed that since Community competence in the field of development aid was not exclusive, the Member States remained free to act collectively, individually or jointly with the Community (Joined Cases C-181/91 and C-248/91 *Parliament v Council and Commission* [1993] ECR I-3685). The same argument was employed in *Lomé* (Case C-316/91 *Parliament v Council* [1994] ECR I-625).

understood as a principle addressed not only to Member State courts but to Member State legislatures as well. Arguably, the Protocol is intended to exclude Member State action within the scope of the Union act, even in the absence of an outright contradiction. Moreover, the Member State duty of *sincere cooperation* extends the prohibition on Member State action to what US doctrine calls obstacle pre-emption: even outside the scope of a Union act, Member States are prohibited from taking action which jeopardizes achievement of the objectives of the act.[61]

Indeed, legal effects largely analogous to the doctrine of pre-emption can be derived from the EU principles of supremacy and sincere cooperation. Hence one might doubt the wisdom of importing the doctrine into EU law in the first place. However, though the pre-emption doctrine by itself does not justify any normative conclusions in EU law, it may still be helpful for systematizing purposes.

General principles

The ECJ has accorded general principles of European law a constitutional status, elevating them to the level of primary law, together with the Treaties.[62] Moreover, as will be discussed in the Epilogue, some general principles, deemed foundational for the Union and its law, seem to occupy a privileged position vis-à-vis other primary law. In addition, some general principles accomplish a second-order justificatory function with regard to other, first-order principles. General legal principles manifest the central role of the ECJ in constitution-making perhaps at its most conspicuous. The Court has both established the normative contents of general principles and determined their position in European law.

Due to the case law origin of general principles, their identity and their specific normative contents and consequences are shrouded in a veil of uncertainty. The Court has never produced even a tentative summary of what it considers to be constitutionally sanctified general principles. Direct effect and primacy, which made *Van Gend en Loos* and *Costa v Enel* so renowned, certainly belong to them. However, in *Van Gend en Loos* and *Costa v Enel* the Court introduced not only the two positioning principles but also two pivotal meta-principles with which it justified its audacious

61 Art. 4(3) TEU lays down, inter alia, that 'the Member States shall facilitate the achievement of the Union's tasks and refrain from any measure which could jeopardise the attainment of the Union's objectives'.

62 Case C-101/08 *Audiolux and Others v Groupe Bruxelles Lambert and Others* [2009] ECR I-9823, Para. 63.

doctrinal innovations: *effectiveness* (*effet utile*) and *uniformity* (unity).[63] These justificatory principles still today form an essential part of the Court's stock argumentative arsenal and must be included among the central elements of the juridical constitution. *Effet utile* in particular possesses international law roots. Yet both principles address specific problems arising from the transnational character of European law and the role of Member State authorities in its implementation. Practically all the major rulings reconfirming or expanding direct effect and primacy, or elaborating such auxiliary principles as the duty of consistent interpretation and state liability, have expressly invoked efficiency or uniformity. The Member State duty of sincere cooperation, which, diverging from effectiveness and uniformity, is explicitly enshrined in the Treaty, is the third justificatory principle which the Court routinely invokes to buttress its case law promoting juridical constitutionalization.

In ECJ jurisprudence, effectiveness has served not only as a justifying meta-level principle for direct effect and primacy but as an independent basis for legal consequences as well. Effective implementation of European law has been argued to require appropriate national legal remedies and procedural guarantees and hence to justify incursions into Member State procedural autonomy. Furthermore, the Court has relied on effectiveness as a justification for criminal law sanctions outside the AFSJ, in the former Community pillar.[64] In Takis Tridimas's words, the principle 'requires the effective protection of Community rights and, more generally, the effective enforcement of Community law in national courts'.[65] The implications of effectiveness relate both to protection of individual rights and to effective enforcement of European law. In most cases, these two perspectives produce similar results: ever since *Van Gend en Loos*, the European juridical constitution has employed the vigilance of individuals over their rights as a means to secure enforcement of European law in national courts. In Lisbon, the constitutional legislator explicitly laid down that 'Member States shall provide remedies sufficient to ensure

63 Although the Court did not yet explicitly name the two principles, they are recognizable for instance in the following reasoning in *Costa v Enel*: 'The executive force of community law cannot vary from one state to another in deference to subsequent domestic laws, without jeopardizing the attainment of the objectives of the Treaty set out in Article 5(2) and giving rise to discrimination prohibited by Article 7.' See also P. Nebbia (2008).

64 The landmark case was C-176/03 *Commission v Council* [2005] ECR I-07879. See on the significance of the justificatory principle of effectiveness for EU criminal law E. Herlin-Karnell (2012).

65 T. Tridimas (2006), p. 418.

effective legal protection in the fields covered by Union law' (Art. 19(1) TEU).[66]

The new provision in Art. 19(1) TEU also manifests the *rule of law*, yet another overarching meta-level principle of the juridical constitution. This shows that in some contexts the principles of the rule of law and effectiveness work in the same direction. Yet they may have contradictory implications as well. In juridical constitutionalization legal certainty has functioned as a counter-principle restricting the expansion of direct effect and primacy, especially with regard to horizontal relations between private parties. It warrants threshold criteria for European norms which may obtain direct effect. It has also provided a justification for refusal by the ECJ to acknowledge horizontal direct effect for directives which have not been properly transposed into national law.

The rule of law principle made its first explicit entry into ECJ jurisprudence in *Les Verts*, where the Court characterized the EEC with the innovative but not wholly felicitous expression 'community based on the rule of law'. The constitutional legislator only enshrined the principle in Treaty law in Amsterdam.[67] In *Les Verts*, the Court identified the rule of law with the availability of remedies and procedures which ensure the conformity of both European and Member State measures with primary Union law. Moreover, the Court stressed the importance of access to justice by private parties to challenge the legality of an act affecting their Community rights or obligations. In its subsequent case law, the Court has relied on the rule of law both as an interpretive principle and as a source for more precise legal standards.[68] Standards of judicial protection include the (sub-)principle of legal certainty, protection of legitimate expectations and the right to an effective remedy, at present guaranteed by not only Art. 19(1) TEU but Art. 47 of the Charter of Fundamental Rights of the European Union (CFREU) as well. In recent jurisprudence, for instance in *Kadi*, the rule of law has been explicitly related to protection of fundamental rights (Para. 316). This link has added a substantive aspect to the principle of the rule of law.

66 See on the principle of effectiveness *ibid.*, pp. 418 ff., and P. Nebbia (2008).

67 Art. 6(1) TEU referred to liberty, democracy, respect for human rights and the rule of law as principles which are common to the EU Member States and on which the Union is founded. A new Art. 7 TEU allowed for EU sanctions in the case of serious and persistent breach of the principles by a Member State, and Art. 49 defined them as criteria for accession to membership in the Union.

68 L. Pech (2010).

As an overarching constitutional principle, the rule of law has its domicile in the juridical constitution, alongside effectiveness, uniformity and sincere cooperation. Through the framing function of the juridical constitution, the principle extends its influence to all the other constitutional dimensions. I shall resume discussing the rule of law in the context of economic constitutionalization (Chapters 5 and 6).

As already indicated, fundamental rights were also introduced into European law by the ECJ as general principles. In Maastricht the constitutional legislator expressly sanctified this constitution-making contribution by the Court. The Lisbon Treaty still retained the provision on fundamental rights as general principles of EU law (Art. 6(3) TEU). Yet the Treaty also accorded the Charter of Fundamental Rights of the European Union the same legal value that the Treaties enjoy. Since Lisbon, the ECJ has shifted its focus in fundamental rights protection to the Charter. However, general principles may still serve the ECJ as an additional normative resource for elaborating EU fundamental rights law, in particular on issues not tackled by the Charter.

3 Perspectivism

Perspectives on legal perspectivism

Perspectivism is an inherent feature of all law. Legal actors always approach the law from a particular perspective, which inevitably affects what they identify as law and how they interpret and apply it. There is no law as such. Law exists only as identified and interpreted by situated legal actors: that is, legal actors embedded in a particular social and cultural context. Although a general characteristic of law, perspectivism is particularly pronounced in transnational law, such as EU law. This is due to the great variety of legal actors and the great variety of the situatedness of these actors. The EU legislator includes not only a transnational bureaucracy, responsible for law drafting, but also Member State ministers constituting the Council in its different compositions, as well as Members of the European Parliament elected from national constituencies; EU law is applied not only by transnational Union courts but also – and even primarily – by the national courts of the Member States, which at the time of writing amount to twenty-eight; and in legal scholarship EU law is discussed not only by specialized EU lawyers but also by representatives of the legal disciplines formed along the traditional divisions of a national legal order: public and private lawyers, criminal lawyers, procedural lawyers, and so on.

How legal perspectivism is conceived of depends on how the situatedness of legal actors is defined. The principal options are distinguished by the dividing line between the internal and external points of view on law. One can either try to specify the situatedness of legal actors by reconstructing the variable determinants of their internal point of view or one can adopt the descriptive and explanatory position of an external observer. The most renowned example of an attempt to account for the situatedness of legal actors through a reconstruction of the internal point of view is Kelsen's pure theory of law. I shall illustrate the other principal option, an analysis of situatedness from the position of an external observer, through two examples: Martti Koskenniemi's version of critical legal scholarship and the theory of autopoietical systems, adopted by disciples of Niklas Luhmann.

Kelsen conceives of the legal order as a hierarchically organized whole, where lower-order norms derive their validity from higher ones: by-laws from laws, laws from the constitution and the (historically first) constitution from a hypothetical, presupposed basic norm (*Grundnorm*). He maintains that all legal actors are bound to assume the existence of a *Grundnorm* which constitutes the ultimate basis for the validity and cognoscibility of the legal order they are applying. Multiple interpretations of the nature of the *Grundnorm* exist; indeed, Kelsen's own accounts of its role vary as well. But a Kantian transcendental aspect, at least, is crucial to an understanding of the function of the *Grundnorm* in the pure theory of law. For Kelsen, the tacit assumption of a *Grundnorm* is a necessary precondition for all legal cognition and all judgments of legal validity. On Kelsen's view, the inevitable perspectivism of law results from adherence by legal actors to the *Grundnorm* of the respective legal order; the *Grundnorm* defines the situatedness of a legal actor.

The Kelsenian approach is an extreme version of the internal point of view. By contrast, Koskenniemi does not try to probe into or reconstruct the normative *Vorverständnis* of legal actors. To the contrary, he shuns discussion of the normative presuppositions or implications of legal speech acts; for him, the grand issues of normatively oriented legal theory – validity or authority and meaning – possess no intrinsic significance. Instead of the illocutionary dimension of legal speech acts, where normative credentials are appraised, Koskenniemi focuses on the perlocutionary, strategic aspect; illocution is subordinated to the strategic, interest-driven aims of perlocution.[1] Legal actors are situated in different legal regimes and institutions, with different and, often enough, conflicting biases and interests. They are active players in the power game of law, and the position which they occupy in this game dictates their perspective on law.

Luhmann's disciples in legal scholarship are also committed to epistemological perspectivism, but instead of institutional biases and strategic interests account for it by reference to the divergent codes and rationalities of social sub-systems. This account is particularly relevant for an

[1] See my criticism of Koskenniemi's position in K. Tuori (2011), pp. 24 ff.

analysis of transnational law. Theorists such as Andreas Fischer-Lescano and Gunther Teubner claim that global social sub-systems produce their particular instances of transnational law, which are enclosed in the perspectival rationality of the sub-system at issue.[2]

Exclusive perspectivism in its Kelsenian, Koskenniemian or Luhmannian variants can see in the relations between different perspectives merely misunderstandings and conflicts created by adherence to a particular *Grundnorm*, institutional biases and strategic interests or the specific code and rationality of a particular social sub-system. But another aspect to these relations exists as well: *interlegality*. Interlegality is particularly important for the functioning of transnational EU law. In Boaventura de Sousa Santos's account, typical of interlegality are 'different legal spaces superimposed, interpenetrated and mixed in our minds, as much as in our actions'. He argues that 'we live in a time of porous legality or of legal porosity, multiple networks of legal orders forcing us to constant transitions and trespassing. Our legal life is constituted by an intersection of different legal orders, that is, by interlegality.'[3] In the mirror of interlegality, legal orders do not appear as self-contained entities; they are seen as mutually overlapping and maintaining a dialogical relation with each other.

In order to capture the interlegality involving cross-perspective dialogue and influences, the situatedness of legal actors should be conceived of in *legal cultural* terms. Legal actors approach the law through a specific legal *Vorverständnis*, which receives its contents from the legal culture they have internalized. Variations of legal culture can be examined in relation to legal orders, legal roles and legal disciplines. Accordingly, legal cultural perspectivism comes in three guises: perspectivism of *legal orders*, perspectivism of *legal roles* and perspectivism of *legal disciplines*.

Perspectivism of legal roles and disciplines is easily discernible in a single national legal system as well, although even there it remains a rather pristine area for legal theory. Perspectivism of legal roles derives from the fact that legal actors perform diverse functions in the legal system and that their particular role as, say, law drafters (legislators), judges, practising lawyers or scholars influences the way they approach the law. In turn, perspectivism of legal disciplines relates to particular fields of law, each with its own doctrinal and theoretical apparatus, in which not only scholars but also other legal actors, such as practising lawyers, specialize. So we have private and public lawyers, international

[2] A. Fischer-Lescano and G. Teubner (2004). [3] B. de Sousa Santos (2002), p. 347.

lawyers, constitutional lawyers, criminal lawyers, and so on. By contrast, perspectivism of legal orders may go unnoticed for those who restrict their theoretical gaze to a single national legal system, while in the context of EU law perspectivism is impossible to ignore. This is due to the problems which legal diversity and pluralism raise in European legal space and the elimination or neutralization of which is one of the main tasks of the juridical constitution of the EU. Accordingly, the main focus in this chapter will lie on the perspectivism of legal orders.

Legal diversity

Let me start with some conceptual clarifications. The perspectivism of legal orders is a consequence of *legal diversity*, defined as the coexistence of multiple legal orders. Legal diversity is not identical to *legal pluralism*. Legal diversity can but need not develop into legal pluralism. 'Legal pluralism' connotes a specific constellation within legal diversity, a constellation where diverse legal orders or systems claim authority within the same legal space: that is, the same geographically delineated social space as the setting for law.

Both legal diversity and legal pluralism should be distinguished from what in Scandinavian debates has been deemed the increased *polycentricity* of law. 'Polycentricity' refers to important developments in the doctrine of legal sources, which determines who is allowed to participate in the continuous discourse specifying the contents of the legal order and what weight the various contributions carry. 'Polycentricity' connotes a multiplication of sources of law; the entry of new participants into the discourse where the ever-changing content of the legal order is determined. Moreover, the weight of individual contributions has changed. Legal sources can no longer be ordered in an unequivocal hierarchical order with formal determinants, as has previously been assumed in, for instance, Scandinavian doctrine; formal authority has been forced to give way to substantive authority.[4]

Growing polycentricity shakes some of the central premises of modern legal theory. Especially hurt is the legal positivism of the Kelsenian or Hartian type with its hierarchical view of law, which implies a hierarchical structure of the state organization as well. Polycentricity questions the fiction of a unitary state will expressing itself in law and jeopardizes the formal, hierarchical principle of order of law. Still, the focus

[4] H. Zahle (1995).

of 'polycentricity' is on a single legal order; it evokes a *plurality of legal sources* and not of legal orders or systems. Polycentricity is certainly a manifest phenomenon in EU law, due to the plethora of its sources and its other specificities, such as the essential role of judicial legislation; the ever-mounting stock of soft-law documents; and reliance on intergovernmental agreements. During the Eurozone crisis, polycentricity took a great leap forward, causing problems for democratic oversight and the rule of law. Moreover, the entry of EU law into the municipal legal order through direct applicability and direct effect has been a crucial factor in enhanced polycentricity at the national level. However, in our present discussion, polycentricity can be left aside and the focus turned towards legal diversity and legal pluralism.

'Legal diversity' refers to the mere parallelism of a plurality of legal orders, without implying anything of either harmonious or conflictual relations among these. Thus, the *black box model* which, according to William Twining,[5] has underpinned much of modern legal theory, depicts legal diversity in terms of self-contained and self-sufficient normative boxes. This model is premised on the coexistence of territorially delineated state legal orders, each of them claiming *exclusive* jurisdiction within their respective territorially defined social spaces, and international law, confined to regulating external relations among sovereign states. As regards internal legal relations, sovereign states are expected to treat each other with respect for the principle of exclusivity: that is, as black boxes. Furthermore, within their territorial confines, states raise the claim of, and mutually acknowledge, the *universal* scope of their exclusive legal sovereignty.

In their respective versions of legal positivism, Hans Kelsen and H. L. A. Hart procured perhaps the most sophisticated formulations of the black box view. Kelsen's hierarchical normative structure, the *Stufenbau*, is, above all, tailored to depict a state legal order: the *Grundnorm* crowning the hierarchy commands obedience to the (historically first) constitution of the state, while the norms on the lower echelons are issued by state organs authorized by the constitution. It is true, though, that Kelsen's world of legal *Sollen* included international law too. He advocated a monist view where both international and national law are subject to the same *Grundnorm*: either that of international law or that of the national legal order. Kelsen's monism with regard to international law does not question the state premises of his construction. International law

[5] W. Twining (2000).

merely regulates relationships between states (national legal orders). Even if the legal *Stufenbau* is construed starting from the *Grundnorm* of international law, international law only provides the national legal order with its validity basis, leaving the national legislator free to decide on the normative contents of that order in compliance with the (procedural) requirements of the state constitution.[6] So in Kelsen's pure theory of law, relations between national and international law are analysed in terms of validity and against two monistic alternatives: either national law derives its validity from international law or vice versa. In turn, in the Hartian framework, the existence of a distinct legal order presupposes particular rules of recognition (a normative doctrine of legal sources), determining the criteria of membership in this order.

Kelsen's account of the necessary, transcendental assumption of a *Grundnorm* which tops the edifice of law and provides it with its validity and normativity can be seen as a depiction of the perspectivism of legal orders. The problems of this depiction are intimately related to the general problems of Kelsen's pure theory of law. Kelsen maintains, and rightly so, that the normative claims of legal speech acts are always made with reference to a specific legal order. Yet the dependence of legal actors on a *referential legal order* should be understood in broader terms than merely as application of surface-level normative material and the doctrine of legal sources determining the legal validity of that material.

Kelsenian perspectivism takes seriously the normativity of law and attempts to articulate the internal point of view of legal actors. But the Kelsenian reconstruction of the *Vorverständnis* of legal actors remains truncated. Kelsen is right in stressing that a doctrine of legal sources which helps to identify valid legal norms is an essential part of legal *Vorverständnis*, as is the law's basic conceptual structure which Kelsen has attempted to pin down as well. But through his leap into the transcendental, Kelsen ahistoricizes historically highly variable cultural phenomena. As the debate on the law's polycentricity has shown, for instance, the doctrine of legal sources is not necessarily hierarchically structured, as Kelsen claims, nor does legal cultural evidence support a thesis of an immutable conceptual skeleton of the law. Perhaps even more serious is Kelsen's silence about the normative elements – general legal principles – in legal culture and in the *Vorverständnis* of legal actors. No layeredness exists in the normative contents of Kelsen's *Stufenbau*. In this respect, the

[6] H. Kelsen (1989), pp. 328 ff.

Stufenbau is a unilevel normative entity, located at the law's surface and excluding the sub-surface, legal cultural layers.

European legal diversity is an important backdrop to European integration. Legal diversity was seen as preventing construction of a Europe-wide marketplace for goods, workers, services and capital. Combating diversity or at least its detrimental consequences has dominated European integration as legal integration. Here the European juridical constitution has availed itself of various means. The primary instrument is EU legislation, ranging from directly effective Treaty provisions to directly applicable regulations and harmonizing directives, issued under the powers established by the Treaties. Furthermore, the central principles of the juridical constitution, introduced by way of ECJ jurisprudence, purport to secure that diversity-fighting EU legislation is realized in Member States. These include the principles of direct effect and primacy, as well as efficacy and uniformity as second-order, justifying master principles. Interpretive principles, which oblige national courts to interpret municipal legislation in conformity with EU law and to treat EU law concepts as autonomous concepts with autonomous meanings, complement the normative armature with which EU law strives to overcome such legal diversity as is considered detrimental to EU policy objectives. The principle of mutual recognition, introduced within the economic constitution through *Cassis de Dijon* and subsequently adopted through political legislation in the security dimension, reacts to legal diversity in Member States. However, it does not target diversity as such but its consequences for cross-border activities. The ECJ is the main guarantor of the uniformity of European law and its integration into national legal orders. The Court mainly performs this role through the preliminary ruling procedure.

European legal instruments reacting to legal diversity are primarily applied by national courts. But due to the perspectivism of legal orders, we are entitled to assume that judges in national courts approach and interpret EU law through their national legal culture: applying the legal concepts, principles and theories inherent in that culture. It is not realistic to suppose that national judges would be able to turn off the deeply ingrained and mainly unconsciously functioning national legal culture when applying European law. The means that EU constitutional law offers for reducing legal diversity are mainly tailored to surface-level law. As a rule, they are not very helpful with regard to legal cultural diversity, which mainly produces its effects through the *Vorverständnis* of legal actors and which even affects the national application of instruments meant to efface surface-level diversity. The doctrine of autonomous EU law concepts and the interpretive principles established in the case law of the ECJ can, though, be argued to aim at reducing legal cultural diversity. But such concepts and principles are like islands in the sea; their impact on the interpretation and application of EU law in national courts is inevitably of a limited nature. The diversity of national legal cultures seems to lead not only to nationally differentiated perspectives on European law but, more dramatically, to a diversity of European laws, cast in different legal cultural moulds.

Where does this leave European integration as integration through and of law? With my legal cultural turn, have I only produced another black box version of legal diversity and the ensuing perspectivism, now rooted in the largely unconsciously functioning *Vorverständnis* of legal actors? Have I only substituted legal cultural idiosyncrasies, guiding interpretation and application of the law, for the Kelsenian *Grundnorm*, Koskenniemian antagonistic strategic interests or Luhmannian system-specific rationalities?

Exclusive perspectivism in its different variants leads to ignoring the phenomena of interlegality that balance the perspectivist diversity of EU law; exclusive perspectivism cannot acknowledge the possibility of interperspective influences and dialogue. A cultural view of legal perspectivism overcomes this shortcoming. Differences in legal culture do not negate the possibility of a common core in nationally differentiated traditions: a common legal *deep culture*, as we can also call it. It is doubtful that the black box model has ever produced an accurate view of the global lawscape. The heyday of modern, sovereign states may have produced some corroboration for it but even then its applicability was restricted to the law's surface level. A major flaw in the hierarchical portrayal of law by such theorists as Kelsen and Hart consists of largely bypassing the cultural levels of law. An examination of the cultural levels underlying surface-level law rapidly dissipates the illusion of self-contained, nationally differentiated legal orders. Ever since the beginning of reception of Roman law in the twelfth century, the cultural foundations of European private law in particular have been of a conspicuously transnational nature.[7] If the idea of self-contained legal orders with sharply definable contours – an idea implicit in Kelsen's pure theory as well as Hart's concept of law – can

[7] The black box model also passes over the important phenomena of colonial legal regimes – a favourite topic of legal anthropologists and sociologists – and global common laws, discussed instructively by H. P. Glenn (2005).

in general be of assistance in mapping our present legal landscape, the applicability of that idea is confined to the surface level of explicit norms. When we turn to the underpinning legal cultural layers, the boundaries of legal orders turn out to be much more porous; no claim of autonomy either can or purports to separate legal orders from each other. No rule of recognition or *Grundnorm* exists which would allow us to draw exact borderlines between legal cultures.

Interlegality is primarily about legal cultural overlaps and interaction. Indeed, EU law is, in a crucial sense, premised on interlegality at the cultural level. Legal traditions common to Member States are an important source of general principles of EU law,[8] and Art. 6(1) TEU explicitly refers to shared constitutional traditions as a basis for fundamental rights principles. In spite of legal-culturally induced perspectivism, misunderstandings and communication gaps, EU law is interpreted and applied in a sufficiently uniform manner across borders to guarantee, for instance, the functioning of the internal market. This would not be possible without similarities, interfaces and overlaps between national legal cultures and the legal *Vorverständnis* of the legal actors of different Member States. We may have diverse EU laws (twenty-eight at present), impregnated by diverse national legal cultures, possibly complemented by 'EU law EU law': that is, EU law as seen from the particular perspective of EU law itself. Still these EU laws are sufficiently alike to make European integration possible.

Legal pluralism

As a rule, relations among national legal orders follow the pattern of 'simple' legal diversity. Legal pluralism enters European legal space together with transnational EU law. Diversity turns into pluralism when state law's exclusive jurisdiction is challenged; when the legal space of a state is transformed into a *hybrid space*[9] where plural and competing claims of authority are raised. Theorists caught in the black box model are unable to conceptualize this step from legal diversity to legal pluralism.

In accordance with the two aspects of law, legal pluralism appears in two shapes: pluralism of legal orders and systems or, expressed in other terms, normative and systemic pluralism. In a *pluralism of legal orders* or *normative pluralism* diverse legal orders claim authority in the same legal

[8] See, e.g., T. Tridimas (2006), pp. 5 ff., and X. Groussot (2006), pp. 17 ff.

[9] The term is borrowed from P. S. Berman (2012).

space. Such a constellation contests not only the hierarchical view of the Kelsenian–Hartian variant of legal positivism but also the exclusivity of state law. Yet the challenge need not be fatal, and state law may still retain its dominance. This is the case when state law defines the conditions for the applicability of non-state law and when enforcement of the latter also falls to state courts.[10] This is how things are in what Twining has called a pluralist state system and where state courts apply different normative orders to different groups of persons.[11] *Pluralism of legal systems* or *systemic pluralism* questions the exclusivity not only of the state legal order but of state legal institutions and practices as well. This occurs when non-state law, claiming authority in the territory of a state, possesses its own court-like, law-enforcing bodies. Evidently, this form of legal pluralism poses the gravest threat to the state-sovereigntist premises of the black box model.

The concept of legal pluralism is originally a contribution of legal anthropological studies of colonial regimes. By contrast, present legal pluralism results from the fairly recent rise of transnational law. Transnational law, with EU law as its most conspicuous epitome, has dealt the final deathblow to the black box model. Transnational law is law beyond the dichotomy of national and international law; it simply does not fit into the compartments of the black box model. In the black box model, legal systems and the reach of their respective claims of authority are differentiated along *territorial* criteria; within its territory, the claim to authority of the state legal system is universal and exclusive. It is universal in the sense of covering all substantive fields of regulation, and it is exclusive in the sense of not recognizing any rival legal authority. By contrast, transnational law follows, not territorial, but *substantive* (functional) criteria of differentiation. Its claim to authority is not universal in its scope but always limited to specific substantive fields. This is true even of EU law, which, in spite of its expansionist tendencies, is bound by the principle of conferral. As a rule, transnational law's claim to authority is not exclusive either. Exceptions to this rule, though, exist, as is proved by Treaty provisions on exclusive EU legislative competence

Conflicts also can and do occur under 'simple' legal diversity, between territorially delineated legal systems, claiming universal and exclusive jurisdiction within their legal space. Still the default assumption is that

[10] See R. Michaels (2005) for discussion of the alternatives for state law to acknowledge the significance of non-state law.

[11] W. Twining (2000), p. 83.

these are mere boundary disputes, relatively few in number and manageable by private international law and choice-of-law rules.[12] Transnational law challenges state law's claim to both exclusivity and universality. Clashes arising from contradictory principles of attribution of legal authority seem inescapable: the substantively limited claim to authority by transnational law contradicts the universal and exclusive claim by state law. Now at issue are not mere border skirmishes, disputes over the exact course of the boundary separating two territorially defined jurisdictions. The battle has moved inland and involves a much more serious controversy. Rival legal orders, with diversely defined jurisdictions and enforced and ensured by at least partly different institutions, are competing for authority in the same territorial and social space: no longer at issue is the territorial demarcation of two legal systems, whose supremacy – sovereignty – within its legal space is uncontested. In clashes between transnational and national law, the battle is waged within the acknowledged legal space of a state, and touches on the very sovereignty of the state and its legal system. A particularly acute crisis is prone to erupt when the claims raised by transnational law touch on issues which in state law are reserved for the constitution. This is the backdrop to European constitutional pluralism, which I will approach through fundamental rights pluralism as its specific manifestation.

European fundamental rights pluralism

Chapter 2 above discussed juridical constitutionalization from the perspective of European law. Direct effect and primacy are principles of European constitutional law, introduced by the ECJ as the European constitutional court. But these principles would have remained mere unilateral declarations if they had not been accepted at the national level; the constitutional speech acts of the ECJ would not have attained their intended perlocutionary effects if their illocutionary force had not been recognized by Member State legal actors. A crucial role in the often-recited (hi)story of the acceptance of the positioning principles of European law was played by ordinary national courts, which bear the main responsibility for implementing and enforcing European law and which, in addition to their tasks in the national legal system, also act as 'ordinary courts within the European Union legal order'.[13]

12 See N. Walker (2008).

13 See on the acceptance by national courts of direct effect and primacy A.-M. Slaughter et al. (1998); K. J. Alter (2001); A. Stone Sweet (2004).

Not only the European constitution but also national constitutions exercise a positioning function. If a vital task for the European juridical constitution is to define European law's relationship to Member State law, national constitutions are faced with the task of positioning the municipal legal system in relation to European law. No *a priori* guarantee exists that Member State and European positioning principles coincide and that Member States embrace the claims of direct effect and primacy of European law. Constitutional courts are key actors in positioning municipal law in respect of EU law. The jurisprudence of ordinary national courts, where direct effect and primacy have found general acknowledgement over the years, represents the ordinary course of affairs in relations between Member State and EU law. By contrast, a somewhat different story emerges from the exceptional jurisprudence of national constitutional courts, their celebrated and widely reported landmark cases which explicitly focus on constitutional positioning principles.

Indeed, in most Member States national constitutional actors have never unconditionally accepted European law's claim to primacy. Member States have articulated the normative premises which govern the relationship of national law to European law through constitutional provisions and the rulings of constitutional courts. Prominent constitutional courts, such as the German and Italian, formulated their basic reservations in the first decades following *Van Gend en Loos* and *Costa v Enel*. Assessing the constitutionality of ratification of the Maastricht Treaty provided a new occasion for specifying these reservations. In the first decade of the present century, ratification of the abortive Constitutional Treaty and the Lisbon Treaty as its stripped-down successor, as well as national implementation of the Framework Decision on the European Arrest Warrant, have again facilitated position-taking for several constitutional courts, including those of such new Member States as Poland and the Czech Republic. The German Constitutional Court is the most important national interlocutor of the ECJ, and its major rulings on the status of European law in the municipal legal order have attracted much resonance among other national constitutional courts.[14] Hence, it is warranted to let the German Court exemplify the perspective of Member State constitutional law.[15]

14 See on the influence of the German Court's *Maastricht* ruling on other constitutional courts J. Baquero Cruz (2008).

15 On the dialogue between the German Constitutional Court and the CJEU see, e.g., D. Thym (2012) and B. Davies (2012).

The provisos of the German Constitutional Court on the primacy of EU law are manifest in the three types of review which the Court has held to be available for assessing the constitutionality of national measures based on EU law:

- *ultra vires* review,
- fundamental rights review, and
- identity review.

In *ultra vires* review, the claim is that the EU measure exceeds Union competence and, therefore, cannot be accorded direct effect or primacy. When exercising *ultra vires* review the Constitutional Court claims jurisdiction to assess the competence basis of EU measures: the famous *Kompetenz-Kompetenz*. In turn, in *fundamental rights review* the Court appraises an EU measure in the light of national fundamental rights law. Finally, in *identity review*, the testing stone is the inviolability of national constitutional identity. I will start from the claims of the German Constitutional Court concerning fundamental rights review, which provided an important impetus towards adding a fundamental rights aspect to European juridical constitutionalization.

Reflecting the limited substantive scope of Community law, no provisions on fundamental rights were included in the Treaty of Rome. However, it soon turned out that in spite of the basic policy orientation of EU law, its national implementation could lead to conflicts with national fundamental rights law. The *Solange* doctrine aimed at safeguarding national fundamental rights protection from the threat perceived to derive from European law's claim of primacy even over national constitutional law; a claim which had been explicitly raised by *Internationale Handelsgesellschaft* in 1970. *Solange* was elaborated by the German Constitutional Court but found counterparts in the constitutional doctrine of other Member States as well.

In *Solange I*, issued in 1974, the German Constitutional Court argued that Art. 24 of the Basic Law, the then constitutional basis for transferring sovereign rights to inter-state institutions, did not authorize amending the fundamental structure of the Basic Law through legislation by an inter-state institution. Fundamental rights are an inalienable, essential feature of the Basic Law and part of its constitutional structure. The Court pointed out that the Community still lacked 'a democratically legitimate parliament directly elected by general suffrage which possesses legislative powers and to which the Community organs empowered to legislate are fully responsible on a political level', and, 'in particular, a codified catalogue of fundamental rights, the substance of which is reliably and unambiguously fixed for the future in the same way as the substance of the Basic Law'. The Court avowed that it would review the compatibility of Community law, relevant to the decision of a German court, in light of national fundamental rights 'as long as the integration process has not progressed so far that Community law also receives a catalogue of fundamental rights decided on by a parliament and of settled validity, which is adequate in comparison with the catalogue of fundamental rights contained in the Basic Law'. However, before filing a reference with the Constitutional Court, the court at issue should obtain a ruling by the ECJ in the preliminary ruling procedure.[16]

Solange II, issued in 1986,[17] reaffirmed that the Basic Law does not allow conferral on international institutions of power to encroach on the identity of the German constitutional order. The Court reasoned that 'an essential part which cannot be dispensed with and belongs to the basic framework of the constitutional order in force is constituted . . . by the legal principles underlying the provisions of the Basic Law on fundamental rights'. If sovereign power accorded to an international institution entails removal of the legal protection offered by the Basic Law, this should be compensated by 'a guarantee of the application of fundamental rights which in substance and effectiveness is essentially similar to the protection of fundamental rights required unconditionally by the Basic Law'. *Solange II* recounted the progress achieved in Community fundamental rights law since *Solange I*, beginning with the ECJ judgments in *Stauder* in 1969[18] and *Internationale Handelsgesellschaft* in 1970,[19] and including the joint declaration on fundamental rights by the European Parliament, the Council and the Commission on 5 April 1977.[20] The Court concluded that it could now revise the position of *Solange I* and formulate a new *Solange* doctrine, with deference to EU fundamental rights review as the starting point. The Court now acknowledged that the European Communities, ECJ case law in particular, generally ensure effective protection of fundamental rights against 'the sovereign powers of the Communities' and that this protection is substantially equivalent to that required by the Basic

16 BVerfGE 37, 271 2 BvL 52/71, 29 May 1974.

17 BVerfGE 73, 339 2 BvR 197/83, 22 October 1986.

18 Case C-29/69 *Stauder v Stadt Uhm* [1969] ECR 419.

19 Case C-11/70 *Internationale Handelsgesellschaft* [1970] ECR 1125.

20 Joint Declaration concerning the protection of fundamental rights and the European Convention for the Protection of Human Rights and Fundamental Freedoms, [1977] OJ C103/1.

Law. The Court declared that in so far as the Communities 'generally safeguard the essential content of fundamental rights' it would no longer review Community legislation by the standard of the fundamental rights contained in the Basic Law.

Since *Solange II*, the fundamental rights dimension of the European juridical and political constitution has been further consolidated. The Maastricht Treaty confirmed the status of fundamental rights as general principles of Community law. The next milestone was the adoption in 2001 of the Charter of the Fundamental Rights of the European Union (CFREU) as a Declaration of the European Council. Lisbon explicitly equated the legal value of the CFREU with that of the Treaties. In turn, post-Lisbon case law has further specified the purport of the horizontal articles, which address the Charter's application to Member State measures and relation to national fundamental rights protection; that is, its direct effect and primacy. The development of EU fundamental rights law has largely quelled the concerns raised from the perspective of the national constitution and lying behind the *Solange* rulings. For Member State constitutional actors, the main worries no longer derive from underdevelopment of EU fundamental rights law but rather the expansion of its scope: its intrusion into fields where national fundamental rights law claims jurisdiction. These worries point in the direction of *ultra vires* review.

Ultra vires review, as formulated by the German Constitutional Court, addresses the *Kompetenz-Kompetenz* issue: the question where the final competence lies to decide on the competence of Union institutions and, ultimately, the EU as a whole. As part of its claim to interpretive autonomy, the ECJ has consequently asserted jurisdiction as to whether Union institutions have acted within the competence established by the Treaties and thus respected the principle of conferral. On the other hand, when Member States as Masters of the Treaties have transferred sovereign rights through the Treaties to the European level, they have acted under the authorization of national constitutions. National constitutional courts claim interpretive autonomy for the national legal system and hence exclusive jurisdiction for themselves over the reach of constitutional authorization. This leads to the conclusion that national constitutional courts are competent to assess whether European measures claiming direct effect and primacy respect the boundaries of constitutional authorization and transferral of sovereign rights. The *Kompetenz-Kompetenz* question receives contradictory answers, depending on whether it is posed from the perspective of the European constitution or the national constitution.

In its jurisprudence, the German Constitutional Court has consequently defended its *ultra vires* jurisdiction with regard to European measures. The importance of the issue has grown in phase with the expansion of the scope of action of European institutions facilitated by, first, ECJ case law and then Treaty revisions, starting with the SEA in 1986. The 1993 *Maastricht* ruling of the German Constitutional Court[21] brought the issue into the limelight, and in its 2009 *Lisbon* judgment the Court reconfirmed its claim to *Kompetenz-Kompetenz*. With reference to the principle of conferral, the Court argued that the EU can only exercise such powers as Member States, in accordance with their national constitution, have transferred to it through the Treaties. Because of the derivative character of its powers, the EU cannot exercise *Kompetenz-Kompetenz* over the Treaties.[22] The Member States remain Masters of the Treaties and possess ultimate jurisdiction over EU institutions acting within the confines of their transferred competences. The Court reiterated its readiness to exert *ultra vires* review when needed with regard to acts adopted by EU institutions. However, it also emphasized the *ultima ratio* nature of this review and announced that it will not be applied as long as – *so lange* – the EU's internal monitoring is able to prevent or correct excesses of competence.[23] Thus, the German court's acceptance of ECJ *ultra vires* supervision is conditional analogously to the *Solange* doctrine of fundamental rights review.

Ultra vires review may be relevant for fundamental rights pluralism as well, in the definition of the reach of EU fundamental rights law in respect of national measures. Where the European juridical constitution finds EU fundamental rights law to be applicable, it treats national courts as 'ordinary courts within the European Union legal order'. Under the principle of primacy, national courts are supposed to set aside national in favour of EU fundamental rights law and act as instruments of EU review. Art. 51(1) CFREU sets out that the Charter is addressed to the Member States when these are implementing Union law. Post-Lisbon case law of the ECJ, most notably *Åkerberg Fransson*,[24] has treated

21 BVerfGE 89, 155, 2 October 1993.

22 According to the BVerfGE *Lisbon* ruling, 'the Basic Law does not authorise German state bodies to transfer sovereign powers in such a way that their exercise can independently establish other competences for the European Union. It prohibits the transfer of competence to decide on its own competence.' 2 BvE 2/08, 30 June 2009, Para. 233.

23 *Ibid.*, Para. 240.

24 Case C-617/10 *Åklagaren v Åkerberg Fransson*, 26 February 2013 (not yet reported).

'implementing Union law' as equivalent in meaning to 'acting in the scope of EU law' in pre-Lisbon jurisprudence on fundamental rights principles. The German Constitutional Court has been quick to react to what it has considered threatening signs of the ECJ expanding its fundamental rights jurisdiction at the expense of national constitutional review and to recall the availability of its *ultra vires* review. Notably, the Court has stressed that even the ECJ, which in the EU constitutional order is expected to watch over the principle of conferral, is a Union institution and itself bound by this very principle.

In *Honeywell*,[25] the German Constitutional Court responded to the ECJ ruling in *Mangold*.[26] The complainant had claimed that in postulating prohibition of age discrimination as a general principle, the ECJ had transgressed the boundaries of interpreting Community law in a manner which was no longer covered by Community competences. In its judgment, the German Constitutional Court reaffirmed the availability of national *ultra vires* review over Union measures and engaged in a detailed discussion of its application to the rulings of the ECJ, in particular in issues related to fundamental rights. In spite of its cooperative tone[27] and the fairly high threshold it set for *ultra vires* review, the Court made clear that it would not accept expansion of EU fundamental rights review through judicial law-making which has no basis in Treaty law or which disregards limitations laid down in explicit provisions. The Court evoked the interpretive principle of openness towards European law (*Europarechtsfreundlichkeit*) which it had elaborated in its previous case law, for instance in the *Lisbon* ruling (Para. 58). *Ultra vires* review presupposes a 'manifest' and 'sufficiently qualified' breach of the principle of

[25] BVerfG, 2 BvR 2661/106, 6 July 2010.

[26] Case C-144/04 *Mangold* [2005] ECR I-9981. The judgment dates from the pre-Lisbon time and was not based on the CFREU but on Directive 2000/78 of 27 November 2000 establishing a general framework for equal treatment in employment and occupation, [2000] OJ L303/16. The CJEU held it to be the responsibility of the national court to guarantee the full effectiveness of the general principle of non-discrimination in respect of age and to set aside any provision of national law which may conflict with Community law, even where the period prescribed for transposition of the directive had not yet expired. In the post-Lisbon *Kücükdeveci*, the Court confirmed prohibition of discrimination based on age as a general principle of Union law and referred as grounds to Art. 21(1) CFREU. Case C-555/07 *Kücükdeveci* [2010] ECR I-365.

[27] In accordance with the spirit of cooperation, the Court declared that it would not accept an *ultra vires* claim before affording the CJEU through the preliminary reference procedure an 'opportunity to interpret the Treaties, as well as to rule on the validity and interpretation of the legal acts in question' (Para. 60).

conferral.[28] The Court argued that the principle of conferral does not preclude the ECJ 'from refining the law by means of methodically bound case-law' (Para. 62). However, the boundaries of legitimate juridical development of the law are transgressed, above all, 'where case-law makes fundamental policy decisions over and above individual cases or as a result of the further development of the law causes structural shifts to occur in the system of the sharing of constitutional power and influence' (Para. 64).

In the end, the Constitutional Court found that in *Mangold* the ECJ had not acted *ultra vires*. Still, the detailed discussion of the applicability of *ultra vires* review to ECJ fundamental rights rulings is a clear reminder that the Court would not approve expansion of European jurisdiction over the borderline drawn in Art. 51(1)–(2) CFREU. *Honeywell* and *Mangold* concerned prohibition of age discrimination as a general principle of EU law. Invoking Art. 51(2) CFREU, the Constitutional Court pointed out that 'even if they guarantee the protection of fundamental rights at Union level, general principles may not expand the field of influence of Union law over and above the existing competences of the Union or indeed establish new tasks and competences' (Para 78).[29]

Another reminder followed in early 2013. In *Åkerberg Fransson*, the ECJ had adopted a rather wide interpretation of when national authorities acted within the scope of EU law. It had claimed jurisdiction to examine whether general national legislation on tax penalties and tax evasion, which had been applied to providing false information concerning VAT, was compatible with the *ne bis in idem* principle laid down in Art. 50 of the Charter. In a decision issued less than two months after *Åkerberg Fransson*, the Constitutional Court held that the German 'Counter-Terrorism Database Act pursues nationally determined objectives which can affect

28 The Court explained this requirement as follows: 'A breach of the principle of conferral is only manifest if the European bodies and institutions have transgressed the boundaries of their competences in a manner specifically violating the principle of conferral . . . , the breach of competences is in other words sufficiently qualified . . . This means that the act of the authority of the European Union must be manifestly in violation of competences and that the impugned act is highly significant in the structure of competences between the Member States and the Union with regard to the principle of conferral and to the binding nature of the statute under the rule of law' (Para. 61).

29 Art. 51(2) CFREU lays down that 'the Charter does not extend the field of application of Union law beyond the powers of the Union or establish any new power or task for the Union, or modify powers and tasks as defined in the Treaties'. See on *Honeywell* and its significance M. Payandeh (2011).

the functioning of the legal relationships under EU law merely indirectly'. Consequently, the Court argued, 'European fundamental rights are from the outset not applicable.' The Court expressly emphasized that *Åkerberg Fransson* does not affect this conclusion. In line with *Honeywell*, the Court characterized European and national fundamental rights review as a cooperative relationship. From this it inferred that *Åkerberg Fransson* 'must not be read in a way that would view it as an apparent *ultra vires* act or as if it endangered the protection and enforcement of the fundamental rights in the member states in a way that questioned the identity of the Basic Law's constitutional order'. The Court explained that it had acted on the assumption that the statements in *Åkerberg Fransson* are 'based on the distinctive features of the law on value-added tax, and express no general view'.[30]

Every legal system claiming autonomy not only defines its relations to other legal systems but also tries to defend its identity. As European legal and constitutional pluralism demonstrates, sovereign legislative rights may be transferred to transnational level, and a transnational court may be conceded at least preliminary and rebuttable jurisdiction over interpretation of the reach of such transfers. Still, a limit exists to the self-limitation of the exclusive and universal claim to authority of a national legal system. If a legal system compromised on what it defines as its identity, it would also compromise on its claim to autonomy.

Several Member State constitutional courts have articulated their reservation to EU law's primacy as *inviolability of national constitutional identity*. The exact terms and the justification may vary but the main idea is approximately the same. Again, the German Constitutional Court is a representative mouthpiece for the Member State standpoint.[31] From the very outset, fundamental rights and identity review have been closely connected in its jurisprudence; indeed, fundamental rights review can be understood as a sub-case of identity review. In Maastricht, the European constitutional legislator heeded Member State identity concerns by an explicit Treaty provision calling for respect for national identity (Art. 6(4)

[30] BVerfG, 1 BvR 1215/07, 24 April 2013. See the Court's Press Release No. 31/2013 of 24 April 2013. See also Editorial comment (2013).

[31] As a brief summary of other constitutional courts' jurisprudence, see A. von Bogdandy and S. Schill (2011) and M. Claes (2013). Especially on the case law of the new Central European Member States, see W. Sadurski (2008) and J. Rideau (2013). For a general review of Member State constitutional law relating to the EU, see C. Grabenwarter (2010).

TEU-Maastricht),[32] and in Lisbon a constitutional dimension was included in this identity. Art. 4(2) TEU lays down that 'the Union shall respect the equality of Member States before the Treaties as well as their national identities, inherent in their fundamental structures, political and constitutional, inclusive of regional and local self-government'. It is probably over-hasty to see in this provision an acknowledgement of the identity reservation with which national constitutional actors had qualified their acceptance of the primacy claim of European law. Still, it is warranted to set the provision in the context of the ongoing constitutional discourse between the EU and the Member States.[33] This, at least, seems to be how the German Constitutional Court sees things. In its *Lisbon* ruling, the Court took notice of the speech act of the Union constitutional legislator. The Court assigned identity review the task of securing respect for 'the inviolable core content of the constitutional identity of the Basic Law'. The Court argued that 'with progressing integration, the fundamental political and constitutional structures of sovereign Member States, which are recognised by Article 4.2 first sentence Lisbon TEU, cannot be safeguarded in any other way'. The Court concluded that 'in this respect, the guarantee of national constitutional identity under constitutional and under Union law go hand in hand in the European legal area'.[34]

But of course, Art. 4(2) TEU does not by itself assure that no future constitutional conflict over national constitutional identity will arise; this would require an additional guarantee of the identity of constitutional identities as interpreted by the ECJ and national constitutional actors. But no such guarantee exists. Still, in two recent cases, the ECJ and its Member State interlocutors have adopted a similar reading of national constitutional identity. If no guarantee for agreement exists, conflict is not inevitable either.[35]

32 As M. Claes (2013), p. 130, has demonstrated, the provision played but a minor role in pre-Lisbon case law.

33 See, however, B. Guastaferro (2012), where the author argues, on the basis of the drafting process, that the provision was primarily intended to address the delimitation of the competences of the Union and the Member States.

34 Para. 240. See also Para. 332, where the Court states that 'the constitutional identity of the Member States is protected by Art. 4(2) TEU and constitutionally safeguarded by the identity review'.

35 In *Sayn-Wittgenstein*, the ECJ 'accepted that, in the context of Austrian constitutional history, the Law on the abolition of the nobility, as an element of national identity, may be taken into consideration when a balance is struck between legitimate interests and the right of free movement of persons recognised under European Union law' (Case C-208/9 [2010] ECR I-13693, Para. 83). Significantly enough, the Court expressly invoked

What further complicates the pluralist constellation between Member State and European claims to authority is the fact that not only each Member State legal system but also the EU legal system keeps watch over its constitutional identity. The ECJ seems to consider the principle of primacy an essential element of this identity as it is asserted in relation to Member State law. In its jurisprudence, the ECJ has asserted primacy for Union fundamental rights law even if this leads to a lower level of protection than is offered by the national constitution. On its face, this interpretation seems to contradict Art. 53 CFREU which intimates that in its field of application, the Charter only defines the bottom line of protection. Art. 53 prohibits interpreting the Charter 'as restricting or adversely affecting' fundamental rights as recognized by, inter alia, Member State constitutions. In *Melloni*, the ECJ firmly rejected the interpretation, which the referring national court had envisaged and which would – in the words of the ECJ – have given 'general authorisation to a Member State to apply the standard of protection of fundamental rights guaranteed by its constitution when that standard is higher than that deriving from the Charter and, where necessary, to give it priority over the application of provisions of EU law' (Para. 56). In the ECJ's account, this would have undermined the principle of primacy, which the Court characterized as an essential feature of EU law, providing that 'rules of national law, even of a constitutional order, cannot be allowed to undermine the effectiveness of EU law on the territory of that State' (Para. 59). The Court presented a new formulation of the normative contents of Art. 53 CFREU. According to the Court, the article 'confirms that, where an EU legal act calls for national implementing measures, national authorities and courts remain free to apply national standards of protection of fundamental rights, provided that the level of protection provided for by the Charter, as interpreted by the Court, and *the primacy, unity and effectiveness of EU law are not thereby compromised*' (Para. 60 – italics added). Here we again face the central principles which *Van Gend en Loos* and *Costa v Enel* had introduced into the European juridical constitution.

Art. 4(2) TEU (Para. 92). In the proceedings in *Melloni* Advocate General Bot and the Spanish authorities agreed that the reading of the constitutional right to fair trial, adopted by the Spanish constitutional court and requiring a right to reopen a criminal case where the defendant has been sentenced *in absentia*, did not bear on Spanish constitutional identity. Case C-399/11, judgment of 26 February 2013 (not yet reported). Opinion of AG Bot in *Melloni*, Paras. 139–42. A dialogical approach to the principle of respect for national constitutional identity has also been adopted by, e.g., L. Besselink (2010) and A. von Bogdandy and S. Schill (2011).

Assertion of the EU's constitutional identity may give rise to a new type of conflict: a clash between Union and Member State constitutional identity. The ECJ may agree with Member State constitutional actors that a particular feature of national fundamental rights law manifests national constitutional identity and hence falls under Art. 4(2) TEU. Yet the Court might conclude that protection of Union constitutional identity overrides respect for national constitutional identity so that, for the sake of the primacy, unity and effectiveness of EU law, Union fundamental rights standards must be applied instead of national ones.

A comprehensive account of fundamental rights pluralism should also include the European Convention on Human Rights (ECHR) and the European Court of Human Rights (ECtHR) as the monitoring body of the Convention legal system. This legal system too is an instance of transnational law which keeps watch over its normative and interpretive autonomy and which raises claims to authority overlapping both Member State and EU fundamental rights law. In the relation between EU fundamental rights law and the ECHR, two instances of transnational law confront each other. Here EU law represents the pole of more general and the ECHR that of more specialized jurisdiction. Mutual positioning comprises three parties: EU fundamental rights law positions itself in respect of not only Member State law but also ECHR law; Member State fundamental rights law positions itself in respect of not only EU law but also ECHR law; and ECHR law positions itself in respect of both EU law and Member State law.

I shall confine myself to some general remarks on how the ECHR complicates the pluralist constellation. The EU is not a party to the ECHR. Art. 6(3) TEU does evoke the ECHR, together with common Member State constitutional traditions, as a source of EU fundamental rights principles, but the ECHR as such has not been incorporated into EU law. Art. 6(2) TEU, though, calls for Union accession to the Convention, but this has not yet transpired. Art. 53 CFREU positions EU fundamental rights law in relation to not only Member State fundamental rights but the ECHR as well. In respect of the ECHR too, Art. 53 intimates that the Charter only defines the bottom line of protection. So long as the EU itself is not a party to the ECHR, the ECHR can pertain to EU measures only indirectly, through Member State implementing measures. It is probable that the ECJ would extend its claim to primacy to ECHR law incorporated into Member State law, so defeating the implication of Art. 53 ECHR. Thus, *Melloni* would be relevant for ECHR law too. It remains to be seen after accession how the

ECJ will specify the position of the ECHR in EU law and with regard to national implementing measures.

In addition to Art. 53, the relationship between the CFREU and the ECHR is governed by the interpretive principle laid down in Art. 52(4): 'In so far as this Charter contains rights which correspond to rights guaranteed by the Convention for the Protection of Human Rights and Fundamental Freedoms, the meaning and scope of those rights shall be the same as those laid down by the said Convention.' However, 'this provision shall not prevent Union law from providing more extensive protection'. These provisions leave room for interpretation: it is not wholly clear which Charter rights correspond to ECHR rights, nor is it always easy to decide which instrument provides more extensive protection.[36]

Because of non-membership of the EU, the ECtHR has not claimed direct jurisdiction over EU measures. However, it has considered itself competent to review Member State implementing measures, even where EU law does not leave room for national discretion. Indirectly, this amounts to an assertion of jurisdiction over compatibility with the ECHR of EU measures too. Here the ECtHR has adopted a position which has often been compared to the *Solange* doctrine of the German Constitutional Court in respect of Union fundamental rights law. The *Bosphorus* ruling of the ECtHR concerned a case which had also been before the ECJ. The Strasbourg Court declared as its default assumption that Union fundamental rights protection is equivalent to that provided for by the ECHR. Accordingly, the Court would refrain from exercising its jurisdiction in cases where a Member State had no discretion in implementing its obligations under EU Law. However, this would hold only so as long as Union substantive guarantees and controlling mechanisms equal those offered by the ECHR and unless a manifest deficit appears in EU fundamental rights protection in a concrete case before the ECtHR.[37] In accession negotiations the EU side has been particularly concerned about preserving the ECJ's interpretive autonomy with regard to both EU measures and national implementing measures. A procedural mechanism has been designed to guarantee that the ECJ can always pronounce on the compatibility of national implementing measures with fundamental rights law before the Strasbourg court issues its ruling.[38] Both the *Bosphorus* doctrine and

36 See the discussion in P. Craig (2013), pp. 232–4.

37 *Bosphorus Airways v Ireland*, No. 45036/98, 30 June 2005.

38 See the perceptive discussion of the Draft Accession Agreement of October 2011 in T. Lock (2012) and the overview in X. Groussot et al. (2011). The Protocol attached to the

a specific procedure for dealing with cases involving EU law are delicate issues not only in the tripartite relationship between the ECtHR, the ECJ and EU Member State courts but also for those signatories of the ECHR which are not members in the EU; the suspicion of double standards, one for the EU and its Member States and another for other Signatory States, is easily aroused. At the time of writing, the final conditions for EU accession are still open, as is the pertinence of the *Bosphorus* doctrine after accession too.

The position of the ECHR in the municipal legal order of the Signatory States varies, depending on, inter alia, the constitutional choice between monism and dualism and, in dualist states, on the hierarchical level of the incorporating act. As a rule, even in states where the Convention enjoys merely a sub-constitutional status, an interpretive principle, comparable to that laid down in Art. 52(4) CFREU, has been adopted which calls for interpreting national fundamental rights in conformity with the Convention. Yet reservations to the ECtHR's interpretive authority are not unheard of either. This holds not only for the *erga omnes* pretensions of Strasbourg case law but even for the legal effects of the Court's ruling in the particular case. Here the German *Görgülü* saga is instructive enough.[39] The question can be posed whether Union accession to the ECHR will, through EU law's supremacy, upgrade the status of the Convention in Member State legal orders in EU law-related issues.

As is inevitable in a pluralist legal constellation, potential for clashes of authority exists even where ECHR law confronts Member State law or EU law. Still, the interpretive principles, adopted by both EU and national fundamental rights law, which require seeking conformity with the ECHR, testify to an aspiration for normative and jurisdictional compatibility and avoidance of conflict, as does the *Bosphorus* doctrine of the ECtHR too. *Görgülü* aside, case law primarily tells of judicial dialogue aiming at normative compatibility between the main fundamental rights actors in European legal space. National constitutional courts routinely refer to Strasbourg jurisprudence, and the ECJ and ECtHR also increasingly invoke each other's rulings. It is not far-fetched to speak of cooperative fundamental rights protection where each of the two transnational branches

Lisbon Treaty and relating to Art. 6(2) TEU explicitly lays down that the accession agreement 'shall not affect the competences of the Union or the powers of its institutions' (Art. 2). The proviso that 'accession shall not affect the Union's competences as defined in the Treaties' is spelled out in Art. 6(2) TEU as well.

39 See B. Peters (2012).

and national review make their contributions. Arguably, this is the ordinary state of affairs, while *Görgülü* and its like are exceptions that should not be allowed to dominate the general picture.

Conflict or dialogue?

'Legal pluralism' connotes a situation where two legal systems raise overlapping claims to authority in the same legal space and where no higher-order principle or arbiter exists to decide on the merits of the rival claims. The risk of an irresolvable conflict always overhangs the pluralist constellation. Hence, a conflictual approach appears to be not only a legitimate but even a natural choice for scholars of pluralism. Indeed, this is the choice of proponents of exclusive perspectivism in its various guises. In their treatment of legal pluralism, they turn into *radical pluralists* who reject the very possibility of a peaceful solution to fundamental conflicts of authority constantly latent in a hybrid legal space. The three varieties of radical pluralism, rooted in three varieties of exclusive perspectivism, condemn legal orders (Kelsenians), regimes (Koskenniemian legal strategists) or systems (Luhmannian autopoietic systems theorists) to their solipsist perspectives, with no prospect of cross-perspective and boundary-breaking contacts. They all end up advocating a new version of the black box model of the legal universe. The boxes are defined differently from the traditional model, and the emergence of transnational law beyond the dichotomy of national and international law may be acknowledged. But self-contained legal orders, regimes or systems remain closed in their boxes.

Exclusive perspectivism and concomitant radical pluralism convey a one-sided and distorted picture of our contemporary legal landscape. True, hegemonic turf wars among legal orders, systems and regimes occur; institutional and professional interests influence legal speech acts; legal actors are committed to their legal order of affiliation; and functionally differentiated legal orders follow divergent rationalities. Still this is not all there is: cooperative relations, cross-boundary dialogue, mutual learning, overlapping and interpenetration exist as well. Legal perspectivism in law is inevitable, but legal solipsism is not. Interlegality offers an alternative to the solipsism of radical pluralisms. Conceiving of this interlegality requires abandoning exclusive perspectivism and portraying perspectivism in legal cultural terms.

Exclusive perspectivists *qua* radical pluralists have been well represented in the discussion on European constitutional pluralism too. In effect, Neil MacCormick, who in the aftermath of the German Constitutional Court's *Maastricht* ruling launched the academic debate, depicted the pluralist constellation in explicit Kelsenian terms. EU law and national constitutional orders, both subject to their respective *Grundnorm* and both claiming interpretive autonomy, inevitably arrive at opposite positions in the *Kompetenz-Kompetenz* issue. In MacCormick's view, 'the interpretative power of the highest decision-making authorities of the different systems must be, as to each system, ultimate'. Hence,

> the constitutional court of a Member State is committed to denying that its competence to interpret the constitution by which it was established can be restricted by decisions of a tribunal external to the system, even one whose interpretive advice on points of EC law the constitutional court is obligated to accept under Article 177 EC. Conversely, the Court is by the same logic committed to denying that its competence to interpret its own constitutive treaties can be restricted by decisions of Member State tribunals.[40]

Still, radical pluralists do not monopolize the field. They are confronted by legal dialogists or *dialogical pluralists*.[41] Radical and dialogical pluralists agree that the issue of ultimate authority must remain unsettled. Both camps reject a hierarchical integrated model in the relations between European and national constitutional law and embrace a *heterarchical* view implying the distinct legal orders model. But where radical pluralists close pluralist legal orders, regimes or systems to one another, dialogical pluralists lay stress on mutual openness and cross-border dialogue. Another difference concerns the basic scholarly orientation: the objectives of radical pluralists are descriptive and explanatory, while the contributions of dialogical pluralists include normative propositions as well.[42]

Indeed, two sides exist to the relationship between overlapping legal orders or systems, such as EU and Member State law: rivalry and conflicts, as radical pluralists point out, but normative openness and mutual dialogue too, as dialogical pluralists emphasize. Interlegality is not only an

40 D. N. MacCormick (1995), p. 265. In a later article, MacCormick held a solution to the constitutional conflict to be possible under international law. D. N. MacCormick (1998).

41 I would include in dialogical pluralists, among others, Neil Walker, Miguel Poiares Maduro, Mattias Kumm and Daniel Halberstam. See N. Walker (2002 and 2006a); M. Poiares Maduro (2003 and 2006); M. Kumm (2005 and 2012); D. Halberstam (2009, 2010 and 2012). As a synthesis of the debate see M. Avbelj and J. Komárek (2012). Nico Krisch can be considered a dialogical pluralist as well. However, he is not a constitutional pluralist: for him, constitutionalism implies hierarchical ordering. N. Krisch (2010).

42 N. Walker (2002), pp. 337–9, has distinguished between epistemic, explanatory and normative pluralism. Epistemic pluralism by and large coincides with what I call legal perspectivism.

essential feature of 'simple' diversity, opening the boxes of territorially delineated national legal orders to reciprocal influences and enabling sufficiently uniform application and interpretation of EU law in Member States. Interlegality is also an essential feature of the pluralist constellation, prevailing in Europe between EU and Member State law, and in fundamental rights comprising even ECHR law. As the history of European fundamental rights law teaches us, conflicts between the ECJ and national constitutional courts are always possible under conditions of constitutional pluralism. But this history also tells about the interlegal side in relations between pluralist constitutional orders: about dialogue, mutual learning and aspiration for normative and jurisdictional harmony. Not only has the ECJ been attentive to the reactions of national constitutional courts and embarked on developing EU fundamental rights law; national constitutional courts, with the German Court as their mouthpiece, have also stressed the cooperative character of fundamental rights protection in Europe. The German Court has acknowledged the ECJ's mandate in Treaty interpretation, invoked the *Europarechtsfreundlichkeit* principle and declared that it does not engage in *ultra vires*, fundamental rights or identity review of EU law before the ECJ has had a possibility to express its view in the preliminary ruling procedure.

Every legal system defends its normative and interpretive autonomy. But adopting the perspective of the referential constitutional order does not exclude acknowledging the perspectivism of the pluralist interlocutor and striving for normative compatibility. As Miguel Poiares Maduro pointed out in his proposal for 'contrapunctual' law, dialogical pluralism presupposes 'the recognition and adjustment of each legal order to the plurality of equally legitimate claims of authority made by other legal orders'.[43] Yet dialogical pluralism is not a mere normative programme. European and national constitutional actors defend their interpretive autonomy, but they have also striven to avoid outright conflicts and managed to maintain a pluralist equilibrium. *Kompetenz-Kompetenz*, fundamental rights protection and respect for constitutional identity are the three main issues where European and national points of view appear to lead to

[43] M. Poiares Maduro (2006) calls on both the European and national legal orders to create the necessary mechanisms to adjust to claims of authority of other legal orders. In a normative respect, he calls for a 'coherent and integrated legal order integrating the decisions of national European legal courts'. Thus, the mission of 'contrapunctual' law would be to manage not only the pluralism of European and national law but also the horizontal diversity of Member State legal orders.

contradictory normative conclusions. However, from the perspective of dialogical pluralism, the history of these issues should be written in terms of horizontal accommodation rather than mutually exclusive pretensions of hierarchical subjection.

Legal perspectivism is not only about watching over the autonomy of the legal order and guarding the authority of its constitution – or *Grundnorm*, as Kelsenians would put it. A legal cultural understanding shows both the deeper roots of perspectivism and the possibility of overcoming the isolationism that labels exclusive perspectivism and radical pluralism. The legal cultural foundations of legal orders not only create the perspectivism working through the *Vorverständnis* of legal actors, they also contain the resources for bridging the perspectives of diverse and pluralist legal orders. Constitutional law also includes cultural layers which impregnate the *Vorverständnis* of the relevant legal actors. Ever since the emergence of modern constitutionalism in the late eighteenth century, constitutional culture has been very much a cross-boundary phenomenon. The fundamental ideas of modern constitutionalism (in the thick normative sense of the term), among which fundamental rights and democracy occupy a prominent position, were launched in the early modern age by enlightenment thinkers and the spokesmen and constitution drafters, especially of the French and American revolutions. During subsequent centuries, universalist ideas received specific interpretations in individual states due to their particular historical trajectories and ethico-political self-definitions. Reference in Art. 4(2) TEU to national constitutional identities implies acknowledgement of constitutional diversity. Member States may display significant differences in their constitutional cultures, differences which are instrumental to their distinct constitutional identities. Art. 4(2) TEU can be read in conjunction with Art. 3(3) TEU: diversity of legal and constitutional cultures forms part of the 'rich cultural and linguistic diversity' which the Union is called on to respect. But national interpretations of the shared universalist basis overlap. That overlap is intimated by Art. 6(3) TEU, which indicates common Member State constitutional traditions as a source of fundamental rights as general EU law principles, and Art. 52(4) CFREU, which defines the role of these traditions in interpreting Charter rights.

Although hardly an argument proving my point, EU Treaty law explicitly evokes the interplay between nationally variable constitutional cultures and a unifying constitutional deep culture, shared not only by the Member States but by the EU as well. Not only does Member State constitutional identity enjoy protection under EU constitutional law, implying at least partially diverging national constitutional cultures; Member States and the EU are also proclaimed to possess a common value basis, which includes central values labelling thick normative constitutionalism, such as respect for the rule of law and human rights (Art. 2 TEU). What Daniel Halberstam – another prominent constitutional pluralist – terms the *embedded openness* of constitutional orders is not only, or even primarily, a matter of conscious effort or particular institutional and procedural arrangements; at the level of constitutional culture it is an inerasable fact. No claim to normative or interpretive autonomy can close the borders of constitutional orders at the cultural levels. A common constitutional deep culture creates the possibility of constitutional dialogue in Europe, prevents latent constitutional conflicts from breaking into the open and, if prevention fails, facilitates their consensual resolution. Although diverse constitutional cultures may have adopted diverse conceptions of key constitutional concepts, European legal actors possess a shared constitutional language, necessary for cross-cultural discourse. Misunderstandings and even overt clashes occur in pluralist relations among key European constitutional actors, such as Member State constitutional courts and the ECJ. They dominate the attention of both the media and European lawyers. Still, they are exceptions to the ordinary course of affairs, which follows the tenets of interlegality.[44]

In sum, I would depict the pluralist constellation in European constitutional space quite differently from exclusive perspectivists. Which aspect of legal development – conflictuality or interlegality – dominates the account is a matter of perspective as well. It is no coincidence that sociologically oriented observers have, from their external perspective, been

[44] Mattias Kumm's version of dialogical pluralism probably comes closest to my account of a unifying and discourse-facilitating deep culture. He stresses the role of shared constitutional principles, universal principles central to liberal democratic constitutionalism, which serve as 'mediating principles for a deeply pluralist structure of public law'. M. Kumm (2012), p. 245. He considers Member State reservations to the primacy of EU law justified when they invoke such universal principles. He argues that 'the point of constitutional pluralism . . . is to create a normative space both for justified institutionalized civil disobedience and justified institutionalized collective conscientious objection'. *Ibid.*, p. 220. N. T. Isiksel (2010) makes a similar point about *Kadi*'s relation to international law: *Kadi* is an act of civil disobedience which is loyal to the principles underpinning international law.

prone to emphasize conflicts and fragmentation as typical of recent developments of law. It should not come as a surprise either that, among legal scholars, the legal strategists among the critical camp have joined forces with sociologists in their depiction of the relationships among legal systems and regimes; they too tend to ignore the internal point of view.

4 Discursiveness

Revolutionary and evolutionary constitutionalism

At the state level, the default position is to approach the constitution as a unitary normative entity.[1] Especially in countries with a formal, written constitution, the tacit understanding is that juridical and political constitutions emerge and develop parallel to each other. By contrast, European constitutionalization has been a differentiated process, displaying diverse temporalities. The putative European constitutions have not appeared simultaneously but, rather, successively, following a certain order. Nor have they followed exactly the same developmental path. Typical of European constitutionalism is – to borrow Ernst Bloch's expression – *Gleichzeitigkeit des Ungleichzeitigen*. This makes a differentiated exploration of constitutional dimensions indispensable.

The upsurge of interest in constitutional theory accompanying the finally abortive Constitutional Treaty involved efforts to apply to the European context the tripartite conceptual cluster of *constituent power* (*pouvoir constituant*), *demos* as the subject of this power and *constitutional moment* as the instance when this power is wielded. These efforts were not particularly successful, but led to a dilution of concepts coined in a specific branch of constitutional culture: revolutionary American and French constitutionalism. We have drifted far from the original conceptual connotations if we define the Member States – *Herren der Verträge* – as a European demos or their treaty-making power as a *pouvoir constituant*

[1] This is not to deny the possibility of a relational analysis which distinguishes between constitutional dimensions in accordance with constitutional objects even at the state level. Indeed, German legal literature abounds with suggestions for particular dimensions of the national constitution, and, as will be shown in Chapter 5, the crucial concept of economic constitution (*Wirtschaftsverfassung*) is of German origin.

the exercise of which has produced the European constitution. The concepts of revolutionary constitutionalism are not transferable to an examination of the European constitution, which has not resulted from the exercise of constituent power by a European demos at an identifiable constitutional moment. Instead of a revolutionary break, the many constitutions of Europe are a continuously evolving outcome of an ongoing process which indeed does include such high-profile manifest occasions as Treaty amendments but is not exhausted by them. Instead of the cluster of revolutionary-tuned concepts of constituent power, demos and constitutional moment, the European constitution(s) should be examined through the evolutionary concept of *constitutionalization*. It is no coincidence that European constitutional scholarship consists to such a great extent of historically oriented expositions. The European constitution is not a standstill phenomenon but should be approached as a multidimensional and multitemporal process of constitutionalization.

Distinct periods can be discerned in European constitutionalization. These receive their particular colouring from a particular constitution: a *pacemaker constitution* as we could put it. Reflecting the temporal and functional primacy of economic integration, the first wave, initiated by the Treaty of Rome, or even earlier by the Treaty of Paris (1951) establishing the European Coal and Steel Community (ECSC), proceeded under the auspices of the economic constitution.[2] The rulings of the ECJ defining the basic principles characterizing Community law as an independent legal system manifested the significance of the juridical constitution: juridical and economic constitutionalization proceeded in tandem. The Maastricht Treaty epitomized the – at least temporary – dominance of the political constitution. In turn, the Amsterdam Treaty (1998), with its new provisions on the Area of Freedom, Security and Justice, inaugurated the prominence of the security constitution, which was further reinforced by 9/11.[3] Finally, the Eurozone crisis catapulted the economic constitution

[2] Arguably, though, in the early 1950s, economic integration was at least partly an *ersatz* solution when political integration proved not to be achievable. See, e.g., Chapters 1 and 2 in M. Gilbert (2012).

[3] Although too much should not be made of the provisions on the values and objectives of the EU, it is worth mentioning that in the present list of objectives in Art. 3 TEU, the provision on the area of freedom, security and justice precedes that on the internal market and other economic (and social) aims. According to Art. 3(2), 'the Union shall offer its citizens an area of freedom, security and justice without internal frontiers, in which the free movement of persons is ensured in conjunction with appropriate measures with respect to external border controls, asylum, immigration and the prevention and combating of crime'.

back to the pacemaker role. However, if the emphasis in the Rome Treaty and the subsequent case law of the ECJ came to lie on what can be called the microeconomic constitution, the crisis has highlighted the role of the second, macroeconomic layer of the European economic constitution. The pacemaker role of the macroeconomic constitution entails that the 'constitutional mutation'[4] launched by the Eurozone crisis is not restricted to the economic aspect. It extends to the political and social dimensions as well; it also affects democracy and transparency, as well as social values and rights.

Related to 'constitutionalization', other process-oriented concepts are also of particular relevance for European constitutional analysis. These include 'transnationalization' and 'individualization'. In important respects, constitutionalization has signified *transnationalization*: superseding intergovernmental institutional and decision-making structures, typical of international organizations, as well as detaching European law from the international law background. However, when examining European constitutionalization, 'transnational' and 'intergovernmental' should not be straightforwardly opposed. It is true that in the institutional organization of the EU, the Commission, the ECJ and the European Parliament make up the transnational core. But even the European Council and the Council of Ministers are institutions of a transnational polity, and the transnational setting leaves its imprint on institutions with an intergovernmental composition too.[5] In turn, the Treaties still possess the dual character of 'a constitutional charter' and an agreement under international law. Moreover, in both the social and security dimensions, international law agreements have played an important role as precursors to constitutionalization through Treaty provisions. In combating the Eurozone crisis, Member States resorted to agreements under international law as an alternative to primary or secondary Union law. The third-pillar Treaty provisions in force from 1993 to 2009 even explicitly constitutionalized international law conventions as an EU legal instrument.

Constitutionalization has implied *individualization*: establishment of direct links between European institutions and European citizens in their diverse attires. From the perspective of European individuals, the multidimensional process of constitutionalization has involved a gradual enrichment of European citizenship, adding successive layers to the initial

[4] E. Chiti et al. (2012), pp. 418 ff.

[5] This is one of the main themes in Luuk van Middelaar's analysis of 'the passage to Europe', L. van Middelaar (2013). It is also Giandomenico Majone's argument for his proposal to substitute 'transgovernmentalism' for 'intergovernmentalism' in the EU context, G. Majone (2009), p. 163.

market citizenship of the economic constitution: the judicial citizenship of the juridical constitution; the social citizenship of the social constitution; and finally the political citizenship which grants individuals not only the specific citizenship rights of the Treaty but European fundamental rights as well. Still, European citizens also remain citizens of Member States, and the relations between European institutions and individual citizens hint at the relevance of the Member State level too.[6]

In Part II, I shall discuss sectoral processes of constitutionalization in the economic, social and security dimensions. These processes possess both a formal and a substantive aspect. In *formal* constitutionalization, the particular field of European law acquires features of higher law: such as anchorage in Treaty law, direct applicability or direct effect and primacy with regard to Member State law, as well as judicial review by the ECJ. Transnationalization and individualization are also indications of formal constitutionalization, although caution should be exercised so as not to identify constitutionalization too simplistically with transnationalization. The formal aspect of sectoral constitutionalization establishes the link – the 'structural coupling' – through which the juridical constitution exercises its framing function and, conversely, sectoral constitutionalization its functional primacy. Because of the differences in respective constitutional objects, the formal criteria of constitutionalization cannot remain wholly identical across the range of sectoral constitutions. In the macroeconomic field, for instance, the legal position of individual economic agents or the role of the ECJ cannot be accorded a significance similar to microeconomic constitutionalization.

Portrayal of *substantive* constitutionalization will be based on the distinction between constitutional doctrine and theory: an EU law application of my claim of the multilayered character of the legal order. A central objective of forays into sectoral processes of constitutionalization is to reconstruct the theory underlying constitutional doctrine. Dimension-specific constitutional theories also include social theoretical elements which act as an interface between constitutional law and the constitutional object.

In sum, 'constitutionalization' is an evolutionary alternative to the revolutionary concepts of *pouvoir constituant*, demos and constitutional moment. Above, I have discerned particular relations among the constitutional dimensions, such as the functional – and temporal – primacy of

[6] Here 'citizenship' is used as a concept of constitutional theory and not in a doctrinal sense referring to Treaty provisions on European citizenship and ECJ jurisprudence expounding their implications.

the economic constitution and the general functional primacy of sectoral constitutionalization in respect of the framing juridical and political constitutionalization. By the same token, I have hinted at a particular internal logic guiding European constitutionalization.[7] As a counterweight, it is important to stress that European constitutionalization should not be reconstructed as a closed, linear and predetermined evolutionary process. Different constitutions may well clash with each other, and constitutional backlashes form part of the picture as well. And even more crucially, one should always bear in mind that the ultimate factors accelerating or impeding constitutionalization are of an extra-legal and extra-constitutional – economic, political and ideological – nature. They may be high-profile, even crisis-like events: such as the fall of the Berlin Wall and the reunification of Germany (the Maastricht Treaty as a high-point of political constitutionalization), 9/11 (acceleration of the development of the security constitution) or the global financial crisis which in the autumn of 2008 broke out following the collapse of Lehman Brothers (the teetering of the Maastricht principles of the European economic constitution). But equally well constitutionalization may be influenced by contingent events which on their occurrence have aroused no public attention but which have, for instance, produced constitutionally relevant case law of the ECJ. While searching for generalizations from an internal constitutional point of view, one should remain sensitive to external impacts and contingent events. Arguably, relations internal to European constitutionalism channel, transform and detract from the influence of external factors, but they should not be mistaken for autonomous, self-sufficient causalities. A constitutional theory, adopting the internal perspective of legal scholarship, should be aware of the limits of its explanatory pretensions and potential.

European constitutional discourse

Law is a thoroughly discursive phenomenon. Law is not only talked about in legal discourses; it is even brought about in and through these discourses. Law as a legal order is produced and reproduced in legal practices. Legal practices – such as law-making, adjudication and legal

[7] My position might be seen as suggesting an affinity to neofunctionalist accounts by political scientists, with their central notion of spillover effects. However, my notion of functional primacy does not imply any quasi-automatic widening and deepening of European integration. For an overview of neofunctionalist views, see A. Niemann and P. C. Schmitter (2009).

scholarship – provide the setting for legal discourse which interconnects diverse legal practices. Different legal practices fulfil different tasks in the legal system; this is reflected in the perspectivism of legal roles. Common legal discourse is a means to overcome this version of legal cultural perspectivism.

The approach to law of legal actors such as the legislator, the judge, the counsellor (the practising lawyer) and the scholar each displays important differences. The legislator sees in law primarily a means of achieving politically defined social objectives, while practising lawyers look at it through extra-legal client interests which they are supposed to promote; both the legislator and the legal counsellor focus on the extra-discursive, perlocutionary effects of legal speech acts, such as statutes and court decisions. Both of them participate in legal discourse and are players in the game of law, but the prizes they are seeking are mainly of an extra-legal character; consequently, they are prone to subordinate the illocutionary aspect of legal speech acts to the perlocutionary aspect. Judges, by contrast, privilege the illocutionary dimension where such criteria as argumentative cogency and normative correctness hold sway. As Klaus Günther has argued, an aspiration to comprehensive normative coherence is inherent in judicial interpretation and decision-making.[8]

In a more detailed discussion, the judicial role should be divided into sub-categories, in accordance with the varying functions of different courts. In a national legal system, the roles of judges of constitutional and ordinary courts, and among the latter supreme and lower courts, display significant differences, with regard, for instance, to the tasks of maintaining the unity and coherence of the legal order and safeguarding its normative foundations. Correspondingly, in the EU legal system the functions of European and national courts diverge in crucial respects. Differences in judicial roles are bound to affect the *Vorverständnis* of judges, the way they tend to conceive of the law. The legal-culturally interpreted perspectivism of judicial roles suggests an explanation for, say, differences in the reception of EU law, especially the principle of primacy, by ordinary and constitutional courts.

What, then, about legal scholars? What is their typical perspective on law? Doctrinal scholars – 'legal dogmaticians' – assist other legal actors through recommendations for interpretation and proposals for systematization. Their focus is clearly on the illocutionary aspect; they appraise the normative credentials of speech acts by other legal actors and claim

[8] K. Günther (1993).

normative correctness for their own contributions. Arguably, the perspective of a doctrinal scholar is close to that of a judge. By contrast, legal theory is a meta-level legal practice and discourse – producing second-order observations, as a Luhmannian systems-theorist would put it – which consciously or unconsciously relates to a particular first-order perspective and gives it a reflexive twist. The first-order perspective may be the normatively (illocutionarily) oriented perspective of a judge or a doctrinal scholar, as is the case both in Kelsenian and Hartian legal positivism and in the principle jurisprudence of, say, Ronald Dworkin or Robert Alexy. But legal theory may also approach the law from a legislator- or counsellor-related meta-perspective. The former may not be so common, but it has animated contemporary endeavours in 'legisprudence' or *Gesetzgebungslehre*.[9] In turn, the point of view of a practising lawyer was the main gateway to law for American realists, as it is for their successors in the Critical Legal Studies movement too. It is this perspective which leads a legal strategist to focus on strategic interests and biases, and to neglect the illocutionary aspect of law. But, of course, legal or constitutional theorists may also try to rise above all the first-order perspectives, encompass them all in their accounts and articulate a general theory of law and legal practices. Whether such an attempt can be successful where no first-order practice is privileged is another question. What, at least, is evident is that even legal and constitutional theorists approach the law through a particular legal *Vorverständnis*.

The law never stands still but is relentlessly changing, in and through never-ceasing legal discourse. In trying to pin down the contents of the law in force, we can only evoke a momentary and transient state of legal discourse. New legal speech acts alter the contents of the legal order and produce continuous turbulence on the surface of law. However, the weight of legal speech acts varies. In an ideal-typical 'mature' legal system, the doctrine of legal sources as an element of the prevailing expert legal culture determines the participants in legal discourse and the significance of their speech acts. A speech act only participates in legal discourse if it is recognized as a legal speech act in other legal speech acts, and this recognition is guided by the doctrine of legal sources implicit in legal *Vorverständnis*.

All this also holds for constitutional discourse. Constitutional law evolves and changes through constitutional speech acts, while the prevailing constitutional culture defines the participants in the discourse

9 As a representative example, see L. Wintgens (2012).

and their respective weight. Speech act theory opens a perspective on European constitutionalization as well. European constitutionalization amounts to a continuous constitutional discourse; an ever-extending chain of constitutional speech acts. Due to the enhanced evolutionary character of the European constitution, application of speech act theory is even more welcome than at the national level. Yet it is also more complicated. Complications arise from at least four particularities of the European constitution.

Firstly, especially as regards the sub-surface, cultural layers, European law is still an emergent legal and constitutional order. No established constitutional theory exists which would unequivocally identify the participants in European constitutional discourse and the import to be attributed to their speech acts. Clearly, though, the most pertinent speech acts originate from the Treaty-making Member States as the European constitutional legislator and the ECJ as the European constitutional court. But although the Founding Treaties make up – in the words of the ECJ – a constitutional charter, the Treaties are not self-evidently dominant constitutional speech acts in the same sense as we are used to thinking of national formal constitutions. Related to the incrementalism of European constitutionalization, the ECJ as the European constitutional court has come to play a more important role in constitution-making than is usual for constitutional courts at state level. Yet this role has hardly been codified in a stable constitutional theory on constitutional sources which would have been sedimented into a European constitutional culture shared by all the relevant constitutional actors.

Secondly, European forums for constitutional discourse display an unprecedented plethora of actors whose speech acts claim constitutional relevance. At the European level too, the constitutional legislator and the constitutional court are the most important constitutional actors and participants in constitutional discourse. However, both the European constitutional legislator and the European constitutional court are composite actors, and their final speech acts – Treaties and Treaty amendments, and constitutional rulings – result from a convoluted discourse the constituent speech acts of which may acquire a constitutional significance of their own. The procedure for Treaty revision consists of interrelated constitutional speech acts by Union institutions and national constitutional bodies, as well as the Convention and the intergovernmental congress as ad-hoc EU bodies (Art. 48 TEU). Furthermore, the Convention in particular may display a composite organization with working groups focusing on specific aspects of proposed amendments and producing reasoned documents. It may happen that subsequent constitutional speech acts relate not only to the final Treaty revision but preceding speech acts too, as, say, sources of interpretive arguments.

Correspondingly, a judgment by the ECJ is an end point in a series of speech acts possessing potential constitutional pertinence even individually. In preliminary rulings, these speech acts include referral by the national court which frames the issue but may also involve substantive arguments aiming to influence the Court. A conspicuous example is the German Constitutional Court's recent referral concerning the legality of the ECB Outright Monetary Transactions programme, the first referral ever by this court.[10] The Statute of the Court grants Member States and Union institutions a right to intervene in cases before the Court. Member States are particularly eager to exercise this right when they consider their sovereignty to be at stake. It also occurs that statements by Member States in landmark cases are picked up and commented on in future constitutional discourse. Of particular importance are opinions of Advocates General, which form the basis for deliberations in the Court but which are published separately. Advocates General operate within a constitutionally enshrined mandate. Under Art. 252 TFEU, the duty of Advocates General is 'to make, in open court, reasoned submissions' on cases where the Statute requires their involvement. In fulfilling their task, Advocates General are expected to act 'with complete impartiality and independence'. They are freer in their reasoning than the Court; their style is more conversational; they can relate to sources excluded by judicial conventions adhered to by the Court; and they can take a broader perspective on ECJ jurisprudence, both past and future, thus stepping out of the confines of the case under consideration. The argumentative leeway of the Court is narrowed not only by judicial conventions and traditions but also by the necessity to reach a consensus. Opinions of Advocates General insert themselves explicitly in ongoing European legal discourse; they include references not only to Luxembourg and other European case law, including rulings by national courts, but legal scholarship as well. Opinions of Advocates General provide an important link in the cooperative enterprise of doctrine elaboration by the ECJ and scholars of EU law. Often enough, the opinions are intended to influence not only the ruling in the case at hand but the development of EU law more generally. The contribution of Advocates General to European constitutional discourse

[10] BVerfG, 2BvR 2728/13, 14 January 2014.

has been particularly important in such constitutionally important fields as citizenship and fundamental rights law.[11]

In particular in countries with long academic traditions in law, legal scholars are influential participants in national legal discourse. Germany is undoubtedly one of these countries, and its Constitutional Court rulings in landmark cases – say, the *Maastricht* and *Lisbon* rulings, or rulings pertaining to the recent Eurozone crisis – abound with references to literature.[12] The tradition of EU legal scholarship in general and EU constitutional scholarship in particular is short; interestingly enough, though, the Hallstein Commission (1958–67) already supported the FIDE association of European law scholars, established in 1961,[13] and the *Common Market Law Review*, still one of the most prominent European law journals, was founded as early as 1963. By now, a transnational community of scholars has emerged who approach EU law from an EU law perspective and who use transnational publication forums, while doctrinal scholarship on EU law, including constitutional law, has increased exponentially. The abortive Constitutional Treaty was a major incitement for constitutional scholarship, but the interest of EU scholars in constitutionally relevant issues has not slackened even after its demise. All in all, contributions by EU law scholars have obtained an acknowledged place in EU legal and constitutional discourse. Growing references to legal literature in opinions of Advocates General are an explicit token of recognition. Scholarly positions most probably influence the final judgments of the Court too, although judicial conventions prevent the Court from explicitly avowing this. As is often the case in national constitutional courts too, 'personal unions' contribute to the impact of legal scholarship. Over the years, many Advocates General and ECJ judges have had an academic background, and it has not been uncommon for them to continue publishing in European law journals or other transnational publication forums while in office. This publication policy has added to the more openly discursive character of EU law compared with many national legal systems where judicial conventions tend to hamper rather than promote judicial participation

11 On the role of Advocates General in European legal discourse, see the papers published in the 2012 issue of the *Cambridge Yearbook of European Legal Studies*.

12 The impact of constitutional scholarship is guaranteed by a kind of personal union as well: academics have always constituted an important member group in the Court's composition. Furthermore, professors often appear as claimants or counsellors, especially in high-profile cases.

13 M. Rasmussen (2012), p. 384.

in legal discourse through personal contributions. Especially when compared with Anglo-Saxon judicial culture, ECJ judgments may still appear rather terse and sometimes even opaque in their reasoning. In this respect, opinions of Advocates General and the publishing practices of judges and Advocates General with an academic background balance the picture.

So the main participants in national constitutional discourse find their counterparts at the EU level: the constitutional legislator, the constitutional court and the community of constitutional scholars. The specific complexity of EU constitutional discourse is largely due to the transnational character of the EU legal and political systems, which accounts for the composite nature of institutional constitutional actors and discourse preceding Treaty revision or an ECJ judgment as a 'final' constitutional speech act. The complexity is further accentuated by the multidimensionality of the European constitution: the *third* factor complicating an analysis of European constitutionalization in a discourse-theoretical framework. Constitutional discourses in distinct constitutional dimensions display particularities which should also be heeded in an examination of European constitutionalization. Sectoral constitutionalization may also be promoted by other institutional actors than the constitutional legislator responsible for Treaty revisions or the ECJ as the constitutional court. In anticipation of the discussions in Part II, let me only allude to the role of the Commission as a Competition Authority in microeconomic constitutionalization; the recent mutations of the macroeconomic constitution through crisis measures by the ECB, the Commission and Member States under their general international law competence; and the significance of the strategies adopted by the European Council for the Area of Freedom, Security and Justice. Sectoral constitutions possess particular discursive networks, which necessitates talking of European constitutional discourses in the plural. Still as a result of the framing function of the juridical and political constitutions, these networks are interlinked as well. This also justifies talking of European constitutional discourse in the singular.

Should we consider even Member State courts participants in EU constitutional discourse? After all, do not national courts also fulfil constitutional functions in the EU legal system when they apply directly effective primary law, including provisions of the EU Charter of Fundamental Rights, or even secondary EU law in judicial review of national legislation? Yes, in a sense, they do. Still, the assumption is that national courts do not make independent contributions to the elaboration of EU constitutional law or EU law in general, but adhere to the readings adopted in ECJ case law. If questions of interpretation arise to which existing case law does not proffer answers, Art. 267 TFEU requires that the courts topping the national judiciary, at the latest, bring the matter before the ECJ, whose constitutional task it is to 'ensure that in the interpretation and application of the Treaties the law is observed'. But it would be erroneous to see in the preliminary ruling procedure – the most important formalized procedure integrating national courts into the European legal system – merely a channel for the ECJ to impose its reading of European law. By framing the constitutional issues brought before the ECJ and from time to time even expressing a tentative substantive position, referring national courts contribute to European constitutional discourse too. Yet the most vital role of national courts in European legal discourse does not relate to their substantive contribution to European constitutionalization. As a rule, the main immediate addressees of ECJ rulings are national courts, and without their recognition the constitutional speech acts of the ECJ would not be able to achieve the expected illocutionary and perlocutionary effects.

The obligation to refer questions concerning interpretation of EU constitutional law for a preliminary ruling by the ECJ extends to national constitutional courts, although these have been rather reluctant to consult their European colleague; considerations of prestige are certainly involved.[14] Hence, instances of a formalized dialogue between the ECJ and a national constitutional court are but rare; an important exception to the rule is the referral concerning the ECB Outright Monetary Transactions programme, which the German Constitutional Court submitted to the ECJ in early 2014.[15] But as our examination of European fundamental rights pluralism has shown, a dialogue between the ECJ and national constitutional courts – especially the German one as the *primus inter pares* – has been instrumental to the development of a particularly important branch of European constitutional law. In its EU law-related judgments, the German Constitutional Court has relied on the yardstick of national constitutional law. Still, the judgments have not been addressed merely to the parties and the national legal community but also, at times perhaps even primarily, to European legal actors (mainly the ECJ). Correspondingly, the 'tacit' addressees of major ECJ rulings touching on, say,

[14] M. Claes (2006), pp. 432 ff. According to Claes, p. 433, by 2006 the Belgian *Arbitragehof* and the Austrian *Verfassungsgericht* were the only national constitutional courts to have submitted a referral.

[15] BVerfG, 2BvR 2728/13, 14 January 2014.

Kompetenz-Kompetenz, fundamental rights review or Member State constitutional identity include national constitutional courts.

An analysis of European constitutionalization should be attentive to the influence of national constitutional courts on, and their reactions to, ECJ rulings, especially in conflict-sensitive issues where European and national claims of authority are prone to clash. European and national constitutional discourses are intertwined. Where an ECJ judgment obviously, even if tacitly, relates to a previous ruling by a national constitutional court – which perhaps for its part has reacted to an earlier ECJ judgment – the latter ruling is acknowledged as a European constitutional speech act as well. Not all the rulings of all the national constitutional courts receive such recognition by European constitutional actors. But those that do should be included not only in national but in European constitutional discourse as well. The pluralist constellation in European constitutional space, accounting for the role that national constitutional courts play in European constitutional discourse, is the fourth and final factor which complicates examining this discourse as a network of interlinked constitutional speech acts.

Perspectives on constitutional discourse

Speech acts consist of three elements or dimensions: locutionary, illocutionary and perlocutionary. A *locutionary* speech act is the act *of* saying or writing; its central characteristic is sense. An *illocutionary* speech act is what I do *by* saying or writing something; illocutionary speech acts include arguing, contesting, promising, baptizing, and so on. Illocutionary speech acts aspire to illocutionary effects (or illocutionary force): acceptance of their illocutionary claims or promises. The *perlocutionary* dimension consists of the consequences of speech acts in the extra-discursive world: of what I achieve *through* saying or writing something. The effects may be intentional – when somebody who is told to shut a window does shut it – but their causal chains may be followed beyond the intentions of the speakers. The distinction between locutionary, illocutionary and perlocutionary speech acts is analytical in nature. A locutionary speech act is also an illocution, an illocutionary speech act is not possible without a locution and the perlocutionary impact of a speech act usually requires that the speech act attains its illocutionary effect.[16]

[16] In my brief presentation of speech act theory I have relied on J. L. Austin (1984) and J. Searle (1988).

In legal discourse, speech acts can only obtain illocutionary force and the status of legal speech acts if they are recognized and assessed as such by other contributions. In the illocutionary dimension, legal speech acts raise particular normative claims which are then assessed in future discourse. Typically, institutional legal speech acts, such as legislative measures and court rulings, claim both formal and substantive validity. If its claim to validity is rejected, the speech act will not be relied on in subsequent legal discourse. Even when the formal validity of a law or ruling is uncontested, its substantive validity can always be challenged anew. To take a conspicuous example, the merits of pivotal rulings of the US Supreme Court – say, *Dred Scott*, *Lochner* or *Brown v Board of Education* – are constantly re-examined in US legal discourse. The same goes for the constitutional landmark decisions of the ECJ: say *Van Gend en Loos*, *Costa v Enel*, *Dassonville* or *Cassis de Dijon*.

The distinction between illocutionary and perlocutionary effects opens and warrants two alternative options for discourse analysis. The focus can be on either normative, illocutionary claims or the perlocutionary extra-discursive effects of constitutional speech acts. In studying constitutional functions – the impact of constitutional speech acts on the constitutional object – we privilege the perlocutionary aspect. In turn, in reconstructing processes of constitutionalization from the internal perspective of European legal discourse, we concentrate on the illocutionary dimension. The distinction between illocution and perlocution is also helpful in explicating how an internal point of view on law differs from an external one. The former focuses on the illocutionary and the latter on the perlocutionary aspect of legal speech acts.

A dissection of the aspects of legal speech acts facilitates contextualizing EU constitutional discourse. The immediate context of a speech act is the argumentative milieu where it relates to other speech acts in the same discourse and engages in ongoing assessment of illocutionary claims; where it argues, criticizes, endorses, attacks or defends itself. The immediate context of EU constitutional speech acts is the discursive network where they are linked to other speech acts making up European constitutional discourse, where their illocutionary pretensions are tested and where illocutionary force is recognized or rejected. The aspired perlocutionary effects exceed the boundaries of this network. Speech acts propelling European constitutionalization are not addressed merely or often enough even primarily to other constitutional actors but have a wider audience where they are expected to find acceptance and intended to produce perlocutionary effects. Depending on the constitutional dimension at issue, constitutional speech acts are also directed at relevant actors in the social field under regulation: European and national political elites, key public and private economic actors, and so on. Moreover, in the intertwined political and juridical constitutions in particular the addressees include the citizenry at large. Neither polity building nor the legitimating constitutional function can be accomplished without constitutional speech acts reaching out to and finding resonance among the general public. A constitutional speech act cannot attain its intended perlocutionary effects if the addressees reject its illocutionary claims or promises. Accordingly, a constitution is not able to secure the legitimacy of a polity if the citizenry does not buy the implicit promises of democracy, citizenship and the rule of law. Inclusion of a wider audience and focus on perlocutionary effects necessitate attention to the rhetorical aspect of constitutional speech; an aspect which is easily ignored when constitutional discourse is examined merely as an elite discourse and when the perlocutionary effects which constitutional speech acts are expected to attain are bracketed.

An analysis of the perlocutionary effects of legal speech acts can also take off from discursive networks. Then legal actors are not understood as participants in a joint normative enterprise but as rivals or adversaries possessing contradictory 'vested' interests; players in an institutional and professional power game of law. The perspectivism of legal roles is then defined in strategic rather than in legal cultural terms. For instance, the ECJ and national constitutional courts are seen as engaged in a hegemonic battle over the privilege to state the law, rather than a cooperative effort to harmonize the illocutionary claims and effects of their speech acts. For legal strategists among constitutional scholars, a seeming consensus between European and national constitutional actors is merely a truce which an overt conflict will sooner or later end.

In comparison with legal language in general, the language of constitutional speech acts displays particular features. Basic constitutional concepts, such as 'democracy', 'sovereignty' or 'constitution' itself, are exceptionally value-laden and evoke enhanced positive or negative value connotations. Employing Quentin Skinner's terms, they are *evaluative-descriptive* or *persuasive* concepts.[17] They are also contested concepts of which alternative conceptions are proposed. Carl Schmitt, writing during the turbulent Weimar Republic, stressed the polemical nature of

[17] Q. Skinner (2002), pp. 148 and 161.

constitutional concepts. 'Words such as state, republic, society, class, as well as sovereignty, constitutional state, absolutism, dictatorship, economic planning, neutral or total state, and so on, are incomprehensible if one does not know exactly who is to be affected, combated, refuted, or negated by such a term.'[18] Schmitt extended his observations beyond the immediate argumentative context of theoretical debates. Using evaluative and, simultaneously, contested and polemical concepts, constitutional theory is – so Schmitt argued – inexorably engaged in the political and ideological battles of its time; expressed in the terms of speech act theory, speech acts by constitutional scholars aspire to perlocutionary effects well beyond discourse among recognized constitutional actors. The persuasive character and perlocutionary value of constitutional concepts make them coveted objects in the power games of constitutional theory; hegemony over the definition of, say, 'democracy' is a crucial stake in these games.

Schmitt published his analysis in an exceptional time and in an exceptionally heated political atmosphere. Still, it reminds us about the adversial aspect of legal discourse; an aspect which is especially accentuated in a field such as constitutional law, with its links to politics and, in the European context, to the foundations of sectoral policies as well. European constitutional discourse is immersed in general debates on the future and direction of European integration, and consequently the implications and potential perlocutionary effects of constitutional speech acts transcend the argumentative context. This raises the stakes in the internal power games of law and provides justification for a conflict-sensitive approach to European constitutional discourse. As we noticed in Chapter 3, the overlapping of transnational and national claims of authority, characteristic of European constitutional pluralism, entails the ever-present possibility of a constitutional conflict. In turn, in our forays into the sectoral constitutions we will time and again see how contentious the underlying constitutional theory is. This controversiality is undoubtedly related to the extra-discursive implications of constitutional theory for European integration.

But potential constitutional conflicts do not negate discursive efforts to attain normative and jurisdictional compatibility between pluralist legal systems, nor is a dialogue between alternative constitutional theories on their respective merits impossible *a priori*. Emphasis on strategic interests

[18] C. Schmitt (1996), pp. 30–1.

and perlocutionary effects, directing attention to constitutional rhetoric and polemics, is a justifiable position. But so is focus on discursively testable normative claims and interlocutionary effects, and on interlegality between legal systems and dialogue between divergent constitutional positions. Again, the coin has two sides.

PART II

Sectoral constitutionalization

5 The triumph of the microeconomic constitution

Origins of a concept

It may seem natural that European constitutional discourse and, by the same token, constitutionalization set off in the economic dimension. In the first decades of its history, say, up to the Maastricht Treaty, European integration was almost exclusively an economic project. This was manifest in the text of the Treaty of Rome, although the Preamble and the objectives enshrined in the Treaty exceeded a narrow economic perspective. Yet the wider objectives too were supposed to be primarily realized by means of economic integration: through a common market, a customs union and common policies.[1] But it was not self-evident that the economic orientation of the Community would be conceptualized with a constitutional vocabulary. The very term 'economic constitution' stems from a particular legal culture, and even there the concept has been highly contested, far from being unanimously accepted or defined. German ordoliberals started portraying the Treaty of Rome in terms of an economic constitution in the early 1960s.[2] However, in the first decades of the Community the term 'economic constitution' was but rarely used by anyone other than German discussants.[3] Only in the 1990s did the term

1 In the Preamble, the Signatory States declared their commitment to laying 'the foundations of an ever closer union among the peoples of Europe' and to strengthening peace and liberty. In turn, Art. 2 of the Treaty laid down that the Community aims not only 'to promote throughout the community a harmonious development of economic activities, a continuous and balanced expansion, an increase in stability . . . [and] an accelerated raising of the standard of living' but also 'closer relations between the states belonging to it'.

2 Thus, Hans von der Groeben, the German Competition Commissioner, already used the term 'economic constitution' in an article published in 1961, H. von der Groeben (1961).

3 An article published by L. J. Constantinesco (1977) is one of the few exceptions.

begin to gain more general recognition, at least partly due to the influence of the European University Institute (EUI) in Florence.[4] By the same token, the ordoliberal reading was downgraded to only one option among others. The underlying premises of Treaty provisions and ECJ jurisprudence have always been contested. The controversies continued, but what changed was the conceptual apparatus: even interlocutors other than German ordoliberals shifted to constitutional language. Ordoliberals used – and still use – 'economic constitution' in a normative sense, connoting a decision for a specific economic model. With the spread of the term, it has acquired a more neutral, descriptive meaning. This will be my choice too, but I shall start by presenting the openly normative ordoliberal notion.

Even if their views have always been contentious, the significance of ordoliberals in developing a theory of the European economic constitution should not be undervalued. Ordoliberals deserve credit in at least four respects. Firstly, though they did not invent the term, they managed to leave a decisive imprint on its conceptual contents for decades. Secondly, they not only aimed at, but even succeeded in, establishing a genuine scholarly dialogue between law and economics, focusing on the respective poles of the constitutional relation of the economic constitution. Thirdly, they were the first to offer a coherent reading of the European economic constitution and to explicate the economic view informing this reading. Fourthly, although they never monopolized interpretation of the Treaty of Rome, their views did influence the microeconomic direction of constitutionalization: that is, the elevation of free movement and competition law to core elements of the economic constitution. Ordoliberals were not always satisfied with the substance of the microeconomic constitution, which was constantly changing through the – at times quite errant – case law of the ECJ. But the microeconomic orientation was certainly to their taste.

Opinions on who, exactly, was the father of the term 'economic constitution' (*Wirtschaftsverfassung*) diverge, but general agreement prevails on the crucial era. This was the Weimar period. One important strand of the debate was initiated by Hugo Sinzheimer, a professor of labour

[4] Reference should be made, in particular, to the doctoral theses of Miguel Poiares Maduro and Julio Baquero Cruz, both educated at the EUI. M. Poiares Maduro (1998) and J. Baquero Cruz (2002). Christian Joerges, a long-time professor at the EUI, has been an important intermediary between German and other European discussion. Of his many writings on the European economic constitution, see C. Joerges (1996 and 2004).

law, politically associated with the trade union movement and the Social Democratic Party. Sinzheimer was involved in parliamentary deliberations on the Weimar Constitution and, as chairman of the committee responsible for provisions bearing on the economy, played an active role in drafting the very provisions in which he then identified the economic constitution.

In its second Part (Fundamental Rights and Duties of Germans), the Weimar Constitution included a section on Economic Life. By 'economic constitution', Sinzheimer did not allude to this section as a whole. Nor did he attach it to the fundamental rights pertaining to individual economic activity, such as the right to property (Art. 153), freedom of contract (Art. 152) and freedom of trade (Art. 151(3)), or to the labour-related provisions, such as Art. 157(1), according to which the 'labour force enjoys the special protection of the *Reich*'. Sinzheimer defined 'economic constitution' in institutional terms, although it is evident that indirectly he also aimed at a substantive reorganization of the economy, in accordance with socialist (social democratic) objectives. Sinzheimer's economic constitution was a reformist version of the council-based organization of power which the radical labour movement had striven for in the revolutionary turmoil of 1917–19. At issue was a multifaceted and multitiered corporatist organization for economic decision-making, intended to supplement the political constitutional bodies.[5]

In the tumultuous history of the Weimar Republic, the corporatist council organization, set out in Arts. 156(2) and 165 of the Constitution, did not live up to the expectations of Sinzheimer and those sharing his aspirations. Worker councils at the shop level were established, as was the National Economic Council, but neither of them played the role envisaged by Sinzheimer and his soulmates. Even the very term 'economic constitution' seems to have temporarily fallen into oblivion: neither in constitutional nor in private law doctrine did it find any niche.[6] Knut Wolfgang Nörr has conjectured that the concept of economic constitution was avoided because it 'had been in a certain way anticipated and

[5] On Sinzheimer, see F. Böhm (1953) and S. Hänninen (2010).

[6] However, the term was picked up and given a different conceptual content by Sinzheimer's younger colleague Franz L. Neumann, who also was politically affiliated with social democrats and had contacts with the trade union movement. In an article first published in 1931, he defined 'economic constitution' as the 'systematic order of state intervention' ('systematische Ordnung der staatlichen Intervention'). F. L. Neumann (1978). This definition, of course, did not add to the allure of the concept among the more conservative mainstream of legal academia.

"occupied" by the content a social-democratic jurist had worked out and authoritatively determined'.[7]

The largely abandoned term was picked up – hijacked, if you want – by a Freiburg group of legal and economic scholars who constituted the nucleus of what came to be called the *ordoliberal* school. The leading economist of the group was Walter Eucken, the leading legal scholar Franz Böhm,[8] who also carried over the concept from the Weimar period to post-Second World War Germany and even the EEC. Some – but not all – of the Freiburg group managed to maintain their academic positions and continue publishing throughout the Third Reich.[9] They were able to establish contacts abroad as well, for instance with Wilhelm Röpke in Switzerland. Moreover, they joined the international neoliberal movement of economists, lawyers, politicians and philosophers, already gathering momentum before the Second World War.[10] After the war, the movement obtained a new organizational nexus in the Mont Pelerin Society, founded in 1948. Friedrich Hayek soon became a leading intellectual figure of the international movement.

The main credit for the renaissance and, by the same token, reconceptualization of 'economic constitution' is due to Böhm. Committed to economic liberalism as he was, Böhm was not interested in an organizational economic constitution but in a constitutional decision in favour of a competition economy, a decision he saw manifested by the freedom of trade, laid down in Art. 151(3) of the Weimar Constitution.[11] Thus, the

[7] K. W. Nörr (1994), p. 351.

[8] Another central legal scholar was Hans Grossman-Doerth. M. Wegmann (2002), p. 104.

[9] Franz Böhm was one of those who had to leave his academic position. See D. J. Gerber (1998), pp. 232–6.

[10] According to Milene Wegmann, the international neoliberal movement, launched at the Walter Lippmann Colloquium in Paris in 1938, was based on three basic ideas of the Freiburg group: (1) the interdependence of the economic, social and legal orders; (2) the fundamental difference between a market economy and an administrative or planned economy; and (3) free and comprehensive competition as the guiding principle of economic policy. The conception of economic policy espoused by the neoliberals included as its central elements: (1) market and price mechanisms as the driving force of a liberal economy; (2) a strong state, independent of interest groups, which creates the legal framework order for securing free competition but which does not interfere in the functioning of market and price mechanisms; (3) liberal interventionism which supports and enforces market forces instead of counteracting them. M. Wegmann (2002), p. 141.

[11] Böhm had worked from 1925 to 1931 in the cartel unit of the Ministry of Economics and thus gathered practical experience of the application of competition law. He already used the concept *Wirtschaftsverfassung* in 1928 in his article *Das Problem der privaten Macht*, F. Böhm (1928).

connotation of the concept was overturned: the other pole of the constitutional relation was no more conceived as an organized economy but as a market economy, based on free competition. Corporatist ideas, which imbued the Sinzheimer version of economic constitution, were regarded as one of the main threats to a market economy. This is a striking corroboration of the often-alleged dual nature and internal contradictoriness of the Weimar Constitution. The contradictory signification of 'economic constitution' and Böhm's taking over and redefining the term coined by Sinzheimer epitomize Schmittian conceptual warfare in practice (see Chapter 4). Ordoliberals aimed at dominance of the conceptual field by introducing both a new vocabulary and a new grammar. In addition to the redefined 'economic constitution', the vocabulary included such conceptual neologisms as, for instance, 'economic power', 'performance-based competition' (*Leistungswettbewerb*) and 'market competition'. These were supposed to be concepts of both economic and legal scholarship and to facilitate the dialogue between the two which the Freiburg School sought to establish. The argumentative grammar, in turn, was based on the interplay between economic and legal ordering.[12]

Indeed, a central tenet of ordoliberalism is the interdependence of economy and law, and, consequently, of economic and legal scholarship. Ordoliberal lawyers have developed a theory of economic law (*Wirtschaftsrecht*) where both the legal and economic aspects of legal institutions, as well as the interaction between the two, were explicitly thematized. This, as we know, is not very common in legal scholarship. However, the deep commitment to the basic neoliberal canons of economic theory added to ordoliberal writings a strong normative flavour, which characterizes ordoliberal views of the European economic constitution as well.

What, then, is the role of state and law in ordoliberal thinking? To put it concisely, their task is to provide the framework *ordo*, necessary for the functioning of the market and price mechanisms of free competition. What is needed is a strong state, but a strong state in the sense of a *Rechtsstaat*, capable of creating and guaranteeing the legal framework for a competence-based market economy. The state should also be strong enough to withstand the pressures of rent-seeking interest groups calling for market-distorting interventions. Such a strong state is a self-limiting state: a state restricting itself to establishing the rules of the game, and confining economic *Ordnungspolitik* to indirect framework

[12] D. J. Gerber (1994), p. 67.

regulation of the economy through general laws, such as banking, bankruptcy or company legislation, as well as, most importantly, competition law. In an institutional respect, ordoliberals put their faith in the legislature, which issues general laws, and the judiciary, which enforces those laws. The executive is the suspect branch of the state, especially if furnished with discretionary powers of intervention. Ordoliberal mistrust does not encompass a quasi-judicial Competition Authority, which functions under clear general rules, respects basic *Rechtsstaat* requirements and is subject to judicial oversight. In effect, in an ordoliberal strong state the legislature does not possess much discretionary power in the economic field either, supposed as it is to pursue a legislative *Ordnungspolitik* giving effect to the economic constitution.[13]

The first-generation ordoliberals were contemporaries of Carl Schmitt, and a comparison with Schmittian ideas might be instructive in highlighting the originality of ordoliberal thinking. Towards the end of the Weimar period, Schmitt introduced the conceptual distinction between 'total state from weakness' (*totaler Staat aus Schwäche*) and 'total state from strength' (*totaler Staat aus Stärke*). In Schmitt's view, the Weimar state was a total state from weakness. It was total in the sense of intervening in all spheres of society. However, these interventions were not a sign of strength but of weakness: the state had fallen prey to interest groups pursuing their particular interests. The pluralism of interest groups threatened to suffocate the independent capacity of the state for action.[14] Ordoliberals shared Schmitt's negative view of the opposite of a strong state: a state controlled by pluralist rent-seeking interest groups and unable to resist the claims these groups raised for economic and social benefits. But where ordoliberals definitely parted ways with Schmitt was the positive characterization of the strong state. For Schmitt, the total state from strength was the authoritarian state he expected of, and obtained from, the post-Weimar future. It had nothing to do with the ordoliberal *Rechtsstaat*, stressing the role of the legislature and the judiciary, and limiting the action field of the executive.[15]

Böhm had certainly read his Schmitt, as had most German legal scholars educated in the 1920s or 1930s. Böhm's conception of the economic

[13] *Ibid.*, p. 48. [14] C. Schmitt (1958) (first published in 1933).

[15] Here Milene Wegmann is certainly right, although in other respects she displays traces of an over-eagerness to deny connections between Schmitt and the ordoliberals. Wegmann (2002), pp. 62 ff.

constitution bears a clear (formal) resemblance to Schmitt's *Verfassungslehre*, which is premised on the distinction between the 'constitution as a decision' or the 'constitution in the positive sense' and 'constitutional laws'. Schmitt defines the constitution in the positive sense as a decision by the people on its specific (political) form of existence.[16] Correspondingly, Böhm conceived of the economic constitution as a *Gesamtentscheidung* (comprehensive decision) on 'the nature (*Art*) and form of the process of socio-economic cooperation'. In the ordoliberal framework, this *Gesamtentscheidung* fell in favour of a market economy based on free competition. When introducing the concept of the economic constitution as a *Gesamtentscheidung* in his *Wettbewerb und Monopolkampf*, Böhm explicitly referred to Schmitt's concept of the political constitution.[17]

Schmitt was deliberately ambiguous about the relation between the constitution in the positive sense and constitutional law. A similar ambiguity pervades Böhm's discussion of how the economic-constitutional *Gesamtentscheidung* relates to explicit constitutional law (the formal constitution). Neither Schmitt nor ordoliberals considered it necessary for the political or economic *Gesamtentscheidung* to be expressly spelled out in the formal constitution; the constitution in the positive sense, as a *Gesamtentscheidung*, was primarily of a substantive rather than a formal character. Thus, the decisive event which for Böhm had signalled Germany's constitutional *Gesamtentscheidung* in favour of a competitive market economy was not an enactment of a formal constitutional rank but the introduction of freedom of trade through the *Gewerbeordnung* of 1869.

It is important to note that even if a link can be established between the economic constitution in the positive sense and the formal constitution, the former cannot be reduced to the provisions of the latter. For Schmitt, the vagueness and aloofness of the constitution in the positive sense created room for constitutional-theoretical and political manoeuvring, even for juxtaposing the two meanings of 'constitution' and justifying violations of (formal) constitutional law in the name of the (substantive)

16 C. Schmitt (2008), pp. 75–9.

17 'From the constitutional law perspective the system of commercial freedom is a constitution of economic life in the positive sense; the introduction of this system thus is an "overall decision" about the kind and form of the economic-social cooperation process in the same sense as Carl Schmitt has called the constitution an "overall decision on the kind and form of political unity".' F. Böhm (1933), p. 107.

positive constitution. Yet again it must be stressed that formal correspondence should not obscure the fact that the normative vision informing ordoliberal concept-formation is wholly different from that espoused by Schmitt.

Böhm underlined that the economic constitution as a *Gesamtentscheidung* imposes an interpretive duty not merely in public but also, and even primarily, in private law. The economic constitution would – and should – unfold much of its legal effects through what today would be called *Drittwirkung* of economic freedom, understood mainly as freedom of competition, confirmed by a constitutional *Gesamtentscheidung*. Böhm was a pioneer in advocating integration, not only of law and economics, but also of public and private law. Private law institutions are instrumental for realization of a constitutional *Gesamtentscheidung*. The public law element of the legal constitution of a free market economy consists of 'the constitutional decision of the legislator as such, i.e. the act of introducing freedom of trade and the included decision for a free performance-based competition', while 'the implementation lies in the hands of the private law judge'. Together the public and the private law elements produce 'a *herrschaftsfreie* order of social cooperation, a market economy governed by performance-based competition'.[18] This *herrschaftsfreie* order is equivalent to what Böhm in his later writings termed 'private law society' (*Privatrechtsgesellschaft*).[19] The objective of creating a social order free of power relations manifests the power-restricting function expected of the economic constitution. As Böhm emphasized, the problem is not only public power but private power as well: private economic power annihilating the preconditions of *Leistungswettbewerb* (performance-based competition) and replacing it with *Behinderungswettbewerb* (impediment-based competition), thus also contradicting the assumption of freedom and equality on which freedom of contract is based. It is no coincidence that Böhm's breakthrough article bore the title *Das Problem der privaten Macht*.[20]

After the Second World War, ordoliberal theorists complemented the justification for free competition with Hayekian ideas of economic knowledge. Through the Mont Pelerin Society, Hayek knit close ties with German ordoliberals, whose younger, post-war generation began to develop and follow a version of ordoliberalism deeply influenced by Hayekian principles. Indeed, many ordoliberal tenets were easily adjusted to a Hayekian theoretical framework. A fundamental consensus existed on the pivotal

[18] *Ibid.*, p. 124. [19] F. Böhm (1966). [20] F. Böhm (1928).

role of competition. Hayek conceives of competition as an indispensable mechanism for providing the decentralized knowledge needed for the functioning of a market economy. Planning and administrative interventions are bound to fail because of the endemic lack of centralized knowledge which results from the high complexity of the economy.[21] Correspondingly, Hayek argues that the role of law should be confined to establishing general framework *rules of just conduct* and not extended to purpose-oriented *rules of organization*. This argument bears a clear affinity to ordoliberal emphasis on general laws and rejection of discretionary administrative measures; here the conceptual precursor presumably lies in Schmitt's distinction between *Gesetz* and *Massnahme*.[22] But Hayek's claim of the spontaneous emergence of framework rules was alien to most ordoliberals, who saw the need for legislative intervention for constructing and maintaining a free market economy. Hayek was suspicious of the ordoliberal idea of a strong state, needed to guarantee the framework *ordo* of a competition-based market economy. Hayek's views on competition law were also quite different from ordoliberal ideas.[23]

In the Third Reich, the ordoliberal reading of the *Gesamtentscheidung* making up the economic constitution did not have any chance to assert itself in the face of continuously expanding state intervention and state-induced cartelization of the economy. Ordoliberals such as Eucken and Böhm opposed the planificatory and *dirigiste* elements of the Nazi economy, as they, from their humanist premises, opposed the regime as a whole. Their hour came after the war, when the German economy lay in ruins

21 However, M. E. Streit and W. Müssler (1995), at 9, emphasize that 'from a constitutional point of view, it is important that competition as a characteristic element of a self-organizing system is not confined to its functional relevance as a discovery procedure'; 'competition is also a controlling device for economic power which is inseparable from the evolutionary market process'.

22 See, e.g., C. Schmitt (1924), pp. 94–6. M. E. Streit and W. Müssler (1995), at 10, refer even to Max Weber's concept of formal rational law and his criticism of tendencies of the law's 'materialization'.

23 While ordoliberals advocate a strong state and vigorous competition law enforcement, including prohibition of cartels and abuse of a dominant position as well as preventive merger rules to protect a competitive market structure, the New Austrian School tends to take a negative or minimalist view of the need for competition law. In Hayek's view, a general cartel prohibition, for instance, is not necessary but it suffices to declare cartels null and void under private law. The New Austrian School opposes monitoring economic power through abuse of dominance regulation or preserving competitive market structures through merger control. See M. E. Streit and M. Wohlgemuth (2000).

and explicit decisions were needed on the direction of the restructuring of the economy. In the post-war intellectual, economic and political search for new coordinates, ordoliberals not only enjoyed scholarly success but won the ear of key decision-makers too; first, the allied administrators and, after their departure, leading politicians such as Ludwig Erhard, the father of the German *Wirtschaftswunder*, a long-time minister of economy and a short-lived prime minister.[24] Ordoliberals could influence German competition law, although not to the extent they wished. But where they did not succeed was in their efforts to have their conception of the 'economic constitution' confirmed in the case law of the German Constitutional Court. Not even the term *Wirtschaftsverfassung* found its way into the Court's jurisprudence, nor did the Court confer constitutional blessing on the ordoliberal view of the substance of Germany's alleged economic constitution. In its 1954 *Investitionshilfegesetz* decision, the Court explicitly stated that the Basic Law, on the one hand, had not opted for any particular economic model, but, on the other hand, did not require of legislation economic policy neutrality either.[25]

The process of economic constitutionalization

Ordoliberal understanding of the European economic constitution relies on the claim that the Treaty of Rome manifested a constitutional *Gesamtentscheidung* in favour of a free market economy relying on performance-based competition. This *Gesamtentscheidung* was supposed to guide

[24] In a speech given in 1961, Erhard famously declared himself to be one of the ordoliberals. M. Wegmann (2002), p. 105. Both Eucken and Böhm were members of the *Wissenschaftlicher Beirat*, assisting the administration of the Western allies. Later on, Böhm continued counselling Erhard's Ministry of Economics and could also further the realization of his ideas as a Member of Parliament. D. J. Gerber (1994), pp. 59–62. See also Gerber's summary: 'For almost two decades, ordoliberal thought . . . played a predominant role in guiding economic policy decisions in Germany . . . The direct influence of ordoliberal ideas reached its apogee in the late1950s and early 1960s when they represented something like orthodoxy among policymakers and thinkers in Germany . . . ' *Ibid.*, p. 68.

[25] BVerfGE 4, 7, 17/18, 20 July 1954. The Constitutional Court reaffirmed its standpoint in 1979 in its *Mitbestimmungsgesetz* decision, BVerfGE 59, 290, 337/38, 1 March 1979. For the USA, cf. Justice Holmes's famous dissent in *Lochner*: 'This case is decided upon an economic theory which a large part of the country does not entertain . . . Constitution is not intended to embody a particular economic theory, whether of paternalism and the organic relation of the citizen to the state or of laissez-faire' (*Lochner v New York* 198 US 45 (1905)). It took the majority of the Court twenty-two years before it came to adopt Holmes's view of judicial restraint in front of economic and social legislation. See also J. Baquero Cruz (2002), p. 37.

interpretation of the Treaty and its implementation through secondary legislation, ECJ case law and Commission competition policy. As will be shown in this chapter, weighty arguments speak for the view that the Treaty did not opt for any specific economic model at either the Community or the Member State level. Accordingly, the European process of economic constitutionalization should be approached in more neutral terms than ordoliberals are willing to adopt. The process possesses two intertwined aspects: one formal, the other substantive. In the *formal* process, the relevant Treaty provisions and principles established by the ECJ were accorded constitutional significance. The *substantive* aspect relates to the contents of economic constitutional law: elaborating the doctrine which specified and complemented the often vague and ambiguous Treaty provisions. The Masters of the Treaties (*Herren der Verträge*) remained silent on the economic constitution for three decades, from Rome until adoption of the Single European Act (SEA) in 1986. And even after the constitutional legislator broke silence, only a few and mainly merely technical amendments have been made to the Treaty provisions on free movement and competition law, which came to be in the focus of economic constitutionalization. In both its formal and substantive aspects, economic constitutionalization has primarily proceeded through the constitutional speech acts of the ECJ.

In the formal respect, four crucial features detached the relevant Treaty provisions and doctrinal principles from the international law template and conferred on them a constitutional label: firstly, direct applicability and direct effect in Member States; secondly, supremacy over conflicting national law; thirdly, creation of rights and obligations for private parties; fourthly, functioning as yardsticks by which the ECJ reviews not only secondary European legislation but also – and even primarily – compliance of national law with European law, thus protecting individual economic rights against possible interference by Member States. By the same token, the ECJ assumed constitutional court functions of judicial review of legislation and protection of individual rights; a kind of Napoleonic self-coronation, we could say.

The formal aspect of economic constitutionalization coincides with the early phase of juridical constitutionalization. Juridical constitutionalization was not an end in itself, but the impetus came from the economic dimension; as *Van Gend en Loos* clearly intimates, the main rationale was to secure effective implementation of the provisions serving the main objective of the Treaty, namely establishment of a common market. Subsequent steps in juridical constitutionalization, which enlarged the scope and consequences of direct effect and granted all European legal instruments primacy over all municipal law, were also mostly motivated by effective implementation of economic constitutional or secondary law. The second-order principles of effectiveness and uniformity have functioned as a bridge linking economic and juridical constitutionalization. From a modest beginning in Art. 12 TEEC, direct effect was extended to cover the vital free movement provisions of the Treaty: first, Arts. 30, 34 and 36 on free movement of goods and, subsequently, even other freedoms as well. The provisions on free movement of capital were last to enter the list.[26]

As argued in Chapter 2, this expansion would not have been possible without loosening the initial threshold criteria for direct effect. In *Van Gend en Loos*, the Court had emphasized that application of Art. 12 TEEC was not dependent on implementing European or national legislation, which made it a suitable candidate for direct effect; it fulfilled the conditions for self-executing rules of international law. But Art. 49 made implementation of free movement of workers dependent on complementary legislation, as did Art. 54 for freedom of establishment and Art. 63 for free movement of services. Direct effect of Treaty provisions was needed no longer only for the original enforcement function but for a legislative function as well. *Van Gend en Loos* had justified direct effect by reference to complementing public enforcement of Treaty law through monitoring by the Commission and other Member States with the vigilance of private litigants. Now direct effect was to compensate for the blockage of secondary legislation in the aftermath of the empty-chairs crisis and the Luxembourg Compromise. ECJ case law had to accomplish what the Treaty had expected of secondary legislation.[27]

The two future sub-branches of European economic constitutional law – free movement and competition law – followed somewhat different paths in both formal and substantive respects. The ECJ introduced direct effect and primacy for the purpose of securing effective and uniform implementation in Member States especially of free movement law. In competition law too, much was left open by the Treaty. Art. 85 TEEC on cartels and Art. 86 on abuse of dominance were expressly addressed to undertakings. Yet Art. 87 presupposed Council regulations or directives to give effect

26 See J. A. Usher (2007).

27 See, e.g., what P. Craig (1992) writes about the legislative function of direct effect. Craig refers to J. H. H. Weiler's (1981) path-breaking analysis of decisional intergovernmentalism and normative supranationalism.

to the principles set out in Arts. 85 and 86. According to Art. 88, until such legislation entered into force, Member States were expected to rule upon cartels and abuse of a dominant position in accordance not only with national law (not all Member States even had a competition law at the time) but also Art. 85 – in particular paragraph 3 on exemptions from the cartel prohibition – and Art. 86 on abuse of dominance. To round up the rather confusing Treaty regulation, Art. 89 required that 'the Commission, as soon as it takes up its duties, ensure the application of the principles laid down in Articles 85 and 86', however, 'without prejudice to Article 88'.

The Treaty provisions left space for divergent readings of a number of important issues: direct applicability of Arts. 85 and 86 in Member States; the relation of the Treaty provisions to national legislation; the division of competences between the Commission and national authorities; and the legal position of undertakings. The Commission, under the direction of German Competition Commissioner Hans von der Groeben, pushed for direct applicability and prevalence over national legislation of the Treaty provisions even before adoption of secondary legislation. Regulation 17/62 included the provisions called for in Art. 87 TEEC and ended the interim period which Arts. 88 and 89 addressed.[28] The Regulation signalled the victory of the Commission position, by declaring Art. 85(1) on prohibition of cartels and Art. 86 on abuse of dominance directly applicable.[29] By contrast, exemption from the cartel prohibition, allowed for in Art. 85(3), required a decision by the Commission; unlike paragraph 1 of Art. 85, paragraph 3 was not directly applicable law under Regulation 17/62 (although it became so when the Regulation was 'modernized' in 2004).[30] The Regulation did not remove all ambiguity concerning the relation of Arts. 85 and 86 to national competition law. Member State authorities were declared to 'remain competent to apply Article 85(1) and Article 86 in accordance with Article 88 of the Treaty', provided that the Commission had not initiated an infringement procedure. But the Regulation, which was issued before *Van Gend en Loos* and *Costa v Enel*, left

28 Regulation No. 17 implementing Articles 85 and 86 of the Treaty, [1962] OJ 13/204.

29 'Without prejudice to Articles 6, 7 and 23 of this Regulation, agreements, decisions and concerted practices of the kind described in Article 85(1) of the Treaty and the abuse of a dominant position in the market, within the meaning of Article 86 of the Treaty, shall be prohibited, no prior decision to that effect being required.' Art. 1.

30 'Subject to review of its decision by the Court of Justice, the Commission shall have sole power to declare Article 85(1) inapplicable pursuant to Article 85(3) of the Treaty.' Art. 9(1).

unclear whether national authorities were not only competent but even obliged to apply Treaty law and whether Treaty law enjoyed supremacy over national law.[31]

In its jurisprudence, the ECJ demarcated the spheres of application of European and national competition law by the trans-border criterion. In 1966 in *Consten and Grundig*, the Court stated that 'the concept of "agreements . . . which may affect trade between Member States" is intended to define, in the law governing cartels, the boundary between the areas respectively covered by Community law and national law'.[32] In 1974 in *Commercial Solvents*, the Court adopted a corresponding position with regard to law on abuse of dominance.[33] The implication was that national authorities, including courts, were obliged to acknowledge the primacy of European law within its scope of application. The primacy of European law on cartels was explicitly proclaimed in 1969 in *Walt Wilhelm*, where the Court invoked the master principles of effectiveness and uniformity and employed expressions reminiscent of its free movement jurisprudence.[34]

It may appear strange that a regulation settled issues of constitutional significance, such as direct applicability and the continuing relevance of Art. 88 TEEC, even after the end of the interim period. The constitutional significance of Regulation 17/62, as well as its successor, Regulation 1/2003, manifests the *Sonderweg* of the constitutionalization of competition law: a *Sonderweg* related to the central enforcement and policy role of

[31] See on the drafting process of Regulation 17/62 L. F. Pace and K. Seidel (2013).

[32] The Court emphasized that what is particularly important for applying Art. 85 TEEC is 'whether the agreement is capable of constituting a threat, either direct or indirect, actual or potential, to freedom of trade between Member States in a manner which might harm the attainment of the objectives of a single market between states'. Case C-56/64 *Consten and Grundig* [1966] ECR 429, Para. 6.

[33] 'The prohibition on abuse of a dominant position, insofar as it may affect trade between Member States, is intended to define the sphere of application of Community rules in relation to national laws.' Case C-6/73 *Istituto Chemioterapico Italiano and Commercial Solvents v Commission* [1974] ECR 223, Para. 4.

[34] 'The EEC Treaty has established its own system of law, integrated into the legal systems of the Member States, and which must be applied by their courts. It would be contrary to the nature of such a system to allow Member States to introduce or to retain measures capable of prejudicing the practical effectiveness of the Treaty. The binding force of the Treaty and of measures taken in application of it must not differ from one state to another as a result of internal measures, lest the functioning of the Community system should be impeded and the achievement of the aims of the Treaty placed in peril. Consequently, conflicts between the rules of the Community and national rules in the matter of the law on cartels must be resolved by applying the principle that Community law takes precedence.' Case C-14/68 *Walt Wilhelm and Others v Bundeskartellamt* [1969] ECR 1, Para. 6.

the Commission, which has no correspondence in free movement law and which accounts for the less intensive involvement of the ECJ.[35] Regulation 17/62 confirmed the direct applicability of Arts. 85 and 86 TEC but, issued as it was before *Van Gend en Loos*, did not pronounce on their direct effect: that is, on the right of competitors or other injured parties to invoke them before national courts. Here a constitutional speech act by the ECJ was needed. In 1974 in *BRT v Sabam*, the Court derived the direct effect of Arts. 85(1) and 86 TEEC from their direct applicability to undertakings.[36] In 2001, *Courage* further reinforced the legal status of competitors and other injured parties with a right to damages.[37]

The ECJ has made a vital contribution not only to the formal but also to the substantive side of economic constitutionalization, in particular in free movement law. The Court has elaborated the doctrines applied in interpretation and application of often ambiguous Treaty provisions, and even introduced doctrinal elements with scarce or non-existent direct support in Treaty law. As many observers have noted, the Court first focused on free movement of goods, which was the doctrinal forerunner among fundamental freedoms. Its privileged position in ECJ jurisprudence was related to its importance for demolishing barriers to cross-border trade

[35] Regulation 17/62 was adopted by the Council but the Commission, in particular DG IV under the direction of von der Groeben, was responsible for the drafting and exerted a decisive influence on its contents. See L. F. Pace and K. Seidel (2013).

[36] Manifesting the still unsettled nature of fundamental concepts of the juridical constitution, the ECJ did not make a clear distinction between direct applicability and direct effect. The Court stated that 'as the prohibitions of Articles 85(1) and 86 tend by their very nature to produce direct effects in relations between individuals, these Articles create direct rights in respect of the individuals concerned which the national courts must safeguard'. The Court also invoked the higher hierarchical position of Treaty law when it argued that a provision in the Regulation requiring Member State authorities to suspend national procedure when the Commission initiates its own infringement procedure could not negate direct effect: 'To deny, by virtue of the aforementioned Article 9, the national courts' jurisdiction to afford this safeguard, would mean depriving individuals of rights which they hold under the Treaty itself.' Case C-127/73 *BRT v Sabam* [1974] ECR 51, Paras. 16–17.

[37] *Courage* granted the right to damages for anyone who has suffered harm as a result of a competition law infringement. The Court argued that 'the full effectiveness of Article 85 of the Treaty and, in particular, the practical effect of the prohibition laid down in Article 85(1) would be put at risk if it were not open to any individual to claim damages for loss caused to him by a contract or by conduct liable to restrict or distort competition' (Case C-453/99 *Courage and Crehan* [2001] ECR I-6297, Para. 26). In *Courage*, the claimant was another undertaking which had been party to the contract restricting competition. In *Manfredi* the right to damages was granted to a consumer (Case C-295/04 [2006] ECR I-6619).

and advancing towards the primary objective of the Treaty: establishment of a common market.

The Court's contribution involves not only constitutionally pertinent concepts and principles but a methodological aspect as well. When assessing the compatibility of national measures with free movement Treaty law, the Court has employed a three-phase methodology. In the first phase, the issue is whether the measure under scrutiny amounts to a *restriction* on free movement. If this is found to be the case, then in the second phase the Court assesses whether the Member State concerned can invoke a legitimate *justification* for the restriction. If the Court accepts the legitimacy of the justification, then at the third stage it subjects the justification to a *proportionality test*, where it weighs the benefits of the justificatory grounds against the costs of the restriction on free movement.

The three-phase reasoning presupposed clarification of the crucial concepts applied in the first and second phases. Definition of 'restriction' hinged on interpretation of Art. 30 TEEC (now Art. 34 TFEU), prohibiting 'quantitative restrictions on imports and all measures having equivalent effect'. In its case law of the first decades, the Court adopted a wide reading of 'measures having equivalent effect'. According to the formula articulated in 1974 in *Dassonville*, 'all trading rules enacted by Member States which are capable of hindering, directly or indirectly, actually or potentially, intra-community trade are to be considered as measures having an effect equivalent to quantitative restrictions'.[38] In 1993, in *Keck*, the Court took a step back and narrowed the definition by introducing the distinction between 'product requirements' and 'sales arrangements'. According to *Keck*, the *Dassonville* formula covers all obstacles to free movement which derive from product requirements applied to goods coming from other Member States where they have been lawfully manufactured and marketed. By contrast, the formula does not pertain to situations where national provisions restricting or prohibiting certain selling arrangements are applied to products from other Member States, provided that the provisions are generally applicable and do not display discriminatory effects.[39]

Art. 36 TEEC (now Art. 36 TFEU) included a list of justifications which Member States can invoke for restrictions on free movement of goods.

[38] Case C-8/74 *Dassonville* [1974] ECR 837, Para. 5.

[39] '... so long as those provisions apply to all relevant traders operating within the national territory and so long as they affect in the same manner, in law and in fact, the marketing of domestic products and of those from other Member States'. Case C-267/91 *Keck and Mithouard* [1993] ECR I-6097, Para. 17.

Reference is made to 'public morality, public policy or public security; the protection of health and life of humans, animals or plants; the protection of national treasures possessing artistic, historic or archaeological value'; and 'the protection of industrial and commercial property'. However, such grounds cannot justify prohibitions or restrictions which 'constitute a means of arbitrary discrimination or a disguised restriction on trade between Member States'. If the Court's definition of 'measures having an effect equivalent to quantitative restrictions' has been wide, in particular in the pre-*Keck* era, as a counterweight it has expanded the scope of justificatory grounds. In 1979 *Cassis de Dijon*, probably the most famous substantive ruling in the chain of economic constitutionalization, complemented the list of Art. 36 TEEC with other 'mandatory requirements'. *Cassis de Dijon* has also been credited with establishing the principle of *mutual recognition*, a central principle of the first, microeconomic layer of the European economic constitution.[40] If a product meets the requirements of 'home state' legislation – 'such as those relating to designation, form, size, weight, composition, presentation, labelling, packaging'[41] – other Member States as 'host states' should not, as a rule, prevent its access to their national markets through different requirements. Only such impediments are allowed which are necessary and proportionate to a legitimate public interest objective. In turn, the principle of mutual recognition has opened the road for *regulatory competition* between Member States.[42]

Roughly coinciding with the Court's more cautious approach to restrictions on free movement of goods – an approach codified in the *Keck* formula – the focus in constitutional free movement jurisprudence shifted to workers and services. Here the Court has again adopted a wide definition of restrictions. In free movement of workers, *Bosman* (1995) is the landmark case.[43] However, after the ECJ embarked on elaborating the implications of citizenship rights, introduced in Maastricht and including free movement, the law on free movement of workers has lost much of its former pertinence. In a methodological respect, the three-phase reasoning applied to free movement of goods has been transferred to other economic freedoms as well. In the field of services, the Court has treated as a restriction any measure which is liable to hinder or make less attractive

40 Case C-120/78 *Rewe v Bundesmonopolverwaltung für Branntwein* [1979] ECR 649 (*Cassis de Dijon*).

41 The list is cited from *Keck*, Para. 15.

42 See N. Reich (1992).

43 Case C-415/93 *Union Royale Belge des Sociétés de Football Association and Others v Bosman and Others* [1995] ECR I-4921.

the provision or receipt of cross-border services or the exercise of the right of establishment; no discriminatory purpose or effect is needed.[44] Corresponding to the notion of mandatory requirements in *Cassis de Dijon*, the Court has departed from the wording of Treaty law and adopted a broader concept of imperative reasons which may justify restricting free movement of services and which may, for instance, include considerations of social policy too.[45]

In sum, substantive constitutionalization within free movement law has transpired through incremental doctrinal construction through ECJ case law. Still, nearly six decades after Rome, the doctrine within this core area of European law remains surprisingly unsettled and – at least in the eyes of many academic observers – incoherent. Though the Court still invokes *Dassonville*, *Cassis de Dijon* and *Keck* and treats them as valid law, commentators complain of vacillation in the application of canonical formulas, facade deductivism and judicial intuitionism. The present relevance of *Keck* has been questioned and the need to add a third category – restrictions on use – to product requirements and selling arrangements has been discussed.[46] Furthermore, some observers have claimed that unhindered *market access* has already replaced the *Keck* formula as the main criterion by which the Court identifies restrictions on free

44 In *Säger*, the Court pointed out that Art. 59 of the Treaty on the freedom to provide services 'requires not only the elimination of all discrimination against a person providing services on the ground of his nationality but also the abolition of any restriction, even if it applies without distinction to national providers of services and to those of other Member States, when it is liable to prohibit or otherwise impede the activities of a provider of services established in another Member State where he lawfully provides similar services'. Case C-76/90 *Säger v Dennemeyer & Co.* [1991] ECR I-4421, Para. 12.

45 In *Säger*, *ibid.*, the Court stated as 'a fundamental principle of the Treaty' that 'the freedom to provide services may be limited only by rules which are justified by imperative reasons relating to the public interest and which apply to all persons or undertakings pursuing an activity in the State of destination, in so far as that interest is not protected by the rules to which the person providing the services is subject in the Member State in which he is established. In particular, those requirements must be objectively necessary in order to ensure compliance with professional rules and to guarantee the protection of the recipient of services and they must not exceed what is necessary to attain those objectives' (Para. 15). With regard to the right to establishment see Case C-55/94 *Gebhard v Consiglio dell'Ordine degli Avvocati e Procuratori di Milano* [1995] ECR I-4165. Roth and Oliver note that 'the case law of the Court of Justice, starting in the 1980s and more so in the 1990s . . . brought a definite move towards a broader concept of restrictions that are to be abolished'. P. Oliver and W. H. Roth (2004), p. 411.

46 The discussion was launched by the Court's rulings in Case C-110/05 *Commission v Italy (Moped Trailers)* [2009] ECR I-519 and Case C-142/05 *Åklagaren v Percy Mickelsson and Joakim Roos* [2009] ECR I-4273. See, e.g., S. Enchelmaier (2007 and 2010).

movement.[47] Focus on market access has also been seen as the doctrinal link between the diverse freedoms. However, convergence of doctrines applied to different freedoms remains a debated issue; over the years, claims of convergence and detachment have alternated among academic discussants. The prevalent impression that debates evoke is great concern over doctrinal coherence with regard both to individual freedoms and to free movement law as a whole.[48] In individual cases, the doctrinal instability surrounding identification of restrictions is complemented by the well-known problems of application afflicting, actually, all three phases of reasoning but especially the proportionality test. Thus, it is difficult, if not impossible, to find a common denominator and measure for justificatory 'benefits' and free movement 'costs'.

A further important issue with constitutional significance pertains to the *ratione personae* of free movement law and its relationship to competition law. On their face, free movement provisions and competition law provisions on cartels and abuse of dominance have different addressees: the former impose obligations on Member States and the latter on undertakings. At quite an early stage of economic constitutionalization, the ECJ faced the question of the relevance of free movement law in horizontal relations between non-state actors and, correspondingly, the significance of competition law for state measures: that is, the potential *privatization of free movement law* and the potential *publicization of competition law*. In *Walrave and Koch* (1974), the Court formulated its basic approach to the horizontal effect of economic freedoms. It argued that free movement 'would be compromised if the abolition of State barriers could be neutralised by obstacles resulting from the exercise, by associations or organizations not governed by public law, of their legal autonomy'.[49] Thus, the ruling identified the functional precondition for horizontal direct effect: collective regulation by exercise of legal autonomy. In the institutional respect, a link to the state has usually been required of the subject of regulation; a link provided by, for example, delegation or authorization. Though a

[47] The criterion of market access had actually been invoked already in *Keck* and *Bosman*. J. Snell (2010) presents the discussion but takes a negative position on market access as a decisive criterion of restrictions on free movement. See also E. Spaventa (2004).

[48] For a general discussion of the coherence of free movement law, see N. Shuibhne (2013).

[49] Case C-36/74 *Walrave and Koch v Association Union Cycliste Internationale and Others* [1974] ECR 1405, Para. 18. See also Case C-415/93 *Union royale belge des sociétés de football association and Others v Bosman and Others* [1995] ECR I-4921, Para. 83; Case C-191/97 *Deliège* [2000] ECR I-2549, Para. 47; Case C-281/98 *Angonese* [2000] ECR I-4139, Para. 32; and Case C-309/99 *Wouters and Others* [2002] ECR I-1577, Para. 120.

string of cases exist which convey the impression of the seemingly consistent application of an established doctrine, in some important cases the Court seems to have retreated from the *Walrave and Koch* criteria, and merely assessed whether the action at issue entailed a restriction on free movement and downplayed the significance of whether the action was attributable to a public or private subject. The most widely discussed cases are *Viking* and *Laval*, where the restriction resulted from trade union action.[50] A shroud of uncertainty overhangs the relevance of free movement law in horizontal relationships too.

By contrast, the doctrine on the relevance of European competition law for state measures – publicization of competition law – seems fairly established: Member States may not enact measures which enable private undertakings to escape their obligations under the Treaty provisions on competition.[51] Even more generally, competition law doctrine, such as it is manifested in ECJ jurisprudence, appears to be rather stable and less volatile than free movement law; any volatility there has been is mainly to be seen in Commission competition policy. All in all, the Court's role has not been as central in competition law as in free movement law. The crucial position of the Commission in competition law has no equivalence in free movement law. The Commission is in charge of enforcing competition law and competition policy in general, and the Court has accorded the Commission a rather wide margin of policy discretion. This largely accounts for the stability and continuity of competition law jurisprudence.

[50] In *Viking* the Court first repeated *Walrave and Koch* and pointed out that 'it is clear from its case-law that the abolition, as between Member States, of obstacles to freedom of movement for persons and freedom to provide services would be compromised if the abolition of State barriers could be neutralised by obstacles resulting from the exercise, by associations or organisations not governed by public law, of their legal autonomy' (Case C-438/05 *International Transport Workers' Federation and Finnish Seamen's Union* [2007] ECR I-10779 (*Viking*), Para. 57). However, it added 'that, contrary to the claims, in particular, of ITF, it does not follow from the case-law of the Court referred to in paragraph 57 of the present judgment that that interpretation applies only to quasi-public organisations or to associations exercising a regulatory task and having quasi-legislative powers' (Para. 64). As G. Davies (2013a), p. 61, notes, 'it is this statement, more than all others, which suggests that horizontal effect encompasses any private actions restricting free movement'. See on the doctrine before *Viking* and *Laval* (Case C-341/05 *Laval un Partneri* [2007] ECR I-11767) J. Baquero Cruz (2002), pp. 105–25, and W. Sauter and H. Schepel (2009), pp. 97–128, and on the discussion of the significance of *Viking* and *Laval*, H. Schepel (2012) and G. Davies (2013b).

[51] Case C-362/88 *GB-INNO-BM v Confédération du Commerce Luxembourgeois* [1990] ECR I-667, Para. 33. See also J. Baquero Cruz (2002), pp. 136–53.

The Court laid down the main doctrinal premises in the pre-Maastricht era, in cases such as *Consten and Grundig* and *Continental Can*. *Consten and Grundig* not only explicated the meaning of 'agreements ... which may affect trade between Member States' in the law on cartels; it also confirmed that competition law protects competition 'as such', irrespective of the concrete effects of an agreement which aimed to prevent, restrict or distort competition.[52] Moreover, *Consten and Grundig* extended the reach of the law on cartels from horizontal agreements between competitors to vertical agreements between actors on different levels of the production chain (e.g. distribution agreements).

In turn, *Continental Can* (1973) opened the constitutional gate for merger control, although only in limited circumstances. In contrast to the Treaty on the ECSC, the TEEC did not include an explicit provision on mergers, and the legality of merger control without explicit Treaty authorization had been questioned. In *Continental Can*, the Court held that Art. 86 could be applied to prohibit mergers that further enhance market dominance of the buyer and eliminate remaining competition in the relevant market. The ECJ rejected the argument that Art. 86 is concerned solely with abusive market behaviour by a dominant firm, and not with structural changes in the market. The Court argued that the distinction between measures which concern the structure of the undertaking and practices which affect the market cannot be decisive, as any structural measure may influence market conditions if it increases the size and the economic power of the undertaking. The Court launched the concept of an *effective competition structure* which it presented as an alternative to direct consumer harm and which was destined to become a key notion in competition law jurisprudence.[53] The Court emphasized that abuse of dominance is not

[52] Case C-56/64 *Consten and Grundig* [1966] ECR 429, Para. 7. The Court emphasized that 'what is particularly important is whether the agreement is capable of constituting a threat, either direct or indirect, actual or potential, to freedom of trade between Member States in a manner which harms the attainment of the objectives of a single market between states'.

[53] Case C-6/72 *Europemballage Corporation and Continental Can Company v Commission* [1973] ECR 215, Paras. 11–12. Accordingly, the Court laid down that 'by prohibiting the abuse of a dominant position within the market insofar as it may affect trade between Member States, Article 86 covers abuse which may directly prejudice consumers as well as abuse which indirectly prejudices them by impairing the effective competitive structure as envisaged by Article 3(f) of the Treaty' (Case C-6/73 *Istituto Chemioterapico Italiano and Commercial Solvents v Commission* [1974] ECR 223, Para. 6). Of more recent case law, see, e.g., Case C-95/04 P *British Airways v Commission* [2007] ECR I-2331, Para. 106: 'as the Court has already held in paragraph 26 of its judgment in *Europemballage and Continental Can*, Article 82 EC is aimed not only at practices which may cause prejudice

restricted to practices which cause direct damage to consumers but covers even practices which are 'detrimental to them through their impact on an effective competition structure'. Hence, a merger may amount to abuse of dominance if an already dominant undertaking further strengthens its position to an extent which 'substantially fetters competition', leaving in the market only undertakings dependent on the dominant one.[54] However, *Continental Can* left a significant loophole as Art. 86 could only be applied in situations where the buyer already had a dominant position before the merger was consummated. This loophole was closed in 1987 by *Philip Morris*.[55] After *Philip Morris* the Commission could claim that it had the power to block mergers it considered harmful. The exact scope of this power was unclear, and the ensuing uncertainty created the momentum that facilitated adoption of the politically very sensitive Merger Regulation by the Council in 1989.[56]

Another important constitutional issue which has occupied the Court is the definition of economic activities which fall under free movement and competition law. This gained in significance in the late 1980s when the Court embarked on subjecting the service sector to internal market law. It is of particular significance for public services in, for instance, healthcare and social security: that is, core areas of national welfare state regimes. It will be discussed in Chapter 7 in the context of the social constitution.

The pre-Maastricht economic constitution came to be centred around free movement and competition law. The Treaty provisions were accorded formal constitutional significance through ECJ jurisprudence, and the Court elaborated and complemented their substance too. In accordance with the constitutive function of the economic constitution and the Court's

to consumers directly, but also at those which are detrimental to them through their impact on an effective competition structure, such as is mentioned in Article 3(1)(g) EC'. See also Para. 63 of Case C-501/06 P *GlaxoSmithKline Services Unlimited v Commission* [2009] ECR I-9291.

54 *Continental Can*, Para. 12. The standard definition, still applied in recent case law, of 'dominant position' was introduced in 1979 in *Hoffmann-La Roche*. It connotes 'a position of economic strength enjoyed by an undertaking which enables it to prevent effective competition being maintained on the relevant market by affording it the power to behave to an appreciable extent independently of its competitors, its customers and ultimately of consumers' (Case C-85/76 *Hoffmann-La Roche v Commission* [1979] ECR 461, Para. 38). Of recent case law, see Case C-52/09 *TeliaSonera Sverige* [2011] ECR I-527, Para. 23.

55 Joined Cases C-142 and C-156/84 *Reynolds v Commission (Philip Morris)* [1987] ECR 115.

56 Council Regulation (EEC) No. 4064/89 of 21 December 1989 on the control of concentrations between undertakings, [1989] OJ L395/1. See on the background to the Merger Regulation T. Käseberg and A. van Laer (2013), pp. 185–9.

teleological method of interpretation, the Treaty provisions on the objectives, tasks and activities of the Community were vital for the often expansive reading of free movement and competition provisions. In addition, Treaty law relevant for the economic constitution comprised provisions on legislative competences. Both free movement and competition provisions created specific legislative competences. These were complemented by the general Community competence to adopt measures harmonizing national legislation for the purpose of establishing or functioning of the common market (Art. 100 TEEC, now Art. 114 TFEU) or eliminating distortions of conditions of competition therein (Art. 101 TEEC, now Art. 115 TFEU). Finally, if these legislative competences were considered insufficient, recourse could also be had to the flexibility clause in Art. 235 TEEC (now Art. 352 TFEU), which allowed for legislative measures in cases where they were necessary for attaining Community objectives but could not be issued under any other article of the Treaty. In effect, the flexibility clause was invoked as a competence basis for the Merger Regulation.

However, political deadlocks hampered pursuit of Community objectives through secondary legislation and reduced the significance of legislative competences. Obstacles to adoption of secondary legislation enhanced the role of ECJ jurisprudence, in particular in free movement law. The law-making role of the ECJ was facilitated by the interlinked processes of juridical and economic constitutionalization, such as conferral of direct effect on Treaty provisions on free movement. As a result of these developments, the pre-Maastricht economic constitution acquired characteristics which warrant the epithet ‘microeconomic’. Its orientation was microeconomic in the sense that both free movement and competition law aim at securing the conditions of market action for individual economic actors. Through the introduction and expansion of the principle of direct effect, fundamental economic freedoms were transformed into individual rights which private parties could invoke before national courts against the respective Member States. In competition law direct effect complemented the obligations of undertakings with justiciable rights of injured parties.

The shift in law-making from secondary legislation to ECJ jurisprudence and the related processes of juridical and economic constitutionalization had significant implications. As a constitutional court, the ECJ can exercise judicial review with regard to both European and national legislation. Clear emphasis has been on review of national legislation. When the ECJ itself exercises a legislative function, a separate European judicial review is excluded. The only theoretical possibility is *ultra vires* review by national constitutional courts, the practical importance of which is bound to remain limited (although, as we saw in Chapter 3, in *Honeywell* the German Constitutional Court recalled this possibility). Moreover, the Court has employed considerably laxer criteria in its review of European than national legislation and has only exceptionally struck down a piece of secondary legislation on *ultra vires* grounds.[57]

The enhanced role of the ECJ in implementing and elaborating the economic constitution provides an institutional explanation for the preponderance of negative over positive integration, as well as for the importance of mutual recognition for overcoming the detrimental consequences of Member State legal diversity. The Court can contribute to removing national obstacles to free movement, but its possibility to promote positive integration is limited. Mutual recognition, one of the important constitutional innovations of the Court, is an alternative to harmonization and positive integration in dealing with legal diversity.

Underlying controversies

In line with 'surface-level' constitutional law in general, Treaty provisions and ECJ jurisprudence in the field of the economic constitution should be read in the light of the underlying theoretical assumptions. Reconstructing the constitutional theory supporting the European microeconomic constitution is not an easy task. The vacillations of constitutional doctrine, in particular in free movement law, reflect contradictory views on its theoretical underpinnings. Due to the Court's less prominent contribution, theoretical controversies in competition law are discernible, not so much in ECJ jurisprudence, but rather in Commission enforcement policy and in the understanding of the role and direction of competition policy in general.

With the experiences from the European Coal and Steel Community (ECSC) fresh in mind, many ordoliberals, perhaps even the majority of them, were sceptical of further European economic integration, fearing

[57] The celebrated case is from the post-Maastricht period, *Tobacco Advertising* of 2000, where the Court annulled the directive and articulated the formula for defining the limits of harmonizing legislative competence (Art. 100 TEC, now Art. 114 TFEU). The Court stated that 'a measure adopted on the basis of Article 100a of the Treaty must genuinely have as its object the improvement of the conditions for the establishment and functioning of the internal market' (Case C-376/98 *Germany v Parliament and Council (Tobacco Advertising)* [2000] ECR I-8419, Para. 84). See S. Weatherill (2011) and J. Snell (2014), pp. 316–21.

strengthened bureaucratic *dirigisme*. The Treaty of Rome left many issues open and facilitated diverging interpretations. The success that ordoliberals achieved in influencing implementation of competition law in particular made them change their views. In Germany they sensed a constant danger of the state being imprisoned by the pluralism of rent-seeking particular interests. Now, eyes were turned towards Europe: perhaps the *ordo* that a competition-based market economy required was attainable in the transnational echelon.[58] In their eagerness to present the Treaty of Rome in terms of an economic constitution, ordoliberals were not deterred by the setback inflicted on them at state level when the Constitutional Court had refused to read an economic *Gesamtentscheidung* into the *Grundgesetz*. Ernst-Joachim Mestmäcker argued that, in contrast to the *Grundgesetz*, the Constitution of the Community has the economy as its direct object and that postulating a corresponding principle of neutrality for the Community would amount to rejecting the very legal content of the Treaty.[59] According to the ordoliberal reading, the Treaty of Rome manifested a *Gesamtentscheidung*, a fundamental decision, in favour of the ordoliberal model of the market economy emphasizing free, performance-based competition.

However, much in the Treaty of Rome and its *travaux préparatoires* contradicts the ordoliberal interpretation and manifests neutrality with regard to models of the economy, albeit with one important exception. In the 1950s, Soviet-type socialist planning economy was still a viable political and economic option, supported by strong communist parties, above all in France and Italy. Competition provisions in particular made it difficult, if not impossible, to reconcile the Treaty with centralized socialist planning economy.[60] Accordingly, all the parties to the controversies over the constitutional theory of the economic constitution shared common microeconomic grounds concerning market behaviour and the market as the basis of the economy. In contrast, the Treaty did not appear to prioritize a particular model of market economy or a particular

[58] Support for European economic integration among neoliberals was far from unanimous. Especially in the initial phase of the ECSC and the first years of the EEC, some neoliberals feared that European integration would entail market-distorting *dirigisme* and bureaucratic interventionism. M. Wegmann (2008).

[59] E.-J. Mestmäcker (2003), pp. 512–13.

[60] In one phase of the preparations, the drafters appeared to include even the option of a socialist economy. The provision which in the Final Treaty became Art. 222 employed the Marxist term of ownership of the means of production: 'Le présent Traité ne préjuge en rien le régime de propriété des moyens de production existant dans la Communauté.' B. Akkermans and E. Ramaekers (2010), p. 300.

variety of capitalism. Both free movement and competition law made ample room for exemptions: Art. 37 TEEC left a space for state monopolies; Art. 90(2) allowed for derogations from competition law for 'undertakings entrusted with the operation of services of general economic interest'; Art. 222 declared that the Treaty 'shall in no way prejudice the rules in Member States governing the system of property ownership'; and competition policy was not the only policy the Community was supposed to pursue.[61]

Disagreements on the underlying constitutional theory are not so much about the microeconomic basis but, rather, about the nature and degree of public interventionism; about the respective organizing tasks of the market and centralized European or decentralized national public intervention. The crucial question is whether the constitutive function of the economic constitution focuses on establishing a common market through a merger of national markets or whether it also presupposes, as ordoliberals claim, a particular model of market economy at both Member State and European levels. In free movement law, the issue is whether the fundamental freedoms aim at (merely) removing cross-border barriers between Member States or imposing a market liberal economic model. With regard to free movement of goods as the 'spearhead' freedom, AG Tesauro's formulation has become a classic: 'Is Article 30 [now Art. 34 TFEU] a provision intended to liberalise intra-Community trade or is it intended more generally to encourage the unhindered pursuit of commerce in individual Member States?'[62] In legal scholarship, Miguel Poiares Maduro has articulated the alternatives as an anti-protectionist or anti-discriminatory and an economic due process approach.[63]

Vacillations in free movement case law reflect the fact that the Court has never taken a clear position on this decisive issue; some rulings are closer to one interpretation, some to the other. The basic controversy determines

[61] See on the 'neutrality' and compromise character of the Treaty of Rome W. Sauter (1998), an article largely written as a rebuttal of the ordoliberal position, as presented in M. E. Streit and W. Müssler (1995). It may, however, be questioned whether the Court still adheres to a neutral position vis-à-vis public ownership. See for a recent ruling on Art. 345 TFEU (previous Art. 222 TEEC) Joined Cases C-105 and C-107/12 *Essent and Others*, judgment of 22 October 2013 (not yet reported).

[62] AG Tesauro in Case C-293/92 *Ruth Hünermund and Others v Landesapothekerkammer Baden-Württemberg* [1993] ECR I-6787, Para. 1.

[63] M. Poiares Maduro (1998). Correspondingly, for Jukka Snell the question is whether free movement law is about discrimination and anti-protectionism or economic freedom. J. Snell (2003).

the frontline which separates ordoliberal or other market liberal readings of the economic constitution from positions which allow for European or Member State interventionism. The primary choice implies divergent views on the extent to which organization of the market should be left to self-regulation and how much space should be accorded to decentralized, Member State, or centralized, European, regulatory intervention. By the same token, the choice also implies how one conceives of the economic rights which directly effective provisions on fundamental freedoms create for individual economic actors: are they rights to access to the markets of other Member States or are they rights to be free from unnecessary public regulation? It can, of course, be questioned whether the Court or its Advocates General have made the theoretical implications clear to themselves in individual cases. But it is evident that the explicit or implicit choice between the basic options has a potential influence on all three phases in free movement reasoning: the import that the trans-border element and protectionist or discriminatory effects are accorded in defining restrictions on freedoms; the scope of legitimate Member State justifications for derogations; and the respective weight bestowed in the proportionality test on the costs of restrictions and the benefits of justificatory grounds.

Different positions in the fundamental controversy lead to different interpretations of the very concepts of market and competition, as used in the Treaty. They also entail divergent views on the role of competition law and its relation to the establishment and functioning of the common (or single) market. Ordoliberals, as the market liberal strand with the most articulated theory of the European economic constitution, were eager to relate market terminology not only to a common market and integration of national markets but to their conception of a free market economy as well. Still, in effect, the principle of an open market economy with free competition, so dear to ordoliberals, was explicitly introduced only in the Maastricht Treaty, which ordoliberals otherwise, because of the additional non-economic objectives and increased policy competences, considered a defeat.[64] If market terminology can give rise to divergent readings, the same is true of the concept of undistorted competition employed in the

64 According to C. Joerges (2004), p. 20, Maastricht turned ordoliberals into an oppositional movement. The Spaak Report (1956), p. 16, made an explicit distinction between common and free markets by pointing out that a common market is not always equivalent to an entirely free market; public interest, as is the case with services, or the nature of production or the market, as is the case with certain agricultural products, may require regulation or establishment of an organization.

Treaty. Here ordoliberals' emphasis is on the level of individual undertakings and on performance-based competition. But another interpretation, corresponding to French positions in the Treaty negotiations and again stressing the trans-border element, is plausible as well. This interpretation aims at creating equal national conditions for competition and thus levelling the playing field for national industries. Evidently, the microeconomic emphasis is more justified in the context of competition law and the harmonizing orientation in the context of policy competences.

Even market liberals acknowledge that markets, including the European internal market, need rules for their constitution, maintenance and functioning. Participants in European discourse on the economic constitution agree that the self-regulatory capacity of the markets has its limits, although they disagree on where, exactly, these limits go. Ordoliberals, for instance, consider indirect framework regulation and interventionism as necessary and desirable for the purpose of constructing and maintaining the market, but condemn direct regulation and interventionism for the purpose of correcting the market.[65] Assuming a basic consensus on the need for rules, the question, then, is who should be charged with issuing them. Jukka Snell has distinguished between three main alternatives: the host country model, the harmonized model and the home country model. In the *host country model*, the responsibility falls on the country where the economic activity takes place. The *harmonized model* relies on centralized European rule-making. Finally, in the third, *home country* model, the rules of the country of origin apply: the rules of the state where a product has been produced or a worker or service provider obtained qualifications. With regard to the basic controversy, the host country model facilitates decentralized regulation and the harmonized model centralized regulation, while the home country model implies the principle of mutual recognition and tends to lead to regulative competition, with the potential consequence of a general reduction of public regulation. Snell discerns in the original common market programme of the Treaty of Rome a propensity for the harmonized model; indeed, this accords with the idea of levelling the playing field and ensuring equal competition conditions in the Member States. However, pursuing Snell's account, the political obstacles to issuance of harmonizing secondary

[65] See M. E. Streit and W. Müssler (1995), pp. 11–13, where a distinction is made between integration by framework activities and integration by intervention, as well as between integration from below and integration from above.

legislation led to a shift to the home country model and its principle of mutual recognition, as canonized in *Cassis de Dijon*. Subsequently, mutual recognition was incorporated into the single market programme of the 1980s.

The position favouring or at least allowing for public interventionism has two variants: one decentralized, the other centralized. Because of its limited capability to contribute to positive integration, the ECJ, however, seems to be left with only two alternatives: decentralized regulation, related to the host country model, and the more market-oriented and competitive approach, related to the home country model. But, of course, even while principally embracing the host country model, the Court can still pursue a market liberal line through an extensive interpretation of restrictions and an emphasis on free movement costs in the proportionality test. With this qualification, Snell's models can be compared to Poiares Maduro's three constitutional theories of the European economic constitution.

These theories involve divergent conceptions of the division of labour between the organizing powers of the market, the Member States and the EC/EU. The *competition model* corresponds to ordoliberal – and other market liberal – views. It trusts the organizing power of the market and mistrusts both national and transnational regulatory powers; it espouses constitutionalization of negative integration, establishing the internal market, and regulatory competition among the Member States.[66] In the interpretation of free movement law, it prioritizes economic due process over anti-protectionist reading. The *centralized theory* reacts to the erosion of Member State regulatory powers, resulting from negative integration, by increasing Community competences. Deregulation at national level is to be compensated through (re-)regulation at European level. The *decentralized theory* stresses the need for market-correcting interventions too, but, mainly for reasons of democracy and legitimacy, advocates the primacy of national regulatory powers. In application of free movement law, it embraces a narrow, anti-protectionist reading of the judicial review of national measures exercised by the ECJ and, under its guidance, national courts.

The Court can adhere to the competition model through an economic due process and to the decentralized model through an anti-protectionist

66 M. E. Streit and W. Müssler (1995) have expressed their preference for the competitive over the centralized model in terms of a choice between integration from below and integration from above.

interpretation of free movement law. But because of the Court's limited possibilities to promote positive integration, the centralized model of positive integration clearly requires measures by the Community legislator. Accordingly, Poiares Maduro concurs with the observation of, inter alia, Fritz Scharpf, that ECJ jurisprudence has primarily aimed at and resulted in furthering negative integration.[67] Still, Poiares Maduro denies that the Court has followed a conscious market liberal agenda, more or less corresponding to the competition model. He conceives of free movement case law in terms of *European majoritarianism* (which appears to correspond to his own normative position, as well): Member State regulatory measures are struck down if they run against a majority view among Member States. At the state level, the standard justification for constitutional review invokes protecting minorities against a potentially oppressive majority. The majoritarian reading of free movement jurisprudence reverses the constellation: European majoritarian policies are allegedly protected against dissenting Member State minority views. Thus, on this reading, ECJ case law promoting negative integration and imposing a European majority position compensates for lack of harmonization through secondary legislation.[68]

European majoritarianism could be seen as a fourth alternative for the constitutional theory of the European economic constitution and, by the same token, as an effort to avoid taking a stand on the basic controversy between anti-protectionism and market liberalism. Yet it is doubtful whether the issue can be circumvented. The basic controversy tends to resurface within the majoritarian position, which can be employed to defend both the anti-protectionist and market liberalist position. The same goes for the market access approach, which has been presented as a third-way option as well. In accordance with the basic alternatives, 'market access' can be understood in two senses: either as access to the national markets of other Member States or as access to the market in general.

Two conclusions can be drawn from the preceding observations. Firstly, doctrinal developments and contributions by various participants in the discourse on the European economic constitution – such as the ECJ, Advocates General and EU law scholars – are always, consciously or unconsciously, explicitly or implicitly, influenced by ideas relating to the underlying constitutional theory. But, secondly and equally importantly, this

[67] F. W. Scharpf (1999 and 2010). [68] M. Poiares Maduro (1998).

constitutional theory has been – and still is – a matter of contestation. Poiares Maduro's observation from 1998 of a continuing dialogue between diverse constitutional theories is still valid.

The above discussion on constitutional theory of the European economic constitution has mainly focused on free movement law. Again, competition law shows particularities which merit a separate examination.

In line with free movement law, the role and orientation of competition law and policy has been afflicted by a fundamental controversy. However, this controversy has left ECJ case law largely untouched.[69] Instead, the opposing positions must be reconstructed from debates on competition policy, for which the Commission is responsible within the margin of discretion granted by the Court. The formal constitutionalization of the competition provisions of the Treaty of Rome, in particular Art. 85 on cartels and Art. 86 on abuse of dominance, can in itself be considered a victory for ordoliberals. All the central features of formal constitutionalization concurred with ordoliberal views: direct applicability by both the Commission and national authorities, and also in terms of obligations of undertakings; direct effect and justiciable rights of competitors and other injured parties; and supremacy of European provisions over national competition law. Substantive constitutionalization too was by and large in harmony with ordoliberal predilections. This holds not only for the extension of competition law to mergers but also for key doctrinal concepts in ECJ jurisprudence, such as 'effective competition structure', and definition of the edge of competition law as protecting competition 'as such' rather than solely as pursuing effects of economic efficiency or prevention of consumer harm.[70] Over the decades, the Court has consistently warranted its interpretations with reference to 'the institution of a system ensuring that competition in the common market is not distorted' with which Art. 3(f) TEEC charged the Community. On a French initiative, the Lisbon Treaty transferred the objective of undistorted competition

[69] However, see Case C-209/10 *Post Danmark*, judgment of 27 March 2012 (not yet reported), where some observers have seen signs of acceptance of the 'more economic' position. E. Rousseva and M. Marquis (2012).

[70] Thus, in 2009 in *T-Mobile Netherlands*, the Court declared that 'Article 81 EC, like the other competition rules of the Treaty, is designed to protect not only the immediate interests of individual competitors or consumers but also to protect the structure of the market and thus competition as such' (Case C-8/08 *T-Mobile Netherlands and Others* [2009] ECR I-4529, Para. 38).

from the Treaty into a Protocol.[71] Still, this has not entailed any change in the Court's argument, proving the post-Lisbon anxiety of ordoliberally oriented scholars unfounded at least in this respect.[72]

Where ordoliberals have not fully succeeded in incorporating their views in the by-now canonical ECJ jurisprudence is in competition law's relation to the common (single) market objective. For ordoliberals, competition law is the most important branch of the microeconomic constitution. Protection of competition is an end in itself: it is expected to guarantee economic freedom, which not only constitutes the basis of the economy but relates it to the foundational moral principles of liberty and equality. As is the case with the market liberal view of free movement law, this leads to a relative downgrading of the significance of the trans-border element. However, this prioritization was difficult to reconcile with the Treaty of Rome and its *travaux préparatoires*. The Treaty clearly set establishing a common market as a primary task for the Community and saw 'the institution of a system ensuring that competition in the common market is not distorted' as a means of realizing that task.[73] The trans-border requirement was enshrined in Arts. 85 and 86 TEEC as explicitly as in free movement provisions.[74] Moreover, as ECJ case law has confirmed, this element is crucial for drawing the boundary between the scope of application of European and national competition law.

71 The Protocol on the internal market and competition states, inter alia, that 'the internal market as set out in Article 2 of the Treaty on European Union includes a system ensuring that competition is not distorted'.

72 For instance in *TeliaSonera*, the Court agued that 'Article 3(3) TEU states that the European Union is to establish an internal market, which, in accordance with Protocol No 27 on the internal market and competition, annexed to the Treaty of Lisbon (OJ 2010 C 83, p. 309), is to include a system ensuring that competition is not distorted' and that 'Article 102 TFEU is one of the competition rules referred to in Article 3(1)(b) TFEU which are necessary for the functioning of that internal market' (Case C-52/09 *TeliaSonera Sverige* [2011] ECR I-527, Paras. 20–1). On ordoliberal concerns, see, e.g., J.-M. Luczak (2009), pp. 382 ff., and J. Drexl (2010), pp. 693–8.

73 Art. 2 defined the task of the Community as follows: 'The Community shall have as its task, by establishing a common market and progressively approximating the economic policies of Member States, to promote throughout the Community a harmonious development of economic activities, a continuous and balanced expansion, an increase in stability, an accelerated raising of the standard of living and closer relations between the States belonging to it.' In turn, Art. 3 listed the activities which the Community should include for the purposes set out in Art. 2. These activities comprised 'the institution of a system ensuring that competition in the common market is not distorted' (Art. 3(g)).

74 The same was true of state aid. Art. 92 TEEC prohibited state aid with actual or potential competition-distorting consequences only if it affected trade between Member States.

The subjection of competition law to the task of establishing the common market was also evident in the Spaak Report, which is the main source of the economic ideas inspiring the Treaty. The Spaak Report argued for merging separate national markets into a common market in order to increase division of work, achieve economic efficiency through economies of scale and enhance the competitiveness of European industries. Distortion of competition had to be dealt with, whether it derived from undertaking behaviour, state aid or legislative diversity among the Member States. Cartels and abuse of dominance had to be prohibited, not for the sake of economic freedom as such, but for the sake of preventing a re-partitioning of the markets which had been opened by free movement law and dismantling of state barriers to cross-border economic activities.[75] This would be – and still is – a standard justification for competition law measures in ECJ jurisprudence, from *Consten and Grundig* onwards.[76]

Two alternative ways exist to achieve theoretical coherence between the two main branches of the European microeconomic constitution: either free movement law is subordinated to competition law or competition law to free movement law and the task of establishing a common market. The former alternative, embraced by ordoliberals, presupposes reading free movement provisions through the general idea of economic freedom, protected against both public and private power. In turn, the latter alternative implies stressing the trans-border element in both free movement and competition law, and deriving the aims of competition law from the task of establishing and maintaining a common (single) market. Evidently, this alternative was more in congruence with the text and *travaux préparatoires* of the Treaty of Rome.

Still, ordoliberals were by and large successful in imposing their views on pre-Maastricht case law; on both the formal and substantive constitutionalization of competition law. This success is conspicuously reflected

[75] Spaak Report (1956), pp. 16–17.

[76] In 2009, *GlaxoSmithKline* reaffirmed the position of *Consten and Grundig* as follows: 'The Court has . . . held, in relation to the application of Article 81 EC and in a case involving the pharmaceuticals sector, that an agreement between producer and distributor which might tend to restore the national divisions in trade between Member States might be such as to frustrate the Treaty's objective of achieving the integration of national markets through the establishment of a single market. Thus on a number of occasions the Court has held agreements aimed at partitioning national markets according to national borders or making the interpenetration of national markets more difficult, in particular those aimed at preventing or restricting parallel exports, to be agreements whose object is to restrict competition within the meaning of that article of the Treaty.' Case C-501/06 P *GlaxoSmithKline Services Unlimited v Commission* [2009] ECR I-9291, Para. 61.

in the congratulatory tone of retrospective appraisals of ordoliberally oriented scholars, such as Ernst-Joachim Mestmäcker, Heike Schweitzer and Josef Drexl.[77] Again it would be overly hasty to conclude that the Court in its jurisprudence or the Council in adopting Regulation 17/62 would have consciously adopted an ordoliberal position.[78] It might be that ordoliberals simply had a temporal and substantive edge over alternative doctrinal and theoretical understandings of European competition law: no rival theory of a similar level of sophistication existed. Controversies there were, but they did not leave their trace in ECJ jurisprudence; rather, they are manifest in the debates on competition policy which the Commission was expected to pursue.

The Treaty depicted implementation of competition law at EEC level as a gradual process. Furthermore, as has already become clear, the Court acknowledged the priority of Commission enforcement and accorded the Commission extensive leeway in interpreting and applying primary and secondary law. Ordoliberals saw – and still tend to see – competition policy as a non-discretional *Ordnungspolitik*, articulating the policy-level conclusions deriving from the constitutional *Gesamtentscheidung* for an open market economy with free competition. This entailed a constitutional primacy of competition policy as *Ordnungspolitik* over other policy fields, which were expected to succumb to the limitations warranted by the superior policy field. Even at the European level, competition policy was not to be a policy field among others but *primus inter pares*. Only in this way could a bulwark be constructed against the influence of corporatist rent-seeking interests on European policies. A doctrinal way to cement the privileged position of competition policy would have been to declare other European policies to be bound by the ordoliberally specified principle of undistorted competition and thus to extend the 'publicization of competition law' from national to European policy. Indeed, ordoliberals, such as Ernst-Joachim Mestmäcker, have repeatedly emphasized that competition law – as well as free movement law too – restricts not only national but European policy- and law-making too.[79]

In pre-Maastricht debates, the ordoliberal position was questioned by those who wanted to leave more space for interventionist national or European policies; here the analogy to the frontlines in debates on the

[77] E.-J. Mestmäcker (2013); K. K. Patel and H. Schweizer (2013a and b); J. Drexl (2010). See also the overall assessment of D. J. Gerber (1994 and 1998).

[78] Ordoliberals were certainly influential in the drafting process of the Regulation, both in the Commission and in deliberations in the Assembly. See L. F. Pace and K. Seidel (2013).

[79] See E.-J. Mestmäcker (2003), pp. 507 ff.

underlying constitutional theory of free movement law is conspicuous. The opponents of the ordoliberals can perhaps be broadly labelled Keynesians, although this hardly does justice to the variety of individual views.[80] The unifying trait was the attempt to topple competition policy from the privileged position to which ordoliberals wanted to elevate it and to treat it as one policy option among others. The bitterest battles were waged between competition and industrial policy. In particular during the economic recession of the 1970s, national or European industrial policy was often called on to rescue industrial sectors in decline, such as the steel and textile industries, and shipbuilding. A rather widespread support for boosting the competitiveness of European industries by facilitating national or European champions also contributed to delay in implementing state aid provisions. Implementation was started in earnest only in the latter half of the 1980s.[81]

Again, the counter-position questioning the ordoliberal reading could find support in the Treaty and its *travaux préparatoires*. After all, the Treaty did include provisions on, for instance, agricultural, transport and regional policy, and the Spaak Report had laid particular stress on aiding underdeveloped regions.[82] Ordoliberals were also alarmed by new policy provisions in the Treaties: the SEA introduced provisions on research and development and the Maastricht Treaty even on industrial policy, the main threat to ordoliberal competition policy in the preceding decades. The Title on industrial policy, though, included – and still includes – the proviso that it 'shall not provide a basis for the introduction by the Union of any measure which could lead to a distortion of competition' (Art. 157(3) TEC, now Art. 119(3) TFEU).

The ordoliberal reaction to the policy provisions of the SEA and the Treaty of Maastricht was divided. In an article published in the aftermath of Maastricht, Manfred E. Streit and Werner Müssler more or less considered the game to be over. On their judgment, the SEA signified a breakthrough for integration by intervention, and Maastricht only added to the distress by creating for Community institutions 'a considerable number of opportunities . . . to formulate discretionary policies incompatible with the principle of undistorted competition'. Streit and Müssler also observed strengthening corporatist tendencies contradicting the fundamental ordoliberal tenet of a strong *Rechtsstaat*-type state: 'a cartelization

80 Cf. S. M. Ramírez Pérez and S. van der Scheur (2013).

81 See on the controversies around industrial policy T. Käseberg and A. van Laer (2013).

82 Spaak Report (1956), pp. 18–19.

of specific interests cooperating with the national governments (ultimately the Council) and a Commission which is principally interested in gaining more influence'.[83] The authors concluded with the sombre foreboding that European economic integration would not live up to ordoliberal expectations: 'The union is likely to develop corporatist structures quite similar to those of the Member States' and 'transform itself from a community under the law to a rent-seeking community'.[84] By contrast, other ordoliberals have sharpened their scholarly weapons and tried to bring the revisions of the Treaties into harmony with the allegedly unchanged *Gesamtentscheidung* through interpretive means.[85] The methodology dates back to the writings of Franz Böhm: the *Gesamtentscheidung* imposes an interpretive duty with regard not only to lower-order legislation but also to *Verfassungsgesetz* provisions which on their face contradict the *Gesamtentscheidung*.

Paradoxically enough, by Maastricht the general neoliberal ideological turn had altered the parameters of the debate and, before long, entailed a reformulation of the basic controversy on the theoretical underpinnings of competition policy. The ordoliberal position, though, remains more or less unchanged: freedom of competition as an individual right; the central role of clear legal rules the enforcement of which is monitored by the Court; and protection of the competitive structure and competition 'as such'. However, since the 1990s, the main adversary no longer consists of proponents of industrial policy or other rival policy fields. After the

[83] Here the authors allude to Treaty provisions on the Economic and Social Committee, and the Committee of the Regions, as well as the provisions in the Agreement on Social Policy (which was incorporated in the Treaty by the Amsterdam Treaty) on the role of the social partners. M. E. Streit and W. Müssler (1995), p. 27.

[84] *Ibid.*, pp. 26–7. Streit and Müssler read into the Treaty of Rome an economic constitution in the *functional* sense, comprising, according to their definition, 'legal rules which are constitutive for or conducive to a specific type of economic system'. But they also use the term 'economic constitution' in another, *descriptive*, sense, referring to all economy-related provisions at the (formal) constitutional level. *Ibid.*, pp. 5–6. The distinction between the functional and descriptive sense of 'the economic constitution' is a new version of the Schmittian distinction between a 'constitution as a decision' or a 'constitution in the positive sense' and 'constitutional laws'. Apparently, for Streit and Müssler, the distance between the ordoliberal *Gesamtentscheidung* and existing Treaty law as *Verfassungsgesetz* or the functional and descriptive economic constitution had, after Maastricht, grown too wide to be crossed by interpretive means.

[85] This has been the line of argumentation to which, for instance, Ernst-Joachim Mestmäcker has clung in his extensive *oeuvre*. See especially the articles collected in E.-J. Mestmäcker (2003). Other representative examples include J.-M. Luczak (2009) and J. Drexl (2010).

neoliberal turn in the 1980s diminished support for public interventionism, the conflict has moved inside competition policy and implementation of competition law. The adversary is, vaguely enough, termed a *more economic approach*. Rule-, rights- and structure-oriented ordoliberals are often labelled traditionalists who hamper application of contemporary economic analysis in the implementation of competition law and competition policy in general.[86] Ordoliberals do not oppose economic analysis in establishing the relevant facts or providing evidence for infringements. But what they do oppose is redefining the very goals of competition law, and replacing protection of an effective competition structure and competition as such with economic efficiency, welfare maximization or prevention of consumer harm.[87]

Though transferred inside competition law enforcement and competition policy at large, the post-Maastricht argument shares important common features with pre-Maastricht debates. Again, ordoliberals can display a relatively coherent conception and can generally find support in the central concepts and methodological premises of ECJ jurisprudence. By contrast, their opponents are hardly a homogenous group, although the influence of US Chicago School and 'post-Chicago' thinking on antitrust law is evident. However, to a large extent it seems to be the common adversary which unites the economists and competition lawyers gathered together under the umbrella of the more economic approach. They have had a decisive influence in and on the Commission, while the Court has refrained from a clear signal of accepting the new approach and has generally stuck to the canonical pre-Maastricht doctrine. Yet some ordoliberal-minded academics, among them Josef Drexl, have already detected worrying omens of an oncoming change.[88] And, indeed, Treaty provisions on derogations from the competition law obligations of undertakings and Member States provide institutional support for the new opponents of the ordoliberal position, as well. Thus, ever since Rome cartels that 'contribute to improving the production or distribution of goods or to promoting technical or economic progress, while allowing consumers a fair share of the resulting benefit', have been allowed exemption from the general cartel prohibition (Art. 85(3) TEEC, now Art. 101(3) TFEU).

For ordoliberals, the more economic approach also implies a threat of downgrading competition policy from a constitutionally superior *Ordnungspolitik* to the level of other European policies; a threat similar to that raised by the pre-Maastricht interventionist camp. If the main objective of

[86] G. Monti (2013). [87] See K. K. Patel and H. Schweitzer (2013b). [88] J. Drexl (2010).

competition policy is defined as economic efficiency, welfare maximization or consumer benefit, how can it still label itself as *Ordnungspolitik* and claim constitutional priority over (allegedly) more mundane policy fields? How would competition policy differ from, say, consumer policy, one of the policy fields with which the Treaties also charge the Union? Ordoliberal concerns are enhanced by some of the novelties of Regulation 1/2003, replacing Regulation 17/62, which by and large had complied with ordoliberal views. The novelties include direct applicability of the provision on exemptions from the cartel prohibition (now Art. 101(3) TFEU), as well as a 'flight from judicial review', exemplified by Commission commitment decisions and guidelines which are not subject to judicial review.[89]

The European economic constitution and national constitutions

Solid arguments exist for rejecting the ordoliberal idea of an economic-constitutional *Gesamtentscheidung*, guiding and even obliging the interpretation and application of European law and imposing a particular model of economy at both the European and the Member State level. Much speaks for the – at least initial – neutrality of the European economic constitution. Still, this does not entail that the economic constitution should be portrayed merely through surface-level constitutional law: explicit Treaty provisions, complemented by ECJ case law and constitutionally relevant speech acts by other European legal actors. Even while rejecting the idea of a *Gesamtentscheidung*, one should not reduce the economic constitution to its surface-level manifestations and ignore the underpinning theories.[90] Yet the preceding discussion has revealed not only the doctrinal instability of free movement jurisprudence in particular, but also how contentious the underlying constitutional theory is in both free movement and competition law. In both fields the main frontline separates advocates of economic freedom and individual economic rights from proponents of wider leeway for public intervention. Neither party has been able to reap a decisive victory, nor would such an end to debates be a credible prognosis.

[89] 'Flight from judicial review' is an expression used by K. K. Patel and H. Schweitzer (2013b), p. 226. See also H. Schweitzer (2007), which discusses the relationship of competition policy with other policy fields in the light of the (then) future Lisbon Treaty.

[90] Here I disagree with Julio Baquero Cruz, who instead of an economic constitution has preferred to talk about the economic provisions of the constitution or economic constitutional law. He defines economic constitutional law as constitutional rules dealing with the organization, structure and processes of economy and identifies EU constitutional law with 'rules, principles, objectives and policies that are fleshed out in a series of concrete Treaty provisions'. J. Baquero Cruz (2002), p. 29.

It is true, though, that ordoliberals could rejoice in the introduction of justiciable economic rights in both free movement and competition law; recognition of the power-restrictive function of both free movement provisions (national regulatory power) and competition law (private economic power); as well as the general microeconomic orientation of economic constitutionalization. But in the end, successful as these developments were, they did not suffice for an unambiguous imposition of a market liberal competition model. The ongoing process of economic constitutionalization has been, and is most likely to remain, a continuing discourse among rival theoretical positions. This is bound to have implications for surface-level doctrine, as manifested by ECJ jurisprudence and EU law scholarship, as well.

The continuing doctrinal and theoretical volatility of the European economic constitution distinguishes it from the ideal-typical constitution of an established democratic *Rechtsstaat*. Typically, state constitutions enshrine fundamental rights without which economic activities in the marketplace would not be possible, such as the right to property, freedom of contract and freedom of trade. These – and other – fundamental rights constrain state economic legislation and policies. But state constitutions do not usually include guideline provisions on economic objectives, tasks and activities, comparable to Arts. 2 and 3 TEEC or the present Art. 3 TEU and restricting economic policy choices. Nor do they grant particular economic legislative or policy competences to the political branches of the state. In line with other economic legislation, regulation of cross-border trade and competition law too are considered matters of ordinary laws, to be issued through majoritarian legislative procedures.

Exceptions to these standards exist. Federal states such as the United States or Australia, for example, possess constitutional principles that police against undue restrictions on inter-state commerce. Other exceptions may be seen particularly in new states or states experiencing a fundamental regime change: such as European post-socialist states, which have wished to make a clear break with the totalitarian past and enter the path of democracy and market economy. In these states, economic guideline provisions in the formal constitution are a rule rather than an exception. To take a random example, Art. 9(3) of the Moldovan Constitution lays down that 'the national economy is based on the interaction of market forces, also on free economic initiative and fair competition'. Deviations from standard constitutions are due to the enhanced constitutive function of post-socialist constitutions: the constitution is supposed to contribute to constructing a market economy, replacing the socialist system. A pronounced constitutive function, aiming at establishing a common European market, relates the Treaty of Rome and its successors to post-socialist national constitutions. European guideline provisions fulfil a restrictive function as well. In accordance with other instances of transnational law, European law raises claims of authority only within a particular substantively limited area, delineated in the guideline provisions. As the ECJ has repeated from *Van Gend en Loos* onwards, Member States have (self)-restricted their sovereignty in favour of the European level, but only in limited fields.

The trans-border element, linked to the common (single) market objective, is conspicuous in free movement and competition law, which are central means of achieving that objective. But this does not explain why these fields of law had to be constitutionalized and not left to the province of secondary legislation, as is mainly the case at state level. The reason lies in the transnational nature of the Community/Union and in the dual nature of the Treaties as both a constitutional charter and agreements under international law. Member States could only be obligated to comply with provisions on free movement and competition law if these were included in an international treaty. The functional orientation of the Community/Union and its legal system accounts for the need to include in the Treaty explicit provisions on legislative and other policy competences. From the very beginning, the principle of conferral has been an integral element in regulating division of competences between European and national levels: the Community/Union can only exercise competences which the Member States have explicitly conferred upon them through an international treaty. So differences between transnational and national polities and legal systems explain the notable differences in economic *materia constitutionis*. Moreover, the wider scope of European economic constitutional law constitutionalizes issues and controversies of economic theory too. At state level, they have their influence on economic policy and legislation but do not usually possess direct constitutional implications.

A further important difference from state constitutions results from the manner in which the ECJ has pushed through the constitutionalization of free movement and competition law. The Court has derived justiciable economic rights from the Treaty provisions on which it has conferred direct effect. By the same token, it has created a new type of constitutionally protected rights, alongside fundamental rights; these constitutional *economic rights* lack correspondence in Member State constitutions. Part of the framework *ordo* that a market economy needs consists of *fundamental rights*, such as the right to property, freedom of contract and freedom of trade. Franz Böhm stressed the importance of freedom of trade in particular in his early writings and dated the German economic *Gesamtentscheidung* back to the issuance of the liberalizing *Gewerbeordnung* in 1869. The fundamental rights indispensable for the markets merged into the European common market are not guaranteed by the European constitution but by Member State national constitutions; here the former relies on support from the latter. Union fundamental rights law has not altered the situation. EU fundamental rights include freedom to conduct business and the right to property (Arts. 16–17 CFREU). However, Union fundamental rights law is applicable only within the scope of Union law and hence cannot frame European market(s) as a whole.[91]

The characteristics of and mutual relations between economic rights, derived from directly effective free movement and competition law, and fundamental rights, protected at both Member State and Union level, raise important theoretical and doctrinal questions. Franz Böhm's doctoral thesis from 1933, *Wettbewerb und Monopolkampf*, includes an interesting discussion on the different focus of human rights and economic freedoms; a discussion which anticipates the EU law distinction between fundamental rights and economic rights. Böhm argues that human rights protect individual freedom as an end in itself. They provide the individual with an 'autonomous, sovereign sphere of freedom', in which 'the individual... has absolute priority over the needs of the social and the state' and which 'has to be protected against interference by the social and the state even if it were in the interest of the social community and the state to restrict the individual freedom'. By contrast, economic freedoms are not protected for the sake of the individual but 'because of their value for the life of the community'. Their primary purpose is not to create individual spheres of freedom but, rather, to organize an area of cooperation. This is the *herrschaftsfreie* order of social cooperation.[92] Böhm also discusses the relationship between freedom of competition and freedom of contract, though leaving open whether the latter belongs to human rights or economic freedoms. He points out that contractual freedom

91 A similar complementary relation prevails between the European economic constitution and national private law systems. Core areas of market-related private law, such as general contract law, still belong to the province of Member States, while Union legislative activities have mainly focused on what has come to be called regulatory private law.

92 F. Böhm (1933), pp. 153–4.

in its 'power-conferring nature' constitutes a prerequisite for exercising freedom of trade. However, the legal institution of competition involves a power-allocating principle, necessary for a *herrschaftsfreie* order where individuals can profit from private property and contractual freedom. Hence, competition must prevail over contractual freedom and general freedom of action. Contractual freedom finds its limit in the higher-ranking principle of performance-based competition; it cannot justify cartel agreements, which amount to abuse of contractual freedom.[93]

Böhm points to the instrumentality inherent in economic rights: individual subjects are granted rights as a means to achieve a wider social (economic) purpose. Economic rights derived from free movement and competition law possess similar instrumentality: they serve the effective and uniform implementation of the European economic constitution and the realization of its objectives. Justiciable economic rights gave birth to judicial and economic (market) citizenship: the first layers of European citizenship. In contrast, fundamental rights are there for the protection of rights-holders, as guarantees of their private and public autonomy, irrespective of any larger economic, social or policy goals; they provide European individuals with a 'thick' European citizenship.[94]

Due to their market-constituting effects, Member State fundamental rights stand in a supportive relation to the European economic constitution. But this relation can be of a conflictual nature too. The ECJ has acknowledged protection of national fundamental rights as a legitimate justification for national measures restricting free movement and European economic rights. In the proportionality test concluding the Court's three-phase methodology, costs suffered by European economic rights are measured against the benefits that national fundamental rights reap from Member State protection. The question is posed from the

[93] *Ibid.*, pp. 120–1.

[94] As E. Spaventa (2009), p. 357, has also stressed, because of this crucial difference, it is important to maintain a clear terminological distinction between economic and fundamental rights. The fact that some of the economic freedoms derived from free movement law were included in the CFREU has not contributed to conceptual clarity. Art. 15(2) CFREU lays down that 'every citizen of the Union has the freedom to seek employment, to work, to exercise the right of establishment and to provide services in any Member State'. According to the Explanations relating to the Charter of Fundamental Rights, [2007] OJ C303/17, this provision 'deals with the three freedoms guaranteed by Articles 26, 45, 49 and 56 of the Treaty on the Functioning of the European Union, namely freedom of movement for workers, freedom of establishment and freedom to provide services'.

perspective of free movement: what needs justification is not a potential violation of a national fundamental right but a potential limitation of a European economic right. Recalling the instrumentality and policy orientation of economic rights, we can note how the Dworkinian distinction between policies, related to collective societal goals, and principles, related to morally laden individual rights, is reversed: justification is called for principles restricting policies and not policies restricting principles. In the case law of the ECJ, national fundamental rights clashing with European fundamental freedoms have ranged from rights pertaining to private autonomy, such as the right to property (e.g. *Hauer*) and human dignity (*Omega*), to rights guaranteeing public autonomy, such as the rights to assembly and expression (*Schmidberger*). In turn, in *Viking* and *Laval* the perceived damage to European freedom of establishment and free movement of services outweighed free exercise of national social rights.[95]

Implications for the political dimension

The functional primacy of the economic constitution can be seen in all the other constitutional dimensions. Especially in the first decades, juridical and economic constitutionalization were closely interlinked; the need to secure the effective and uniform implementation of free movement and competition law provided the decisive impetus for this intertwined process. In the social dimension, the triumph of the microeconomic constitution has imposed restrictions on both European and national welfare policy, and the opening of internal borders to promote free movement of workers has been a central backdrop to the emergence of a security dimension in European constitutionalism. These developments will be addressed in chapters to come. Here the focus will be on institutional and political implications.

In the political dimension, ordoliberals have advocated a strong state which matches the criteria of a liberal *Rechtsstaat* and does not fall prey to corporatist rent-seeking interests. In such a strong state, legislation consists of general framework rules, which procure the necessary *ordo*

[95] Case C-44/79 *Hauer v Land Rheinland-Pfalz* [1979] ECR 3727; Case C-36/02 *Omega Spielhallen- und Automatenaufstellungs-GmbH* [2004] ECR I-09609; Case C-112/00 *Eugen Schmidberger, Internationale Transporte und Planzüge* [2003] ECR I-05659; Case C-438/05 *International Transport Workers' Federation and Finnish Seamen's Union* [2007] ECR I-10779 (*Viking*); Case C-341/05 *Laval un Partneri* [2007] ECR I-11767.

for a free market economy and performance-based competition, and are enforced by an independent judiciary. A quasi-judicial Competition Authority abiding by the general rules of competition law can well complement judicial supervision. By contrast, discretionary executive powers should be strictly avoided.

The crucial European institutions for elaborating and implementing the microeconomic constitution are the ECJ and the Commission as a Competition Authority. In the absence of a political legislature meeting their criteria, ordoliberals have accepted the ECJ's role as not only enforcing but even as introducing general rules. The original ordoliberal programme not only claimed constitutional superiority for competition law and competition policy as an *Ordnungspolitik* implementing the economic constitution as a *Gesamtentscheidung*; it also called for an independent and strong but, by the same token, rule-bound enforcement authority. Initially, ordoliberals placed great hopes in the Commission where they exercised considerable influence during the Presidency of Walter Hallstein and Hans von der Groeben's mandate as the Competition Commissioner. Still, in the longer run that dominance could not be maintained. The Commission is a hybrid institution: it combines traits of independence of an expert body, representation of Member States and parliamentary responsibility. Its profile of an independent expert body is difficult to reconcile with the other features. Fearing the influence of interventionist policies and corporatist interests, ordoliberals have not nurtured unreserved trust in the ability of the Commission to live up to their expectations. Occasional suggestions for transferring competition law enforcement to a new Competition Authority, independent also from the Commission, have not come as a surprise.

In such an institutional setting, and confining European integration to its economic dimension, ordoliberals have seen no need for democratic input legitimacy; under these conditions, no democratic deficit exists. In the ordoliberal account, the legitimacy of the microeconomic constitution – and, indeed, European integration as a whole – cannot be categorized within the alternatives of input and output legitimacy. Assessing competition law – the central sub-field of the ordoliberal version of the microeconomic constitution – by output legitimacy would entail capitulating before the 'more economic' approach and abandoning rule and rights orientation. Ordoliberals are proponents of what I have called substantive legitimacy: the economic constitution, with its *Gesamtentscheidung* for an open market economy with free competition, is allegedly anchored in the values of freedom and equality, characteristic of the value basis of modern society. Competition theory, as exposed by Poiares Maduro and corresponding to an ordoliberal *Gesamtentscheidung*, implies a negative view of European political constitutionalization aiming at European-level democratic arrangements.

On the other hand, ordoliberals have employed democratic input legitimacy as a determinant of the division of competences between European and national levels. In general, ordoliberals are suspicious of discretionary policies, although some variance exists in their views of the need to complement socially favourable market outcomes with particular social policy measures. The ordoliberal competition model is premised on a belief in the expected welfare-increasing effects of the market economy, but at least in certain of its versions, it is also ready to accept limited market-compensating social measures. This is manifested by the notion of the social market economy, coined by Alfred Müller-Armack for internal German use but finding in Lisbon, rather belatedly, its way to Art. 3(3) TEU.[96] But if social policy there will be, it should not be exercised at the European but at the national level. In line with other discretionary policies, social policy entails a requirement of democratic input legitimacy, and such legitimacy can be found only at the national level. Consequently, social policy should be maintained under Member State sovereignty. The same goes for industrial policy, the traditional bête noire for ordoliberals.[97] The argument is circular: because the EU possesses merely restricted tasks, it does not need democratic legitimacy, and because it does not possess democratic legitimacy, its tasks must remain restricted. One may even doubt the sincerity of the argument. Through the European *ordo*, ordoliberals have wished to limit market-interfering interventionism at not only the European but the national level as well. And, in effect, ordoliberal hopes have not been wholly misplaced, as is proven by the

[96] According to Alfred Müller-Armack, a social market economy is aimed at elevating 'soziale Gerechtigkeit mit und neben der Freiheit zum integrierenden Bestandteil unserer künftigen Wirtschaftsordnung' and at combining 'das Prinzip der Freiheit auf den Markt mit dem des sozialen Ausgleichs'. M. Wegmann (2002), p. 75. But the objective of a social market economy has always entertained a rather uneasy relation with the basic tenets of ordoliberalism, and a widespread view among ordoliberals seems to have been that at the national level, too far-reaching concessions in the social direction were being made. This view is related to the perception of a constant danger of the state being imprisoned by the pluralism of rent-seeking particular interests. For a sceptical assessment of the transfer of Müller-Armack's notion to the European level, see C. Joerges and F. Rödl (2004). See also G. Monti (2013), who points out that two ordoliberal readings of 'social market economy' exist.

[97] See, e.g., E.-J, Mestmäcker (2003), pp. 517–18. See also the summary of the ordoliberal position in W. Sauter (1998), p. 57.

microeconomic turn of the economic constitution, accompanied by successful negative integration through ECJ case law and the *Ordnungspolitik* of the Commission.

As Poiares Maduro and Snell have indicated, all the alternative constitutional theories of the microeconomic constitution have important implications in the institutional and political dimension. Competition theory, propounded by ordoliberals and more or less corresponding to Snell's home country model, tends to lead to a *gouvernement des juges* (or *des experts*), justified by claims to substantive legitimacy (ordoliberals) or output-based expert legitimacy. In free movement law, the competition or home country model is prone to adopt an extensive interpretation of restrictions on free movement and downplay the importance of the transborder element. It tends to open a wide space for judicial second-guessing of democratically adopted Member State legislation, and to enhance the position of both European and national judges at the expense of national legislatures.

The decentralized theory of the European microeconomic constitution – Snell's host country model – allows for Member State interventionism, respects national democratic mechanisms and limits the expansion of judicial power. Of the three alternatives the centralized or harmonized theory is most concerned about European democratic deficit. This is the case especially with those versions of centralized theory which leave room for European interventionism transcending market construction and maintenance. It is no coincidence, then, that in Maastricht increased European competencies were accompanied by efforts to strengthen European democratic input legitimacy. However, the European project has also been theorized in terms of an apolitical regulatory state which primarily claims output legitimacy, to be guaranteed by economic or other technocratic expertise. In line with the ordoliberal position, this theory too is suspicious of the EU adopting discretionary objectives and tasks which presuppose direct democratic legitimacy, impossible to attain at the European level.[98]

Art. 114 TFEU (previous Art. 100 TEEC) is the central competence basis for harmonizing European legislation. This article has preserved the requirement that harmonizing measures should serve the establishment or functioning of the internal market. In its *Tobacco Advertising* case law, the ECJ has confirmed the continuing validity of this requirement. As Gareth Davies has noted, purposive competences, such as the one created by

[98] G. Majone (2009 and 2014).

Art. 114 TFEU, constrain democratic choice of legislative purposes and tend to lead to technocratic predominance in law drafting. Although references to non-economic interests have been added to Art. 114,[99] their leeway is restricted by the need for an internal market connection. Thus, drafting secondary legislation tends to reproduce the asymmetry afflicting free movement jurisprudence: non-economic interests are treated as derogations from economic ones.[100] These are important observations. However, as long as the EU remains a transnational polity and legal system with a functionally limited claim of authority, purposive competences are there to stay; only the establishment of a federal state would abolish them. But even in a transnational polity it is vital to keep a vigilant eye on the legitimate reach of expert knowledge. Examining in the next chapter the constitutional implications of the Eurozone crisis will give me an opportunity to resume discussing this issue.

99 According to Art. 114(3) TFEU, 'the Commission, in its proposals envisaged in paragraph 1 concerning health, safety, environmental protection and consumer protection, will take as a base a high level of protection, taking account in particular of any new development based on scientific facts. Within their respective powers, the European Parliament and the Council will also seek to achieve this objective.' Interestingly enough, by invoking scientific facts the provision seems to seek to confer a technocratic label on legislation promoting non-economic interests as well; expert knowledge is to occupy a prominent position here, too.

100 G. Davies (2013a).

6 Mutation of the macroeconomic constitution

The Maastricht Treaty launched a process of macroeconomic constitutionalization. The Eurozone crisis, which erupted in spring 2010 or – if we include the preceding financial crisis – in late 2008, proved that in crucial respects the principles agreed on in Maastricht were based on assumptions which did not stand the test of reality. The crisis produced a significant constitutional mutation, the impacts of which have not been confined to the macroeconomic constitution but have encompassed other constitutional dimensions as well.[1]

From Rome to Maastricht

The economic constitution which emerged from the Treaty of Rome and the subsequent constitutional speech acts by European institutions, such as the ECJ as the constitutional court, received a clear microeconomic emphasis, centred as it was around free movement and competition law. Yet the Treaty included provisions on macroeconomic policy as well, and in the Spaak Report macroeconomic objectives occupied a prominent place. However, monetary and economic policy remained under Member State sovereignty, and as the Treaty provisions were not backed up by legal competences, procedures or sanctions, they had mostly a soft-law character. This considerably weakened their practical significance. The provisions were largely a compromise between ordoliberally oriented German and more *dirigiste* French views.

In ordoliberal thinking, price stability is essential for an open market economy with free competition; only a stable price mechanism is

[1] In this chapter, I have been able to draw on the constitutional analysis of Kaarlo Tuori and Klaus Tuori (2014).

capable of accomplishing its informational and incentive functions that provide for rational and efficient allocation of resources under decentralized decision-making by households and companies. In his *Grundsätze der Wirtschaftspolitik*, Walter Eucken – the leading ordoliberal economist – elevated a functioning price system to an essential criterion of all measures of economic policy and, by the same token, to the basic principle of economic constitutional law. Furthermore, primacy of monetary policy headed his list of the constitutive principles of an economic system based on competition.[2] Indeed, price stability, along with equilibrium of overall balance of payments and maintenance of confidence in the currency, was expressly mentioned in Art. 104(1) of the Rome Treaty as an aim for Member State economic policy. But exchange-rate and monetary policy objectives were not the only aims the Treaty expected Member States to heed. As a concession to *dirigiste* views, primarily advocated by French negotiators, ensuring a high level of employment was mentioned as well, and even conjunctural policy was explicitly evoked.[3]

Within the microeconomic field, a central task of European law and a central impetus for the intertwined process of juridical and economic constitutionalization lies in overcoming Member State legal diversity or at least combating its detrimental effects. In the macroeconomic field, a central issue consists in overcoming Member State policy diversity. The Spaak Report called for a convergence of efforts to maintain monetary stability, a high level of employment and economic activity.[4] As a token of the importance laid on such convergence, Art. 2 TEEC placed progressive approximation of Member State economic policies alongside establishment of the common market as a means to achieve overarching Community objectives. In turn, Art. 3 laid down that the activities of the Community included 'the application of procedures by which the economic policies of Member States can be coordinated and disequilibria in their balances of payments remedied'. Furthermore, Art. 6(1) provided that 'Member States shall, in close cooperation with the institutions of the Community, coordinate their respective economic policies to the extent necessary to attain the objectives of this Treaty.' This obligation was

2 W. Eucken (1952), pp. 254–5.

3 According to Art. 103(1), Member States were supposed to regard their conjunctural policies as a matter of common concern, and to consult each other and the Commission on measures to be taken in the light of the prevailing circumstances. The Common Agricultural Policy was, of course, the most conspicuous example in the Treaty of the influence of (French) *dirigiste* views.

4 Spaak Report (1956), p. 23.

reiterated in the Title on Economic Policy. Still, no effective means of ensuring coordination were created.[5]

The most far-going Community competences concerned Member State exchange-rate policy and balance of payments. Art. 107(2) TEEC granted the Commission power to react and to authorize the other Member States to take necessary countermeasures in case a Member State altered its exchange rate inconsistently with the objectives set out in Art. 104 and thus seriously distorting conditions of competition. Where a Member State was in difficulty with regard to its balance of payments, or was seriously threatened with such difficulties and these were liable to jeopardize the functioning of the common market or progressive implementation of the common commercial policy, available Community measures comprised granting mutual assistance. Art. 108 TEEC, providing for such assistance, is a predecessor to present Art. 143 TFEU, which allows for assistance to non-euro Member States facing difficulties in their balance of payments.[6]

In pursuing monetary and exchange-rate objectives, Member States benefited from the Bretton Woods system, which mostly managed to support national efforts to keep inflation low and to prevent dramatic exchange-rate fluctuations. In the late 1960s, when the Bretton Woods system showed the first signs of decline, an effort was made to realize the policy convergence called for by the opening provisions of the Treaty by establishing an economic and monetary union. However, no serious effort was ever made to implement the proposals which the Werner Group put forth in 1970.[7] On the road from Rome to Maastricht the major results in

[5] Art. 103(2) did, though, give the Council the power to issue, on the proposal of the Commission, directives in case a Member State did not respect the obligation to consider its conjunctural policy as a common concern. However, no provision for possible sanctions was included. In turn, Art. 105(2) established a Monetary Committee with advisory status 'in order to promote co-ordination of the policies of Member States in the monetary field to the full extent needed for the functioning of the common market'. It was supposed 'to keep under review the monetary and financial situation of the Member States and of the Community and the general payments system of the Member States and to report regularly thereon to the Council and to the Commission'. In addition, it was expected to deliver opinions to the Council and the Commission at the request of these institutions or on its own initiative. The Member States and the Commission each appointed two members of the Committee.

[6] Unilateral protective measures were also allowed, either as a precaution or, on the Commission's authorization, where the Council had not granted mutual assistance or where this had proven insufficient.

[7] Werner Committee, 'Report to the Council and the Commission on the realization by stages of economic and monetary union in the Community', 8 October 1970.

coordinating Member State policies were achieved in exchange-rate policy as a European continuation of Bretton Woods, although the European Monetary System (EMS) was not able to prevent the currency crisis which hit several Member States in 1992–3.[8]

After approval of the Single European Act in 1986 and adoption of the objective of realizing the single market before the end of 1992, discussion on economic and monetary union resumed. In congruence with the Werner Group, the Delors Committee argued for economic and monetary union starting from the implications and needs of the microeconomic constitution; economic and monetary union would complement the single market and address its consequences, such as the growing interdependence of national economies.[9] Yet, in the end, EMU was established as a central part of the Maastricht package, whose aim was to further political rather than economic integration. In a somewhat paradoxical way, economic and monetary union was subordinated to political objectives but its implications in the dimension of a political union were more modest than the Werner Group, in particular, would have preferred.

In line with the gradual establishment of the common market under the Treaty of Rome, the Maastricht Treaty conceived of the launch of EMU as a stepwise process; the Treaty provisions would be implemented in three phases. However, not only implementation but the macroeconomic constitution itself must be approached as a process. Constitutionalization began but did not end in Maastricht. Maastricht was the moment of the European constitutional legislature; subsequently, other European institutions have contributed to constitutional development. Before the acceleration of constitutional mutation during the Eurozone crisis, the main constitutionally significant speech acts were the Stability and Growth Pact (SGP), concluded in 1997 in anticipation of the approaching third stage in implementing EMU, as well as the ECJ ruling in 2004, *Commission*

[8] The EMS was established in December 1978 and subsequently complemented by the introduction of the Exchange Rate Mechanism (ERM) and the European Currency Unit (ECU). Resolution of the European Council of 5 December 1978 on the establishment of the European Monetary System (EMS) and related matters, Compendium 1979, p. 42; Council Regulation No. 3181/78 of 18 December 1978 relating to the European Monetary System, [1978] OJ L379/2; and Council Decision No. 78/1041 of 21 December 1978 amending Decision 71/143/EEC setting up machinery for medium-term financial assistance, [1978] OJ L379/3.

[9] Committee for the Study of Economic and Monetary Union, 'Report on an economic and monetary union in the European Community', 17 April 1989.

v Council, which dealt with the sanctions regime of the excessive deficit procedure,[10] a central element of the SGP.

Because of their different focus, the criteria for constitutionalization must differ between the macroeconomic and microeconomic dimensions. The macroeconomic constitution is not about economic action by individual economic actors but about macroeconomic policies and policy objectives, European competences and Member State obligations, as well as procedures where European competences are employed and Member State obligations monitored. Within the macroeconomic field, state obligations cannot be transformed into individual rights, and constitutionalization criteria such as direct effect are not applicable. The decisive criterion must be sought in growing Europeanization, in transfer of competences to the European level and a corresponding reduction of Member State sovereignty, as well as specification of Member State obligations and buttressing these by an effective sanctions mechanism. As with the microeconomic constitution, direct applicability of European law does play a role; however, obligations are imposed, not on private parties but on state institutions. What is also important is increased coherence, without which we could hardly talk of a distinct constitutional (sub-)dimension. The Maastricht macroeconomic provisions were intended to make up a coherent constitutional basis for constructing an economic and monetary union. Again the constitutive function of the economic constitution stands very much in the foreground.

The Maastricht principles

The major change brought about by the Maastricht Treaty was the introduction of a common monetary policy; Europeanization of monetary policy had been the central item on the agenda of both the Werner Group and the Delors Committee, the two main expert bodies paving the way for EMU. Art. 3(1)(c) TFEU lays down that the Union has exclusive competence in monetary policy for Member States whose currency is the euro.[11] The German perception had a clear impact on the definition of monetary policy objectives, as well as the institutional position of the

[10] Case C-27/04 *Commission v Council* [2004] ECR I-6649.

[11] In this chapter, references will mainly be to the TFEU. Treaty revisions subsequent to Maastricht have left the relevant provisions more or less untouched.

European Central Bank (ECB) and the national central banks, forming the European System of Central Banks (ESCB). Even initially recalcitrant German ordoliberals, many of whom had been quite sceptical about EMU and the common currency, gradually made their peace with the loss of the Deutsche Mark and the Bundesbank as the guarantor of its stability. In accordance with the monetarist tenet, Arts. 119(2) and 127(1) TFEU elevate price stability to the primary objective of monetary and exchange-rate policy. General economic policies in the Union may only be supported if this can be done without prejudice to price stability. Arts. 119(2) and 127(1) also relate monetary policy to the basic principles of the first layer of the European economic constitution: an open market economy and free competition. Invoking these principles testifies to the continuing primacy of the microeconomic constitution and recalls price stability as a vital element of the framework conditions called for by ordoliberals.

Institutional provisions on monetary union aim to secure the enhanced independence of both the ECB and national central banks, not only in euro states but in other Member States too. Most importantly, Art. 130 TFEU sets out that neither the ECB nor national central banks 'shall seek or take instructions from Union institutions, bodies, offices or agencies, from any government of a Member State or from any other body'. Correspondingly, Union institutions and Member States shall 'respect this principle and not to seek to influence the members of the decision-making bodies of the European Central Bank or of the national central banks in the performance of their tasks'. In the 1980s, central bank independence, a vital precept of ordoliberalism and an essential feature of the Bundesbank model, had gained more general support among economists and central bankers themselves. Yet politically it was far from a self-evident premise. Here Germany, however, managed to drive through its standpoint against the hesitation of, primarily, France. ECB objectives, tasks and competences are strictly defined in the Treaties and in the Statute, concurring with the general principle of conferral pertaining to the division of competences between the Union and Member States. Art. 127(1) TFEU defines the objectives of monetary policy, prioritizing price stability and invoking the basic principles of the microeconomic constitution. In turn, Art. 127(2) enumerates the basic tasks of the ECB: defining and implementing the monetary policy of the Union; conducting foreign-exchange operations; holding and managing the official foreign reserves of the Member States; and promoting smooth operation of payment systems. The wording of Art. 127(5)[12] intimates that the main responsibility for prudential supervision remains with national authorities. However, Art. 127(6) facilitates conferring on the ECB specific tasks in the prudential supervision of credit institutions and other financial institutions with the exception of insurance undertakings.

Unlike monetary policy, the Maastricht Treaty retained Member State sovereignty in fiscal and economic policy. In effect, due to loss of control over monetary policy instruments, the significance of national fiscal policy grew in, for instance, reacting to asymmetric, country-specific economic shocks. Still, according to the Maastricht provisions Member State sovereignty in fiscal and economic policy is not absolute but conditioned by specific constraints. A latent tension inhered in the Maastricht principles which defined the position of national fiscal policy. On the one hand, its importance increased, which required sufficient leeway for Member State decision-makers. On the other hand, its potential spillover effects, especially with regard to common monetary policy, were seen to require European constraints.

The Founding Treaties, now as before, presuppose that Member States heed the viewpoints of other Member States and the Union as a whole in their economic policies; in other words, internalize the externalities of their policies. Member States are supposed to 'conduct their economic policies with a view to contributing to the achievement of the objectives of the Union' (Art. 120 TFEU). They should regard their economic policies as a matter of common concern and are expected to coordinate their policies within the Council (Art. 121(1)).[13] Instead of legal rules and formal sanctions, the multilateral surveillance procedure provided for by Art. 121 TFEU adheres to what has come to be called the open method of coordination: legally non-binding broad guidelines; peer review through the Council; and likewise legally non-binding country-specific recommendations. In principle, the multilateral surveillance procedure covers Member State economic policy as a whole. Yet the Stability and Growth Pact clearly

[12] 'The ESCB shall contribute to the smooth conduct of policies pursued by the competent authorities relating to the prudential supervision of credit institutions and the stability of the financial system.'

[13] The basic provision is in Art. 2(3) TFEU: 'The Member States shall coordinate their economic and employment policies within arrangements as determined by this Treaty, which the Union shall have competence to provide.' Art. 5(1) TFEU repeats Member States' obligation to coordinate their economic policies within the Union and adds that 'to this end, the Council shall adopt measures, in particular broad guidelines for these policies'. It also lays down that 'specific provisions shall apply to those Member States whose currency is the euro'.

defined fiscal policy as the main target of the procedure. Thus, it must be placed in the context of the other means by which the Maastricht macroeconomic constitution purports to guarantee that Member States pursue the objective of sound public finances, explicitly enshrined in Art. 119(3) TFEU, and obey the fiscal discipline which European monetary policy prioritizing price stability presupposes.

The 'basic safeguards against fiscal profligacy',[14] introduced by the Maastricht Treaty, include the no-bailout clause precluding shared liability for government debt across Member States or by the Union (Art. 125(1) TFEU). The no-bailout clause addresses the issue of moral hazard. It was intended to function as a barrier to reckless borrowing by sovereigns and reckless lending by credit markets which the expectation of a bailout by the Union or other Member States in case of default could induce. The no-bailout clause gives expression to Member State fiscal responsibility, i.e. their exclusive liability for their fiscal commitments; a constitutional principle which is the reverse of Member State fiscal sovereignty. The prohibition of central bank financing in Art. 123(1) TFEU serves the purpose of sound public finances, but can – in line with the bailout prohibition – be read as a manifestation of Member State fiscal liability too. It also belongs to the package which was designed to ward off moral hazard in government spending and borrowing. The convergence criteria which have to be met before a Member State is eligible for the euro were designed with a view to securing sound public finances as well.The criteria refer to price stability, general government deficit and debt, and stability of both the exchange rate and the long-term interest rate level (Art. 140(2) TFEU).

Finally, Treaty provisions on the multilateral surveillance and excessive deficit procedures implied continuous monitoring of Member State policy by the Commission and the Council. The procedures were expected to curb and – in case of failure – keep track of and put a stop to Member State deviation from the path of prudent fiscal policy. The Treaty basis for the excessive deficit procedure lies in Art. 126 TFEU and the complementary Protocol. In line with the multilateral surveillance procedure, the emphasis in the excessive deficit procedure, in its original shape, was on peer review and soft-law instruments. Yet even in Maastricht formal sanctions were also made available against delinquent states. Art. 126 TFEU assigns the Commission the task of monitoring development of the budgetary situation and the stock of government debt in the Member States. In particular, the Commission is expected to examine compliance

[14] L. Schuknecht et al. (2011).

with budgetary discipline, employing criteria based on the reference values of government deficit and debt, which the Protocol has fixed at 3 and 60 per cent of gross domestic product, respectively. Subsequent measures laid down in Art. 126 TFEU target budgetary deficits. The decision on the existence of an excessive deficit is taken by the Council. As an ultimate recourse, the Council can impose a non-interest-bearing deposit and fines of appropriate size on a Member State which does not comply with its recommendations concerning deficit-reducing measures.[15]

After Maastricht, the next major step in the process of macroeconomic constitutionalization was the Stability and Growth Pact, which added new thrust to the Treaty provisions on multilateral surveillance and excessive deficit procedures. The Pact consists of a legally non-binding, political resolution of the European Council and two regulations, translating political guidelines into legal language.[16] The Pact does not possess formal constitutional status, but is based on the Maastricht principles and acts out some of their implications, particularly with regard to the excessive deficit procedure. The Resolution of the European Council as the political basis of the Pact made clear the prevalence of Europeanized monetary policy, aiming at price stability, over national fiscal policy. The European Council underlined 'the importance of safeguarding sound government finances as a means to strengthen the conditions for price stability and for strong sustainable growth conducive to employment creation', and declared it 'necessary to ensure that national budgetary policies support stability oriented monetary policies'. The multilateral surveillance procedure, set out in Art. 121 TFEU and further specified by Regulation 1466/97, constitutes the preventive arm of the Stability and Growth Pact. The corrective arm, which is supposed to take over if preventive measures do not lead to expected results, is centred round the excessive deficit procedure. Regulation 1467/97, dealing with the corrective arm, did not introduce new measures but complemented the already quite detailed provisions in the Treaty and the Protocol by regulating the timetable for the diverse phases

15 For a discussion of the Stability and Growth Pact in its original form see F. Amtenbrink and J de Haan (2003).

16 The term 'Stability and Growth Pact' is misleading in the sense that no legal intergovernmental agreement exists. Resolution on the Stability and Growth Pact of Amsterdam, 17 June 1997, [1997] OJ C236/1; Council Regulation No. 1466/97 of 7 July 1997 on the strengthening of the surveillance of budgetary positions and the surveillance and coordination of economic policies, and Council Regulation No. 1467/97 of 7 July 1997 on speeding up and clarifying the implementation of the excessive deficit procedure, [1997] OJ L209/1. On the negotiations leading to the Pact see M. Heipertz and A. Verdun (2010), pp. 19–41.

and measures of the procedure, and by further specifying the deposits and fines which can be imposed on a Member State for failing to correct its excessive deficit.

Underlying economic assumptions

Provisions on macroeconomic objectives, aggregate values and policies are not staple elements of state constitutions, although recent provisions on balanced budgets, for instance in the German Basic Law, have partly altered the general picture.[17] Still, the general starting point at the state level is constitutional neutrality in economic policy. The principle of neutrality is based on the recognition that economic policy involves value choices, that policy decisions cannot be derived in a self-evident way from generally accepted, objective economic truths and that rival economic theories may lead to different policy conclusions. Hence, controversial policy choices, based on controversial economic theories, should not be fixed at constitutional level but should be left to democratic political decision-making. Constitutional enshrinement would grant economic policy a privileged position vis-à-vis, for instance, social policy. Both the micro- and macroeconomic layers of the European economic constitution diverge from the standard state template. Macroeconomic objectives, including primacy of the monetary policy objective of price stability, the entry criteria for EMU and exactly defined reference values for national fiscal policy, are not unequivocally determined or universally accepted economic givens. It is no wonder, then, that conflicts over proper economically informed constitutional theory label not only microeconomic but macroeconomic constitutionalization too.

A major issue for contestation has been the relationship between monetary and other economic policy, as well as the proper locus of the latter in the division of competences between European and national levels. In the aftermath of the Werner Report, published in 1970, two main approaches to monetary integration distinguished themselves, soon enough labelled Monetarist and Economist. The Monetarist camp, not to be confused with monetarism as a school of thought in economics, argued that monetary union would facilitate deeper integration. As both a necessary and a sufficient condition for the functioning of the EU as a single market and, by

[17] In Germany the amendment was adopted in 2009. Other European countries with a constitutional debt brake include Austria, Italy, Poland, Spain and Switzerland. See the overview in F. Fabbrini (2013).

the same token, approaching what was called an optimal currency area, monetary union would precede and induce further political and economic integration. The Monetarist view was widespread among French politicians, who were keen to end Bundesbank domination in the European economy. By contrast, the Economists conceived of monetary union as a potential result of preceding political and economic integration; a final step on the long road of integration. The Economist position was common particularly among German economists, as well as officials at the Bundesbank and the Ministry of Finance. They emphasized the significance of monetary policy for economic policy in general and saw in monetary stability a major building block of the economic framework as a whole.[18]

The result consecrated in Maastricht was a compromise between the two camps. The mainly German Economists managed to include a list of economic criteria to be fulfilled before a country can accede to EMU and to introduce a Bundesbank type of central banking model with an overriding emphasis on price stability.[19] Ordoliberals tended to see monetary policy as a constitutionally privileged field of non-discretionary *Ordnungspolitik*, analogous to competition policy, where both goals and means were 'objectively' given and which thus could and should be left to the care of politically independent expert institutions. This time ordoliberals were not alone in their views: the model of independent and inflation-alert central banking had begun to gain wider currency during the 1980s, which contributed significantly to acceptance of the Bundesbank model.

German Economists had emphasized that monetary union required far-reaching economic and political integration among participating Member States. However, they had to settle for a few key areas of economic convergence. The convergence criteria set only two major preconditions for a common currency. Eligible members in EMU were expected to have their public finances in reasonable shape and to have reached a certain level of monetary stability. Strictly speaking only the latter prerequisite required economic convergence. Convergence in the area of monetary stability was checked from three angles. Firstly, the annual inflation rate should not exceed the average of the three countries with the lowest inflation by more than 1.5 per cent. Secondly, the exchange-rate criterion presupposed that future EMU members would participate in the ERM for two years without major realignments. This criterion was expected to test the

[18] See D. Marsh (2011), pp. 45–6.

[19] O. Issing (2008), pp. 6–12.

credibility of monetary stability from an external perspective. The third criterion for monetary stability required that the long-term interest rate should not exceed the average interest rate of the three countries with the lowest inflation rate by more than 2 per cent. In turn, the criteria for public finances contained ceilings for general government deficit and debt, but did not presuppose rapprochement of national fiscal policies. Government deficit was not to exceed 3 per cent of GDP, and debt was to remain under 60 per cent of GDP.

The fact that economic convergence was not included among the Maastricht criteria reflects the Monetarist view that a single currency would over time lead to necessary convergence and that EMU would in due time approach an optimal currency area. Less clear were the grounds on which the Monetarist optimists based their confidence. German Economists continuously made the case that some level of fiscal and political integration would be needed for monetary union to work. Yet no serious attempt was made to facilitate major fiscal transfers in EMU or to introduce EU-level social policy measures with similar effect, optimally financed by procyclical EU-wide taxes. So it appears that the optimistic expectation of EMU developing into an optimal currency area was based on assumptions of increased flexibility and simultaneous easing of asymmetric, country-specific shocks.

For monetary stability, fiscal policy is the crucial non-monetary field of economic policy. The Maastricht model opted for national sovereignty over and responsibility for fiscal policy, with certain safeguards against negative externalities and moral hazard. Because of their different locus, little room was reserved for a dialogue between fiscal and monetary policy. Treaty provisions on fiscal policy, complemented by the Stability and Growth Pact, aimed to ward off risks for monetary stability. In economic history, the major risk had arisen from monetizing government debt, so that an explicit prohibition of central-bank financing was included in the Maastricht Treaty (now Art. 123(1) TFEU). Furthermore, it was realized that in EMU governments could have means for and incentives to deficit financing well beyond the previous situation. The no-bailout clause of the Treaty (now Art. 125(1)), as well as the Stability and Growth Pact, aimed to combat this moral hazard.[20]

After the Europeanization of monetary policy and the non-availability of exchange-rate and monetary-policy instruments for national purposes, the importance of fiscal policy as a national instrument for adjusting to

[20] O. Issing (2008), pp. 193–5.

asymmetric internal and external shocks has grown. However, this aspect was accorded surprisingly little attention in the run-up to the Maastricht Treaty. Another major issue determining the position of fiscal policy in the Maastricht architecture concerned redistribution. A broad consensus prevailed over the highly restricted role of redistribution between Member States; the EU in general or EMU in particular was not to become a 'transfer Union'. For historical and cultural reasons, internal redistributive mechanisms and welfare regimes varied greatly in Member States. Welfare policy also stood at the very heart of national political debates, concentrated around the annual budgetary process. Redistribution is the meeting point of fiscal and social policy, as well as democratic self-assertion. In Maastricht, no attempt was made to harmonize national redistributive systems or to create Union-level redistributive functions.

The disciplining effect of financial markets on Member States was a thoroughly discussed topic in the long hatching process of EMU. The emerging consensus appeared to be that the discipline imposed by the financial markets and backed up by the prohibition on bailouts was a necessary condition for prudent Member State fiscal policy. Yet the Delors Report, for instance, was explicit in its assessment that market discipline alone would not suffice. Much hope was laid on the potential of the excessive deficit procedure as an additional guarantee of sound public finances. In total, the drafters of the Maastricht (macro)economic constitution took the possibility of reckless public finances seriously and defined it as a major risk for stability and balanced growth. The artillery of the Treaty provisions on economic and especially fiscal policy was directed against irresponsible short-term behaviour by national governments, which would ultimately be detrimental to the longer-term interests of their own constituencies, as well.

Before EMU, financial markets in most EU countries were largely national. The main question was whether institutional reforms were needed in banking supervision and, if they were, whether the ECB should be assigned centralized functions. The Bundesbank opposed central-bank supervision, invoking the moral hazard risk which could ensue from the expectation by banks that the central bank would not only exert supervision but also employ monetary policy instruments to rescue them.[21] The resulting conclusion was to continue with the existing decentralized framework, with amplified emphasis on cooperation between national supervisors. The probability of a major banking crisis was also held to

21 H. James (2012), p. 291.

be low. EMU was presumed to enhance financial stability. Financial markets would become more synchronized, and integration would produce larger and more liquid markets, which are less prone to failures and less affected by the crash of individual institutions and which make for better risk diversification.

From crisis prevention to crisis management

The Eurozone crisis erupted in spring 2010 but was preceded by the global financial crisis triggered off in 2007–8. The crisis proved the mistaken basis of many of the central economic assumptions for the Maastricht principles of the macroeconomic constitution. The Eurozone had not developed into an optimal currency area, and a uniform monetary policy tended to have contradictory effects in countries with different economic structures and in different phases of economic development. Expectations of the combined effect of financial market discipline and European surveillance procedures for Member State fiscal prudence turned out to be overly optimistic. Moreover, potential problems caused by the intertwinement of national financial markets as well as the inter-linkage between sovereign debt and private financial institutions were underestimated. Economic reality showed that the Maastricht framework should be amended; consequently, a constitutional mutation was launched. Except for the amendment to Art. 136(3) TFEU, European measures were not labelled as constitutional revisions, and the amendment, which concerned the establishment of a permanent stability mechanism, was a relatively minor element in the whole. However, the constitutional implications of the measures are evident. The ECJ discussed some of these, but not all, in its *Pringle* judgment in November 2012, the Court's major constitutional speech act pertaining to the crisis.[22]

European reactions to the crisis fall into three categories. Firstly, rescue packages were assembled to pull the worst-hit countries out of the most acute difficulties, and financial stability mechanisms were established. The objective was not merely to provide emergency assistance but also to avert contagion and to enhance the confidence of financial markets in the euro area of its ability to cope with the situation. Secondly, emergency measures and building financial and institutional capacity to meet future

[22] Case C-370/12 *Thomas Pringle v Government of Ireland*, judgment of 27 November 2012 (not yet reported).

crises were flanked by efforts to strengthen European-level economic governance. Here the aim was to remedy the insufficiencies and inefficiencies of the Maastricht constraints on national fiscal economic policy, which had proven unable to prevent turmoil erupting in spring 2010. Thirdly, interventions by the ECB supported and complemented by other emergency measures, at times even playing a decisive role. Measures in all three categories have contributed to a constitutional mutation and shaken central Maastricht principles. I shall start from the constitutional implications of rescue packages and stability mechanisms.

The possibility of bailout had never been seriously discussed in the run-up to Maastricht, and no resolution mechanism for fiscal turmoil was included in the macroeconomic constitution. Hence, aggravation of the Greek debt crisis in early 2010 largely caught the EU and the euro states unprepared. The Maastricht macroeconomic constitution was based on the assumption that safeguards against fiscal imprudence in Arts. 123–5 TFEU, the convergence criteria of EMU and the Stability and Growth Pact would suffice to ensure fiscal stability and to impose the necessary restraint on euro-area Member States, although these still retained fiscal policy sovereignty. The procedure for mutual assistance established by Art. 108 of the Treaty of Rome still existed, and indeed had been activated after the financial crisis exploded. However, it only allows for financial assistance to non-euro states facing difficulties in their balance of payments (Art. 143 TFEU).[23] For resolving a sovereign debt crisis in a euro state, legal experimentalism was needed.

The rescue packages and stability mechanisms adopted during the sovereign debt crisis display both common and divergent traits. The shared features embrace reliance on intergovernmental legal and institutional structures. Here the only exception is the financially rather insignificant European Financial Stability Mechanism (EFSM), which was established on 11 May 2010 by a Council regulation,[24] issued under the emergency provision of Art. 122(2) TFEU.[25] Another common feature is the conditionality of assistance: financial assistance has been provided on the

[23] Financial assistance under Art. 143 TFEU has been provided to Latvia, Romania and Hungary.

[24] Council Regulation (EU) No. 407/2010 of 11 May 2010 establishing a European financial stabilization mechanism, [2010] OJ L118/1.

[25] This provision lays down that 'where a Member State is in difficulties or is seriously threatened with severe difficulties caused by natural disasters or exceptional occurrences beyond its control, the Council, on a proposal from the Commission, may

condition that the recipient country signs a Memorandum of Understanding (MoU), committing itself to spending cuts, taxation measures and structural reforms. Furthermore, the IMF was involved in diverse forms of financial assistance, from loans to Greece in May 2010 to establishment of the European Stability Mechanism (ESM), which ended the period of legal experimentalism. The IMF not only made a significant financial contribution but participated in drafting the conditions of assistance and in monitoring compliance with them. The Commission, the ECB and the IMF made up the Troika, dominating much of the media coverage of the – at times dramatic – rescue operations.

Where the mechanisms diverge is in their exact legal form; here the experimentalism labelling European reactions is highly conspicuous. Broadly speaking, management of the crisis has given rise to two types of intergovernmental agreement. Firstly, there are agreements with a primarily private law character. This category comprises the agreements for the first Greek rescue package – the Loan Facility Agreement and the Intercreditor Agreement – and the Framework Agreement on the European Financial Stability Facility (EFSF), functioning from summer 2010 to summer 2013, when it was replaced by the ESM.[26] Secondly, the Treaty on the ESM was concluded under public international law, as was also the case with the Treaty on Stability, Coordination and Governance (TSCG), which falls under efforts to tighten European economic governance. A clear-cut division is complicated by the fact that agreements in the first category also possess features which point in the direction of public international law and which are of relevance from the perspective of EU law as well. Differences between agreements under private law and agreements under public international law may be important for national constitutional law,[27] but less so for EU law. From the EU law perspective, the default position for both types of agreement is Member State freedom of action: Member States may conclude agreements between themselves under both public international law and private law, if no ground to the contrary can be derived from EU law.

grant, under certain conditions, Union financial assistance to the Member State concerned'.

26 The consolidated version of the Framework Agreement is available on the EFSF website under legal documents.

27 In Member States, some uncertainty is noticeable as to the legal character of the agreements and the necessity for their parliamentary approval. In Finland, the agreements making up the first Greek rescue package were not submitted to Parliament for approval, but the EFSF Framework Agreement was. In Germany, none of these agreements were approved by the Bundestag.

The legal status of the Member States providing assistance also varies from one mechanism to another. In the Greek aid package of May 2010 the assisting states appear as creditors, in the EFSF as guarantors for loans issued by the EFSF and in the ESM as shareholders, while in the EFSM the liability of Member States is restricted to their contributions to the EU budget. These differences may have constitutional implications at both European and Member State levels, but from the perspective of beneficiary states they are largely irrelevant. Rather, what matters for the recipient states and their population is the foremost common feature of the mechanisms, which was also spelled out in the amendment to Art. 136 TFEU: the *strict conditionality* of financial assistance. The MoUs which the beneficiary states have been obliged to sign not only define in aggregate terms required cuts in public expenditure but also determine how those cuts should be allocated. In addition, the MoUs indicate market-liberally oriented structural reforms.

The main substantive constitutional question that the rescue packages and stability mechanisms raise is their concurrence with the explicit prohibition on bailouts in Art. 125(1) TFEU. This was a major issue in *Pringle* too. Essentially, the Court embraced a two-telos interpretation of the no-bailout provision. The Court adopted the prevailing view among academic commentators and argued that 'the prohibition laid down in Article 125 TFEU ensures that the Member States remain subject to the logic of the market when they enter into debt, since that ought to prompt them to maintain budgetary discipline' (Para. 135). The Court emphasized that the main function of the provisions on economic policy in the TFEU, especially Arts. 123–5, is preventive, 'to reduce so far as possible the risk of public debt crises'. But the no-bailout provision serves a higher objective as well: namely, the *financial stability of the euro area as a whole*. This objective seems to harmonize crisis prevention, which includes the prohibition on bailouts, with crisis resolution, which may require measures deviating from that prohibition. The conclusion is that interpretation and application of the no-bailout clause should not prevent attaining the higher-level objective it shares with crisis management. The Court set out two criteria which financial assistance by a stability mechanism such as the ESM must meet in order to be compatible with Art. 125(1). Firstly, it must be indispensable for safeguarding the financial stability of the euro area as a whole, i.e. the higher objective of economic policy provisions; and, secondly, it must be subject to strict conditions (Para. 136). The second requirement is necessary for preventing the prospect of future financial assistance creating a new risk of moral hazard.

Pringle not only constitutionally sanctioned the rescue packages and mechanisms produced by the experimentalism of the preceding two and a half years. It also confirmed that the macroeconomic constitution had been complemented and modified by three new elements: firstly, with regard to Member State fiscal policy, the macroeconomic constitution provides not only for crisis prevention but for crisis management as well; secondly, preventive fiscal policy constraints and crisis resolution share the same higher objective of the financial stability of the euro area as a whole; and, thirdly, crisis resolution by means of financial assistance for the purpose of financial stability is only permitted if accompanied by strict conditionality.

The amendment to Art. 136 TFEU must be linked to the constitutional mutation confirmed by *Pringle*. The amendment procedure was closely intertwined with establishment of the ESM. However, the amendment only entered into force after the ESM had already been founded and, consequently, could not constitute the competence basis for the Treaty establishing the ESM. Accordingly, many commentators, including AG Kokott in *Pringle*,[28] have emphasized the merely declaratory nature of the amendment. European Council Decision 2011/99 on the amendment preceded *Pringle*, although it only entered into force on 1 May 2013, that is, after the issuance of *Pringle*. It is tempting to read the amendment and *Pringle* together and see both these constitutional speech acts as serving the same purpose: constitutionally sanctifying the innovations which legal and institutional experimentation in management of the Eurozone crisis had brought about. Amended Art. 136(3) lays down that 'the member states whose currency is the euro may establish a stability mechanism to be activated if indispensable to safeguard the stability of the euro area as a whole. The granting of any required financial assistance under the mechanism will be made subject to strict conditionality.' The three constitutional innovations to be distilled from *Pringle*'s treatment of the no-bailout clause are present in the amendment as well: constitutionalization of crisis management; postulation of a second-order telos of the (financial) stability of the euro area as a whole; and constitutionalization of the requirement of strict conditionality, which helps to harmonize financial assistance with the primacy objective of the ban on bailouts.[29]

[28] Case C-370/12 *Thomas Pringle v Government of Ireland*, judgment of 27 November 2012 (not yet reported), view of AG Kokott, Para. 65.

[29] With regard to the postulated second-order telos of the Treaty provisions on EMU, *Pringle*, in harmony with the majority of legal and political documents produced during the crisis, evokes financial stability. The amendment, by contrast, has dropped the

The constitutional mutation confirmed by *Pringle* and the amendment to Art. 136 TFEU signified retreat from a central Maastricht principle: namely, exclusive liability of each Member State for its own debts. Now the principle is valid only for good, but not bad, times.

Strengthening European economic governance

The Maastricht model implied not only the principle of national fiscal liability but also its reverse: Member State fiscal and economic sovereignty. Sovereignty, though, was not absolute, but the Treaties, complemented by the Stability and Growth Pact, imposed restrictions, especially on national fiscal policy. These restrictions served the overriding objective of monetary stability. The starting point, however, was that the Union would play a merely coordinating role in non-monetary economic policy. Accordingly, the means the Union had at its disposal to influence Member State policies consisted primarily of soft-law instruments, typical of what later came to be called the open method of coordination. The central role of the Council emphasized the peer review character of monitoring procedures. Indeed, Art. 121(1) TFEU indicates the Member States as the subjects of coordination and the Council merely as the forum where Member States exercise it. The only exception to soft-law governance was adopted in Art. 126(11) as an *ultima ratio* means in the excessive deficit procedure. The Council could oblige a Member State which had failed to comply with a previous Council decision to make a non-interest-bearing deposit of an appropriate size with the Union and even impose a fine. The coordinating role of the Union in principle covered economic policy as a whole, but as the Stability and Growth Pact made evident, its clear emphasis lay in fiscal policy: more precisely, in managing budget deficit and sovereign-debt rates.[30]

epithet 'financial' and refers merely to the 'stability of the euro area as a whole'. Perhaps too much should not be made of this divergence, which could be purely accidental. This assumption finds corroboration in the fact that when discussing the amendment in *Pringle*, the Court alternates between the two terms.

30 In 2005 the Stability and Growth Pact was watered down by amendments to the two regulations, which increased the discretion of the Commission and the Council in the multilateral surveillance and excessive deficit procedures. This occurred as a reaction to application of the excessive deficit procedure to Germany and France; that is, the two biggest Member States. The Commission took to the Court the Council decisions not to adopt the formal instruments contained in the Commission recommendations. However, the Court only took a position on the issue whether Art. 104 TEC (now Art. 126 TFEU) or Regulation 1467/97 enabled a decision to hold the procedure in abeyance and came to a negative conclusion. Case C-27/04 *Commission v Council* [2004] ECR I-6649.

Rescue packages and funds have had consequences not only for the principle of Member State fiscal liability but also for Member State fiscal and economic sovereignty. Most obvious is the curbing of the sovereignty of the crisis states. All forms of assistance, starting from the Greek loan facility and ending with stability support by the ESM, have been premised on 'strict conditionality'. The Memoranda of Understanding or Programmes of Adjustment which the beneficiary countries have had to sign have contained not only general, aggregate, reference values on, say, public spending or the level of taxation, but also rather detailed provisions on how spending cuts should be allocated and deficits financed.[31] With their reference to strict conditionality, *Pringle* and the amendment to Art. 136 TFEU have made explicit the constitutional status of the curtailment of sovereignty which beneficiary states must accept as a price for financial assistance. But rescue packages and mechanisms have had grave repercussions for the fiscal sovereignty of assisting states as well. Their financial liabilities, both taken separately for each instrument and in total, are huge. This has created constitutional problems in, for example, such Member States as Germany and Finland where the constitution enjoys high prestige in political and legal culture. The main constitutional issues relate to national sovereignty, the fiscal powers of Parliament and democratic legitimation of decision-making in fiscal policy. Member State constitutional concerns clearly attest to the close intertwinement of European and national constitutional developments: now from the perspective of national constitutional law.[32]

Strengthening European economic governance as the second branch of European responses to the crisis has led to further relativization of Member State sovereignty. The measures have addressed all Member States. Yet the crisis has also led to the erection of a particular Eurozone regime, including specific treatment of the worst-hit states. The main legal instruments used in the reinforcement of European surveillance of Member State policies are the six-pack legislation, consisting of five regulations

[31] This goes for Greece, Ireland, Portugal and Cyprus. Spain constitutes an exception, because the scope of its MoU is confined to the financial sector.

[32] In Finland, the Constitutional Law Committee of Parliament has repeatedly emphasized that liabilities should be assessed as a whole, in order to appraise the encroachment on Parliament's fiscal powers and the possible endangering of the state's ability to cope with its constitutional obligations. In addition, the risk connected to liabilities should also be taken into account. Indeed, such a holistic approach is needed, although it is difficult to execute, due to the different legal and economic nature of liabilities and the variation in the respective risks. See on the German and Finnish constitutional reactions to crisis measures Kaarlo Tuori and Klaus Tuori (2014), pp. 197–204.

and one directive, plus the two-pack of two regulations and the Fiscal Compact; that is, Title III of the Treaty on Stability, Coordination and Governance (TSCG). The six-pack and two-pack regulations introduced obligatory deposits and fines in monitoring procedures in the preventive arm under Art. 121 TFEU, as well as reversed majority voting in both the preventive arm and the corrective arm under Art. 126 TFEU. These changes have emphasized the role of formal sanctions and enhanced the position of the Commission in relation to the Council. Due to the new status of the Commission, it is difficult to conceive any longer of the Member States as the subjects of coordination. Monitoring has moved away from peer review and soft-law mechanisms, typical of the open method of coordination.

Simultaneously, the scope of monitoring has been enlarged. The Stability and Growth Pact put the emphasis of the multilateral surveillance procedure under Art. 121 TFEU on fiscal policy. The new excessive imbalances procedure, introduced by the six-pack, aims to cover all the main sources of economic imbalance and opens surveillance towards general economic policy.[33] Furthermore, economic governance under the original Stability and Growth Pact did not address annual budgetary processes, but the focus was on medium-term fiscal planning. Nor was Member State procedural budgetary autonomy affected. However, the Protocol on the excessive deficit procedure, attached to the Treaty of Maastricht, set out a general duty for Member States to ensure that national procedures in the budgetary area enable them to meet their Treaty obligations. Yet before the Eurozone crisis this general duty was not given any specific thrust through secondary legislation. The first intrusion into the procedural autonomy of Member States was effected by the Directive on requirements for Member State budgetary frameworks (2011/85),[34] based on the delegation in Art. 126(14) TFEU and belonging to the six-pack.

The Directive retained the focus on multiannual budgetary planning. It aimed to secure that national procedures are consistent with the Stability and Growth Pact and promote compliance with the reference values on budget deficit and public debt. Regulation 1175/2011 extended European monitoring from medium-term budget planning, focusing on aggregate objectives, to annual budgetary planning.[35] Two-pack

[33] Regulation No. 1176/2011 of 16 November 2011 on the prevention and correction of macroeconomic imbalances, [2011] OJ L306/25.

[34] Council Directive No. 2011/85 of 8 November 2011 on requirements for budgetary frameworks of the Member States, [2011] OJ L306/25.

[35] Council Regulation (EU) No. 1175/2011 of 8 November 2011 amending Council Regulation 1466/97, [2011] OJ L306/12.

legislation goes still further and obliges euro-area Member States to submit an annual draft budgetary plan for the forthcoming year to the Commission and the Euro Group. Although the Commission has no power to take legally binding decisions, its opinions are expected to put strong pressure on Member States. Moreover, opinions addressing 'particularly serious non-compliance' with European budgetary policy obligations will be made public.[36] The inroad into the procedural aspect of national budgetary autonomy opened by Directive 2011/85 has been widened by two further instruments. Firstly, the two-pack not only extended European monitoring to the annual budget process, but also includes provisions on, inter alia, the timeline of the national budget process. Secondly, the main thrust of the Fiscal Compact – the most important Title of the Treaty on Stability, Coordination and Governance – is to create national guarantees to ensure that Member States respect the rules on balanced budget and limited sovereign debt. The Fiscal Compact entrusts the Commission, other Member States and the Court with the task of monitoring the adequacy of these guarantees.

In sum, the constitutional mutation incited by the crisis has altered the character of European economic governance, in particular in the Eurozone. Decisive steps have been taken, from soft-law instruments to formal sanctions; the strengthening of the position of the Commission, together with formal sanctions, has stripped governance of many of its peer review features; the scope of surveillance has been enlarged from fiscal to general macroeconomic policy; and in fiscal policy, monitoring has been extended from multiannual planning to both substantive and procedural aspects of annual budgetary processes. It is true, though, that Member States still retain the final formal decision over their budgets. Still, European constraints have been considerably enlarged and deepened beyond those adopted in Maastricht. This has occurred in tandem with redefinition of the second-order objective of the Treaty provisions on economic policy: its reformulation as financial stability or simply stability, instead of price stability.

The new roles of the ECB

During the financial and fiscal crises, the ECB assumed tasks which made all the central monetary policy principles of Maastricht teeter: the primacy of the price-stability objective, the independence of the ECB and

[36] Regulation No. 473/2013 of 21 May 2013 on common provisions for monitoring and assessing draft budgetary plans and ensuring the correction of excessive deficit of the Member States in the euro area, [2013] OJ L140/11.

the narrow definition of its mandate. In Maastricht, the main responsibility for the stability of the financial system was retained with national authorities. Active ECB involvement in re-establishing financial stability has shaken this premise. By the same token, it has raised concerns of moral hazard, which may jeopardize both the primacy of the price-stability objective and the independence of the ECB. These concerns are further aggravated by the supervisory role of the ECB in banking union.

The ECB Securities Markets Programme from May 2010 – replaced by the Outright Monetary Transactions (OMT) programme in September 2012 – compromised on the narrow definition of the ECB mandate in terms of monetary policy focusing on price stability, and the deep ECB involvement in country-specific rescue operations and in the functioning of stability mechanisms in the Eurozone problematized the principle of independence.[37] In the Securities Markets and Outright Monetary Transactions programmes, the Maastricht relationship between European monetary policy and national fiscal policy was reversed: the needs of the latter have determined the objectives pursued by the former.[38] By the same token, the ordoliberal tenets of the non-political character of central bank policy and of the self-evident truth of price stability as the focus of that policy suffered a severe blow.

The Maastricht Treaty set stability as a major economic objective. However, it was explicitly expressed in terms of price stability. In Arts. 119(2) and 127(1) TFEU, price stability is specified as the primary objective of monetary policy, entrusted to the ECB. Yet it would be erroneous to restrict the significance of price stability merely to narrowly defined monetary policy. As the Stability and Growth Pact made clear, fiscal constraints for the purpose of sound public finances were also designed to serve the higher-order objective of price stability.[39] Restrictions on national fiscal sovereignty, imposing fiscal discipline and securing sound public finances, were expected to create in national fiscal policy the presuppositions required by common, transnational, monetary policy aiming at price stability. Arguably, the euro-area crisis has in a constitutionally significant way replaced price stability with financial stability as the overriding

[37] Decision of the ECB of 14 May 2010 establishing a securities market programme (ECB/2010/5), [2010] OJ L124/8; ECB, 'Press Release', 'Technical Features of Outright Monetary Transactions', 6 September 2012.

[38] This has been the refrain particularly in German criticisms of the ECB. As a representative example, see A. Belke (2010).

[39] See Council Resolution (EC) of 17 June 1997 on the stability and growth pact (Amsterdam), [1997] OJ C236/1.

objective which European economic policies, including the monetary policy of the ECB, are expected to serve. The objective of financial stability of the euro area as a whole has been the main justification invoked for rescue packages and stability mechanisms, and it also played a major role in ECB operations in the financial and fiscal crises. In February 2014 the German Constitutional Court submitted a referral to the ECJ for a preliminary ruling on the compatibility of OMT with EU primary law.[40] At the time of writing the ECJ had not yet issued its ruling. It remains to be seen whether the Court will invoke this higher-order telos to warrant the ECB exceeding the Treaty-based focus on monetary policy and price stability, analogously to its justification for retreat from another central Maastricht principle; namely, Member State fiscal liability as manifested in the no-bailout clause.[41]

The *ESMA* ruling of the ECJ[42] shows that financial stability as a constitutional principle has implications for the microeconomic constitution too. The same can be said of the banking union which straddles the micro- and macroeconomic dimensions of the European economic constitution. The banking union responds to the invalidation of Maastricht assumptions regarding financial markets: to deepened financial integration, cross-border spillover effects of banking crises and the vicious circle interlinking banking and sovereign debt. But through free movement of financial services and capital, as well as freedom of establishment, regulation of financial markets relates to the microeconomic constitution as well.[43] The two elements of the banking union already decided on

40 BVerfG, 2 BvR 2728/13, 14 January 2014.

41 The referral includes a lengthy discussion on interpretation of EU Treaty law. The central claims are that OMT, firstly, does not classify as monetary policy but pursues objectives of economic policy and, hence, exceeds the ECB mandate; and, secondly, stands in contradiction with the prohibition on central bank financing, set out in Art. 123 TFEU. See on the referral the discussions in the special issue of the *German Law Journal*, 15(2) (2014).

42 Case C-270/12 *United Kingdom v Parliament and Council*, judgment of 22 January 2014 (not yet reported). The main issue was whether the European Securities and Markets Authority (ESMA) could have been established under Art. 114 TFEU which allows for harmonizing measures having as their objective the establishment and functioning of the internal market. The Court invoked the objective of guaranteeing financial stability within the Union when arguing that the powers of intervention of the ESMA were compatible with the rules governing the delegation of powers laid down in Arts. 290 TFEU and 291 TFEU (Paras. 84–6).

43 Indeed, the regulation **establishing** the single resolution mechanism (SRM) is based on Art. 114 TFEU and is thus supposed to serve harmonization for the purpose of the establishment or functioning of the internal market. The appropriateness of the legal basis has been a matter of controversy. *ESMA* can be interpreted to have shown a green

are the single supervisory mechanism and the single resolution mechanism. The single supervisory mechanism (SSM) consists of a network of the ECB supervisory function and national supervisory bodies.[44] The single resolution mechanism (SRM) complements harmonization of national mechanisms. It includes a single resolution authority and a European Resolution Fund. The Fund will be financed through levies on banks which participate directly in the single supervision mechanism; backing up the Fund by means of an ESM credit line was also discussed, but in the end rejected.[45] It appears that the same fate awaits the third element of the banking union, envisioned in the reform plans presented by the Commission and the Van Rompuy Working Group in late 2012: a deposit guarantee scheme which would involve a single European deposit guarantee fund.[46]

Debates on banking union have reawakened controversies over the economic assumptions underlying the macroeconomic constitution. Fears of moral hazard ensuing from the ECB supervisory function and doubts about its compatibility with the enhanced independence of the ECB have been widespread, in particular among German officials and economists. In the single resolution mechanism and the – at least for the time being – abandoned deposit guarantee scheme, critics have discerned signs of a development towards a transfer union. National banking sectors have varying degrees of undisclosed losses, so that mutualization of risks is dreaded to lead to fiscal transfers. Such a prospect would be even more likely if plans for mutualization of sovereign debt in the form of Eurobonds were adopted.[47] Criticism by German economists of the

light to the use of Art. 114 even for creating the SRM, which includes establishment of a European Resolution Authority. Invoking Art. 114 is justified by the claim that the SRM complements the harmonization of national resolution mechanisms. Regulation No. 806/2014 of 15 July 2014, [2014] OJ L225/1.

44 The Regulation conferring supervisory tasks on the ECB is based on Art. 127(6) TFEU, which allows for entrusting the ECB with 'specific tasks in the prudential supervision of credit institutions and other financial institutions with the exception of insurance undertakings'. Council Regulation (EU) No. 1024/2013 of 15 October 2013 conferring specific tasks on the European Central Bank concerning policies relating to the prudential supervision of credit institutions, [2013] OJ L287/63.

45 National contributions to the fund will be only gradually mutualized, in accordance with an international agreement among the participating states.

46 European Commission, 'A Blueprint for a Deep and Genuine Economic and Monetary Union – Launching a European Debate, Communication from the Commission', 30 November 2012, COM (2012) 777 final/2; European Council, 'Towards a Genuine Economic and Monetary Union', 5 December 2012, 120/12.

47 However, such a step would obviously conflict with the no-bailout clause of Art. 125(1) TFEU which, under the *Pringle* doctrine, is still constitutionally valid at other than crisis times.

ECB Securities Markets and Outright Monetary Transactions programmes proves that elevating financial stability to the overarching principle of the macroeconomic constitution is contentious as well, especially if this principle is used to justify the ECB's stepping outside monetary policy focusing on price stability. The German Constitutional Court's referral to the ECJ concerning the legality of OMT gives expression to a similar criticism, now dressed in legal garb.

Present debates are not confined merely to the focus and independence of ECB policy or the desirability of moving towards a transfer union. The familiar contradiction between market liberals – including ordoliberally oriented discussants – and proponents of European or national interventionism for the sake of competitiveness, economic growth and combating unemployment, has resuscitated as well. Critics have contested the economic premises of the emphasis on fiscal prudence in European economic governance. Perhaps the severest criticism has been directed at the austerity policy and market liberal reforms imposed on crisis states through the strict conditionality of financial assistance and also manifest in Commission decisions taken in the European monitoring procedures covering other Member States. In reactions to the far-reaching schemes of an economic union proposed by the Commission and the Van Rompuy Working Group in autumn 2012, even the pre-Maastricht constellation of Economists and Monetarists shows signs of revival. In accordance with the Economist position during the preparations for Maastricht, many of the initiatives strive at advancing the emergence of an integrated economic area – an optimal currency area.

The constitutional basis of the Eurozone regime

Above, our focus has been on the substantive mutation of the macroeconomic constitution, provoked by the Eurozone crisis. However, in line with other processes of sectoral constitutionalization, macroeconomic constitutionalization possesses not only a substantive but a formal aspect as well; a formal aspect which links it to the European juridical constitution. In this dimension, responses to the Eurozone crisis have raised two important issues: the constitutional basis of a particular legal regime of the Eurozone and the role of the rule of law in the macroeconomic field. I shall start with the first issue and discuss the rule of law principle in the next section.

The Maastricht provisions on EMU were premised on the assumption that Member States would join as soon as they fulfilled the convergence criteria. In effect, this was considered a legal obligation, except for the UK and Denmark who had negotiated opt-outs confirmed in separate Protocols attached to the Maastricht Treaty. Yet, though still heeding the principle of the unity of the EU, the Maastricht Treaty also launched a bifurcation of the macroeconomic constitution which shows no signs of being dissolved; indeed, rather the contrary: the economic constitution of the euro area is not identical to that applicable to non-euro Member States.

The expectation that all Member States would join EMU after fulfilling the convergence criteria has not been realized. The UK and Denmark have stuck to their formal derogations and Sweden has refused to enter, obtaining a political, *de facto* derogation. Furthermore, not all Member States accepted in the eastern enlargement are likely to hurry to join. The TFEU Chapter on the euro area, adopted in Lisbon,[48] reflects resignation in front of a lingering bifurcation of the Union into the euro area and non-euro Member States. The Chapter expressly constitutionalizes a separate legal and institutional framework for the euro area. It facilitates particular secondary legislation on the preventive and corrective arms of the Stability and Growth Pact, and formalizes the Euro Group; that is, the euro-area composition of the Ecofin Council.

The Eurozone crisis has reinforced legal and institutional diversification within the macroeconomic dimension. This has occurred partly through targeted secondary legislation issued under Art. 136(1) TFEU, partly through international agreements among the euro states. Secondary legislation has been prioritized in strengthening European economic governance, while in constructing rescue packages and stability mechanisms recourse has been had to international law instruments. Exceptions to this rule exist, though: the European Financial Stability Mechanism, the role of which was rather insignificant, was established by a regulation, and the focus of the Treaty on Stability, Coordination and Governance is on economic governance.

The multilateral surveillance and excessive deficit procedures under Arts. 121 and 126 TFEU address all Member States. However, the crisis was seen to require stricter fiscal discipline especially in euro states. Eurozone regulations, as integral elements in the six-pack and two-pack, have enhanced the sanctions mechanisms of European monitoring procedures by raising the level of existing deposits or fines and introducing new ones, and by strengthening the position of the Commission through reversed

[48] Ch. 4 of Title VIII TFEU (Provisions specific to Member States whose currency is the euro).

majority voting where the Council can only overturn Commission recommendations by a qualified majority. The regulations were issued on the basis of Art. 136(1), together with Art. 121(6) TFEU. The same competence basis was indicated for the two-pack regulation which established Commission power to monitor the annual draft budgets of the Eurozone states. Art. 136(1) sets out the delegation as follows:

In order to ensure the proper functioning of economic and monetary union, and in accordance with the relevant provisions of the Treaties, the Council shall, in accordance with the relevant procedure from among those referred to in Articles 121 and 126, with the exception of the procedure set out in Article 126(14), adopt measures specific to those Member States whose currency is the euro:

(a) to strengthen the coordination and surveillance of their budgetary discipline;
(b) to set out economic policy guidelines for them, while ensuring that they are compatible with those adopted for the whole of the Union and are kept under surveillance.

The Eurozone regulations manifest a very liberal reading of this provision. The delegation has been interpreted to warrant establishing new competences for EU institutions with regard to Eurozone states, such as power to impose deposits and fines or to monitor annual budgets in procedures under Art. 121 TFEU. This seems to collide with the wording of Art. 136(1), which intimates that the specific measures adopted for euro states must respect not only the procedures established in Arts. 121 and 126 TFEU but also the substance of the relevant Treaty articles. If creating new competences is allowed for EU institutions to strengthen coordination and surveillance of budgetary discipline in euro states, it is difficult to see how the limits of those competences should be defined. How deep or wide might permissible encroachments be on the sovereignty of euro states in fiscal and economic policy? And then, what about the procedural rules issued under Art. 136(1) TFEU? May these deviate from those laid down in the Treaties? Here a negative answer would appear to be warranted by both the wording of Art. 136(1) and the hierarchical supremacy of Treaty provisions over secondary legislation.[49]

[49] Art. 121(6) TFEU, too, has been interpreted in a way which seems difficult to justify in the light of its wording and scope. In the context of Regulation 1173/2011 on the effective enforcement of budgetary surveillance in the euro area, as well as the two-pack Regulations, Art. 121(6) has been invoked as a competence basis for provisions which deal not only with the preventive arm consisting of the multilateral surveillance procedure, but also the corrective arm of the excessive deficit procedure. Clearly, the reason for such innovative interpretation lies in the explicit prohibition in Art. 136(1)

Pringle examined European economic governance solely with regard to its implications for the constitutionality of intergovernmental stability funds, such as the ESM. In neither *Pringle* nor any other ruling has the ECJ taken a position on the reach of Art. 136(1) TFEU and thereby clarified the existing constitutional possibilities of erecting a specific regime of economic governance for the Eurozone. The extensive interpretation by the EU legislator of Art. 136(1) TFEU hints at an ongoing constitutional mutation in this field too; a mutation aimed at removing obstacles to a further differentiation of Eurozone legislation.

Use of international agreements in establishing stability mechanisms, in laying down rules applicable to financial assistance and – in the case of the TSCG – even in complementing primary and secondary EU legislation on economic governance raises constitutional concerns the potential implications of which exceed the macroeconomic constitution.[50] Contrary to *Van Gend en Loos* and *Costa v Enel* or *Kadi*, at issue now is not the positioning of the European legal system with regard to international law, but the use of international agreements as an instrument of European law-making. This issue touches on the doctrine of pre-emption, discussed above in Chapter 2 as a sub-principle of the supremacy of European over national law. After Lisbon, the doctrine finds an explicit basis in Art. 2(2) TFEU and the related Protocol on shared competences. It is also buttressed by the Member State duty of sincere cooperation. The starting point in assessing Member State powers in financial assistance or economic governance is clear: Member States, acting individually or in concert, do not need an explicit competence basis in the Treaties. They are free to act, provided that no legal obstacles deriving from EU law exist.[51] Their

to take recourse to Art. 126(14) which establishes the Council's power to issue complementing rules on the excessive deficit procedure.

50 Establishing a banking union will entail a third case of using international agreements as a means of European law-making. The Regulation on the single resolution mechanism will be complemented by an international agreement among the participating states on the mutualization of national compartments of the resolution fund.

51 This point has been made by many in academic debate on the crisis measures; see, e.g., C. Calliess (2011), pp. 213 and 222. It was also spelled out by AG Kokott in Para. 125 of her views in *Pringle*: 'In particular however, measures taken by the Union and measures taken by the Member States are in different contexts. For Union measures, in accordance with Article 4(1) and the first sentence of Article 5(1) TEU, the principle of conferred powers applies, while for the actions of Member States the principle of comprehensive power applies. In that light, Articles 122(2) and 143(2) TFEU empower the Union to grant credit facilities; a power which the Member States on the other hand

competence is assessed not on the principle of conferral but on the principle of comprehensive powers.[52] A potential legal obstacle relates to the doctrine of pre-emption. The question is whether Union financial assistance under Art. 122(2) TFEU, which was the Treaty basis indicated for the regulation establishing the EFSM, or secondary legislation or other measures of economic governance under Arts. 121, 126 and 136 TFEU prevent Member States from taking comparable action.

In the US doctrine of pre-emption, the focus is on legislative acts. At least according to their wording, the Treaty provisions on exclusive and shared competences also primarily concern legislation and adoption of other legally binding acts. Reference is to acts which are legally effective within Member States and where pre-emption encroaches on Member State legislative sovereignty. The Treaty provisions focus on legislative competences, which have been in the spotlight of scholarly discussion as well. However, the relevance of these provisions must be extended to Member State treaty-making power too. In discussing the division of competences between the Union and the Member States, it does not matter whether the latter adopt legally binding acts acting separately or jointly through agreements *inter se*.[53] The fact that in establishing and administering stability mechanisms, such as the EFSF and the ESM, Member states have not acted individually but in concert does not affect the possible applicability of the pre-emption doctrine.

Yet the fact that the focus of this doctrine is on legally binding acts and legislative sovereignty raises doubts as to its relevance for economic policy. Here the main task of the Union is to facilitate coordination among Member States. Both Treaty provisions and secondary legislation, which includes the original regulations of the Stability and Growth Pact as well as the six-pack and two-pack, lack direct effect within Member States and are largely irrelevant for their internal legislative sovereignty. This points to the irrelevance of the dichotomy of exclusive and shared competences for economic policy. And indeed, in the general provisions of the TFEU, Union economic policy competences are regulated outside this

do not need. To infer, from the fact that powers are conferred on the Union to grant credit facilities and that those powers are subject to restrictive conditions, that there is a comprehensive prohibition preventing the Member States from granting loans would be at variance with the principles relating to the division of powers between Member States and the Union.'

52 This is a principle not explicitly mentioned in the Treaties but evoked, for instance, by AG Kokott in Para. 125 of her views in *Pringle*.

53 For the purposes of the present discussion, treaties involving non-Member States – treaties *cum tertiis* – can be ignored.

dichotomy.[54] In *Pringle*, the ECJ brushed aside the claimant's argument related to shared competence.[55]

Yet EU legislation and other EU measures evidently restrict Member State freedom of action in constructing European procedures and mechanisms for financial assistance and economic governance through international agreements. However, instead of a pre-emption doctrine built on Treaty provisions on shared competence and the related Protocol, the restrictions should, more appropriately, be derived from the general EU law principles of supremacy and sincere cooperation. As argued in Chapter 2, the principle of supremacy is not restricted merely to the primacy of EU law over conflicting national law in cases pending before national courts. It extends to national legislatures, restraining them from enacting legislation contradicting EU law. In turn, the duty of sincere cooperation enshrined in Art. 4(3) TEU, which obliges Member States not only to 'facilitate the achievement of the Union's tasks' but also to 'refrain from any measure which could jeopardise the attainment of the Union's objectives', expands the restrictive effects even further: to all measures jeopardizing the objectives of EU legislation or other EU measures. In economic policy, the principles of supremacy and sincere cooperation entail normative consequences which come close to what in the pre-emption doctrine has been called rule and obstacle pre-emption. By contrast, they do not appear to give rise to such a prohibition for Member States to

54 Art. 2(3) contains the principal provision on coordination of economic policy: 'The Member States shall coordinate their economic and employment policies within arrangements as determined by this Treaty, which the Union shall have competence to provide.' This provision follows those on exclusive (Art. 2(1)) and shared (Art. 2(2)) competences. The areas of the Union's exclusive competences are enumerated in Art. 3 and shared competences in Art. 4 TFEU. Again, economic policy coordination, together with coordination of employment and social policy, is left outside this distinction and subsumed under a specific provision in Art. 5. Art. 5(1) repeats the Member State obligation to coordinate their economic policies within the Union and adds that 'to this end, the Council shall adopt measures, in particular broad guidelines for these policies'. It also lays down that 'specific provisions shall apply to those Member States whose currency is the euro'.

55 In *Pringle*, the claimant contended that economic policy is a shared competence, and that Arts. 2(3), 119 to 121 and 129 TFEU confer on Union institutions the power to coordinate economic policy. Mr Pringle further claimed that the conditionality of stability support by the ESM serves the same function as the recommendations under Arts. 121 (multilateral surveillance) and 126 TFEU (excessive deficit procedure). Therefore, he concluded, the ESM is in breach of Art. 2(2) TFEU, which stipulates that Member States are entitled to act in an area of shared competence only to the extent that the Union has not exercised its competence. The Court did not accept the argument and did not even consider it necessary to examine whether the EU law concept of shared competence is applicable to economic policy.

take action within the scope of Union measures as seems to derive from the Treaty provisions and the Protocol on shared (legislative) competence, not to speak of anything resembling field pre-emption. But if restrictions exist, they concern both individual and joint Member State action, as does pre-emption in areas of shared competence too.

In accordance with the above conclusion, *Pringle* confirmed that Union financial assistance under Art. 122(2) TFEU, including the conditions attached to it, or secondary legislation or other measures of economic governance under Arts. 121 and 126 TFEU do not prevent Member States from pursuing crisis resolution through intergovernmental agreements under private or international law. For instance, establishing the EFSM through Regulation 407/2010 is not an obstacle to Member States creating stability mechanisms, such as the EFSF or the ESM, which aim at similar objectives of crisis resolution as the Regulation and Union assistance. Nor do Arts. 121 and 126 TFEU, complemented by secondary legislation, bar provisions in intergovernmental agreements on the conditionality of financial assistance, contrary to what Mr Pringle argued. Yet the principles of supremacy and sincere cooperation entail that intergovernmental agreements or measures taken under them may not contradict EU primary or secondary legislation or other EU measures. This also means that the conditionality of financial assistance must be congruent with the country-specific guidance in the multilateral surveillance procedure under Art. 121 and the excessive deficit procedure under Art. 126. Moreover, harmony is required with conditionality under Regulation 407/2010, establishing the Union financial stability mechanism, the EFSM.[56]

Viewpoints concerning the Member State duty of sincere cooperation and the supremacy of EU law are of pertinence with regard to the Treaty on

[56] The Court states in Para. 121 of *Pringle* that 'the Member States remain free to establish a stability mechanism such as the ESM, provided however that, in its operation, that mechanism complies with European Union law and, in particular, with measures adopted by the Union in the area of coordination of the Member States' economic policies'. The Court's reasoning, though, is not persuasive. The Court emphasizes that 'the ESM is not concerned with the coordination of the economic policies of the Member States, but rather constitutes a financing mechanism', and that 'the conditionality prescribed . . . does not constitute an instrument for the coordination of the economic policies of the Member States' (Paras. 110–11). This is not convincing: certainly, financial assistance falls under economic policy and certainly the Member States coordinate their economic policies when establishing a joint mechanism for providing such assistance through an international agreement.

Stability, Coordination and Governance too.[57] Yet the particular contents of the TSCG occasion some additional comments. If economic policy were examined within the dichotomy of exclusive and shared competences, the TSCG would have to be seen as a rather clear breach of pre-emption. The Fiscal Compact, which makes up Title III of the TSCG, addresses issues which lie in the focus of Art. 126 TFEU, the Protocol on the excessive deficit procedure and the respective secondary legislation under the Stability and Growth Pact. In turn, Title IV (Economic Policy Coordination and Convergence) regulates issues within the scope of Art. 121 TFEU and complementary secondary legislation.

The TSCG raises two further pre-emption-related constitutional issues. Originally, the Fiscal Compact was intended to substitute for a Treaty amendment which would have imposed on Member States an obligation to introduce a debt break in their constitutions but which in December 2011 was blocked by the UK. Supremacy of EU law precludes provisions in international agreements between Member States which conflict with the Founding Treaties. But is complementing the Treaties possible? Or are there issues that fall under the exclusive competence of the EU constitutional legislator? Do the Founding Treaties exert a pre-emptive effect with regard *inter se* to agreements between Member States, by reserving certain topics for EU constitutional law?

Largely due to the constitutional concerns of some Member States, including Finland, in its final form the Fiscal Compact no longer entails

[57] The TSCG includes provisions which are aimed at guaranteeing respect for the principles of sincere cooperation and supremacy of EU law. Art. 2(1) TSCG invokes the principle of sincere cooperation: 'This Treaty shall be applied and interpreted by the Contracting Parties in conformity with the Treaties on which the European Union is founded, in particular Art. 4(3) of the Treaty on European Union, and with European Union law, including procedural law whenever the adoption of secondary legislation is required.' Furthermore, Art. 2(2) TSCG, in accordance with the supremacy of EU law, lays down that 'the provisions of this Treaty shall apply insofar as they are compatible with the Treaties on which the Union is founded and with European Union law' and that they 'shall not encroach upon the competences of the Union to act in the area of the economic union'. Yet the TSCG includes a particular provision whose compatibility with Union law is questionable: Art. 7, where the euro states commit to supporting proposals or recommendations by the Commission, where it considers that a euro state is in breach of the deficit criterion in the framework of an excessive deficit procedure, and adopting a reversed majority vote among themselves. It is difficult to see how such an obligation under international law, introducing a voting procedure in clear contradiction to Art. 126 TFEU, in combination with Art. 16(3) TEU, could permit the Contracting Parties to fully respect the procedural requirements of the Foundational Treaties, as Art. 7 TSCG also implies.

any legal obligation to amend national constitutions, and its provisions could arguably have been adopted as EU secondary legislation; if necessary, in the procedure for *enhanced cooperation* which the Treaties have provided since Amsterdam. Now the question is whether Member States are free to resort to agreements under international law in subject matters of the Treaties after adopting *secondary* EU legislation has proven to be politically impossible. Considering the focus of the TSCG, the situation under discussion is fundamentally different from channelling to a Member State in fiscal distress financial assistance from other Member States. Financial stability mechanisms, such as the EFSF or the ESM, have coordinated Member State action outside the Treaty framework. The Founding Treaties do not include any specific competence basis which would facilitate EU legislation for such purposes, nor has the amendment to Art. 136 TFEU, expressly justifying establishment of an intergovernmental stability mechanism, created one. The financial justification for the intergovernmental option is obvious too. The Union, with its limited budgetary resources, does not possess the fiscal capacity needed for maintaining financial stability and buttressing the common currency. Recourse to intergovernmental assistance appears to be not only legally justified but even fiscally necessary.[58] By contrast, the TSCG addresses issues of Union action which clearly belong to the scope of the Founding Treaties and which have already been submitted to quite dense secondary legislation. Here the reason for picking the intergovernmentalist way was simply the veto by the UK – and later the Czech Republic – which blocked the Union way.

The gravest constitutional doubts concerning intergovernmental agreements within the scope of the Founding Treaties relate to sidestepping the procedural requirements which have to be respected in amending the Treaties or in drafting and adopting secondary legislation. These requirements aim to engage all the major EU institutions, including the European Parliament, and grant a voice to all Member States. In the post-Lisbon era, national parliaments have a right to intervene in the legislative procedure too. By contrast, drafting, adopting and implementing intergovernmental agreements involve merely the contracting parties. These, in turn,

58 The establishment of the EFSM through Regulation 407/2010, though, shows that the Union framework allows for quite flexible arrangements, including credit-market financing. However, involving only the euro states in a stability mechanism functioning under the EU budget might have been constitutionally difficult.

are represented primarily by governments, while parliamentary input depends on the provisions of the national constitution. If political negotiations aiming at consensus among all Member States fail, should not the Member States who still want to push ahead rely on the procedure the Treaties have expressly reserved for such a situation: namely, enhanced cooperation within the EU?[59] I shall approach the issue by examining, firstly, the arguments presented in the literature for the continuing availability of the intergovernmental option even where enhanced cooperation is constitutionally possible; and, secondly, the scope of enhanced cooperation, as it emerges in the light of *Pringle*.

Bruno de Witte's main argument in support of his view that the intergovernmental way is legally open after Amsterdam too is that to exclude this option would be 'a drastic curtailment of Member State treaty-making competences that cannot be assumed to have taken place in the absence of any clear indication in the founding treaties'.[60] Because of the Treaty provisions on enhanced cooperation, this argument is not as convincing in the post- as it perhaps was in the pre-Amsterdam era. De Witte clearly perceives the main reasons for the continuing allure of the intergovernmental way: 'i) the legal conditions for taking the "outside" route are less onerous than the conditions set for intra-EU closer cooperation and ii) Member States preserve, when acting under international law, complete control over the negotiation process and almost complete control over the implementation and enforcement of the obligations which they accept in the agreement'.[61] But he does not seem to accept the circumvention argument. He explains the severity of the conditions for enhanced cooperation as follows: 'as the closer cooperation delivers the keys of the powerful EU/EC engine to a group of Member States, such a move should be allowed less liberally than "old-fashioned" recourse to the more modest instruments of international law'.[62] But if a group of Member States entrust EU institutions with implementation tasks through an intergovernmental agreement, as is the case with the TSCG, they endeavour to have the best of both worlds: recourse to the 'powerful EU engine' within a regime established under the less onerous conditions of public international law.

Thus, a powerful case can be made for Member States not being allowed to resort to intergovernmental agreements where enhanced cooperation is legally possible. The available scope of enhanced cooperation is defined

[59] Cf. the questions posed by P. Craig (2012).
[60] B. de Witte (2001), p. 40. [61] *Ibid.*, p. 33. [62] *Ibid.*, p. 57.

in Arts. 20(1) TEU and 329(1) TFEU.[63] In *Pringle*, the ECJ adopted a rather strict interpretation of the possible scope of enhanced cooperation. The Court's reasoning seems to imply that for enhanced cooperation to be possible, it does not suffice that the matter for cooperation falls under an area of shared competence, as the wording of Art. 329(1) TFEU appears to imply. What is further required is that a specific competence basis for Union action can be identified (Paras. 166–9). But the Court's reasoning also implies that if this condition is met the argument related to the primacy of enhanced cooperation is relevant.

The legal leeway for a separate Eurozone regime and the possibility of a two-speed Europe, with the Eurozone escaping to its own way of deepened integration, depends on the position taken on the constitutional issues raised in this section: the reach of Eurozone legislative measures under Art. 136(1) TFEU; the scope of enhanced cooperation and its relationship to international agreements among Member States; and the relevance of the doctrine of pre-emption and the principles of supremacy and sincere cooperation as potential restrictions on Member State treaty-making power. Neither the constitutional legislator – the Member States as *Herren der Veträge* – nor the ECJ as the Union constitutional court has yet brought clarity to these fundamental issues.

Still a Union based on the rule of law?

As argued in Chapter 5, the microeconomic constitution deals with the behaviour of individual economic actors, which has enabled the central role of the law and the courts. The field of the macroeconomic constitution, with its focus on objectives, aggregate economic values and policies, is much less susceptible to juridification. Objectives and aggregate values may, though, be fixed in seemingly exact terms, such as the upper limits for government deficit or debt, set out in the Protocol on the excessive deficit procedure, or the convergence criteria as the test for membership in EMU. However, attainment or non-attainment of these objectives

63 According to Art. 20(1) TEU, 'Member States which wish to establish enhanced cooperation between themselves within the framework of the Union's non-exclusive competences may make use of its institutions and exercise those competences by applying the relevant provisions of the Treaties.' In turn, Art. 329(1) TFEU lays down that enhanced cooperation can be established between Member States 'in one of the areas covered by the Treaties, with the exception of fields of exclusive competence and the common foreign and security policy'.

depends on a great number of individual policy decisions and external factors which simply cannot be exhaustively regulated by law. Hence even exactly defined objectives and values must leave room for exceptions in order to allow for unpredictable and uncontrollable external factors and to facilitate timely reactions by decision-makers.

Procedures lend themselves more easily to legal regulation than substantive policies, but the practical impact of mere procedural regulation may be rather weak. This is especially the case if the procedures adhere to the open method of coordination. In particular before the Eurozone crisis, much of the Treaty law on fiscal and economic policy had a soft-law character. Correspondingly, the courts, European or national, have hardly played any role in implementing or further elaborating the European macroeconomic constitution. Before *Pringle*, the only ruling of the ECJ explicitly pertaining to the macroeconomic constitution was *Commission v Council* in 2004, which led to loosening up the excessive deficit procedure. *Pringle* is the single most important constitutional speech act which the Eurozone crisis has produced. Yet it mainly confirms the constitutional mutation which had already occurred, while landmark rulings in the field of the microeconomic constitution, such as *Dassonville* or *Cassis de Dijon*, really created new constitutional law.

Reliance on expert bodies is a common characteristic of both layers of the European economic constitution. Within the microeconomic constitution, the key players are the courts – the ECJ and national courts feeding it with their references and transmitting its jurisprudence into national law – and the Commission as the European Competition Authority. In the field of the macroeconomic constitution, the position of the Court has been rather peripheral. However, here the Maastricht Treaty introduced another body relying on expert knowledge and output legitimacy, and insulated from democratic political pressures: the European Central Bank. In addition, the Commission holds a vital position in coordinating and monitoring Member State economic and fiscal policies. Macroeconomic constitutionalization has especially strengthened the standing of the Commissioner for Economic and Monetary Affairs and the Directorate-General subordinated to that office. In both the micro- and macroeconomic fields, basic principles and objectives have been regulated at constitutional (Treaty) level, while operationalizing and – at least to a certain extent – complementing them has been left to independent experts. However, the role of legal expertise is more marginal in the macroeconomic dimension than it has been in free movement law in particular.

In free movement law, the ECJ has assumed the task of elaborating constitutional principles and filling in the blanks. Relying on its mandate to create and maintain an effective rule of law, the ECJ has provided the necessary legal experimentalism with regard to unforeseen situations; hence the slogan 'integration through law'.[64] The Court has been able to introduce its doctrinal innovations in unspectacular cases and free from political pressure or media attention. In the macroeconomic field, hardly any doctrinal tradition exists, and judicial decision-making cannot be based on undisputed, verifiable facts either. Assessing the consequences of alternative readings of Treaty provisions would presuppose an economic expert knowledge which the Court simply does not possess. In divergence from free movement law, but few cases touching upon the macroeconomic constitution come before the ECJ, and those which do tend to be politically heavily loaded. The ECJ has only been able to exercise restricted *ex post* control. Indeed, perhaps the main burden of legal scrutiny has fallen to Member State level. However, the level of activity of constitutional courts and other institutions responsible for national constitutional review varies, depending, firstly, on differences in national constitutional doctrine on, for instance, parliamentary budgetary sovereignty and social rights; and, secondly, on the particularities of national systems of constitutional review, such as the extent to which they allow supervision of European measures. Furthermore, Member State review does not apply European but national constitutional standards.

A discussion of the EU in terms of the rule of law or community of law is riddled with conceptual difficulties. This is due not only to the well-known polysemy of 'the rule of law' but, more profoundly, the collusion of two traditions whose interrelationship is not easy to grasp. Indeed, the German expressions *Rechtsgemeinschaft* and *Rechtsstaat* are more instructive than their English counterparts. Often enough both German terms are translated into 'the rule of law', thus obliterating their conceptual difference. On the other hand, 'community of law' as a translation for *Rechtsgemeinschaft* is not very informative either, because it lacks any established conceptual content. In *Les Verts*, the ECJ introduced a veritable terminological mishmash, 'a community based on the rule of law', clearly trying to capture something of the conceptual content of both *Rechtsgemeinschaft* and *Rechtsstaat*.[65]

64 Probably first used by M. Cappelletti et al. (1985).

65 'It must . . . be emphasized . . . that the European Economic Community is a Community based on the rule of law, inasmuch as neither its Member States nor its institutions can avoid a review of the question whether the measures adopted by them are in conformity with the basic constitutional charter, the Treaty. In particular, in Articles 173 [now 263 TFEU] and 184 [now 277 TFEU], on the one hand, and in Article 177 [now 267 TFEU], on

The Treaties do not employ the term 'community of law' or 'a community based on the rule of law'. In contrast, ever since Maastricht explicit reference has been made to the rule of law or, in the German version, *Rechtsstaatlichkeit*. In the Preamble to the Treaty on the European Union, the Member States declare that they draw 'inspiration from the cultural, religious and humanist inheritance of Europe, from which have developed the universal values of the inviolable and inalienable rights of the human person, freedom, democracy, equality and the rule of law', and confirm 'their attachment to the principles of liberty, democracy and respect for human rights and fundamental freedoms and of the rule of law'. In Art. 2 TEU, the rule of law is included in the values on which the Union is declared to be founded and which are proclaimed to be common to all Member States. These values are referred to in several other Treaty provisions, and a commitment to their promotion is a condition for accession to the Union (Art. 49 TEU). Art. 7 TEU sets out the procedure to be followed in case of a clear risk of a serious breach of those values by a Member State. In turn, the preamble to the Charter of Fundamental Rights asserts that 'the Union is founded on the indivisible, universal values of human dignity, freedom, equality and solidarity', and 'based on the principles of democracy and the rule of law'. All in all, Treaty provisions and value proclamations, complemented by the case law of the ECJ repeatedly reconfirming the principle, leave no doubt as to the status of the rule of law as an overarching constitutional principle. It finds its main location in the juridical constitution but, in accordance with the framing function of this constitutional dimension, pertains to all the other dimensions too, including the economic one.

The German notion of *Rechtsstaat* and the English (Anglo-American) principle of the rule of law have different roots, which still, despite a rapprochement during the twentieth century, influence their understanding in the respective legal cultures. Yet they share a common core: they both aim at preventing arbitrary use of power.[66] And it is this common core which also facilitates a conceptual synthesis in EU law, acceptable to different legal cultures. However, the rule of law is not the same as

the other, the Treaty established a complete system of legal remedies and procedures designed to permit the Court of Justice to review the legality of measures adopted by the institutions. Natural and legal persons are thus protected against the application to them of general measures which they cannot contest directly before the Court by reason of the special conditions of admissibility laid down in the second paragraph of Article 173 of the Treaty.' Case C-294/83 *Les Verts v Parliament* [1986] ECR 1339, Para. 23.

[66] See Ch. 7 in K. Tuori (2011).

Rechtsgemeinschaft. It really makes a difference whether we discuss the EU in terms of *Rechtsgemeinschaft* or *Rechtsstaat(lichkeit)*.

The portrayal of the Community as a *Rechtsgemeinschaft* goes back to Walter Hallstein, the first President of the Commission. For Hallstein, the Community was a *Rechtsgemeinschaft* in three senses. It was a creation of law (*Rechtsschöpfung*), it was a source of law and it was a legal order.[67] The foremost of these connotations was the first one: the Community as a creation of law. Here Hallstein evoked the central role of law as the means and object of integration; the reason why European integration has so often been characterized as a legal project, in spite of its basic economic orientation. *Rechtsgemeinschaft* refers, firstly, to the community of states: instead of being simple relations of power, the mutual relations of the Member States and their relations to the Community are governed by law. But, secondly, the connotation of *Rechtsgemeinschaft* possesses a societal aspect too, and bears an echo of the ordoliberal conception of the marriage of economy and law. The *ordoliberal* conception of market economy with free, performance-based competition implies an *ordo* of general legal rules giving rise to individual economic rights and restricting not only discretionary and interventionist public power but also competition distorting private economic power. Creation and maintenance of such an *ordo* presupposes a strong *Rechtsstaat*-type state. But it is also expected to engender a *herrschaftsfreie* social order. In this wider, societal connotation Hallstein's *Rechtsgemeinschaft* comes close to Franz Böhm's *Privatrechtsgesellschaft*.[68]

In sum, *Rechtsgemeinschaft* has both a public and private aspect. It refers not only to the relations of Member States to the Community/Union and among themselves; it also alludes to the vertical relations of market actors to centralized European and decentralized national public power, as well as the horizontal relations among themselves. What is missing in the context of the macroeconomic constitution is the societal or private aspect of *Rechtsgemeinschaft*. But as we have seen, even in the remaining public aspect the power of law is inevitably limited. With the prominence of the macroeconomic constitution the Union has lost much of its quality of a *Rechtsgemeinschaft*.

In its original, Hallsteinian sense, *Rechtsgemeinschaft* is a descriptive rather than a normative notion. The rule of law or *Rechtsstaatlichkeit*, by contrast, is undoubtedly a normative principle, even in the EU. The rule of law, as developed in the Anglo-Saxon tradition, and Continental, mainly

[67] See I. Pernice (2001). [68] See F. Böhm (1966).

German, *Rechtsstaatlichkeit* aim to prevent arbitrary power, and – as is often added – to safeguard rights of the individual. In the EU context, however, the rule of law must be examined in the tripartite relations between the Union, Member States and individual subjects. Even in the EU, the implications of the rule of law are most often discussed from the perspective of individual subjects. For these, the rule of law provides protection against arbitrary use of power by both the Union and Member States (when these act in the scope of EU law). This is the main perspective from which the ECJ has elaborated on the contents of the rule of law. As Laurent Pech has summarized the case law, 'the Court essentially equates the rule of law, as a constitutional principle . . . with judicial review (as it gives effect to the rule of law) and judicial protection of individual rights and in particular, the individual's fundamental rights'.[69] But protection of individuals does not exhaust the significance of the principle in the EU. It is also relevant for relations between the Union and Member States, although its content cannot remain exactly the same as in discussing safeguards for individuals. Thus, fundamental rights – the substantive element in the rule-of-law notion employed by the ECJ – lose relevance and must be replaced – so I suggest – with the powers or sovereignty rights of Member States.

Within the field of the macroeconomic constitution, the emphasis in the implications of the rule-of-law principle lies in Union–Member State relations. For the sake of discussing the repercussions of recent constitutional mutation, I propose to unpack the principle into three main normative elements:

- protection of Member State powers,
- the principle of legality and
- accountability.

The principle of conferral is the primary constitutional safeguard for Member State competences. It applies both to the Union as a whole and to each Union institution. Under Art. 5(2) TEU, 'the Union shall act only within the limits of the competences conferred upon it by the Member States in the Treaties to attain the objectives set out therein', while 'competences not conferred upon the Union in the Treaties remain with the Member States'. Correspondingly, Art. 13(2) TEU lays down that 'each institution shall act within the limits of the powers conferred on it in the Treaties'. The principle of conferral is complemented by *subsidiarity*

69 L. Pech (2010), p. 380.

which is supposed to govern Union action in areas outside Member State exclusive competence (Art. 5(3) TEU).

The principle of conferral has not been able to prevent erosion of Member State sovereignty in non-monetary economic policy or the ensuing reduction of national latitude in core fields of social policy. The edge of the principle of conferral can be blunted through a liberal reading of Treaty provisions on Union and institution competences; this is what has largely occurred in the application of Arts. 121, 126 and 136 TFEU for the purpose of tightening European economic governance, as well as in interpreting the mandate of the ECB (Art. 127 TFEU). Furthermore, the principle of conferral can be rendered ineffective by recourse to international agreements, which has been the dominant option in rescue packages and stability mechanisms. The strict conditionality of financial assistance, whereby recipient states 'voluntarily' accept restrictions on their sovereignty, tends to undermine the principle of conferral as well. Even in economic governance, the efficacy of *ultra vires* review, focusing on transgressions of competence, can be doubted, not only because of the general laxity of ECJ *ultra vires* review of Union measures but also because of the vagueness of the Treaty provisions on economic policy competences.

Judicial control in the shape of *ultra vires* review is a necessary guarantee of respect for the principle of conferral. In economic governance within the institutional and legal framework of the EU, Member States can bring an action before the ECJ pursuant to, and within the limits set out by, Art. 263 TFEU.[70] As regards rescue mechanisms, the EFSF Framework Agreement included provisions on dispute settlement and access to justice, and so does the Treaty on the ESM. Still, judicial control over, say, the conditions of financial assistance on the initiative of recipient states can be deemed quite illusory, also due to the duress under which states receiving financial assistance find themselves and which leaves them little choice but to accept the conditionality of assistance.

The principle of conferral specifies the principle of legality with regard to the competences of the Union and its institutions. Yet the implications of legality are not exhausted by the requirement of a competence basis in

[70] The ECJ possesses jurisdiction over the legality of, inter alia, acts of the Council, of the Commission and of the European Central Bank, other than recommendations and opinions. In addition to EU institutions, actions can be brought by Member States 'on grounds of lack of competence, infringement of an essential procedural requirement, infringement of the Treaties or of any rule of law relating to their application, or misuse of powers' (Art. 263 TFEU).

the Treaties but have a wider scope. As can be read from Art. 13(2) TEU, the principle of legality addresses even the procedures, conditions and objectives of action.[71] In addition, as has been emphasized in both the Anglo-Saxon and the German tradition, the principle implies particular qualities of the rules which are supposed to govern administrative action. In an influential article, Joseph Raz, clearly taking his cue from Lon Fuller's account of the 'internal morality of law',[72] has argued that legal norms must be prospective, adequately publicized, clear and relatively stable, and that law-making too should be guided by open, stable, clear and general rules.[73] It is easy to agree with Raz's criteria. Only such rules can accomplish the two purposes of legality: providing reliable *ex ante* guidance and facilitating *ex post* control. However, a further requirement should be added: the addressees must have a factual possibility to adjust their behaviour to the rules.

Due to the extreme complexity of the rule-work emerging from the Eurozone crisis, it can hardly be deemed to meet the rule of law requirement of clarity. Often enough, the rules are characterized by a peculiar combination of apparent exactness and great ambiguity. This applies, for instance, to provisions on budget deficits and sovereign debt: exact reference values are accompanied by vaguely formulated exceptions. Provisions on the procedure of economic imbalances follow the same pattern: the scoreboard the Commission is supposed to employ in its monitoring activities involves exact parameters but their application allows for wide discretion. What makes this discretion particularly worrying from a rule of law perspective is that it is backed by formal sanctions. Doubts can also be raised as to whether euro states with their essentially reduced macroeconomic arsenal can do much to improve the situation and to adjust their behaviour to rules and decisions.

The principle of legality implies access to justice, and, indeed, this is the crucial rule of law requirement the ECJ has emphasized in its case law. The jurisprudence of the ECJ is mostly related to individual subjects, but access to justice is also vital in controlling rules and decisions addressed to Member States. I have already commented on problems affecting *ultra vires* judicial review. Substantive review, in turn, requires that decisions can be conceived of as resulting from the application of legal rules. Even if based primarily on non-legal, say, economic considerations, they should

[71] 'Each institution shall act within the limits of the powers conferred on it in the Treaties, and in conformity with the procedures, conditions and objectives set out in them.'

[72] L. L. Fuller (1969).

[73] J. Raz (1979), pp. 214–15.

also be accessible to analysis in terms of legal rationality. In the field of the macroeconomic constitution this is but very rarely the case, and for easily understandable reasons. Both monetary and non-monetary policy must react to rapidly changing economic situations and heed a wide range of economic variables. This makes it extremely difficult – and, many observers would add, economically even irrational – to try to govern economic policy with legal rules. It lies in the very nature of independent expert bodies, such as the ECB and the Commission, that the rules they employ in their decision-making are not supposed to be so much legal as scientific by nature. Even when these bodies overstep their expert role and adopt the features of a politician, the value judgments they make within their mandate are often not judicially controllable. The same, of course, holds for institutions which possess an even primarily political character, such as the Council. At both supranational and national level, courts have no choice but to leave a wide margin of appreciation to politicians and experts. This is a potential source of severe tensions, if expert institutions deviate far from the justified, rule-of-law-based expectations of Member States and their constituents. If these tensions do not find other than judicial means to dissolve, the legitimacy of the macroeconomic constitution may be jeopardized.

So, to arrive at the third component I have discerned in the rule of law, the reach of judicial accountability in the field of the macroeconomic constitution is necessarily limited. This makes the functioning of other forms of accountability, such as public and political accountability, important even from a rule of law perspective. Unfortunately, here one confronts the hurdles to accountability raised by the complexity of the issues, the fragmented rule-work and institutional structure, as well as deficient transparency.

Legitimacy concerns

The institutional and political implications of macroeconomic constitutionalization possess both similarities to and differences from the repercussions of the microeconomic constitution. In the macroeconomic field, no problem of *gouvernement des juges* exists, but *gouvernement des experts* is certainly an important issue. Clear affinities exist between the positions of, on the one hand, the Court and the Commission as the Competition Authority in the microeconomic field and, on the other hand, the ECB and the Commission as supervisor of national policies in the macroeconomic field. However, before turning to the role of expert bodies I shall discuss the problems that the recent constitutional mutation has posed for the democratic legitimation mechanisms of the EU.

Democratic input legitimacy in the EU relies on two channels. Direct input legitimacy is channelled mainly through European elections and the European Parliament. Direct input legitimacy suffers from well-known problems related to the lack of a European demos united by a common constitutional culture and identity and involved in citizenship practices in a Europe-wide public sphere. The main burden in guaranteeing democratic input legitimacy for EU policies has fallen on the indirect, two-level mechanism where national democratic procedures hold a key position. In its *Maastricht* ruling, the German Constitutional Court stressed that because of the largely lacking sociological and cultural presuppositions of a European demos, European democracy can have but a supportive function as the 'peoples of individual States convey democratic legitimation via national parliaments'. Hence, the German constitutional law principle of democracy imposes limits on the extent to which functions and powers can be transferred to the European level.[74]

Indeed, democratic arguments played a significant part in determining the division of competences between the national and transnational level in Maastricht. A major reason for leaving the economic union incomplete and not paying heed to Economist forebodings was the perceived need for democratic input legitimation for fiscal and other economic policies; that need, in turn, could only be satisfied at the Member State level. In its *Lisbon* ruling, the German Constitutional Court not only confirmed its assessment that because of the weak democratic foundations of the Union, under the Lisbon Treaty too the necessary democratic legitimation for Union action derives mainly from national procedures. Pointing to the pivotal political role of the budgetary process and in particular parliamentary debate on the budget, the Court also explicitly included public revenue and expenditure among the areas of 'democratic formative action' which must remain under Member State sovereignty.[75]

As the German Constitutional Court has repeatedly stressed, Member State fiscal sovereignty is not only a central principle of the Maastricht macroeconomic constitution but a principle of national constitutional law as well;[76] it is necessary for the sake of democratic legitimacy at

[74] BVerfGE 89, 155, 2 October 1993. [75] BVerGE, 2 BvE 2/08, 30 June 2009.

[76] This has also been the central premise of the Constitutional Law Committee of the Finnish Parliament in its opinions on European measures to combat the Eurozone crisis. However, both the German Constitutional Court and the Finnish Constitutional

both the European and the national level. This normative argumentation has its sociological counterpart in Fritz Scharpf's observations on the two-level legitimation structure of the EU. The effects of European policies on European citizens have been mediated through Member States, and citizens have confronted EU institutions, policies or the impacts of these policies in their daily lives not directly, but indirectly, via Member State action. Consequently, Member States have borne the main responsibility for providing input legitimacy for the EU as well. This they have largely been able to accomplish, due to national democratic procedures and the controlling power of national parliaments, electorates and civil societies.

Scharpf has also pointed to how the Eurozone crisis and the measures taken to combat it have affected the functioning of the two-level legitimation mechanism. The citizenry has experienced the consequences of European policies without the dampening and legitimating mediation of national democratic procedures: 'In the present euro crisis . . . the shield of legitimacy intermediation has been pushed aside as citizens are directly confronted with the massive impact of European policies – and with their manifest lack of democratic legitimacy.'[77] In crisis states, governments and parliaments implement the austerity programmes agreed on by the Troika of the Commission, the ECB and the IMF, giving effect to the strict conditionality of assistance. National democratic institutions are widely conceived of as mere executors of policies imposed from the outside. In these circumstances, parliamentary and electoral mechanisms are hardly able to procure input legitimation even for national decision-making, not to speak of channelling that legitimation to the European level. In assisting Member States too, the European level is increasingly held responsible for policies affecting citizens, and the national parliament is not seen to possess much leeway in their implementation. Despite the dominant intergovernmentalism in both creation and administration of

Law Committee have consented to significant curtailing of national budget autonomy. Kaarlo Tuori and Klaus Tuori (2014), pp. 196–204.

77 '[T]he higher level of the European polity is generally beyond the horizon of citizens' expectations and political demands; it is not the target of public debates and party competition, and most importantly, it is not vulnerable to electoral sanctions . . . Citizens will not usually know the origin of the rules with which they are asked to comply, but they know that the only government which they might hold politically accountable is their own. In effect, therefore, national governments must generally bear the full burden of political accountability for unwelcome exercises of governing authority, regardless of how much European law may have contributed to these.' F. Scharpf (2012), p. 19.

rescue packages and stability mechanisms, reduced national sovereignty has hampered the functioning of the two-level legitimation mechanism. The discontent in both recipient and assisting states, which finds expression in, for instance, the electoral success of populist parties riding on nationalistic and anti-European themes in both national and European elections, testifies to increasing legitimation problems.

Two alternative responses exist to the legitimacy dilemma of fiscal and economic policy which has resulted from the gradual erosion of national sovereignty in these two fields, and the consequent shrinking of the legitimating power of national democratic procedures. The first of these is to redefine fiscal and economic policy and negate their need for democratic input legitimation. This strategy implies de-politicizing fiscal and economic policy, labelling them fields of non-political expertise where decisions should be grounded in objectively given economic parameters. Thus, the model already applied to monetary policy would be extended to non-monetary economic policy as well. The door to redefinition was already opened ajar by the Maastricht constraints on national fiscal policy, relying on quasi-objective, quantitative reference values. However, the reference values still left the content and size of the public sector to national discretion, as long as it was considered to be prudently financed. The expansion and deepening of European economic governance and the increasing substantive and procedural requirements imposed on national budgetary frameworks have widened the crack and enhanced the non-political features of fiscal policy. The new excessive imbalances procedure, with its scoreboard of macroeconomic parameters monitored by the Commission, has extended the tendency of de-politicization to general macroeconomic policy.[78]

The strategy of de-politicization has obvious limits. The need for democratic input legitimation arises from the redistributive effects of fiscal and economic policy. European citizens have experienced these effects very profoundly during the Eurozone crisis which has but intensified

[78] This tendency has taken institutional forms as well. Proposals for creating independent budget offices or councils at both the Member State and European level have abounded. With adoption of the two-pack, they have reaped their first practical results. Eurozone states are obliged to establish independent bodies monitoring compliance with fiscal rules. These must be structurally independent or 'endowed with functional autonomy *vis-à-vis* the fiscal authorities of the Member State' in charge of monitoring the implementation of national fiscal rules. Regulation No. 473/2013 of 21 May 2013 on common provisions for monitoring and assessing draft budgetary plans and ensuring the correction of excessive deficit of the Member States in the euro area, [2013] OJ L140/11, Arts. 2(1) and 5.

the call for democratic legitimacy. Redefinition of fiscal and economic policy signifies an effort to shift the emphasis from democratic input legitimation towards output legitimation, guaranteed by non-political, independent experts. But even if concrete results testifying to the benefits of increasing the weight of non-political expertise were to be seen, legitimacy expectations cannot be manipulated at will from above.

The obvious alternative to de-politicization would be to try to remedy the proverbial democracy deficit at the European level. In this respect, developments during the Eurozone crisis have not been very encouraging. The European Parliament and the national parliaments have been accorded but a peripheral position in both financial stability mechanisms and European economic governance, while intergovernmental institutions and expert bodies have held sway. Still, the weak formal position of the European Parliament in both financial stability mechanisms and European economic governance is not the only and, arguably, not even the main obstacle to democracy at the European level. The major problems now as before concern sociological and cultural presuppositions: the still embryonic European civil society and public sphere, as well as the weak self-identity and frail mutual solidarity of European citizenry. If the Eurozone crisis has in general had positive consequences for democracy, one of these could be awakening a sense of European interconnectedness both in the media and among the general public. Unfortunately, this in itself positive development has been tainted by a nationalistic distortion: more often than not, events in other Member States and in Europe at large have been observed through the lenses of narrowly conceived national interests. The European elections in spring 2014 clearly testified to this nationalistic bias. On balance, the crisis has probably done more to destroy than create sociological and cultural presuppositions for the emergence of a European demos, the subject of European democracy. One of the crucial issues for the future of European integration is how to end the inopportune marriage between rising European awareness and mounting nationalism.

In the Maastricht framework, the ECB, enjoying constitutionally guaranteed independence, was supposed to be the central expert body responsible for implementing the macroeconomic constitution. Indeed, from an ordoliberal perspective monetary policy aiming at price stability epitomizes similar non-political *Ordnungspolitik* as competition policy within the microeconomic constitution. And just as non-discretionary competition policy is expected to enjoy supremacy over other, discretionary policies, the same holds for non-discretionary monetary policy. Differing from competition policy, Treaty law explicitly lays down the exactly defined and limited focus of monetary policy; its superiority with regard to Member State fiscal and economic policy; and the independence of the ECB as the expert body charged with the execution of this branch of *Ordnungspolitik*.

Although the German Bundesbank had in practice enjoyed great independence, this independence was never explicitly constitutionally anchored. By contrast and somewhat paradoxically, the independence and monetary stability focus of the ECB has been explicitly enshrined in German constitutional law. According to Art. 88 of the Basic Law, amended to enable ratification of the Maastricht Treaty, the Bundesbank's 'tasks and powers can, in the context of the European Union, be transferred to the European Central Bank which is independent and primarily bound by the purpose of securing stability of prices'. In the *Maastricht* ruling, the German Constitutional Court defined EMU as primarily a monetary union, which the Treaty governs as 'a community committed to long-term stability, in particular to monetary stability'. The Court pointed out that assignment of monetary policy to an independent European central bank restricts Member State sovereign rights and the democratic legitimation deriving from the electorate of Member States. The Court characterized monetary policy in rather ordoliberal terms as 'a substantial political sphere which supports individual liberty by maintaining the value of currency, and influences public finances and those areas of politics dependent on them by controlling the money supply'. In the Court's view, modifying the scope of the principle of democracy through Art. 88 of the Basic Law is justified not only by German experience but by a truth of economic science as well: 'it takes account of the special factor, established in the German system and also scientifically proven, that an independent central bank is more likely to protect monetary value, and therefore the general economic basis for national budget policy and private planning and disposition, while maintaining economic liberty than are sovereign governmental institutions'.[79]

Independent expert bodies are exempted from the coverage of democratic input legitimation. This calls for both specific justification and a compensatory guarantee of legitimacy. The justification is based on a belief that expert functions require application of scientific or quasi-scientific knowledge and tools. Experts are expected to perform their

[79] BVerfGE 89, 155, 12 October 1993.

tasks independently from external, particularly political, influences. The input information processed by experts is solely defined by the 'scientific' needs of their functions. As scientific rationalization leaves only one available option, no room or need exists for political decision-making. Courts of law are the classic epitome of an independent expert function, competition authorities a later example. The independent expert role of central banks is an even more recent phenomenon, with its underpinning intellectual foundation laid only in the 1970s.

The ordoliberal view of economic freedom providing substantive legitimacy for the economic constitution resurfaces in the *Maastricht* ruling of the German Constitutional Court as a justification for entrusting stability-focused monetary policy to an independent European central bank. But if we try to assess the legitimacy claim of expert bodies within the alternatives of input and output legitimacy, the emphasis is on the latter. Independent courts are expected to safeguard individual rights and the rule of law in general; independent competition authorities are expected to ensure an open market economy with free competition; and independent central banks are expected to guarantee monetary stability and facilitate economic prosperity. Furthermore, these institutions are supposed to produce their expected outcome in virtue of their expertise: their knowledge of the juridical or scientific laws which govern their field of action and which they apply in a non-discretionary way. Here lies the justification for their independence: expert bodies must be shielded from all influence which would derail them from rigorous and disinterested employment of their expertise. This justification also holds for the independence of the ECB.

Instead of supervision and guidance by European or national political authorities, the ECB was expected to maintain necessary accountability through the transparency and trustworthiness of its actions. However, the picture became blurred in the course of the financial and fiscal crises, as the ECB was involved in actions concerning the banking sector and Member State fiscal positions. The decisions the ECB has taken in its new fields of action hardly live up to the model of rational application of scientific information and exclusion of value judgments. The major issue, of course, is how sound the underlying premises justifying the position of independent expert bodies, such as the ECB, really are; how objective are the objectives and means of the policy field involved. The more the premise of objectivity and the concomitant claim of the absence of alternatives are contested and the more value choices are perceived to play a role, the more expert legitimacy as a variant of output legitimacy loses of its power.

Accusations of transgressing legitimate boundaries and of imposing value choices under the guise of neutral expertise are familiar from criticism of the judiciary; the ECJ, the main institutional actor in implementing and elaborating the first layer of the European economic constitution, has not been spared from such accusations either. It is inevitable that similar reproaches are directed at the ECB too. It may be debated whether even the aim and policies of price stability correspond to objectivist premises. But especially if the ECB ventures outside the framework of monetary policy aiming at price stability, criticism of the bank for overstepping its mandate and including value judgments in its decision-making is inevitable.[80] By the same token, its institutional position and the related legitimacy presuppositions will inevitably be put under scrutiny.

The possibility that the ECB exceeds its Treaty-based monetary policy mandate is particularly disconcerting in Germany, where the Constitutional Court has elevated ECB independence and focus on price stability to constitutional requirements for German participation in EMU. This is the central backdrop to the preliminary ruling referral to the ECJ concerning the ECB Outright Monetary Transactions decision and the rather conspicuous *ultra vires* intimations the referral includes. As conjectured above, the ECJ might justify its decision by invoking the new overarching principle of financial stability of the Eurozone as a whole. Due to the crisis-induced mutation of the European macroeconomic constitution, this might be regarded as a valid justification from an EU law perspective. But it is questionable whether it is equally valid from the perspective of the German constitution. The referral implies that no corresponding mutation has occurred at the national level and that the German constitution has not relativized price stability through postulating a higher-level stability objective.

In addition to the ECB, the Commission also emerges from the Eurozone crisis more powerful than ever. The Commission has been a central actor in country-specific rescue measures, and even the European Stability Mechanism relies not only on its own institutional structure but on the Commission too. Along with the IMF and the ECB, the Commission is the third limb of the famous Troika, which drafts and monitors financial assistance programmes. Tightening, re-modelling and expanding European economic governance, especially in the Eurozone, has increased the

[80] A central topic in Christopher Lord's discussion on the legitimacy of the monetary union consists of the consequences of the ECB's alleged move from rule-based to discretionary decision-making, C. Lord (2012).

competences of the Commission and left the Council, the epitome of intergovernmentalism, in the shadow. The Commission has become the main EU institution in monitoring and coordinating procedures under Arts. 121, 126 and 136 TFEU. At the same time, the focus of its competences has shifted towards country-specific monitoring.

The institutional position of the Commission has always been marked by a fundamental ambivalence. From Rome to Lisbon, the Commission has been treated mainly as an expert body. Yet the fact that the Member States have possessed the right to nominate the Commissioners has added a distinct intergovernmental flavour to it. But as the Commissioners are not, despite the procedure for nomination, supposed to act as representatives of the Member States, the characteristic of an expert body has prevailed. This is also how the present Founding Treaties portray the Commission.[81] A third, parliamentary feature has been introduced by the provisions on election of the President of the Commission by the European Parliament; the vote of consent in the Parliament preceding appointment of the Commission; the collective responsibility of the Commission before the Parliament; and the availability of a motion of censure of the Commission. Such a peculiar constitutional combination of features of an expert, intergovernmental and parliamentary institution entails that in terms of legitimacy expectations too the Commission is a hybrid body. The picture is further complicated by the multiplicity of Commission functions: different functions may imply different roles and legitimacy expectations. In competition policy, the role of independent expert has traditionally been particularly accentuated, although German observers in particular have at times doubted whether the Commission has been able to execute this role.

Great uncertainty seems to reign over how the increased tasks and powers of the Commission in economic governance and fiscal crisis resolution should be defined. The quasi-automatic sanction regime with reverse majority voting in the Council has enhanced the expert function of the Commission in fiscal and economic monitoring procedures. Still, open contestation of the economic theory underlying the conditionality of financial assistance and country-specific economic governance has

[81] Art. 17(3) TEU lays down that 'in carrying out its responsibilities, the Commission shall be completely independent' and that 'the members of the Commission shall neither seek nor take instructions from any Government or other institution, body, office or entity'. Furthermore, in Art. 245(1) TFEU, Member States pledge to respect the independence of the members of the Commission and not seek to influence them in the performance of their tasks.

undermined belief in objective, scientifically proven foundations of austerity programmes and supply-side reforms.[82] It is increasingly difficult to present the goals and means of fiscal and economic policy as objectively given, admitting of no alternatives and involving no value choices. The practice of the major European parties presenting their candidates for the Commission Presidency, adopted in the 2014 European elections, points to a reinforcement of the parliamentary element and perhaps even implies contestation of the value-free, technocratic nature of crisis management and economic governance.

[82] The contributions of such academic observers as Paul de Grauwe have been complemented by the self-criticism of the IMF for the Troika measures in Greece. See P. de Grauwe (2011 and 2013); P. de Grauwe and Y. Ji (2013); IMF (2013).

7 The European social constitution: between solidarity and access justice

Is there a European social constitution?

Does the European constitution include a social dimension? And, if so, what are its characteristic features?

Treaty law contains provisions on social values and objectives, social policy competences and even social rights.[1] Ever since the Treaty of Rome, social values and objectives have occupied a prominent place in 'surface-level' constitutional law, alongside economic objectives. In the Preamble to the Treaty of Rome, the Signatory States declared their resolution 'to ensure the economic and social progress of their countries by common action to eliminate the barriers which divide Europe' and affirmed 'as the essential objective of their efforts the constant improvement of the living and working conditions of their peoples'. In line with the Treaty of Rome, the Preamble to the TEU-Lisbon invokes promotion of both economic and social progress, and assures that advances in economic integration will be accompanied by parallel progress in other fields. The value basis of the EU, as defined in Art. 2 TEU, comprises values relevant for social policy, such as justice, solidarity and equality between men and women. Furthermore, Art. 3 TEU includes social objectives and, in defining economic objectives, refers to their social implications as well; it even introduces the term 'social market economy', familiar from German post-Second World War debates. Ever since Rome, the Treaty has also included a Social Policy Title, which has gradually been amended into the shape it received in Lisbon and where legislative competences have been established too. Social rights are a later addition; here the decisive breakthrough was only made with the Lisbon Treaty, which explicitly equated the constitutional status

[1] I am here applying the useful classification introduced by F. Rödl (2010).

of the Charter of Fundamental Rights of the European Union, including its Solidarity Chapter, with that of the Treaties. In sum, EU primary law involves guideline provisions on Union social objectives, provisions on social policy competence and, at present, even provisions on social rights.

Still, doubts have been raised whether these provisions justify talk of a social dimension in the European constitution. Doubts rest on two main grounds. For many observers, socially oriented Treaty provisions, as well as secondary legislation, are of a patchwork character and not animated by a coherent social policy view which would lend individual provisions the necessary degree of coherence. Starting in the late 1980s, *l'espace sociale Européen*, social Europe, the European social self or the European social model have been intensively discussed, not only among European academics and NGOs, but within EU institutions and in their policy documents as well. Still, it is highly questionable whether a distinct and commonly shared basic normative understanding of social policy, capable of sustaining individual Treaty provisions, has emerged from these debates. I largely agree with this assessment, especially with regard to the policy fields which lie at the core of national welfare regimes, such as social security and healthcare.

Another consideration also seems to negate the existence of a European social constitution. The emphasis in the European project has been and, to a large extent, still is on economic integration. This has left its mark on European constitutionalism. Here too the focus has been on the economic aspect; the economic constitution has enjoyed and, to a large extent, still enjoys primacy over a putative social dimension. Union social policy has suffered from a fundamental imbalance between Treaty provisions on social and economic issues. Unlike Treaty provisions on free movement and competition law – that is, the core of the (micro)economic constitution – provisions on social policy have not enjoyed direct effect. Furthermore, macroeconomic constitutionalization – so the argument continues – has only added to the constitutional disparity between economic and social policy. Social policy provisions are not backed up by a similar monitoring and sanction regime as in particular fiscal policy. Such a disparity has turned the social constitution into a constitutional underdog, which has but very rarely been able to assert itself in conflicts with the economic constitution. The disproportion between economic and social constitutional law is a European-level phenomenon unknown to national constitutions, which usually accord economic and social viewpoints equal constitutional status in political discourse and decision-making.

I concede the pertinence of both arguments: the lack of a shared normative vision of social Europe and the subjugation of social policy considerations to the needs of economic integration and constitutionalism. Yet I would like to claim that they tell not so much of the absence of a social constitution as of two of its main characteristic features: the *primacy of the national welfare state* and *subordination of the social to the economic constitution.*

In all its dimensions, European constitutionalization should be examined in the interrelationship between the transnational European constitution and the national Member State constitutions. This general premise possesses special importance in the social dimension. The European economic constitution has always relied on a presupposition of the existence of national redistributive mechanisms. National welfare policies, embodying diverse conceptions of social justice, have been a presupposed, silent partner in European constitutionalism and must necessarily be included in a discussion of the European social constitution. The underlying assumption in Rome was that the Treaty would achieve its social goals through the increased economic prosperity which the common market would produce and which would then be redistributed through national welfare mechanisms. As Florian Rödl has argued, leaving national mechanisms of distribution and redistribution intact was an integral part of the social compromise between capital and labour which supported the European project.[2]

The macroeconomic constitution, the foundations of which were laid in Maastricht, also presupposes national welfare policies. Europeanization of monetary policy has entailed that exchange-rate and monetary-policy instruments are not available for the purposes of national economic policies. This has increased the importance of fiscal policy as a key national instrument for adjusting to asymmetric internal and external shocks. Of particular importance are so-called automatic stabilizers: that is, countercyclically altering revenues and expenditures, such as taxes and welfare spending.

In European debates, social and fiscal policies are often seen as inseparable. If one remains with the Member States, the other should remain as well. And, correspondingly: if one were to be transferred to the European level, the other should follow. But in figuring out which policy field should take the lead, positions have diverged. In debates on EMU, the Economists – those who emphasized that monetary union was impossible without economic union – pointed to the need for Europeanized

[2] F. Rödl (2010).

fiscal policy and argued that this would entail Europeanization of social policy as well. On the other hand, those who wanted to retain national welfare regimes under national sovereignty were well aware that this required fiscal policy sovereignty too. The German Constitutional Court has approached the close relationship between fiscal and social policy from the perspective of the national constitution. In its *Lisbon* ruling, the Court indicated that 'particularly sensitive for the ability of a constitutional state to democratically shape itself' are, inter alia, 'fundamental fiscal decisions on public revenue and public expenditure, the latter being particularly motivated, inter alia, by social policy considerations'.[3]

The *Lisbon* ruling is a token of the jealousy with which Member States have guarded their sovereignty in social policy, especially as regards core welfare services with a redistributive effect, such as social security and healthcare. In line with fiscal policy, Treaty revisions have retained social policy under Member State sovereignty. The primacy of the national welfare state in the core welfare services has been explicitly enshrined in Treaty law, as has the principle of European neutrality with regard to national welfare models. Thus, the provisions which the Union may adopt within its limited legislative competence under Art. 153 TFEU 'shall not affect the right of Member States to define the fundamental principles of their social security systems and must not significantly affect the financial equilibrium thereof'. In turn, Art. 168(7) TFEU assures that 'Union action shall respect the responsibilities of the Member States for the definition of their health policy and for the organization and delivery of health services and medical care'; 'the responsibilities of the Member States shall include the management of health services and medical care and the allocation of the resources assigned to them'. Accordingly, ever since the Treaty of Rome, provisions on social policy have emphasized soft measures of coordination, instead of legislative competences. In Art. 4(2) TFEU, social policy is included in shared competences, but only 'for the aspects defined in this Treaty'. For other aspects, Union competences are confined to coordinating Member State policies (Art. 5 TFEU). Union legislative competences, granted by the Social Policy Title of the Treaty, focus now as before on labour law issues; in other areas, the clear accent is on coordination.

So the European economic constitution in both its micro- and macroeconomic dimensions relies on support from Member State redistributive

[3] BVerfG, 2 BvE 2/08, 30 June 2009, Para. 252.

mechanisms and, through explicit Treaty provisions, professes impartiality in respect of the Member State right to choose a particular welfare model. However, as I shall argue in this chapter, one of the many tensions of European constitutionalism is that the processes of constitutionalization subsequent to Rome and Maastricht have diminished the very leeway for national redistribution which the European economic constitution presupposes. The three alternative constitutional theories discussed by Miguel Poiares Maduro – the competition or market model, and the centralized and decentralized interventionist models – involve different social policy implications (see Chapter 5). Because of limited European competences, the main choice in social policy is between more or less market reliance. National social policy sovereignty implies that the choice is up to Member States. But the more the emphasis in European free movement and competition law shifts towards the competition model, the more difficult it becomes for Member States to maintain welfare models based on an extensive role of the public sector. Correspondingly, the more Member State fiscal policy sovereignty is restricted, the less space is left for public welfare financing.

Overall, a social dimension can be discerned in European constitutionalism, but only if we include the national level in the discussion. In addition, an important qualification must be attached to the claim of lack of a unifying normative vision at the European level. To a certain extent, this claim falls prey to the familiar fallacy of uncritically applying a state template to European developments. Observers who have stressed the fragmented and patchy nature of European measures have mainly focused on the core fields of national welfare policy: namely, social security and healthcare. But, arguably, the particular contribution of the EU social legislator has concentrated on areas which in the national setting lie on the fringes of the welfare state: on what Hans-W. Micklitz has called *European regulatory private law*. And, as Micklitz contends, European regulatory private law might be imbued with a definite normative vision of its own: a particular notion of justice which Micklitz terms *access justice*.[4]

My central claim in this chapter is that the social dimension of European constitutionalism does display distinct features and principles; these, however, are not identical to those characteristic of a national welfare state. Two basic tensions permeate the social dimension. On the one hand, the primacy of the national welfare state is but with difficulty

[4] H.-W. Micklitz (2011a).

reconcilable with the prevalence of the economic constitution. On the other hand, European access justice confronts the solidaristic social justice underpinning national welfare regimes; a confrontation that may have conflictual consequences.

Why does the national welfare state have primacy?

Many explanations exist for insistence of the European constitutional legislator on the primacy of the national welfare state. These relate to democratic legitimacy and the boundedness of solidarity; cultural, ideological and economic differences among Member States; and the fiscal resources that welfare policies presuppose.

Social policy, especially in the key areas of social security and healthcare, is about redistribution based on value choices, and such redistribution entails an enhanced need for democratic legitimacy. As long as the EU is afflicted by a democratic deficit, this need can only be met at the national level. A shift of emphasis in social policy from national to European level would only aggravate the existing legitimacy deficit. Moreover, it could jeopardize the overall legitimacy of national political regimes which in post-war Western Europe has largely derived from the fair (re)distribution of increasing prosperity through welfare state mechanisms. As the democratic input legitimacy of the Union is mainly guaranteed by national democratic procedures, Member State legitimacy problems would have repercussions at the European level as well.

Redistributive welfare policy reflects a solidaristic notion of social justice. Solidarity as a moral or ethical principle is intimately linked to solidarity as a sociological fact. Redistributive social policy draws on and presupposes solidarity among the members of the polity. Solidarity in the sociological sense of the term builds on common history, values and identity. In spite of increasing and intensifying cross-boundary ties among European citizens, up to now the necessary cultural basis for such solidarity has only existed at the national level. This has inevitably made the post-Second World War welfare state a national project. In turn, cultural divergences and particular national historical trajectories and traditions account for differences in welfare state ideologies and normative commitments; for different specifications of social justice and its implications. Member State welfare regimes manifest varying perceptions of the respective tasks of the state, the market and the third sector, as well as of the respective weight of financial transfers and public services in kind as instruments of social policy.

Comparative research has shown the great ideological, institutional and financial divergences of national welfare regimes. The relative homogeneity among the six original Bismarckian welfare states has long since been broken, and it is futile to search for a uniform European Social Model shared by the Member States. Scholars have proposed diverse groupings, starting from Gosta Esping-Andersen's by now classic division into Anglo-Saxon liberal, Central and Southern European corporatist, and Nordic social democratic welfare states.[5] Cultural diversity, resulting in bounded solidarities and divergent conceptions of social policy, goes a long way to explaining the tenacity with which Member States try to shield their welfare regimes, both within the Union constitutional and ordinary legislature and before the ECJ as the Union constitutional court.

Redistribution through welfare state measures would not be possible without sufficient fiscal resources. A central principle of the European macroeconomic constitution is Member State fiscal sovereignty, which covers the right of taxation. The Maastricht Treaty and the subsequent establishment of the Economic and Monetary Union left this principle intact. The Eurozone crisis has opened inroads into Member State sovereignty, but the decisive step in the direction of Europeanizing fiscal policy and building up Union fiscal capacity has not been taken. Hence, the EU simply does not possess the indispensable fiscal means to act as a transnational welfare state, nor is a fiscal union a likely prospect for the foreseeable future. For the German Constitutional Court, for instance, the inextricably intertwined fiscal and social policy competences belong to the core area of national sovereignty which democracy as an inviolable principle of the national constitution prohibits from being transferred to the transnational level.[6]

Even where the EU possesses legislative competences in social policy, their use outside the coordination of cross-border social security and healthcare has been scarce. Reaching necessary consensus on legislative measures, in particular outside such fields of 'encapsulated federalism' as labour law and anti-discrimination law,[7] is extremely difficult, due to Member State sovereignty concerns, the cultural, ideological, institutional and financial variance of national social policy regimes, as well as economic divergences, all greatly accentuated by the eastern enlargement. This is not only an explanation for the continuing primacy of the national welfare state, but also the backdrop to the structural asymmetry

[5] G. Esping-Andersen (1990). [6] BVerfG, 2 BvE 2/08, 30 June 2009, Absatz-Nr. (1 - 421).

[7] The term 'encapsulated federalism' is used by W. Streeck (1995).

which in the EU favours judicial before political law-making and negative before positive integration.[8] It also explains why European social policy, especially in fields central for national welfare states, is a favoured province of the open method of coordination, conferring on it a voluntaristic label.[9] Indeed, the open method of coordination is perhaps the main contribution of the social dimension to the institutional aspect of European political constitutionalization.

From the very beginning, the primacy of national welfare states and the sovereign option of Member States to choose their specific regime have been pivotal principles of European constitutionalism. Let us examine how these principles have fared under the strain of the functional prevalence of the economic constitution.

Restrictions on free movement

Considerable repercussions for the social dimension have been inflicted by both the microeconomic constitution, centred around free movement and competition law, and the macroeconomic constitution, centred around the Maastricht EMU provisions and significantly amended during the Eurozone crisis.

The microeconomic constitution may impose limitations on national welfare regimes in two ways: firstly, by treating national social policy measures as restrictions on free movement or competition, and, secondly, by subjecting national welfare services themselves to internal market law. The jurisprudence of the ECJ has been crucial in staking out the boundaries of Member State sovereignty in social policy. Through the prism of negative integration, the Court has examined Member State socially oriented legislation as a potential restriction on fundamental economic freedoms or undistorted competition.

In applying the three-phase reasoning which the Court has developed in its free movement jurisprudence, the crucial questions are: Firstly, what constitutes a restriction on free movement? And, secondly, what constitutes an acceptable justification for such a restriction? As may be recalled, the *Dassonville* formula, adopted by the ECJ in 1974, included a wide definition of national measures which could have an effect equivalent to that of quantitative restrictions on free movement of goods. The definition stated

[8] F. W. Scharpf (1999 and 2010).

[9] W. Streeck (1995). See on the open method of coordination in the social dimension K. A. Armstrong (2010).

that 'all trading rules enacted by Member States which are capable of hindering, directly or indirectly, actually or potentially, intra-community trade are to be considered as measures having an effect equivalent to quantitative restrictions'.[10] Through the *Dassonville* doctrine, the ECJ extended its constitutional jurisdiction to socially motivated national legislation in the fields of, say, consumer or worker protection or public health, where the Community did not at that moment enjoy legislative competence. Judicial legislation pursuing negative integration did not acknowledge the boundaries of legislative competence for positive integration.[11]

On the other hand, the mandatory requirements which under *Cassis de Dijon* define acceptable Member State justifications for restricting free movement of goods, include 'in particular... the effectiveness of fiscal supervision, the protection of public health, the fairness of commercial transactions and the defence of the consumer' (Para. 8).[12] With the qualification 'in particular', the formula intimates the openness of the list of mandatory requirements. Hence, even if social rights or other social viewpoints were not expressly invoked in *Cassis de Dijon*, the ECJ may still recognize them as mandatory requirements. Indeed, especially after Maastricht, the ECJ has conceded the relevance of social policy justifications. It has referred to Treaty provisions on social objectives and argued that the Union serves not only an economic but also a social purpose. However, in line with other mandatory requirements, social viewpoints have yet to prove their force in the proportionality test – a 'cost–benefit' assessment – which constitutes the final phase in the Court's argument.[13] It is perhaps worth noting that the ECJ has not – at least not explicitly – included in the

10 Case C-8/74 *Dassonville* [1974] ECR 837, Para. 5.

11 See, e.g., M. Poiares Maduro (2000). Of course, the Court has not always ruled against national legislation, as for instance *Sunday Trading* case law proves. See H.-W. Micklitz (2005).

12 Case C-120/78 *Rewe v Bundesmonopolverwaltung für Branntwein* [1979] ECR 649 (*Cassis de Dijon*), Para. 8. *Cassis de Dijon* is memorable for introducing not only the doctrine of mandatory requirements but also mutual recognition. The latter doctrine opened the way for regulatory competition among Member States with its potential 'horizontal' impact on national welfare regimes.

13 In 1995, *Gebhard* formulated the proportionality test in the context of freedom of establishment as follows: 'national measures liable to hinder or make less attractive the exercise of fundamental freedoms guaranteed by the Treaty must fulfil four conditions: they must be applied in a non-discriminatory manner; they must be justified by imperative requirements in the general interest; they must be suitable for securing the attainment of the objective which they pursue; and they must not go beyond what is necessary in order to attain it'. Case C-55/94 *Gebhard v Consiglio dell'Ordine degli Avvocati e Procuratori di Milano* [1995] ECR I-4165, Para. 37.

proportionality test any democracy or sovereignty premium constraining second-guessing national social legislation by a transnational court.

After the Delors Commission published its White Paper on completing the internal market in 1985[14] and the Member States acting as a constitutional legislature adopted the SEA in 1986, the attention of the Court started to shift from goods to free movement of services and freedom of establishment. In the field of services too, the ECJ has established itself as a constitutional court, competent to assess and, after a proportionality test, declare socially oriented national legislation or comparable measures which it deems an unjustifiable restriction on free movement incompatible with EU law. However, to counterbalance a rather extensive definition of restrictions on free movement, the Court again went beyond the wording of the Treaty in defining acceptable Member State justifications under the heading of imperative reasons. Imperative reasons may include considerations of social policy too.[15] The widely debated *Viking* and *Laval* rulings possess many aspects, not all of them particularly favourable for national social rights. However, these rulings are also memorable for an explicit recognition of social purposes as a potential justification for restricting free movement of services or freedom of establishment.[16]

[14] COM 85 (310) final.

[15] In *Säger*, the Court stated as 'a fundamental principle of the Treaty' that 'the freedom to provide services may be limited only by rules which are justified by imperative reasons relating to the public interest and which apply to all persons or undertakings pursuing an activity in the State of destination, in so far as that interest is not protected by the rules to which the person providing the services is subject in the Member State in which he is established. In particular, those requirements must be objectively necessary in order to ensure compliance with professional rules and to guarantee the protection of the recipient of services and they must not exceed what is necessary to attain those objectives.' Case C-76/90 *Säger v Dennemeyer & Co.* [1991] ECR I-4421, Para. 15. With regard to the right to establishment see *Gebhard*. Roth and Oliver note that 'the case law of the Court of Justice, starting in the 1980s and more so in the 1990s . . . brought a definite move towards a broader concept of restrictions that are to be abolished'. P. Oliver and W. H. Roth (2004), p. 411.

[16] In *Viking*, the Court stated that 'since the Community has . . . not only an economic but also a social purpose, the rights under the provisions of the Treaty on the free movement of goods, persons, services and capital must be balanced against the objectives pursued by social policy, which include, as is clear from the first paragraph of Article 136 EC, inter alia, improved living and working conditions, so as to make possible their harmonisation while improvement is being maintained, proper social protection and dialogue between management and labour'. Case C-438/05 *International Transport Workers' Federation and Finnish Seamen's Union* [2007] ECR I-10779, Para. 79. See also Case C-341/05 *Laval un Partneri* [2007] ECR I-11767, Paras. 104–5. Some observers have emphasized that in comparison with preceding case law, the Court engaged in more nuanced balancing between economic and social rights and did not treat the latter as

Viking and *Laval* applied a proportionality test, not to national legislation, but to collective trade union action. In the Nordic countries they were largely experienced as threatening the exceptionally vital role which trade unions and collective agreements have played in those countries, not only in determining terms of labour in a narrow sense, but labour-related social policy in general. Still, in standard cases socially oriented measures which the Court examines as potential restrictions on free movement consist of state legislative or administrative measures. Usually these are not located in the core area of the national welfare state but remain on the outer ring of labour and consumer law and general measures promoting public health.[17]

Extension of internal market law to welfare services

Censuring national social legislation for restricting free movement and infringing on trade union freedom of action may justly be seen as limiting Member State social policy sovereignty and the right to decide on the regime through which that sovereignty is exercised. Still, a potentially much more serious threat to Member State autonomy in choosing the national welfare model arises from subjecting healthcare and social security themselves to free movement and competition law. The ECJ's turn to services since the late 1980s has not excepted social security or healthcare. In its rulings, the ECJ habitually refers to Treaty provisions confirming Member State sovereignty in these crucial areas of national welfare regimes. However, the Court has not considered the provisions an obstacle to application of free movement or competition law. This has cleared the ground for the primacy of the economic over the social constitution and for a corresponding internal hierarchy in Treaty law.[18]

possessing a *prima facie* inferior ranking with regard to the former. See, e.g., L. Azoulai (2008).

17 *Cassis de Dijon* itself concerned national legislation with a public health objective.

18 In *Watts*, for instance, the Court first invoked the present Art. 168(7), confirming Member State sovereignty in the field of public health, but then added an important qualification: 'That provision does not, however, exclude the possibility that the Member States may be required under other Treaty provisions, such as Article 49 EC, or Community measures adopted on the basis of other Treaty provisions, such as Article 22 of Regulation No 1408/71, to make adjustments to their national systems of social security.' Case C-372/04 *Watts v Bedford Primary Care Trust and Secretary of State for Health* [2006] ECR I-04325, Paras. 146–7. In the rulings on social security schemes, the refrain is that 'according to settled case-law, Community law does not detract from the power of the Member States to organize their social security systems'. This is followed by the qualification that 'the Member States must comply with Community law when

In applying free movement or competition law to welfare services, the first issue concerns the qualification of the service involved: is it an *economic service* for the purposes of free movement and competition law? According to Art. 57 TFEU, 'services shall be considered to be "services" within the meaning of this Treaty where they are normally provided for remuneration'. For the ECJ the essential characteristic of remuneration is that it constitutes consideration for the service. Remuneration need not necessarily be paid by the recipient but can, for instance, be covered by insurance. In turn, in defining the field of its application competition law employs the concept of undertaking. For the Court, an undertaking is any entity engaged in economic activity, regardless of its legal status and the way it is financed. An activity is considered economic if it is, or could be, performed in a competitive market. The scope of free movement and competition law is largely identical: if a service is treated as economic for the purposes of competition law, it is provided for remuneration and falls under free movement law too.[19] In both free movement and competition law, the decisive dividing line runs between economic and non-economic services. Most of the case law of the ECJ specifying this line in healthcare focuses on free movement, while the categorization of social security services has primarily been discussed under competition law. Yet competition law is relevant for healthcare too, as is free movement law for social security.

An important string of healthcare cases has dealt with cross-border healthcare: more specifically, the right of a patient to reimbursement from the social security scheme of the country of affiliation for treatment received in another Member State. In a number of cases, the Court has held that both ambulatory healthcare and treatment received in hospital are services for the purposes of free movement. After affirming the applicability of free movement law, the Court has proceeded to discuss refusal of reimbursement as a potential restriction on the freedom to provide – and receive – services. The fact that the country of affiliation has adopted a National Health Service (NHS) system, based on publicly owned hospitals providing a health service free of charge or for symbolic compensation, does not affect the relevance of freedom of movement law for cross-border healthcare. What is essential is the character of the service received in the other Member State. Services in an NHS system are not of an economic

exercising that power'. See, e.g., Case *C-157/99 Geraets*-Smits *v Stichting Ziekenfonds and* Peerbooms *v Stichting CZ Groep Zorgverzekeringen* [2001] ECR I-0473, Paras. 44–5.

19 G. Davies (2006), pp. 15–17.

character, nor are public hospitals providing them undertakings for the purposes of competition law.[20] This does not, however, relieve an NHS country from its obligation to reimburse costs of healthcare services of an economic nature received in another Member State. I shall come back to this case law when discussing coordination of cross-border welfare services.

The need to locate social security schemes with regard to the boundary separating non-economic from economic services has arisen in cases where a person or a company covered by a compulsory scheme has refused to pay a contribution, claiming that compulsoriness violates constitutional competition law. Starting from *Poucet and Pistre*,[21] the ECJ has developed a set of yardsticks for judging whether or not a social security fund is an undertaking and subject to competition law. The Court has argued that as social purposes can be realized through economic, market-oriented, and non-economic action, a social purpose as such does not exempt a fund from the application of competition law. What appears to be the decisive criterion for exemption is the solidarity principle, adhered to in financing the scheme and determining the benefits. Solidarity may take diverse forms. It may be internal and confined to the clients of the fund; that is, its beneficiaries and contributors. It may also extend beyond clients and be manifest in external subsidies from the state – taxpayers – or from other funds. Crucial for both internal and external solidarity is that financing is not based on 'capitalization'[22] and that the benefits which clients receive are not directly linked to their contributions. Social purpose and non-profit making are relevant but not conclusive considerations.

The provisions in Art. 106 TFEU (previously Art. 90 TEC) lay down a general prohibition for Member States to enact or to maintain in force any measure concerning public undertakings and undertakings with special or exclusive rights which would be contrary to Treaty rules, in particular competition law and the prohibition of discrimination on the basis of nationality. If the Court has found a social security fund to be an undertaking, it has moved to examining whether the compulsoriness of the scheme amounts to an exclusive right within the meaning of Art. 106(1) TFEU and,

20 Case T-319/99 *FENIN* [2003] ECR II-357, Paras. 39–40.

21 Joined Cases C-159/91 and C-160/91 *Poucet v Assurances Générales de France and Caisse Mutuelle Régionale du Languedoc-Roussillon and Pistre and Caisse Autonome Nationale de Compensation de l'Assurance Vieillesse des Artisans* [1993] ECR I-637.

22 In the Court's case law, 'capitalization' refers to dependence of entitlements on contributions paid and the financial results of the scheme.

if it does, whether it constitutes an unjustified restriction on competition. Art. 106(2) TFEU allows restricting competition in favour of 'undertakings entrusted with the operation of services of general economic interest' if restrictions are necessitated by the particular tasks assigned to the undertakings. In *Albany*, the Court held it to be decisive whether the exclusive right of a social security fund and the ensuing restriction on competition are 'necessary for the performance of a particular social task of general interest with which that fund has been charged'.[23]

A social function or financial solidarity have not sufficed to exclude a social security scheme from the concept of undertaking. By contrast, the Court has deemed these features relevant when assessing the justifiability of a restriction of competition deriving from the compulsoriness of a social security scheme. In *Albany*, the Court first invoked the essential social function that the supplementary pension scheme under scrutiny fulfilled within the pension system of the country concerned. Secondly, in the Court's assessment the fund displayed a high level of (financial) solidarity, which rendered its services less competitive than comparable services provided by insurance companies and went towards justifying its exclusive right. The Court inferred that 'the removal of the exclusive right conferred on the Fund might make it impossible for it to perform the tasks of general economic interest entrusted to it under economically acceptable conditions and threaten its financial equilibrium' (Paras. 109–11).

The treatment of core welfare services in EU law and Commission documents is labelled by notable conceptual fuzziness. Bringing social security schemes under the concept of *services of general economic interest*, employed by the Treaty provision now in Art. 106(2) TFEU, may seem somewhat surprising. The standard reading of the concept mainly invokes infrastructure services which are vital for the economy in general, such as telecommunications and other network industries or postal and transport services. In characterizing the rationale behind special treatment for services of general economic interest, the Court too has stressed considerations of economic and fiscal policy.[24] In contrast, the general interest that

[23] Case C-67/96 *Albany International BV v Stichting Bedrijfspensioenfonds Textielindustrie*, with joined Cases C-115/97, C-116/97 and C-117/97 [1999] ECR I-5751, Para. 98.

[24] 'In allowing, in certain circumstances, derogations from the general rules of the Treaty, Article 90(2) of the Treaty seeks to reconcile the Member States' interest in using certain undertakings, in particular in the public sector, as an instrument of economic or fiscal policy with the Community's interest in ensuring compliance with the rules on

welfare services promote is chiefly non-economic rather than economic in character.

The Court's reasoning in treating social security schemes as services of general economic interest has been sparse. In *Albany*, an essential factor for the justifiability of the restriction on competition was whether the exclusive right of a pension fund 'may be justified under Article 90(2) of the Treaty as a measure necessary for the performance of a particular social task of general interest with which that fund has been charged'. This intimates that 'performance of a particular social task of general interest' would suffice to bring the service under 'services of general economic interest', which would in effect imply collapsing 'social' into 'economic'. But another reading of the Court's case law is possible as well: when privileging undertakings entrusted with services of general economic interest, Member States are free to pursue other objectives, including social policy objectives too.[25] But even if social interests can legitimately be pursued, should it not, as a precondition for exemption, first be established that the undertaking fulfils a general economic interest as well? It may well be that compulsory social security funds can be shown to further not only social but also general economic interests. However, in *Albany*, for instance, the Court bypassed this issue. It is hard to avoid the impression that in order to promote application of the microeconomic constitution to services, the Court has preferred to employ a wide definition of 'economic activity' and 'undertaking', but, as a counterbalance, has also wanted to acknowledge the relevance of solidarity-related justifications for compulsory social security schemes. This has required a liberal interpretation of 'services of general economic interest' and the exemption from the constraints of competition law facilitated by the Treaty.

In many Member States, services-related ECJ jurisprudence raised concerns about their sovereignty over the organization and financing of core welfare services. The amendments which the constitutional legislator introduced through the Treaty of Amsterdam reflect these concerns. Yet they did not diffuse the conceptual haziness surrounding welfare services;

competition and preservation of the unity of the common market.' Joined Cases C-115/97 to C-117/97 *Brentjens' Handelsonderneming BV v Stichting Bedrijfspensioenfonds voor de Handel in Bouwmaterialen* [1999] ECR I-6025, Para. 103.

25 Indeed, in *Brentjens* for instance the Court argued that 'in view of the interest of the Member States thus defined they cannot be precluded, when determining what services of general economic interest they entrust to certain undertakings, from taking account of objectives pertaining to their national policy or from endeavouring to attain them by means of obligations and constraints which they impose on such undertakings' (Para. 104).

rather the contrary. The Treaty included services of general economic interest among the shared values of the Union and pointed to their role in strengthening social and territorial cohesion. It also obliged the Union and the Member States to secure that 'such services operate on the basis of principles and conditions, particularly economic and financial conditions, which enable them to fulfil their missions' (Art. 16 TEC-Amsterdam). The Lisbon Treaty amended this provision by entrusting the ordinary legislator with the task to 'establish these principles and set these conditions without prejudice to the competence of Member States, in compliance with the Treaties, to provide, to commission and to fund such services' (Art. 14 TFEU).

A Protocol attached to the Lisbon Treaty introduced into constitutional law the concept of *services of general interest*, already employed in Commission documents. Art. 1 of the Protocol deals with services of general economic interest within the meaning of Arts. 16 and 106(2) TFEU, while Art. 2 addresses *non-economic services of general interest*. Art. 2 assures that 'the provisions of the Treaties do not affect in any way the competence of Member States to provide, commission and organize non-economic services of general interest'. This was clearly intended to alleviate Member State worries about their autonomy in organizing core welfare services. However, the legal significance of the concept of non-economic services of general interest and the assurance provided by Art. 2 of the Protocol remains unclear. Non-economic services which do not meet the criteria of an economic service fall outside the scope of competition (and free movement) law anyway, whether these services pursue a general interest or not; hence, the article seems to be of a merely declaratory character. Another problem arises from the ostensibly exhaustive character of the dichotomy of non-economic services of general interest and services of general economic interest. Services might exist which are to be considered economic for the purposes of competition (and free movement) law and which serve a general interest of other than an economic nature. The only way to maintain the exhaustiveness of the division between services of general economic interest and non-economic services of general interest is to ignore the epithet 'economic' in interpreting the general interest which warrants application of Arts. 16 and 106(2) TFEU and Art. 1 of the Protocol. And, indeed, as argued above, in its case law on Art. 106(2) TFEU (previous Art. 90(2) TEC) the ECJ has not been interested in establishing the economic character of the general interest that economic social services pursue.

In its effort to ensure implementation of free market and competition law in the service sector, the Court has enjoyed the support of the Commission, expressed in Commission communications and legislative initiatives, largely aiming at codifying the jurisprudence of the Court. The most debated legislative initiatives have been the proposals for the 2006 Services Directive and the 2011 Patients' Rights Directive. Several Member States pushed to exclude welfare services from the Services Directive. In the end, healthcare was explicitly left out but social security schemes were not: if they meet the criteria of economic services the Directive is relevant. As regards healthcare, the Preamble to the Services Directive states that cross-border healthcare would be addressed in another legal instrument (Recital 21). That instrument turned out to be the Patients' Rights Directive.[26] Both directives were issued under Art. 114 TFEU, allowing harmonization for the purpose of the establishment or functioning of the internal market.[27] This manifests the fact that a central backdrop to both the Services Directive and the Patients' Rights Directive lies in furthering economic integration and implementing the microeconomic constitution, rather than distinct social policy considerations.

Welfare services for mobile workers and citizens

Above, we discussed two instances where Member State social policy has been subordinated to the European economic constitution: case law where national social policy measures have been treated as restrictions on free movement and case law where national welfare services have themselves been assessed under free movement or competition law. Our overview of constitutional developments promoting negative integration has shown the essential role of judicial legislation. As the Services Directive and the Patients' Rights Directive exemplify, political legislation has mainly stepped in only *ex post*, codifying ECJ jurisprudence.

The distinction between negative and positive integration does not necessarily coincide with that between market construction and market

26 Directive No. 2006/123 of 12 December 2006 on services in the internal market, [2006] OJ L376/36; Directive No. 2011/24 of 9 March 2011 on the application of patients' rights in cross-border healthcare, [2011] OJ L88/45.

27 The conceptual situation has been further complicated by the concept of social services of general interest which the Commission has employed in its documents but which does not appear in Treaty provisions or ECJ rulings. See Communication from the Commission, Implementing the Community Lisbon Programme: Social services of general interest in the European Union. COM (2006) 177 final.

correction. Positive integration can aim not only at market correction but at market construction as well. This, arguably, is the case with much of the EU secondary legislation pursuing either coordination or harmonization of national welfare regimes.

In the negotiations paving the way for the Treaty of Rome, *harmonization* of social security was expressly rejected, and the Community was granted legislative competence even for *coordinating* national social security only to the extent deemed necessary for establishing the common market.[28] Coordination did not aim at distinct social targets but was seen in instrumental terms, as a means serving economic integration. The only specific social legislative competence in the Treaty was located not in the Social Policy Title but in the Free Movement Title; that is, among provisions of economic law rather than social constitutional law. The instrumental tone is conspicuous in the wording of Art. 51 TEEC (now Art. 48 TFEU), which obliged the Community legislator to adopt 'such measures in the field of social security as are necessary to provide freedom of movement for workers'.

The wording of the Treaty provision implies that it does not possess direct effect but presupposes secondary legislation. Thus, Art. 51 belonged to those Treaty provisions on free movement which did not meet the initial threshold criteria that the ECJ set for direct effect. However, the expansion of direct effect has encompassed provisions on free movement of workers as well.[29] Consequently, the ECJ has played an important role in developing constitutional law on cross-border social security too. In turn, case law has induced legislative amendments. In cross-border social security, the ECJ has pursued the integrationist line which has in general labelled its reading of the core provisions of the microeconomic constitution. Still, perhaps slightly paradoxically, liberal interpretation of primary and secondary law has also contributed to detaching cross-border social security from the internal market perspective.

The Court has adopted an extensive interpretation of both the personal and substantive scope of the central legislative instrument issued under Art. 51 of the Treaty of Rome: Social Security Regulation 1408/71.[30] The Court gradually expanded the personal reach of the Regulation from

28 C. Barnard (2011), pp. 642–5.

29 In *Angonese*, direct effect was extended to horizontal relations as well (Case C-281/98 [2000] ECR I-4139).

30 Council Regulation No. 1408/71 of 14 June 1971 on the application of social security schemes to employed persons and their families moving within the Community, [1971] OJ L149/2.

migrant workers and their dependants to all economically active persons, as well as future and former workers, such as students and pensioners. In the Court's interpretation, the substantive scope, in turn, comprises not only traditional 'Bismarckian' labour-related benefits, mostly of a contributory character, but reaches out to non-contributory benefits as well.

Originally, the *Leitbild* of social security coordination was the mobile worker.[31] The inclusion of students in the early 1990s already diverged from that initial *Leitbild*, but the decisive turning point came with the introduction of European citizenship in Maastricht. The mobile European citizen emerged as the new dominant *Leitbild* guiding the cross-border right to social security. In spite of the loosening of dependence on the economic constitution, this development did not signal a triumph of 'genuine' social policy objectives. Even after the citizenship turn, social policy was devised on other than social policy premises, and again coordination of social security schemes was conceived of in instrumental terms. Now the general aim was to promote mobility, not merely of economically active persons for the sake of economic integration, but of European citizens in general for the sake of broader societal integration.

Introduction of European citizenship was due to a speech act by the constitutional legislator, but it was the Court that drew the social policy conclusions.[32] Acting as a constitutional court, the Court in its case law on cross-border social security rights set aside Regulation 1408/71 and invoked the right of EU citizens 'to move and reside freely within the territory of the Member States', explicitly enshrined in the Treaty (now Art. 21(2) TFEU). As the ECJ ruled in *Baumbast*,[33] this Treaty provision possesses direct effect; hence, realization of the citizenship right of free movement does not depend on secondary legislation. When an EU citizen exercises the Treaty-based right of movement, this brings her within the scope of the Treaty provision prohibiting discrimination on the grounds of nationality (now Art. 18 TFEU) as well. This line of argument opened access for mobile European citizens to social security benefits in the Member State of residence. However, the Court has also shown understanding towards the Member States' wish to ward off 'welfare tourism' and consequent strain on their welfare systems. The Court has made the eligibility of foreign

31 I have borrowed the term *Leitbild* from H.-W. Micklitz (2011a).

32 See on ECJ citizenship jurisprudence S. Sankari (2013).

33 Case C-413/99 *Baumbast and R v Secretary of State for the Home Department* [2002] ECR I-7091.

nationals for social benefits dependent on additional criteria, reflecting the firmness of the bond with the state of residence. Still, all restrictions on the social rights of mobile citizens are subject to a proportionality test, which ultimately decides their justifiability.

The substantive reach of the right to social benefits derived from European citizenship is larger than the cross-border rights granted under Art. 51 of the Treaty of Rome and the Social Security Regulation. It covers in principle all social benefits, including social assistance, which was expressly excluded from the scope of Regulation 1408/71. The constitutional basis is different too. Diverging from workers' rights to social benefits, the Treaty does not explicitly presuppose secondary legislation on citizenship rights. Still, complementary secondary legislation has been issued on citizens' freedom of movement and adjacent rights to social benefits. Secondary legislation, though, does 'little more than codify the jurisprudence of the European Court of Justice'.[34] The Court has formulated its doctrines as a constitutional court and based them directly on the Treaty, so that the doctrines narrow the leeway of the political legislator. Furthermore, because of the direct effect of the Treaty provisions on citizenship, freedom of movement and non-discrimination, the list of rights expressly guaranteed to citizens by secondary legislation is not necessarily exhaustive.

Healthcare belongs to the core welfare areas where Member States have been especially attentive to their sovereignty and where the clear emphasis in Union policy lies in soft law and the open method of coordination. Coordination of cross-border healthcare is an exception to this rule and constitutes a parallel case to coordination of social security. Again, social policy decisions have been taken outside the Treaty framework for social policy and primarily on other than social policy premises. And again, the institutional driving force has been the ECJ, while the contribution of the political legislator has mainly been reduced to codifying case law. The Treaty basis for the Court's activism has, though, been different.

[34] D. Damjanovic and B. de Witte (2009). The relevant directives are Directive No. 2004/38 of 29 April 2004 on the right of citizens of the Union and their family members to move and reside freely within the territory of the Member States, [2004] OJ L58/77, which replaced residence directives dating from pre-Maastricht time, and Regulation No. 883/2004 of 29 April 2004 on the coordination of social security systems, [2004] OJ L166/1, which not only amended Regulation 1408/71 but extended the scope of the provisions to economically non-active European citizens exercising their freedom of movement.

Instead of the provisions on worker or citizen mobility, primary Treaty support has been the provision on freedom to provide services (now Art. 56 TFEU).

As long ago as 1984, in *Luisi and Carbone*, the ECJ established that the Treaty-guaranteed freedom to provide services implies the freedom to receive them.[35] Still, in cross-border healthcare the main legal issue has not been freedom to receive healthcare services in another Member State as such, but the obligation of the home country to reimburse those services from its public insurance system. In 1998 in *Kohll* and *Decker*,[36] the Court ruled that healthcare funded by a public insurance system is covered by free movement law. EU citizens are entitled as service recipients to cross-border healthcare financed by their home country insurance system, provided that the service in question is in general covered by that system. Acting once more as a constitutional court, the ECJ set aside the restrictions that Regulation 1408/71 imposed on export of healthcare benefits and based its rulings directly on Treaty law on free movement.[37] Subsequently, the Court has specified the main principles defining cross-border access to healthcare services, thereby progressively adjusting and widening the conditions originally laid down by the legislator in Regulation 1408/71. The Court has formulated all the crucial parameters of the scope, conditions and funding of cross-border healthcare. Again, what has remained for the Union legislator is codification of case law; this was accomplished through the Patients' Rights Directive.[38] In line with the Services Directive, the Patients' Rights Directive was issued under Art. 114 TFEU, 'since the majority of the provisions of this Directive aim to

[35] Joined Cases C-286/82 and 26/83 *Luisi and Carbone v Ministero del Tesoro* [1984] ECR 377.

[36] Case C-120/95 *Decker v Caisse de Maladie des Employés Privés* [1998] ECR I-1831; Case C-158/96 *Kohll v Union des Caisses de Maladie* [1998] ECR I-1931.

[37] Under the Regulation reimbursement by the home insurance system presupposes urgency of treatment and prior authorization from the patient's competent insurance institution. In *Kohll* and *Decker*, the Court found the requirement of prior authorization justified only if it is meant to address 'the risk of seriously undermining the financial balance of the social security system' or if it pursues the protection of public health by 'maintaining a balanced medical and hospital service open to all', while ensuring 'the maintenance of a treatment facility or medical service on national territory'. This has led to a distinction between hospital care and ambulance care. As a rule, prior authorization can still be required for the former but not for the latter.

[38] The main codificatory purpose was openly spelled out in the Preamble. The objective of the Directive was stated to be 'to achieve a more general, and also effective, application of principles developed by the Court of Justice on a case-by-case basis' (Recital 8). Of course, as J. Baquero Cruz (2011), p. 98 has remarked, the Court's jurisprudence may leave room for different interpretations. Invoking it may also serve tactical purposes.

improve the functioning of the internal market and the free movement of goods, persons and services' (Recital 2 of the Preamble).

The Preamble to the Directive evokes Member State responsibilities for both 'healthcare to citizens on their territory' and 'the definition of social security benefits relating to health and for the organization and delivery of healthcare and medical care and social security benefits, in particular for sickness'. The Preamble also declares that the Directive respects and is without prejudice to the freedom of each Member State to decide what type of healthcare it considers appropriate. Furthermore, any objective of encouraging patients to seek treatment outside their Member State of affiliation is denied. Yet, in a rather contradictory way, the Preamble also includes in the objectives of the Directive establishment of rules for facilitating access to safe and high-quality cross-border healthcare and ensuring patient mobility in accordance with the principles established by the ECJ (Recitals 4, 7 and 10). And, indeed, patients' rights as defined in the Directive are rights of mobile patients and aim at transforming patient mobility within the Union from legal principles set out in ECJ case law into a living reality. In spite of ECJ jurisprudence, starting from *Decker* and *Kohll* in 1998, patient mobility has remained relatively low and has had but a minor financial impact on Member State social security and healthcare systems.[39] It remains to be seen whether the Directive and its implementation will bring about a more significant change.

Denationalization and deterritorialization of welfare services

As many observers have remarked, expansion of rights to cross-boundary welfare services has led to a tendency of denationalizing and deterritorializing national welfare regimes. Depending on the chosen welfare model, this tendency can have grave consequences for national social policy.[40]

The familiar general groupings of European welfare states, starting from Esping-Andersen's typology, are of limited help in analysing the potential consequences. What, instead, is decisive is the method of financing and organizing social and healthcare services. In healthcare, the main dividing line goes between National Health Service (NHS) and insurance-based systems. In the former, healthcare services are publicly funded and delivered, while patients pay merely nominal or symbolic remuneration. In the latter, public insurance schemes reimburse to patients the costs

[39] See D. Martinsen (2005a), p. 1046, and G. Davies (2011).
[40] See in particular D. Martinsen (2005a and b) and A. Menéndez (2009).

of publicly or privately delivered and financed services. In social security, a related distinction separates residence-based from insurance-based systems. In a residence-based model, a person is entitled to social benefits on the basis of citizenship or habitual residence. Most benefits are not dependent on individual contributions but are universally granted and financed through taxation. In a social insurance model, employees are insured against basic risks in accordance with *lex loci laboris*. Social benefits are primarily financed by, and depend on, individual contributions.[41] In practice, distinctions between NHS and insurance-based healthcare or residence-based and insurance-based social security are not necessarily clear-cut, so that one and the same system may combine features from both sides of the dividing line.

In its rulings on cross-border social security and healthcare, the ECJ routinely pays lip service to Member State sovereignty in choosing welfare models. Still, denationalization and deterritorialization evidently affect different models in different ways. Denationalization manifests itself in the opening of national welfare services for non-nationals: first mobile workers and their family members; then other economically active nationals of other Member States moving across borders; and finally all European citizens exercising their Treaty-based right of movement. This has had repercussions particularly for residence-based social security, a traditional hallmark of Nordic welfare states, which have been forced to modify their rules on eligibility for social security benefits: above all, to drop the nationality requirement within the scope of the Social Security Regulation. Furthermore, Member States have also been obliged to extend the coverage of both NHS and insurance-based systems of public healthcare beyond their own nationals and long-time residents. As the ECJ put it in *Grzelczyk*, cross-border rights to welfare services have entailed 'a certain degree of financial solidarity between nationals of a host Member State and nationals of other Member States'.[42]

Denationalization is supplemented by deterritorialization. If denationalization has opened national social security and healthcare systems for non-nationals, deterritorialization has allowed participants of national systems to receive social security benefits or healthcare services in other Member States. Regulation 1408/71 adopted the principle of exportation within its field of application and facilitated cross-border healthcare, but

41 D. Martinsen (2005a), pp. 1038–9.

42 Case C-184/99 *Grzelczyk v Centre Public d'Aide Sociale d'Ottignies-Louvain-la-Neuve* ECR [2001] I-6193, Para. 44.

only after authorization by the Member State of affiliation. The case law of the ECJ, starting with *Kohll* and *Decker* and codified in the Patients' Rights Directive, gradually expanded the possibility of exit; that is, it facilitated searching for healthcare in another Member State than the country of affiliation. If residence-based models have been under particular pressure in social security, in healthcare insurance-based systems are more easily adaptable than NHS systems to the combined effects of expanded possibilities of entry of patients from other Member States and exit of patients covered by the national system.

Denationalization and deterritorialization have been accompanied by EU-induced amendments to national legislation and modifications in national social security or healthcare models. Still, indirect impacts may be more important than legal obligations to introduce changes to national welfare regimes. EU law does not oblige Member States to revise their fundamental choices between residence- and insurance-based social security or between NHS and insurance-based healthcare. But, arguably, insurance-based social security and healthcare can be more flexibly geared up for the liberalization driven by the Court and the Commission. Liberalization backed up by ECJ constitutional jurisprudence has given a boost to those trends in organizing and financing welfare services which the Commission in its 2006 Communication labels modernization[43] and which Gareth Davies has characterized as a shift from provision to regulation.[44] Denationalization and deterritorialization may influence the substantive reach and level of welfare services too. The prospect of non-nationals entering publicly financed welfare regimes with the ensuing additional financial burdens or the enlarged territorial exit of nationals at the expense of the Member State of affiliation may function as an efficient brake to introducing new benefits or enlarging the scope or raising the level of existing ones. Instead of upgrading, the general tendency in Member States seems rather to be towards downgrading.

At the most fundamental level, denationalization and deterritorialization may strike at the solidarity foundations of national welfare regimes. 'Solidarity' is a polysemic term, with diverse conceptual meanings. For the purposes of the present discussion, it is vital to draw a distinction between two significations. The first of these has been prevalent in ECJ

[43] Communication from the Commission, Implementing the Community Lisbon programme: Social services of general interest in the European Union. COM (2006) 177 final.

[44] G. Davies (2006), p. 53.

assessment of the economic or non-economic character of social services: 'solidarity' in the technical sense of financial redistribution among the participants in a healthcare system or a social security scheme, or among taxpayers at large. Such financial solidarity is grounded in, and reflects, solidarity in a deeper, ethical and sociological sense: solidarity as a bond of mutual allegiance among members of society. In healthcare, NHS and insurance-based systems are both premised on solidarity, in the sense of both financial redistribution and an underlying socio-ethical bond. In social security, financial solidarity is evident in both residence- and insurance-based systems. By contrast, solidarity in the socio-ethical sense is more manifest in a residence- than an insurance-based system. This is due to the bounded nature of the solidarity which has underlain national welfare state projects: a solidarity uniting nationals living in the territory of a nation state. The future of the social dimension in Europe is overshadowed by the danger that denationalization and deterritorialization will undermine the ethical and sociological foundations of national welfare states, without initiating compensating developments at the European level.[45]

Denationalization and deterritorialization expand financial solidarity beyond national citizenry and territory. This may corrode the socio-ethical solidarity which made financial solidarity – and the welfare state in general – possible in the first place. Of course, no *a priori* obstacles exist to extending the boundaries of the solidarity community too. But this cannot be done overnight, by fiat, but requires arduous social and cultural developments. Here European integration still has a long way to go.

Consequences of macroeconomic constitutionalization

European macroeconomic constitutionalization, launched in Maastricht, has further curtailed Member State leeway in social policy. Due to the close intertwinement of redistributive social policy with fiscal policy, the fiscal constraints introduced by the Maastricht EMU provisions and significantly reinforced as a reaction to the Eurozone crisis have reduced the latitude for national social policy too. Yet, in a slightly contradictory way, one of the background assumptions supporting the Maastricht principles of the macroeconomic constitution was that Member States would create sufficient room for manoeuvre for their automatic stabilizers in economic downturns; thus they would give effect to the enhanced

[45] See also A. Menéndez (2009).

macroeconomic function which national fiscal policy possesses in EMU after Member States have lost control over monetary policy instruments. As automatic stabilizers on the public expenditure side are largely identical to legal entitlements to social benefits, fiscal leeway would have protected national social security regimes too. However, due to national failures or the exceptional features of the Eurozone crisis, fiscal leeway seems to have been exhausted in the middle of the economic downturn. Instead of relying on the automatic-stabilizer function of social expenditure, Member States, especially those hit worst by the crisis, resorted to cutting social benefits; under 'strict conditionality' this was even a legal obligation for states receiving financial assistance.

A common currency in a non-optimal currency area calls for high labour market flexibility. Because of limited labour mobility and intra-euro-area fiscal transfers, increasing labour market and wage flexibility has been deemed necessary to manage adverse country-specific developments which common monetary policy cannot address. Indeed, during the Eurozone crisis measures aimed at enhancing labour market and wage flexibility were a staple in the Memoranda of Understanding implementing the strict conditionality of financial assistance.[46] Yet imposing such measures on countries caught up by the crisis has jeopardized national labour market arrangements and their ability to find adequate policy solutions. The measures have implied a general tendency of shrinking the freedom of social partners and tariff agreements in wage-setting and putting pressure on social benefits, especially unemployment benefits. If in general it were justified to invoke a European social model, manifested by Community/Union positions on social policy over the decades, labour orientation and a central role for social partners would certainly form part of its essential elements. Even before the outbreak of the Eurozone crisis, macroeconomic constitutionalization, combined with the repercussions of globalization, had instigated a significant change in Union labour law and labour market orientation. The crisis provided new impetus to the market liberal tenets of marketization and flexibilization as central premises of European macroeconomic governance. The effects of official market liberalism are not confined to the crisis states but extend to the Eurozone as a whole.[47] These developments are an important aspect of the

[46] K. Busch et al. (2013). For an analysis of Greek measures see A. Koukiadaki and L. Kretsos (2012).

[47] Thus, for instance, the scoreboard indicators on which the Commission bases its sanction-backed monitoring within the macroeconomic imbalance procedure, include, inter alia, a three-year percentage change in nominal unit labour costs, with thresholds

shift in emphasis between liberal and social market economies towards the former;[48] a shift which questions the constitutional principle of EU neutrality with regard to 'varieties of capitalism'.

In addition to requirements of labour market and wage-setting liberalization and flexibilization, austerity programmes have curbed the social policy sovereignty of crisis states through detailed and focused obligations to cut social expenditure and public sector wages. Indeed, social spending has been a major target in measures aiming to reduce the budget deficit and public debt. The massive impact of European measures on the labour and welfare regime of, especially, the crisis states raises the question of the protective role of social rights.

In addition to provisions on, firstly, Union objectives and values and, secondly, Union competences, social rights represent the third limb of socially oriented Treaty law. Social rights are a latecomer in European constitutional law. During the activism of the Delors era, efforts to balance the single market orientation with a social dimension led to adoption of the Community Charter of the Fundamental Social Rights of Workers in 1989. Juridically, the Charter, which was adopted as a Declaration of the European Council with the UK opting out, is a misnomer; one of the contributions of the social dimension to the plethora of European hard- and soft-law instruments. In the Maastricht Treaty, the Community Charter of the Fundamental Social Rights of Workers was granted explicit constitutional significance: Art. 136 TEC (now Art. 151 TFEU) included a reference both to this Charter and to the European Social Charter of the Council of Europe.[49] In addition, in the Preamble to the TEU the Member States confirm their attachment to fundamental social rights as defined in the two Charters. The next steps in the constitutionalization of social rights in EU law consist of adoption of the EU Charter of Fundamental Rights and confirmation of its constitutional status in Lisbon. Under the heading *Solidarity*, the Charter devotes a particular Chapter

set at +9 per cent for euro-area countries. European Commission website, 'MIP Scoreboard', last updated 13 November 2013.

48 F. W. Scharpf (2010).

49 'The Union and the Member States, having in mind fundamental social rights such as those set out in the European Social Charter signed at Turin on 18 October 1961 and in the 1989 Community Charter of the Fundamental Social Rights of Workers, shall have as their objectives the promotion of employment, improved living and working conditions, so as to make possible their harmonization while the improvement is being maintained, proper social protection, dialogue between management and labour, the development of human resources with a view to lasting high employment and the combating of exclusion.'

to social rights. However, the Charter has adopted a distinction between principles and rights in Art. 52(5), the clear intent being to lower the status of social rights to mere principles and water down their legal significance.[50]

In its case law, the ECJ has acknowledged the European Social Charter of the Council of Europe as one of the sources of inspiration for the common European tradition which defines fundamental rights as general legal principles of EU law. Yet the Court has been wary of basing its rulings on a provision of this Charter or the solidarity provisions in the EU Charter of Fundamental Rights (CFREU). So the position of social rights in EU law remains rather weak. In such famous cases as *Laval*[51] and *Viking*[52] where social rights have clashed with rights emanating from fundamental freedoms, the social dimension has rested on Member State law. Yet these rulings are important for EU social rights too, as they, for instance, explicitly acknowledged the right to strike as a principle of EU law even before Lisbon.

Despite the rather weak position of social rights in EU law, it would be erroneous to label them merely as constitutional soft law. The renewed European Charter of Social Rights belongs to the common constitutional heritage which, in accordance with Art. 6(3) TEU, determines the contents of fundamental rights as general principles of EU law. What is even more important is that the provisions on solidarity rights of the EU Charter, similarly to other Charter provisions, are legally effective and 'addressed to the institutions, bodies, offices and agencies of the Union' so that these are to 'respect the rights, observe the principles and promote the application thereof in accordance with their respective powers' (Art. 51(1) CFREU). Furthermore, according to an explicit provision of the Charter, even provisions containing principles are 'judicially cognisable' in interpreting Union measures, as well as national measures in the scope of EU law, and assessing the legality of such measures (Art. 52(5) CFREU). The relevance

[50] In accordance with this distinction, (subjective) rights must be respected and principles observed (Art. 51(1)). Principles may be implemented through legislative or executive acts. They become significant for courts only when these interpret or review such acts. They do not give rise to direct claims for positive action by Union institutions or Member States authorities (Art. 52(5)). See on the distinction P. Craig (2013), pp. 217–21, where the author argues that 'any of the Charter provisions dealing with social matters can be properly thought of as rights, capable of individual legal enforcement'.

[51] C-341/05 *Laval un Partneri* [2007] ECR I-11767.

[52] C-438/05 *International Transport Workers' Federation and Finnish Seamen's Union* [2007] ECR I-10779.

of the Charter for the austerity programmes imposed on the crisis states through the Memoranda of Understanding, drafted and monitored by the Troika, might be questioned on the ground that the Commission and the ECB were not acting under their Treaty powers but under those conferred on them by intergovernmental agreements. However, the main contents of the MoUs have been repeated in Council decisions under Arts. 126 or 136 TFEU, which the Charter clearly covers.

Pringle includes a position on the significance of the Charter for the European Stability Mechanism, but only in relation to Member States. The Court referred to the provision in Art. 51(1) CFREU, which confines the Charter's application to Member States to implementation of Union law, and stated that in establishing a stability mechanism like the ESM the Member States are not implementing EU law.[53] No conclusions can be drawn from *Pringle* on the pertinence of the Charter to action by EU institutions within or in relation to stability mechanisms. Nor does *Pringle* say anything on the Charter's relevance for Member States implementing MoUs. At least after an MoU has been confirmed by a Council Decision taken under EU law, a Member State can be claimed to be implementing EU law within the meaning of Art. 51(1) of the Charter when giving effect to the MoU. This would entail the relevance of solidarity rights for Member State measures. At the time of writing the ECJ has yet to take a position on the issue.[54]

According to the prevalent view of social rights, manifest in, for instance, the so-called Limburg principles, in times of austerity social rights function as criteria of prioritization in the allocation of spending cuts.[55] Yet no reference to either the Solidarity Chapter of the EU Charter on Fundamental Rights or to the renewed European Social Charter can

[53] Case C-370/12 *Thomas Pringle v Government of Ireland*, judgment of 27 November 2012 (not yet reported), Paras. 179–80. It should also be noted that *Pringle* was issued before the entry into force of the amendment to Art. 136 TFEU. The amendment explicitly provides for a Member State right to establish a stability mechanism. It remains an open issue whether the Court would in the present legal situation still consider that in establishing a stability mechanism, such as the ESM, Member States do not implement EU law in the meaning of Art. 51(1) of the Charter.

[54] Future financial assistance will involve applying the two-pack provisions on the macroeconomic adjustment programme which Member States requesting assistance must prepare and which the Council approves. This will make the connection of the MoUs to EU law even clearer.

[55] Limburg Principles on the Implementation of the International Covenant on Economic, Social and Cultural Rights, UN Doc. E/CN.4/1987/17, available in *Human Rights Quarterly* (1987).

be found in the abundant legal documents which the Eurozone crisis produced, except for one mention of the right to collective bargaining and action in a two-pack regulation.[56] In the face of failure of fundamental rights monitoring within the EU, other transnational or international supervisory bodies have had to step in. These, however, possess less influence and have no jurisdiction over Union action or intergovernmental stability mechanisms. All they can do is to criticize national authorities which have had but little latitude in implementing the strict conditionality imposed on them.[57]

Within the crisis states, austerity measures and labour market reforms have led to litigation before national courts. In general, the results have been meagre. The courts have exercised judicial restraint and displayed far-going understanding of government defences invoking economic emergency and the strict conditionality of financial assistance. The most important exception consists of rulings by the Portuguese Constitutional Court, which have struck down national austerity measures as violating constitutionally protected social rights.[58]

In sum, social rights have proved to be rather toothless in resisting or redirecting spending cuts or structural labour market reforms weakening the position of social partners and collective bargaining. This general conclusion covers all levels of social rights protection, whether European, international or national. With regard to the conditionality of European financial stability assistance, the primary deficiency is lack of a Union-level monitoring mechanism and the apparently non-existent commitment of key Union institutions.

[56] The two-pack Regulation No. 473/2013 of 21 May 2013 on common provisions for monitoring and assessing draft budgetary plans and ensuring the correction of excessive deficit of the Member States in the Euro area, [2013] OJ L104/11, which, inter alia, introduces economic partnership programmes for Member States in the excessive deficit procedure, evokes the role of social partners in wage setting. According to Art. 1(2) of the Regulation, its application must be in full compliance with Art. 152 TFEU, where the role of the social partners is recognized. Recommendations issued under the Regulation must respect national practice and institutions for wage formation. Here an explicit reference is made to Art. 28 of the Charter, where the right of collective bargaining and action is enshrined.

[57] The European Committee of Social Rights, which monitors Signatory States' observance of the renewed European Charter of Social Rights, has been perhaps the most active supervisory body. It has issued five decisions on complaints submitted by Greek trade unions and other NGOs, and included critical observations in its assessments of country-specific reports. The International Labour Organization (ILO) has been another energetic actor in the field of labour-market reforms and tariff autonomy. Kaarlo Tuori and Klaus Tuori (2014), pp. 239–40.

[58] See the following rulings by the Court: 353/2012, 178/2013, 474/2013 and 413/2014.

Regulatory private law

In many respects, Union social policy measures – at least those executed through hard-law means – reverse the order of binaries typical of national welfare states. In the context of national welfare states, we are used to thinking of social policy in terms of market correction and decommodification. By contrast, in the EU social policy seems to be subjected to the purposes of market construction, promoting commodification rather than decommodification. In this section, I discuss another reversal: that of centre and periphery.

The credo of the national welfare state is to guarantee basic welfare services, such as social security and healthcare, to the citizenry as a whole. If in general one is entitled to talk about an independent EU contribution to social policy, its focus lies elsewhere: not on redistributive services in the kernel of national welfare regimes but, rather, on regulatory measures on their outer ring. Instead of redistribution, the emphasis is on regulation: on regulatory private law. Diverging from the standard situation at state level, in the EU this branch of law is also constitutionally anchored.

Four particular fields of regulatory private law have gradually stood out: labour law, consumer law, anti-discrimination law and law on universal services. In these fields, European law has advanced to positive integration through harmonization of Member State legislation. The political legislator has played a central role, although in anti-discrimination law in particular the ECJ has also been able to assert itself. Compared to market-constructing negative integration through judicial legislation or equally market-constructing coordination of cross-border social security and healthcare, positive integration through regulatory private law has gained greater independence from the logic of economic constitutionalization.[59]

The general market dependence of Union social policy, though, explains its characteristic labour orientation, noticeable already in the Treaty of Rome. This orientation was conspicuous, not only in the provisions on migrant workers, but also in the Social Policy Title. The Title did not, however, create specific legislative competences. Harmonization of labour law, or other socially oriented legislation, was possible only under Art. 100 of the Treaty (now Art. 114 TFEU); that is, merely on condition that it could be

[59] In the following exposition, I have greatly benefited from Hans-W. Micklitz's writings, in particular H.-W. Micklitz (2011a and b).

justified as promoting the establishment or functioning of the common market or, put differently, in terms of realizing the economic constitution. The main impetus for including social policy provisions in the Treaty in the first place had lain in presuppositions of economic integration, such as guaranteeing equal conditions of competition for industries in different Member States. Still, Art. 100 TEEC, the use of which seemed to confirm subordination of the social dimension to economic integration, was able to provide the competence basis for legislation pursuing a more independent transnational social policy too. Practically any step in harmonizing labour law or other social legislation could be argued to further the establishment or functioning of the common market through levelling the playing field of economic actors in different Member States. However, especially as the relative social policy homogeneity of Member States had broken down after the first enlargement in 1973, the intricacy of finding the necessary consensus in the Council was an effective impediment to extensive social policy harmonization.

In spite of this political hurdle, in the wake of widespread labour unrest the first wave of labour directives was adopted in the 1970s under Art. 100 TEEC, pursuant to the first Commission Social Action Programme of 1974.[60] The second wave was facilitated by the Single European Act, which entered into force in 1987 and introduced qualified majority voting in the Council for harmonizing measures which aimed at completing the internal market (Art. 100a TEEC). Moreover, the SEA created a particular competence basis for minimum directives in the field of worker health and safety (Art. 118a(2) TEEC).[61] Still, persistent disagreements among Member States on the ideological, institutional and financial bases of social policy hampered agreement on far-reaching objectives and measures. Nevertheless, the social policy achievements of the Delors era include the Community Charter of Fundamental Social Rights of Workers. Although the Charter lacked immediate legal effect, it proved instrumental for development of the social dimension through further harmonizing labour law directives.[62]

[60] Council Resolution of 21 January 1974 concerning a social action programme, [1974] OJ C13/1.

[61] The 1989 framework directive on health and safety of workers was based on this provision. Directive No. 89/391 of 12 June 1989 on the introduction of measures to encourage improvements in the safety and health of workers at work, [1989] OJ L183/1.

[62] In order to achieve the objectives set out in the Charter, the Commission adopted a Social Action Programme, COM (89) 568 final. This led to a number of labour-related directives, adopted under Art. 118a TEEC.

The Social Protocol and the adjacent Agreement on social policy, attached to the Maastricht Treaty, gave a further boost to labour law harmonization. By the same token, the rather peculiar constitutional arrangement – another *sui generis* contribution of the social dimension to the European juridical constitution – which was resorted to in the face of a new opt-out by the UK led by Mrs Thatcher, manifested once again the difficulty of obtaining consensus among Member States on ideologically sensitive social issues. The Social Protocol initiated the last intensive period in the development of European labour law. The Agreement significantly expanded the scope of minimum harmonization directives, requiring merely qualified majority in the Council, and created, under the requirement of unanimity, new legislative competences in the field of, for instance, social security and social protection of workers.[63] The Treaty of Amsterdam not only ended the special regime by incorporating the provisions of the Agreement on social policy but also introduced a new Employment Chapter. This signalled a shift of focus from labour law to employment policy, and, by the same token, from hard law to soft law and the open method of coordination.[64] At the time of drafting the Charter of Fundamental Rights of the European Union the heyday of European labour law had already ended. Still, the import of labour-related social issues in the EU is evident in the Solidarity Chapter of the Charter, headed as it is by six labour-oriented articles.

Labour law was already an established field of law in Member States when the Community embarked on its legislative activism. Still, in particular in the period from the mid-1970s until the late 1990s, European support was essential for the efforts of typical national labour law coalitions, consisting of social democratic parties, trade unions and academic labour lawyers. Particularly in the 1990s, European labour law occupied an important position in the programme(s) for Social Europe.

In turn, anti-discrimination law is an original EU contribution to regulatory private law. The Treaty of Rome included two provisions related to discrimination. Art. 7 (now Art. 18 TFEU) prohibited discrimination

63 Between 1994 and 1997 four Directives were adopted under the Protocol, among them Directive No. 94/45 of 22 September 1994 on the establishment of a European Works Council or a procedure in Community-scale undertakings and Community-scale groups of undertakings for the purposes of informing and consulting employees, [1994] OJ L64/72 and Directive No. 97/81 of 15 December 1997 concerning the Framework Agreement on part-time work concluded by UNICE, CEEP and the ETUC, [1998] OJ L014/9.

64 See also the assessment of C. Barnard (2011), pp. 657–8.

based on nationality 'within the scope of application of this Treaty, and without prejudice to any special provisions contained therein'. This provision can only be applied together with other provisions and its significance in, for instance, free movement law is reduced by specific anti-discrimination provisions. Prohibiting discrimination on grounds of nationality was clearly linked to opening national markets to economic actors coming from other Member States and provided an argument for an anti-protectionist reading of free movement law. But of course, Art. 7 TEEC cannot be bypassed in a search for the roots of anti-discrimination as a general principle of EU law.[65] In addition, as we saw above, the provision has played a role in the ECJ's development of the rights of mobile citizens.

Pace Art. 7 TEEC, another Treaty provision came to have more importance for anti-discrimination law. In a sense, anti-discrimination law is an accidental offshoot of labour-oriented constitutional law. The Social Policy Title of the Treaty of Rome involved a provision on equal pay (Art. 119, now Art. 157 TFEU), which, in line with other provisions in the Title, was originally intended to promote economic integration by equalizing Member State conditions of competition. However, its subsequent destiny was to provide the constitutional basis for gradually widening anti-discrimination case law and secondary legislation. Constitutionally anchored anti-discrimination law is a primary example of social constitutional law severing its roots in the economic constitution and adopting a more independent teleology. Differing from labour law, the main credit for this development is due not to the political legislator, but to the ECJ. This fact may balance an over-straightforward view of the ECJ as a champion of negative integration and economic constitutionalization.

In the mid-1970s' *Defrenne* cases, the ECJ assigned direct effect to the Treaty provision on equal pay. The Court also at least partly detached the provision from the logic of economic constitutionalism and argued that it had both economic and social functions. A quarter of a century later, in 2000 in *Deutsche Post*, the Court finally established that in the teleology the provisions on social objectives outweigh economic ones.[66]

Until Amsterdam, the Treaty basis for combating other than nationality-based discrimination remained meagre, consisting only of the equal pay

[65] Art. 7(2) (now Art. 18(2) TFEU) also established a legislative competence to adopt rules designed to prohibit discrimination on nationality grounds. The competence has never been used.

[66] Case C-43/75 *Defrenne v Sabena* [1976] ECR 455. Joined Cases C-270/97 and C-271/97 *Deutsche Post v Sievers and Schrage* [2000] ECR I-929, Para. 57.

provision, which the Court, though, interpreted rather liberally. The provision did not establish any legislative competence. The anti-discrimination directives which the Community legislator issued, starting from the mid-1970s, were based on market-harmonizing competence (now Art. 114 TFEU) and the auxiliary competence established by the flexibility clause (now Art. 352 TFEU). The Amsterdam Treaty signified a turning point in the constitutionalization of anti-discrimination law and its definition in wider terms. The Treaty obliged the Community to aim to eliminate inequalities and to promote equality between men and women in all its activities (now Art. 8 TFEU). It also laid down a wider obligation to 'combat discrimination based on sex, racial or ethnic origin, religion or belief, disability, age or sexual orientation' (now Art. 19 TFEU).[67] Finally, the EU Charter of Fundamental Rights includes a particular Equality Title.[68] Reinforcement of the constitutional basis has been followed by renewed legislative and judicial activism.[69] A distinctive strand in ECJ case law consists of rulings on age discrimination, with *Mangold* as the most hotly debated.[70]

67 Legislative measures, however, were retained behind the threshold of unanimity in the Council. This did not concern measures aiming at equality between men and women with regard to labour market opportunities and treatment at work, which were included in the social policy legislative competence under Art. 137 TEC (now Art. 151 TFEU). Under the present Art. 19 TFEU, only harmonizing measures still require unanimity.

68 In addition to general provisions on equality before the law (Art. 20) and prohibition of discrimination (Art. 21), the Title comprises specific provisions on cultural, religious and linguistic diversity (Art. 22); equality between women and men (Art. 23); the rights of children (Art. 24) and the elderly (Art. 25); and integration of persons with disabilities (Art. 26). The prohibition of discrimination contains the same list of forbidden grounds as the provision now in Art. 19(1) TFEU, but, diverging from the latter provision, keeps it open-ended. Open-endedness also separates the provision on equality between women and men in Art. 23 of the Charter from the equality mandate of Art. 151 TFEU.

69 New directives include Directive No. 2000/78 of 27 November 2000 establishing a general framework for equal treatment in employment and occupation, [2000] OJ L303/16; Directive No. 2000/43 of 29 June 2000 implementing the principle of equal treatment between persons irrespective of racial or ethnic origin, [2000] OJ L180/22; Directive No. 2004/113 of 13 December 2004 implementing the principle of equal treatment between men and women in the access to and supply of goods and services, [2004] OJ L373/37; and Directive No. 2006/54 of 5 July 2006 on the implementation of the principle of equal opportunities and equal treatment of men and women in matters of employment and occupation, [2006] OJ L204/23. The three first Directives were adopted on the basis of Art. 13 TEC, while Directive 2006/54 is based on the social policy legislative competence under Art. 141(3) TEC.

70 Case C-144/04 *Mangold v Helm* [2005] ECR I-09981. For a critique of *Mangold* see R. Herzog and L. Gerken (2008).

In line with labour law, consumer law existed at least in some Member States before the Community's entry into this field of regulatory private law. Here the Community contribution was to provide a fledgling and insecure area of legislation with new impetus. The Treaty of Rome was silent on consumer policy, so that Art. 100 TEEC was resorted to as a competence basis for the first harmonizing directives. The Commission White Paper in 1985 and adoption of the SEA in 1986 were decisive for the constitutionalization of consumer policy too. Completion of the internal market was seen to require flanking support from not only labour law but consumer law as well. Art. 100a TEEC, which introduced qualified majority voting for measures aiming to realize the internal market, expressly enshrined the objective of a high level of consumer protection. The Maastricht Treaty introduced a particular Consumer Policy Title, consisting of one article, which in slightly modified form has been incorporated in the TFEU as Art. 169. In line with its predecessors, Art. 169 TFEU not only establishes specific legislative competence but in addition refers to general competence for harmonizing measures to complete the internal market (now Art. 114 TFEU). In practice, the specific competence has had minor pertinence, while most directives have been issued under the general harmonizing competence. At present the constitutional foundation of consumer policy includes a provision in the Solidarity Chapter of the CFREU, according to which Union policies should ensure a high level of consumer protection (Art. 38). Such constitutional privileging lacks correspondence at the state level and testifies to the prominence of consumer protection within EU social policy.

According to Hans-W. Micklitz, the *Leitbild* of initiatives taken between 1975 and 1985 was the weak consumer, which gave consumer policy a clear social flavour. The White Paper and the SEA linked consumer policy to the overriding objective of completing the internal market, which left its impact on the legislative activism of the 1990s.[71] Micklitz argues that consumer law gradually lost its protective orientation, while the *Leitbild* of

[71] This activism produced an impressive number of directives, such as Directive No. 90/314 of 13 June 1990 on package travel, package holidays and package tours, [1990] *OJ L158/59;* Directive No. 93/13 of 5 April 1993 on unfair terms in consumer contracts, [1993] OJ L95/29; Directive No. 94/47 of 26 October 1994 on the protection of purchasers in respect of certain aspects of contracts relating to the purchase of the right to use immovable properties on a timeshare basis, [1994] *OJ L280/83;* Directive No. 97/7 of 20 May 1997 on the protection of consumers in respect of distance contracts, [1997] OJ L144/19; Directive No. 98/27 of 19 May 1998 on injunctions for the protection of consumers' interests, [1998] *OJ L166/51; and* Directive No. 1999/44 of 25 May 1999 on certain aspects of the sale of consumer goods and associated guarantees, [1999] OJ L171/12.

the weak consumer retreated in the face of the now emerging image of a 'European consumer who shops across borders in a relaxed though attentive and self-responsible manner'. The Lisbon Council of 2000, which set the objective of making the EU the most competitive market worldwide, brought about yet another turn in consumer policy. The new *Leitbild* arising from Commission initiatives is 'the economically efficient consumer which has to operate no longer merely in a European but in an international environment'.[72] After the Lisbon Council, a number of important consumer directives have been adopted, culminating in the Consumer Rights Directive in 2011.[73]

The shift of emphasis in EU consumer law is partly balanced by the social aspects of a new field of law where the Union – in line with anti-discrimination law – has played a vanguard role: law on universal services. Law on universal services is a by-product of implementation of internal market rules in the service sector, but has subsequently acquired social features which cannot be reduced to the logic of market liberalization.

The constitutional background to law on universal services lies in the competition law provisions on public undertakings (now Art. 106 TFEU), which were amended in Amsterdam by new provisions on services of general economic interest and in Lisbon by the Protocol on services of general interest. As may be recalled, Member States are prohibited from enacting or maintaining in force any measure concerning public undertakings and undertakings with special or exclusive rights which would be contrary to Treaty rules, in particular competition law and the prohibition of discrimination on the basis of nationality. However, an exemption is made for services of general economic interest. Undertakings which have been entrusted with operating these services are subject to Treaty rules, in particular on competition, only 'in so far as the application of such rules does not obstruct the performance, in law or in fact, of the particular tasks assigned to them'. Still, the privileged position of these undertakings may not affect the development of trade to such an extent as would be contrary to the interests of the Union. Typical examples treated as services of general economic interest are network industries, such as

72 H.-W. Micklitz (2011a), pp. 30–3.

73 Directive No. 2011/83 of 25 October 2011 on consumer rights, [2011] OJ L304/64. Another distinct feature of the last phase in the development of consumer law is replacement of minimum with full harmonization. This has not only been the policy of the Commission, but was also embraced by the ECJ in its *Gysbrechts* ruling (Case C-205/07 *Gysbrechts and Santurel Inter* [2008] ECR I-9947).

telecommunications, electricity and gas; postal services; water supply and waste water services; treatment of waste; and transport services.[74]

Following adoption of the SEA, the Commission's urge to complete the internal market in the service sector too did not spare services of general economic interest. Under the protection of Treaty provisions, these services had been provided by public undertakings and undertakings with special or exclusive rights. A major justification for these arrangements had been the guarantee of universal access to services. Resorting to its general market-constructing harmonizing competence, the Community legislator initiated a rapid liberalization of services of general economic interest, starting from telecommunications and other network industries. Universal service law, ensuring access to services even in competitive markets, is meant to compensate for the loss by service providers of their privileged status.

The Treaty amendments adopted in Amsterdam and Lisbon provided the law on universal services with an explicit constitutional basis. As already explained, the Treaty of Amsterdam obliged the Union and Member States to secure that services of general economic interest 'operate on the basis of principles and conditions, particularly economic and financial conditions, which enable them to fulfil their missions', while the Lisbon Treaty introduced an additional mandate for the ordinary legislator to 'establish these principles and set these conditions without prejudice to the competence of Member States, in compliance with the Treaties, to provide, to commission and to fund such services' (Art. 14 TFEU). As was shown above, the legal significance of the concept of services of general interest employed by the Protocol attached to the Lisbon Treaty is ambiguous, as indeed is the concept of non-economic services of general interest also implied by the Protocol. For services of general economic interest, the Protocol may have more legal relevance, especially in guiding the interpretation of Arts. 14 and 106(2) TFEU. Art. 1 of the Protocol specifies the shared values of the Union in respect of services of general economic interest within the meaning of Art. 14. What is notable is that the values are mainly defined from the perspective of end users and include 'a high level of quality, safety and affordability, equal treatment and the promotion of universal access and of user rights'. The Protocol, together with Art. 36 of the EU Charter of Fundamental Rights, has explicitly entrenched the principle of universal services in EU constitutional

[74] Ever since the Treaty of Rome, transport policy has been subject to particular Treaty provisions, establishing even legislative competence (now Title VI TFEU).

law. Art. 36 CFREU lays down that 'the Union recognises and respects access to services of general economic interest as provided for in national laws and practices, in accordance with the Treaties, in order to promote the social and territorial cohesion of the Union'. The provision is located in the Solidarity Chapter of the Charter, which expressly places it in the context of the social constitution.

Neither Art. 36 CFREU nor Art. 1 of the Lisbon Protocol creates justiciable rights for users of services of general economic interest. However, as Micklitz has argued, Art. 36 CFREU should be read together with secondary legislation on services of general economic interest, such as telecommunications, postal services, electricity, gas and transport, which adopted the idea of universal services: 'The respective directives are all united in the idea that the new consumer should and must have access to the new competitive market and that access must be understood as an individually enforceable right.' Thus, a case can be made for an enforceable right of access to services of general economic interest. However, as Micklitz continues his argument, the addressee of such a right would not be the service provider but the Member State responsible for implementing the directive at issue.[75]

Another question, also discussed by Micklitz,[76] is whether the idea of universal services can be developed into a general principle of EU law. As regards services of general economic interest, Art. 36 CFREU and Art. 1 of the Protocol point to an affirmative answer. Arguments can be produced to support extending the principle also to services which do not perhaps meet the criteria of general economic interest but which in contemporary society are vital for social inclusion and participation, such as financial and internet services. If these arguments were accepted, Member States would, as a general principle of EU law, be required to ensure universal coverage of such services at a certain quality level and at affordable prices, even where this is not (yet) expressly spelled out in secondary legislation.

Two notions of justice: complementary or conflicting?

Comprising labour law, anti-discrimination law, consumer law and law on universal services, European regulatory private law may seem a

75 Micklitz regards this situation as exemplifying what Norbert Reich has termed 'Rights without Duties', that is, EU rights which cannot be enforced against the 'correct' addressee. H.-W. Micklitz (2011a), p. 41; N. Reich (2010), p. 56.

76 H.-W. Micklitz (2011a), pp. 41–2.

heterogeneous legal branch. But this would be a false impression: European regulatory private law is united by a social orientation and by a particular conception of justice which sets it apart from typical national welfare state legislation. This is the conception which Micklitz has termed *access justice*.

Whatever else the European social constitution may be about, it is also about the division of labour between the market and decentralized, national, or centralized, transnational, public policies. In the social dimension, the tasks assigned respectively to the markets, the Member States and the Union may be informed by three alternative, ideal-typical notions of justice. The first of these is *market justice* or allocative justice: whatever is the outcome of market mechanisms is just. Here the role of the state or the transnational polity is reduced to securing the general framework conditions for market mechanisms, such as the rights to property and freedom of contract. This is the realm of F. A. Hayek's rules of just conduct or Robert Nozick's libertarianism.[77] The second alternative is *access justice*, as Micklitz has termed it. As a rule, functioning markets do not emerge spontaneously but presuppose particular market-constructing measures by a polity. Furthermore, left to themselves, market mechanisms may lead to self-detrimental results by eliminating some economic agents from the marketplace and barring the (re-)entry of others. Public policy promoting access justice furthers market construction, combats exclusion and seeks to facilitate the (re-)entry of economic agents to the marketplace as entrepreneurs, workers or consumers. The third alternative is social justice, which implies correction of the distributive outcomes of the markets. As redistribution through welfare policies presupposes solidarity in both a financial and a socio-ethical sense, we can also call our third alternative *solidaristic social justice*.

Libertarian market justice entails a minimum state with practically no social responsibilities; a social constitution based on market justice would be a contradiction in terms. The value basis of national welfare states with their emphasis on social security and healthcare consists of solidaristic social justice. By contrast, EU social law is largely tailored to pursue, not redistributive social justice, but access justice: facilitating (re-)entry to the marketplace. This objective is conspicuous in regulatory private law, especially in labour law, consumer law and law on universal services, but also in those parts of anti-discrimination law which address market participation. It is evident in the coordination of cross-border social

77 F. A. Haeyk (1982); R. Nozick (1975).

security and healthcare as well. Originally, coordination of national social security schemes aimed at furthering worker mobility and realizing free movement of workers. The citizenship turn modified the determinants of access justice: now at issue is access to wider societal integration, redemption of the promise of European citizenship and realization of free movement of citizens. In turn, judicial and political legislation on cross-border healthcare purport to guarantee access to services for migrant patients: their entry to the transnational marketplace of healthcare services.

The prevalence of access justice in EU social policy can be deemed yet another example of primacy of the economic constitution over the social constitution. Market-constructing or market-maintaining social policy, manifesting access justice, supports the market-constructing and market-maintaining function of economic constitutional law. If we try to identify the conception of justice underlying the microeconomic constitution, centred around free movement and competition law, this would fall under access justice. Free movement law is supposed to create Europe-wide markets and to eradicate obstacles which national policy measures might pose to that objective. In turn, competition law aims to prevent accumulation of private power which would distort the functioning of market mechanisms and shut out competitors on illegitimate grounds or prevent the entry of new market participants.

Are national solidaristic social justice and transnational access justice complementary or conflicting principles? European regulatory private law does not affect the workings of core welfare services, left to the care of Member States. The fundamental social compact underlying European economic integration also intimates a complementary relation between the two conceptions of justice: transnational markets were supposed to produce increased prosperity, while national redistributive mechanisms were supposed to ensure just allotment of that prosperity. But things have not turned out to be so simple. Often enough, conflicts between economic constitutional law and national social legislation can be re-categorized as conflicts between two types of rights – transnational economic rights established by free movement law and national social rights – and two notions of justice – transnational access justice and national solidaristic social justice. This is one way of depicting the essential issue in, say, *Viking* and *Laval*. The access justice of freedom of establishment and free movement of services collided with, and finally prevailed over, the Nordic welfare model; that is, the Nordic regime for promoting solidaristic social justice. We have perceived an analogous tension permeating the case law on cross-border healthcare, the constitutional anchorage of which lies in free movement of services: guaranteeing access to cross-border services for mobile patients through the obligation of reimbursement by the country of affiliation may jeopardize the solidaristic foundations of national healthcare. Similar consequences may ensue from cross-border social security, the coverage of which has expanded from mobile workers and their dependants to mobile citizens, and the subjection of social security funds to competition law. Denationalization and deterritorialization of social security and healthcare in the name of access justice may threaten the solidaristic basis of national welfare regimes.

It is conceivable that, especially after Lisbon, European fundamental social rights could buttress the position of national welfare regimes, with their underpinning notions of solidaristic social justice, against the European economic constitution and market-constructing measures. They could add to the solidaristic scale in the weighing which the Court applies in assessing Member State restrictions on free movement or competition law. After all, the social rights of the Solidarity Chapter are also covered by Art. 51(1) of the Charter, which lays down that the institutions, bodies, offices and agencies of the Union must respect the rights, observe the principles and promote the application thereof. Whether Union social rights will attain a role in the defence of national welfare regimes remains to be seen. The fact that they have been almost totally ignored by both EU institutions and Member States as a potential counterweight to the implications of the macroeconomic constitution during the recent Eurozone crisis does not give reason for much optimism among defenders of social rights.

8 The insecure security constitution

The paradox-ridden relationship between the constitution and security

Modern constitutions have an ambivalent relation to security. Security considerations have often – in a Hobbesian way, we might say – weighed heavily among the objectives of a new political formation and its constitution; that is, behind the *constitutive* functions of the constitution. That was the case with the US Constitution, for instance. Security objectives, such as insuring domestic tranquillity and providing for common defence, occupy a prominent place in the Preamble:

> We the People of the United States, in Order to form a more perfect Union, establish Justice, insure domestic Tranquility, provide for the common defence, promote the general Welfare, and secure the Blessings of Liberty to ourselves and our Posterity, do ordain and establish the Constitution for the United States of America.

Yet constitutions fulfil not only constitutive but *restrictive* functions too: state constitutions are expected to discipline the use of public power, primarily through fundamental rights, alongside democratic and judicial control. The restrictive function, closely related to the ideas of a democratic *Rechtsstaat* (a constitutional democracy), focuses on executive bodies and activities related to internal and external security, i.e., police and armed forces. For the restrictive function, security as embodied in such institutions and activities is not something to be brought about by the constitution but something pre-existing it; something that must be subordinated to constitutional forms, procedures and limitations. However, constitutionalization has not been an easy task, due to the specific nature of security activities: they belong to the executive domain, consist of factual rather than normative measures and seem to escape the reach of the legislative function. We shall note these features resisting constitutionalization and juridification in general in the security dimension of the EU too.

Some constitutions put more emphasis on the constitutive and others on the restrictive function, but as a rule, state constitutions are expected to accomplish both of them. Even if the accent is on the constitutive function, constitutions also impose restrictions on security agencies and activities. Restrictions are necessary for managing what might be called the first paradox of a security constitution: if unchecked, security agencies are prone to turn themselves into security threats for citizens.

A further paradox inheres in the restrictive function. A constitution is supposed to curtail security activities and bring them under democratic and judicial supervision. However, security objectives are allowed to justify curbing the effect of those very restrictions and monitoring mechanisms, even suspending them. This dialectic between fundamental rights and security considerations can be seen in both *limitations* on and *derogations* from fundamental rights; a distinction adopted, for instance, in the European Convention on Human Rights (ECHR). Limitations are allowed even under conditions of 'normalcy', whereas derogations are justifiable only in a *state of emergency*. Arts. 5–11 of the Convention include clauses on the grounds warranting limitations to rights, and some clauses explicitly invoke security grounds, such as national security or public safety.[1] In turn, derogation, i.e., temporary suspension of rights, 'in time of war or other public emergency threatening the life of the nation' is provided for by Art. 15 of the Convention.[2]

In standard cases, states of emergency are justified by security exigencies. In addition to suspending the protection offered by fundamental

[1] Thus, Art. 8(1) guarantees everyone's right to respect for private and family life, home and correspondence. In turn, according to Art. 8(2), 'there shall be no interference by a public authority with the exercise of this right except such as is in accordance with the law and is necessary in a democratic society in the interests of *national security, public safety* or the economic well-being of the country, for the prevention of disorder or crime, for the protection of health or morals, or for the protection of the rights and freedoms of others' (italics added).

[2] The contrast between limitation and derogation has been relativized by the restrictions international human rights instruments impose on derogations. It could be argued that derogation should not be seen as a suspension of rights but as a specific type of restriction available only during a threat to the life of the nation. See on derogation under the UN Covenant on Civil and Political Rights Human Rights Committee, General Comment 29, States of Emergency (Article 4), UN Doc. CCPR/C/21/Rev.1/Add.11 (2001).

rights, a state of emergency may also entail empowering the executive at the expense of the legislature, and adjourning democratic and judicial control of security organs. In sum, states of emergency – or states of exception, as they also are called – imply setting aside the fundamental constitutional principles defining a democratic *Rechtsstaat*. A security constitution centred around the doctrine of state of emergency has traits of an anti-constitution: another paradox in the relations between security and the constitution!

For both the constitutive and restrictive function, security is an extra-constitutional objective, a *common good*, which public authorities are expected to produce under constitutional restrictions and supervisory mechanisms but which also justifies limiting or even suspending these constitutional guarantees. However, in recent decades, a tendency to transform security into a fundamental *right*, equal in rank to traditional liberty rights, has made itself manifest. Such a transformation would shake the doctrinal foundations of a liberal *Rechtsstaat*: a previously extra-constitutional collective good, the main target of the restrictive function of modern constitutions, would be turned into an inherent element of the restrictive system of fundamental rights. Evidently, the list of paradoxes attached to a putative security constitution must again be amended!

In total, a basic ambiguity permeates the relationship between security and the constitution. Security seems to be unable to find a stable location with respect to the constitution and to establish itself either within or outside the constitution. But if, in spite of these paradox-ridden relations, we still engage in a search for a security constitution, how should we proceed? The natural way would appear to be to point to individual constitutional provisions relating to security and to label their assemblage the security constitution, as, indeed, has been done in post-9/11 debates, especially in the United States. In these debates, the term 'security constitution' or 'national security constitution' has been employed at the state level, although rather hesitantly.[3] Candidates for inclusion in such a 'surface-level' constitution comprise, for instance, provisions concerning decisions on war and peace; on armed forces; and on states of emergency and emergency powers. In the European Union, ever since Maastricht the Treaties have involved distinct Titles or Chapters on Common Foreign and Security Policy (CFSP) as well as issues of internal security too. So arguably

[3] See, e.g., J. Mazzone (2005). A precursor to the present usage of the term is Harold Koh's study of the US national security constitution in the aftermath of the Iran-Contra affair of the late 1980s. H. H. Koh (1990).

at present the European security constitution consists of Title V of Chapter III TFEU (Area of Freedom, Security and Justice), complemented, perhaps, by security-related provisions in Title I TEU. But if 'security constitution' is understood, as I think it should be, in more substantive terms than just as an additive or enumerative category, then a minimum degree of coherence uniting individual constitutional provisions should also be required. In effect, some observers have claimed that, constitutionally speaking, the AFSJ does not amount to more than a fragmented collection of policy provisions. No justification exists – so the argument continues – for elevating the AFSJ above other EU policy domains and privileging it with the status of a distinct constitutional dimension, comparable to, say, the European (micro)economic constitution. A crucial testing-stone in the search for a European security constitution is whether a unifying background concept(ion) of security exists which injects coherence into the amalgamation of security-related Treaty provisions.

We have already noticed how contentious is the underlying constitutional theory in the various dimensions of the European constitution. The security dimension is no exception. In this dimension, the main formal criteria of constitutionalization pertain, on the one hand, to legal and political *transnationalization* at the expense of international law and institutional intergovernmentalism, and, on the other hand, to individualization: *subjectivization* of the individual in the two senses of the term. Both these criteria hint at substantive controversies concerning the foundations of the putative security constitution.

In the security dimension, the process of detaching from international law has been particularly arduous. The reason is obvious: security issues touch on the heart of the traditional understanding of state sovereignty, which includes, as Max Weber famously put it in the very definition of 'state', state monopoly over the use of legitimate violence. Lingering features of international law arrangements and enhanced institutional intergovernmentalism testify to Member State sovereigntist concerns. As these concerns are more accentuated in some Member States than others, they have led to legal and institutional fragmentation: a complicated system of opt-outs and opt-ins. Potential tensions between the transnational and the national characterize European constitutionalization in all its dimensions, but they are especially pertinent in the security dimension.

The dialectic between the constitutive and restrictive function of the constitution is reflected in the dual position of European individuals. A tension between security considerations and fundamental rights permeates the security constitution, implying two different perceptions of the individual: the individual is treated as both a *security risk* and as a *citizen* endowed with fundamental rights.

In line with other constitutional dimensions, the security constitution fulfils a positioning function and, again in line with other constitutional dimensions, with regard both to Member States and the rest of the world. Ever since Maastricht, the Treaty on the European Union has included a Title on Common Foreign and Security Policy (CFSP). Below, following the focus of preceding chapters, my focus will be on internal Union security and the relations between the European and Member State level. This choice is also warranted by the low degree of juridification of the external security dimension; to a great extent, CFSP is the province of 'high politics' in the European Council and the Council of Foreign Ministers. As Art. 31(1) TEU explicitly sets out, adoption of legislative acts is excluded. In turn, Art. 275 TFEU precludes ECJ jurisdiction with respect to CFSP provisions or acts adopted on that basis.[4]

From Trevi to Maastricht

From the very beginning, since Paris 1951, European integration possessed a prominent security aspect. One of the major objectives – if not *the* major objective – of integration was to guarantee peace among former enemies through reinforcing their economic ties. Accordingly, in the Preamble to the Treaty of Rome the Signatory States defined pooling their resources as a means 'to preserve and strengthen peace and liberty'. But peace was a second-order, extra-Treaty objective, comparable to Hobbesian security as the rationale behind polity-building and constitution-making. Achieving this objective would be the work of the economic constitution and not a separate security constitution.

Security considerations entered the domain of what would develop into the European microeconomic constitution through the justificatory regime of free movement law. The provisions on economic freedom explicitly allow for Member State derogations on security-related grounds. Free movement of goods does not 'preclude prohibitions or restrictions on imports, exports or goods in transit justified on grounds of public

[4] An exception is made for reviewing the legality of Council decisions providing for restrictive measures against natural or legal persons. The background to this exception lies in the case law concerning Union implementation of the UN post-9/11 sanctions regime, with *Kadi* as the most famous ruling. Joined Cases C-402 and C-415/05 P, *Kadi and Al Barakaat International Foundation v Council and Commission* [2008] ECR I-6351.

morality, public policy [in French, *ordre public*] or public security' (now Art. 36 TFEU). And, correspondingly, free movement of workers is subject to 'limitations justified on grounds of public policy (*ordre public*), public security or public health' (now Art. 45(3) TFEU).[5]

Such exemption clauses did not give rise to a distinct security dimension but remained an integral part of economic constitutional law. Furthermore, they unfolded their effects at the Member State rather than the European level; indeed, they aimed at preserving Member State sovereignty in security-related questions. However, free movement of workers has played an intermediary role between the economic and security dimensions, as it has in the interrelations between the economic and social constitutions too. Particularly relevant is the clause permitting Member States to restrict free movement of workers on grounds of *ordre public* and public security. Member States perceived worker mobility and opening of internal borders as a potential threat to security, which required vigilance over border-crossing movements of persons potentially jeopardizing *ordre public* or public security. Samuli Hurri argues that this led to the birth of a European individual whose legal status was defined outside the dichotomy of the law of nationals and the law of aliens.[6] What is significant for our present discussion is that this European individual was born as a problem: as a security threat.

Hurri locates the birth of the European individual in the 1970s, when the ECJ issued its pivotal rulings on interpretation of the derogation clause in the provision on free movement of workers. This was the decade when terrorism appeared as a major security risk in Europe: the decade of intensified activity of the IRA in Northern Ireland and elsewhere in the UK; ETA in Spain and France; Black September and the *Rote Armee* in Germany; and *Brigade Rosse* and extreme-right terrorism in Italy. The upsurge of terrorism was also a central backdrop to the Trevi framework, one of the 'laboratories' where border-crossing security cooperation was experimented with in advance of any constitutional mandate.[7] The Trevi framework anticipated many pertinent traits of the EU security dimension: not only the

[5] Similar clauses pertain to the right to establishment and capital movement. Treaty provisions on the right to establishment or measures based on them do not 'prejudice the applicability of provisions laid down by law, regulation or administrative action providing for special treatment for foreign nationals on grounds of public policy, public security or public health' (now Art. 46(1) TFEU). The limitation clause concerning capital movement is applicable in 'a situation of disturbances in the functioning of the capital market' (now Art. 66(1) TFEU).

[6] S. Hurri (2014). [7] J. Monar (2001).

initial experimental nature of cooperation 'in the shadow of the Treaties' but also the perseverance of intergovernmentalism and the weight of state-sovereigntist obstacles to transnationalization; the importance of cooperation and networking among Member State security officials; and exchange of information as a central operational modus.

The Trevi framework was founded by Member State Ministers of Justice and Home Affairs in 1975. The objective was to combat terrorism through exchange of information about training, equipment and organization of police action. In the mid-1980s the fight against football hooliganism and serious organized crime, such as drug trafficking, arms smuggling and large-scale bank robberies, was added to the tasks of specialist Working Groups, composed of security professionals from the participating states. Ministers of Justice and Home Affairs were responsible for policy development and overall review of cooperation. Trevi was intergovernmental cooperation with emphasis on technical issues and information sharing among Member State security officials, and subject only to international law. The problems to which Trevi initially responded, such as terrorism or football hooliganism, were not directly related to the establishment or functioning of the common market. In its last phase the Trevi network was associated with the Schengen process, where the link to economic constitutionalization was evident.

The Schengen Agreement, concluded in 1985, anticipated completion of the internal market project, scheduled for the end of 1992. Removal of internal border controls was seen to require compensatory security-related measures, which were included in the Convention on the Implementation of the Schengen Agreement, signed in 1990.[8] The Convention was an agreement under international law, manifesting the typical pioneer function of international law instruments in the security dimension. Schengen introduced another distinctive feature of the security dimension, which also has its backdrop in state-sovereigntist concerns: territorial fragmentation or so-called *variable geometry*. Recourse to an international law agreement instead of European legislation was motivated not only by issues of competence but also by the doubts of some Member States in respect of abolishing internal border controls. In effect, the Schengen Agreement and Convention were originally signed by only five Member States. The Schengen *acquis* was integrated into the framework of EU law through a Protocol attached to the Amsterdam Treaty (1998), but

[8] The 1990 Convention only entered into force on 1 September 1993, with its application beginning as late as 26 March 1995.

this was accompanied by a complicated system of opt-outs and opt-ins, so that by no means did it spell the end of variable geometry. The Schengen Convention included provisions on external border controls, visas and residence permissions, and asylum applications;[9] on police cooperation, including cross-border police operations; mutual assistance in criminal matters; application of the *ne bis in idem* principle; extradition; narcotics; as well as on firearms and ammunition. In addition, the Convention established the Schengen Information System, which reflects the importance of data processing and information exchange for the security dimension.

Neither Trevi nor Schengen had any anchorage in Treaty law. Only in Maastricht did the security dimension receive a place in the 'constitutional charter' within the new three-pillar structure of the Union. A particular Title on Cooperation in the Fields of Justice and Home Affairs – the third pillar of the Union – acknowledged internal security as a separate policy field, irreducible to the economic constitution. Justice and Home Affairs were, though, still defined as derivative from free movement of persons, one of the cornerstones of the economic constitution. However, Maastricht enlarged the personal scope of free movement to European citizens, and by the same token, enhanced its potential security consequences.

The Justice and Home Affairs Title listed nine policy areas as matters of common interest and subjects of cooperation.[10] Still, in light of the transnationalization criterion, constitutionalization made but modest progress. Third-pillar provisions were impregnated by intergovernmentalism and recourse to international law instruments. An explicit bow in the direction of state sovereigntism was made by declaring that the provisions 'shall not affect the exercise of the responsibilities incumbent upon Member States with regard to the maintenance of law and order

[9] Rules on the Member State responsible for examining asylum applications were included in another international law agreement, the Dublin Convention of 1990.

[10] These areas were: (1) asylum policy; (2) rules governing the crossing by persons of the external borders of the Member States and the exercise of controls thereon; (3) immigration policy and policy regarding nationals of third countries; (4) combating drug addiction in so far as this is not covered by (7)–(9); (5) combating fraud on an international scale in so far as this is not covered by (7)–(9); (6) judicial cooperation in civil matters; (7) judicial cooperation in criminal matters; (8) customs cooperation; (9) police cooperation for the purposes of preventing and combating terrorism, unlawful drug trafficking and other serious forms of international crime, including if necessary certain aspects of customs cooperation, in connection with the organization of a Union-wide system for exchanging information within a European Police Office (Europol). Art. K.1.

and the safeguarding of internal security'. Administrative information exchange and consultation were to be the main operational modus in areas of common interest (Art. K.2). Decision-making in the third pillar rejected the Community method, based on the agenda-making privilege of the Commission and the supervisory role of the ECJ and also presupposing the involvement of the European Parliament. The main third-pillar institution was the Council, and the requirement of unanimity, with only few exceptions, enhanced the prevalent intergovernmentalism (Art. K.3).[11] The Treaty granted the Commission only limited initiative, and in the areas where it was competent, it shared the initiative with Member States (Art. K.4). The main legal instruments at the disposal of the Council were international law conventions which the Council could recommend to Member States for adoption in accordance with the national constitution.[12] Somewhat paradoxically, conventions under international law could induce steps in the transnational direction: if the conventions did not provide otherwise, implementing measures could be adopted by a majority vote among the contracting parties.[13] As a rule, the ECJ did not possess jurisdiction within the third pillar (Art. K.3(2)).[14]

Maastricht did not immediately affect the Schengen Convention, which remained outside the umbrella of Treaty law and was not applicable in all Member States. However, in visa policy replacing Schengen by EU legislation was made possible.[15] In addition, the Justice and Home Affairs Title

[11] The Council was assisted by a Coordinating Committee – the so-called K.4 Committee – consisting of senior officials of the Member States (K.4(1)). The present successor to the K.4 Committee is COSI, the Standing Committee on operational cooperation on internal security, set up by Council Decision No. 2010/131 of 25 February 2010.

[12] The Council could also adopt joint positions and joint actions, whose exact legal effect, however, remained unclear. See S. Peers (2007), pp. 16–17.

[13] Another possibility to adopt majority voting was provided by Art. K.6. The Council, acting unanimously on the initiative of the Commission or a Member State, could decide to apply Art. 100c TEC to action in areas referred to in Article K.1(1)–(6). Art. 100c TEC granted the Council, starting from 1 January 1996, the power to adopt measures related to visa policy with a qualified majority.

[14] Art. K.6 provided the European Parliament with a consultative role. The Presidency and the Commission were obliged to inform the Parliament of discussions within Justice and Home Affairs. The Presidency was expected to consult the Parliament on the principal aspects of activities and ensure that its views were duly taken into consideration. The Parliament could also ask questions of, or make recommendations to, the Council. Finally, the Parliament was supposed to hold a debate each year on the progress made in implementation of the areas referred to in the Title on Justice and Home Affairs.

[15] Art. 100c TEC laid down that 'the provisions of the conventions in force between the Member States governing areas covered by this Article shall remain in force until their content has been replaced by directives or measures adopted pursuant to this Article'.

sanctified the variable geometry of the security dimension, already manifested by Schengen. Closer cooperation between two or more Member States was possible 'in so far as such cooperation does not conflict with, or impede, that provided for in this Title' (Art. K.7).

The significance of Amsterdam

The Treaty of Amsterdam signified a new boost to the constitutionalization of the security dimension. Internal security was explicitly included among EU objectives, although in the Preamble to the TEU and in Art. 2 TEU it was still subordinated to the primary objective of free movement of persons. In the amended Preamble, the Member States declared their resolution to 'facilitate the free movement of persons, while ensuring the safety and security of their peoples, by establishing an area of freedom, security and justice'. A corresponding objective was added to Art. 2 TEU: 'to maintain and develop the Union as an area of freedom, security and justice, in which the free movement of persons is assured in conjunction with appropriate measures with respect to external border controls, asylum, immigration and the prevention and combating of crime'.

Amsterdam changed the designation of the internal security dimension into the Area of Freedom, Security and Justice (AFSJ) and split the provisions concerning this area into two. Provisions on police and judicial cooperation remained in the Treaty on the EU as the third pillar of the Treaty architecture. A free-standing security objective opened the new Title: 'Without prejudice to the powers of the European Community, the Union's objective shall be to provide citizens with a high level of safety within an area of freedom, security and justice by developing common action among the Member States in the fields of police and judicial cooperation in criminal matters and by preventing and combating racism and xenophobia.' Cooperation was extended to crimes with no inherent cross-border aspect, which constitutionalized developments within the Trevi framework and its successor, Europol.[16] The envisaged high level of safety was to 'be achieved by preventing and combating crime, organized or otherwise, in particular terrorism, trafficking in persons and offences against children, illicit drug trafficking and illicit arms trafficking, corruption and fraud' (Art. 29 TEU).

[16] Europol, which had replaced Trevi, had been established on the basis of an explicit provision in the Maastricht Treaty (Art. K.1(9) TEU).

In Amsterdam, matters directly related to free movement of persons, such as external and internal borders, visas, asylum and immigration, were transferred to the Community pillar. Still, this did not deprive them of all their state-sovereigntist and intergovernmental features. Firstly, the new Title of the Treaty on the EC reconfirmed the assurance that Member State responsibilities in maintaining law and order and safeguarding internal security would not be affected (Art. 64(1) TEC). Secondly, AFSJ issues of the Community pillar were subject to a transitional regime for five years. During this period, the Council acted unanimously on a proposal from the Commission or on the initiative of a Member State and after consulting the European Parliament. After the transitional period, the Council could act only on the initiative of the Commission; the Commission, however, was obliged to examine any request by a Member State that it submit a proposal to the Council. Thus, a step towards the Community method was taken, but not a full step. Yet the Title also opened the possibility of further integration. The Council could, through a unanimous decision, transfer AFSJ policy fields to the co-decision procedure, which entailed qualified majority voting in the Council and the involvement of the European Parliament, as well as jurisdiction of the ECJ (Art. 67 TEC). In 2004, this *passerelle* clause was applied to asylum and immigration. The typical fragmentation of the security dimension was manifested by the opt-outs granted to the Member States most worried about their national sovereignty: the UK, Ireland and Denmark. These countries were also accorded special treatment in the Protocol integrating the Schengen *acquis* into the EU framework. The Amsterdam Treaty retained the possibility of closer cooperation between Member States too, which was now regulated by general TEU provisions.

Intergovernmental features were even more pronounced in the fields which remained in the third pillar and under the Treaty on the EU. While the AFSJ Title of the TEC introduced intergovernmental elements into the Community pillar, the stripped-down Title VI TEU brought some transnational traits into the third pillar. The Council was granted the power to decide that police cooperation and judicial cooperation in criminal matters fell under the procedures laid down in the AFSJ Title of the TEC. Provisions on the legal instruments at the disposal of the Council also took a step in a transnational direction. International law conventions were still provided for, but they found an alternative in framework decisions, a juridical novelty of the Amsterdam Treaty. Framework decisions could be adopted for the purpose of approximation of the laws and regulations of the Member States. They were similar to directives in the Community pillar in binding Member States as to the result to be achieved but leaving to national authorities the choice of form and methods. However, an explicit provision denied them any direct effect; here the drafters had had an eye on ECJ case law on directives. A similar disclaimer applied to decisions, which the Council could adopt for other purposes consistent with the objectives of the Title than approximation of Member State laws and regulations.[17] Diverging from conventions, framework decisions, although requiring a unanimous Council, did not fall under international law. In practice, they superseded conventions as the primary legal instrument of the third pillar.[18] Their importance was still enhanced by the *Pupino* ruling, which accorded a framework decision a legal effect similar to the indirect effect of Community directives.[19] All in all, in the pre-Lisbon era juridical constitutionalization took interesting sidesteps in the security dimension.

A further sign of transnationalization, related to juridical constitutionalization, was the extension of ECJ jurisdiction into the third pillar. The Court was granted jurisdiction to issue preliminary rulings on the validity and interpretation of framework decisions and decisions, as well as on the interpretation of conventions and on the validity and interpretation of measures implementing them. Yet accepting the Court's jurisdiction was optional for Member States, which could restrict the competence to request a preliminary ruling to the highest courts or extend it to all courts and tribunals: again a token of the power of state sovereigntism, contributing to the constitutional mishmash of the AFSJ. The Court was explicitly denied jurisdiction to review the validity or proportionality of operations carried out by the police or other law enforcement services of a Member State or the exercise of Member State responsibilities in law and order maintenance and in safeguarding internal security (Art. 35 TEU).

That these responsibilities were incumbent on Member States was reconfirmed in Amsterdam (Art. 33 TEU). However, police cooperation was no longer confined merely to mutual consultation, data processing and information exchange, but reached out to operational cooperation between law enforcement services, thus constitutionalizing the inroads into national sovereignty already accepted by Schengen states. State sovereigntism, though, retained an impact: authorities of a

[17] Decisions fell under the requirement of unanimity in the Council, but only a qualified majority was needed for measures implementing them. Decisions were adopted, e.g. to set up Europe-wide bodies or networks, to facilitate cross-border activity of Member State authorities and to implement conventions. S. Peers (2007), p. 36.

[18] See S. Peers (2007), pp. 33–6.

[19] Case C-105/3 *Pupino* [2005] ECR I-5285.

Member State could only operate in the territory of another Member State in liaison and in agreement with the authorities of that State (Art. 32 TEU). Another important opening of the Amsterdam Treaty pertained to harmonization in criminal and criminal procedural law; a traditional core area of state legislative sovereignty. Common action in judicial cooperation included ensuring such compatibility in national legislation as was necessary to improve cooperation in procedural and enforcement matters and facilitate extradition between Member States. It also included 'progressively adopting measures establishing minimum rules relating to the constituent elements of criminal acts and to penalties in the fields of organized crime, terrorism and illicit drug trafficking' (Art. 31 TEU).

The Amsterdam Treaty created a decisive impetus to activities in the security dimension, which rapidly gained a high ranking on the legislative and policy agenda of the EU. New agencies and networks were established, while administrative cooperation, which had been exercised ever since the establishment of Trevi, was intensified.[20] In the eyes of many observers, the AFSJ became the most dynamic field of the EU in the post-Amsterdam era. The new guiding role of the European Council, whose position had been enshrined in the Maastricht Treaty, was a token of the political significance accorded to the AFSJ. In October 1999 in Tampere, Finland, the European Council adopted the first comprehensive programme for activities in this area, followed by the Hague Programme in 2004 and the Stockholm Programme in 2010.[21] The Tampere Conclusions introduced in the security dimension the principle of *mutual recognition* which subsequently found application in, for instance, the Framework Decision on the European Arrest Warrant (EAW).[22] Just as in free movement law within the economic constitution, mutual recognition balances between transnationalism and intergovernmentalism. Unlike in harmonization,

20 Art. 34(1) TEU obliged Member States to inform and consult one another within the Council with a view to coordinating their action and to establish collaboration between the relevant departments of their administrations.

21 Tampere European Council, 15 and 16 October 1999 – Conclusions of the Presidency, *Bulletin of the European Union* No. 10/1999; The Hague Programme – Strengthening Freedom, Security and Justice in the European Union, [2005] OJ C53/1; The Stockholm Programme – an Open and Secure Europe Serving and Protecting Citizens, [2010] OJ C115/1. Unlike the case in the first pillar, where the role of the European Council was entrenched in Art. 13 TEU, the position of the European Council in the third pillar was not based on an explicit Treaty provision. Only in Lisbon, the role of the European Council in AFSJ matters was enshrined in a separate Treaty provision (Art. 68 TFEU).

22 2002/475/JHA.

the Member States retain sovereignty over national legislation, but they are obliged to acknowledge the legal effects of the legislation and decisions of other Member States. The programmes adopted by the European Council have been complemented by Commission action plans, manifesting the further intrusion of the Commission into the (former) citadel of intergovernmentalism.

More than twenty framework decisions were adopted within the third pillar before the entry into effect of the Lisbon Treaty. In addition to the European Arrest Warrant, framework decisions pertained, for instance, to terrorism, environmental crimes, sexual exploitation and child pornography, and drug trafficking.[23] At the institutional level, the constitutional position of Europol was strengthened through explicit provisions in Title VI TEU. Europol is the institutional site for police cooperation, data processing and mutual exchange of information and experience. Eurojust was established as a corresponding site for cooperation among public prosecutors, and in Nice a Treaty basis was created for this agency too (Art. 31(2) TEU). New post-Amsterdam agencies within the AFSJ include Frontex, operating in the field of external border guarding; the European Asylum Support Office (EASO); the European Anti-Fraud Office (OLAF); the European Police College (CEPOL); and the European Monitoring Centre for Drugs and Drug Addiction (EMCDDA). The agencies are supplemented by networks of security professionals, a characteristic feature of the EU security dimension.[24] Another important aspect in reinforcement of the AFSJ is extension of information systems, a development which was launched even before Maastricht by the Schengen Information System. The end result is a hardly controllable, fragmented whole, with obvious overlaps among its constituent parts.[25]

The 9/11 attacks fell in the post-Amsterdam period. The EU reacted rapidly. The Justice and Home Affairs Council met on 20 September 2001 and agreed on a package in the fight against terrorism, which was endorsed the next day by the European Council. The conclusions of the European Council included the need for a European definition of terrorism, which was provided on 13 June 2002 by the Framework Decision

[23] S. Peers (2007), pp. 35–6.

[24] These include, for example, the European Crime Prevention Network (EUCPN), the Police Chiefs Operational Task Force, the Counter Terrorism Group, the Police Working Group on Terrorism and the European Judicial Network.

[25] Information systems include Schengen Information System I and II, the European Union Visa Information System (VIS), the Customs Information System (CIS) and the Europol Information System.

on Combating Terrorism. The 'jewel in the crown of the EU's response to the terrorist attacks'[26] was the EAW Framework Decision, adopted by the Council simultaneously with the terrorism decision. Anti-terrorism measures were taken within other pillars too. Implementation of UN Security Council Resolutions 1373 (28 September 2001) and 1390 (16 January 2002) fell under the first pillar of Common Foreign and Security Policy and the second, Community pillar. On 27 December 2001, the Council adopted two common positions under the first pillar, which focused on the fight against financing terrorism, such as freezing funds of individuals and organizations suspected of terrorist contacts and included in lists annexed to the common positions. The Community pillar was involved through Council regulations on implementation of the CFSP common positions.[27] EU reactions to 9/11 and the bomb explosions in Madrid (2004) and London (2005) also included the European Security Strategy and the European Union Counter-Terrorism Strategy, which the European Council adopted on 12 December 2003 and 30 November 2005, respectively. Moreover, a particular EU Counter-Terrorism Coordinator was appointed and such networks of security professionals as the Counter-Terrorism Group and the Police Working Group on Terrorism were created.[28] On the external front anti-terrorist cooperation with the United States was greatly intensified in the aftermath of 9/11.

Although 9/11 had a weighty impact on development of the security dimension, it can hardly be considered a decisive turning point. Anti-terrorism had stood high on the agenda ever since the launch of Trevi, and some of the major legislative measures adopted in the aftermath of 9/11 had been drafted before the World Trade Center towers fell in New York; this applies, for instance, to the Framework Decision on the European Arrest Warrant. The attacks of 9/11 or the subsequent attacks in Madrid and London did not leave any immediate trace in Treaty law.

26 S. Douglas-Scott (2004), p. 223.

27 Council Regulation No. 2580/2001 of 27 December 2001 on specific restrictive measures against certain persons and entities with a view to combating terrorism was adopted on the same day as the first-pillar common positions, [2001] OJ L344/70. A further common position and an implementing regulation focusing on Al-Qaeda and the Taliban were adopted on 27 May 2002. All common positions and corresponding regulations have been frequently amended.

28 The Counter-Terrorism Group functions under the auspices of the Joint Situation Centre (JSC or SitCen), an intelligence body – at times called the CIA of the EU – which is part of the CFSP structure and, since 2010, integrated with the European External Action Service. The SitCen is expected to provide the Council with information on issues of (external) security, in the form of early warnings and assessments.

However, the Solidarity Clause in Art. 222 TFEU can be traced back to the attacks. Furthermore, Art. 75 TFEU was expected to clarify competences in the fight against the financing of terrorist activities.[29] Despite the potential importance of the Solidarity Clause, the indirect constitutional implications of anti-terrorism measures are probably more important. They concern the pillar structure and the dividing line between transnationalism and intergovernmentalism. Combating terrorism was seen to require complementary measures in diverse pillars, as is shown by the simultaneous adoption of first-pillar common positions and Community-pillar regulations on financing terrorism. Anti-terrorist policy also questioned the separation of external and internal security, the former confined within the first pillar, and the latter divided between the Community pillar and the rump third pillar. Furthermore, legal measures approved in the wake of 9/11 gave rise to constitutionally important case law in both the EU and Member States. In their decisions on implementation of the EAW Framework Decision, several Member State constitutional courts addressed fundamental issues concerning the relationship between EU law and national constitutional law.[30] On the side of the EU, *Kadi* reaffirmed the autonomy of EU law from international law, clarified the role of fundamental rights in security measures, and even pronounced on relations between the pillars and the competence basis of Community regulations on financing terrorism.

Lisbon and after

For the purposes of this chapter, the (hi)story of EU security-related constitutional law can be brought to an end with a brief summary of the security-related provisions of the Lisbon Treaty. I will start with the Solidarity Clause (Art. 222 TFEU).

[29] These had been a side aspect in *Kadi*. Art. 75(1) TFEU lays down that 'where necessary to achieve the objectives set out in Article 67, as regards preventing and combating terrorism and related activities, the European Parliament and the Council, acting by means of regulations in accordance with the ordinary legislative procedure, shall define a framework for administrative measures with regard to capital movements and payments, such as the freezing of funds, financial assets or economic gains belonging to, or owned or held by, natural or legal persons, groups or non-State entities'. According to Para. 2, 'the Council, on a proposal from the Commission, shall adopt measures to implement the framework referred to in the first paragraph'. Para. 3 can be considered a reaction to the fundamental rights problems which the ECJ had also addressed in *Kadi*. It provides that the legal acts referred to in the Article shall include necessary provisions on legal safeguards.

[30] See E. Guild (2006), J. Komárek (2007a) and M. Fichera (2011).

The Solidarity Clause not only possesses deep symbolic significance but extends solidarity obligations to military resources which Member States are expected to put at the disposal of the Union. The Clause calls for joint action in a spirit of solidarity by the Union and its Member States in preventing and responding to terrorist attacks and in assisting a Member State hit by a natural or man-made disaster. The Union should mobilize all the instruments at its disposal, including military resources which Member States have made available. Assistance following a terrorist attack or natural or man-made disaster presupposes a request by the political authorities of the Member State concerned. The Council decides on the measures on a joint proposal by the Commission and the High Representative of the Union for Foreign Affairs and Security Policy. A decision that has defence implications requires unanimity. Thus, even when acting in a spirit of solidarity, the Union is expected to heed state-sovereigntist concerns![31]

As the Solidarity Clause demonstrates, the Lisbon Treaty pushed further the piecemeal constitutionalization of the security dimension. Yet it did not eradicate all remnants of intergovernmentalism, nor did it cut the ties linking the security dimension to free movement. In the Preamble to the TEU and in the Treaty itself, security remains subordinated to the primary objective of facilitating free movement of persons. Still, significantly enough, offering citizens an area of freedom, security and justice has been upgraded in the list of objectives and now precedes establishment of the internal market (Art. 3(2–3) TEU). This reflects the new prominence of security in the post-Amsterdam era, as does the explicit enshrinement in the Treaty of the strategy role which the European Council had already exercised in Tampere in 1999 and in The Hague in 2004.[32]

The Lisbon Treaty abolished the pillar structure, integrated the AFSJ into the institutional structure of the former Community pillar and extended the use of Community legislative instruments and procedures to fields which the Amsterdam Treaty had still left to the truncated third pillar of police and judicial cooperation. The jurisdiction of the Court was accordingly amended. In consequence, regulations and directives can now be

[31] On the significance of the solidarity clause, see S. Myrdal and M. Rhinard (2010).

[32] According to Art. 68 TFEU, 'the European Council shall define the strategic guidelines for legislative and operational planning within the area of freedom, security and justice'. The Solidarity Clause includes a further constitutional sanction of the role of the European Council in defining the EU's security strategy. Art. 222(4) stipulates that 'the European Council shall regularly assess the threats facing the Union in order to enable the Union and its Member States to take effective action'.

adopted in all policy fields of the AFSJ. As a rule, they are approved in the ordinary legislative procedure, involving a Commission initiative, a co-decision of the European Parliament and qualified majority voting in the Council. These are important developments for transnationalization and constitutionalization of the security dimension. However, the TEU still emphasizes the primary responsibility (and sovereignty) of Member States in the security field. Art. 4(2) lays down that the Union 'shall respect their essential State functions, including ensuring the territorial integrity of the State, maintaining law and order and safeguarding national security' and that 'in particular, national security remains the sole responsibility of each Member State'. Moreover, exclusion of Member State security measures from the Court's jurisdiction is reconfirmed in Art. 276 TFEU.

The TFEU Title on the AFSJ also makes several concessions to state sovereigntism and intergovernmentalism. AFSJ measures are supposed to respect not only fundamental rights but the different legal systems and traditions of the Member States as well. The specific objectives listed in the Title accord primacy to Member State action but call for mutual trust and solidarity too. Common policy on asylum, immigration and external border controls is to be based on solidarity between Member States,[33] while in criminal matters and access to justice emphasis is on the principle of mutual recognition; harmonization of criminal laws can be resorted to only 'if necessary'.[34] The Title also re-invokes the reference to 'the responsibilities incumbent upon Member States with regard to the maintenance of law and order and the safeguarding of internal security' which has accompanied constitutionalization of the security dimension from its Maastricht beginnings (Art. 67 TFEU).

Provisions on policy competences too defer to state sovereignty as well. Art. 67(4) TFEU declares that Member State power concerning the geographical demarcation of borders will be left intact. Accordingly, Art. 79(5) proclaims that the Member State right to 'determine volumes of admission of third-country nationals coming from third countries to their territory in order to seek work, whether employed or self-employed', will not be affected. In the legislative procedure, Member States have retained

[33] The principle of solidarity to be followed in policies on border checks, asylum and immigration is enshrined in Art. 80.

[34] The principle of mutual recognition is confirmed in Art. 81(1) concerning judicial cooperation in civil matters having cross-border implications and in Art. 82(1) concerning judicial cooperation in criminal matters.

a residue of their power of initiative: legislative acts can be adopted within the AFSJ, not only on a proposal by the Commission, but also on the initiative of a quarter of the Member States.

Finally, the powers of EU agencies and authorities of other Member States in police and judicial cooperation are accompanied by substantive and procedural qualifications which also heed state sovereigntism. Operational action by Europol or authorities of other Member States must be carried out in liaison and in agreement with the authorities of the Member State or States whose territory is concerned. The main function of Eurojust and Europol remains to provide a site for coordination and cooperation between Member State authorities and professionals. Prosecutorial cooperation under the auspices of Eurojust does not cover 'formal acts of judicial procedure', which are to be carried out by competent national officials (Art. 85(2) TFEU).[35] The Treaty, though, enables developing Eurojust into a European Public Prosecutor's Office, responsible for 'investigating, prosecuting and bringing to judgment, where appropriate in liaison with Europol, the perpetrators of, and accomplices in, offences against the Union's financial interests'. Such an agency would also exercise 'the functions of prosecutor in the competent courts of the Member States in relation to such offences'. However, such a move in a transnational direction requires surmounting an intergovernmental threshold. It requires a special legislative procedure involving unanimity in the Council and consent by the European Parliament. The procedural hurdle is still higher for extending the mandate of the European Public Prosecutor's Office to serious crime having a cross-border dimension. In addition to a unanimous decision by the European Council, the consent of the European Parliament and consultation with the Commission is needed (Art. 86 TFEU).

A special legislative procedure, including a unanimous Council decision and consultation with or consent from the European Parliament,

[35] According to Art. 85(1) TFEU, 'Eurojust's mission shall be to support and strengthen coordination and cooperation between national investigating and prosecuting authorities in relation to serious crime affecting two or more Member States or requiring a prosecution on common bases, on the basis of operations conducted and information supplied by the Member States' authorities and by Europol.' Correspondingly, 'Europol's mission shall be to support and strengthen action by the Member States' police authorities and other law enforcement services and their mutual cooperation in preventing and combating serious crime affecting two or more Member States, terrorism and forms of crime which affect a common interest covered by a Union policy' (Art. 87(1) TFEU).

must be followed even in other matters where action by EU agencies or authorities of other Member States has been considered to be particularly sensitive for national sovereignty. These include judicial cooperation in family law questions with cross-border implications (Art. 81(3));[36] extension of the list of serious crimes with a cross-border dimension where minimum rules on the definition of criminal offences and sanctions may be established through directives adopted in the ordinary legislative procedure (Art. 83(1–2)); and operational cooperation among Member State police, customs and other specialized law enforcement services (Art. 87(3)). As a counterbalance, some of the provisions facilitate a minimum of nine Member States proceeding with enhanced cooperation; a token of variable geometry, characteristic of the security dimension.

Harmonizing criminal and criminal procedural law through minimum rules falls under the ordinary legislative procedure. But here too emergency brake clauses address state-sovereigntist sensitivities. If a member of the Council considers that a draft directive would affect fundamental aspects of its criminal justice system, it may request that the draft be referred to the European Council. If that happens, the ordinary legislative procedure will be suspended and can only be resumed if the European Council reaches a consensus. In case of disagreement, nine Member States can proceed with enhanced cooperation with the draft directive (Arts. 82(3) and 83(3) TFEU).

In total, even after Lisbon the AFSJ possesses conspicuous intergovernmental features and defers to state-sovereigntist concerns. Yet, since Maastricht, progress in the transnational direction has been considerable, and inroads have been made even into the hard core of traditional national sovereignty in policing, and criminal and criminal procedural law. State-sovereigntist sensibilities account for the complex system of opt-outs and opt-ins with which the AFSJ seems not to be able to dispense and which are provided for in Protocols annexed to the Lisbon Treaty. Coherence within the AFSJ has increased due to abolition of the pillar structure and the 'communitarization' of the former third pillar. But this increased coherence finds its counterweight in the fragmentation brought about by opt-outs and opt-ins, as well as possibilities for enhanced cooperation provided by provisions on special legislative procedure and emergency brakes.

[36] Art. 81(3) TFEU includes a *passerelle* clause which allows for transferring aspects of family law with cross-border implications under the ordinary legislative procedure.

From state of emergency to security

We have been able to observe an advancing constitutionalization of the security dimension at the Treaty level starting in Maastricht from the declaration of a number of security issues as common interests of the Member States, and ending up in Lisbon with the upgrading of security objectives and the 'communitarization' of the entire AFSJ field. Moreover, we have followed the institutional build-up, often enough antedating Treaty-level constitutionalization: the establishment of EU agencies, information systems and networks for administrative and professional cooperation. But, as we have also seen, by no means has the development been unequivocal. Persistent state-sovereigntist concerns explain the concessions which even the Lisbon Treaty makes to intergovernmentalism and the lingering juridical peculiarities that constitutionalization in the security dimension shows in comparison with the (micro)economic constitution and the former Community pillar.

Individual Treaty provisions do not yet make up a security constitution. What is also needed is sufficient coherence in security-related constitutional law: a coherence deriving from an underlying conception of security issues. My search for such coherence bears some resemblance to the constructivism of the Copenhagen School of security studies. The central premise of the Copenhagen School is that what is called security or a security problem does not have any objective, independent existence but results from a naming, from a speech act by a securitizing actor: 'by definition, something is a security problem when the elites declare it to be so'.[37] This is not an innocent declaration, an innocent speech act, but implies the need of and, by the same token, a justification for extraordinary measures to maintain or restore security: 'Security is the move that takes politics beyond the established rules of the game and frames the issue either as a special kind of politics or as above politics.'[38] In legal terms, 'politics beyond the established rules of the game' corresponds to a *state of exception* (state of emergency) and extraordinary *emergency measures* permitted during such a state.

The emphasis on the explicit declaration of a security problem – or, to use a more dramatic term, an existential threat – and the link from

37 O. Waever (1995), p. 54.

38 Another formulation by the same authors is the following: 'by labeling it as security, an agent claims a need for and right to treat it by extraordinary means'. H. Buzan et al. (1998), p. 26.

there to the right to take extraordinary measures brings the Copenhagen School close to Carl Schmitt's ideas of sovereignty and state of exception. The Schmitt citation index is probably topped by the opening sentence of *Politische Theologie*: 'Souverän ist wer über den Ausnahmezustand entscheidet.'[39] Post-9/11 developments have launched a new wave of debates on the concept of state of exception and the pertinence of Schmitt for understanding and conceptualizing reactions to terrorism. No agreement has been reached on even the fundamental question whether a state of exception should be, or in general can be, conceived of in constitutional terms or whether it is located beyond the law and the constitution. The debates, where Walter Benjamin's and Jacques Derrida's theorizing on the relationship that law maintains with violence has also been brought in, touch on fundamental paradoxes in the very foundation of law and the constitution, and certainly possess great legal philosophical interest.[40] They also illuminate the uneasy relation that security holds with the constitution and the difficulty in defining a fixed place for the former with regard to the latter.[41]

This is not the right place to intervene in the legal philosophical discussion on sovereignty, state of exception and the constitution. I would only wish to stress the relevance of the constructivist approach and its account of the typical consequences that a declaration of a state of exception or an emergency is intended to justify. These include an at least partial suspension of fundamental rights, the rule of law and separation of powers; that is, the basic constitutional principles which define a democratic *Rechtsstaat*. In addition, I would also stress the wider cultural presuppositions of security-related speech acts and their success. These speech acts are not Schmittian *Entscheidungen aus Nichts*[42] but are dependent on the cultural factors which inform the *Vorverständnis* of 'securitizing actors'. Nor do the speech acts succeed in their justificatory intent if they do not find (cultural) resonance among the political and legal elites, as well as the public at large.

The Copenhagen School is aware of the importance of the cultural context of securitizing speech acts. By contrast, what the Copenhagen School can be criticized for is holding – in Schmitt's wake – on a sharp distinction between state of exception and normal times. Here it follows traditional

[39] C. Schmitt (1985), p. 11. 'The sovereign is the one that decides on exception.' C. Schmitt (2004), p. 5.

[40] W. Benjamin (2004); J. Derrida (1990).

[41] One of the most-cited contributions is G. Agamben (2005).

[42] Decisions from nothing.

constitutional doctrine which has seen in the state of exception and concomitant emergency powers the main constitutional response to security concerns (in other words, they are viewed as constitutional means to suspend the constitution). But, as many observers have contended, the boundary separating exceptional from normal times has become increasingly blurred,[43] although by no means have arguments from emergency and constitutional emergency powers exhausted all their relevance. Nor does a strict demarcation correspond to the rationale of the European security constitution. It is true, though, that the Solidarity Clause in Art. 222 TFEU invokes a pending emergency. Yet it does not adhere to the Continental European constitutional tradition, which includes the requirement of an explicit declaration of a state of emergency and the consequent (partial) suspension of such constitutional basics as fundamental rights, the rule of law and separation of powers.[44] Tellingly enough, no emergency provision comparable to Art. 15 of the European Convention on Human Rights or Art. 4 of the UN Covenant on Civil and Political Rights was included in the EU Charter of Fundamental Rights.[45]

What, then, has been the argumentative device which has facilitated lowering the wall separating exceptional from normal times, and emergency measures from normal legislation? The concept of security has played a major part in this development. Under justification by security exigencies, normal legislation has in many countries acquired features

[43] This point has frequently been made by, for example, Oren Gross. See O. Gross (1998) and (2000) and O. Gross and F. Ni Aolain (2001).

[44] Another AFSJ provision which makes reference to a pending emergency pertains to sudden inflows of immigration. Art. 78(3) lays down that 'in the event of one or more Member States being confronted by an emergency situation characterized by a sudden inflow of nationals of third countries, the Council, on a proposal from the Commission, may adopt provisional measures for the benefit of the Member State(s) concerned'.

In addition, Art. 122 TFEU includes two provisions which evoke emergency situations but which are part of economic rather than security constitutional law. Para. 1 covers, for instance, crises in energy supply: 'Without prejudice to any other procedures provided for in the Treaties, the Council, on a proposal from the Commission, may decide, in a spirit of solidarity between Member States, upon the measures appropriate to the economic situation, in particular if severe difficulties arise in the supply of certain products, notably in the area of energy.' As noted in Chapter 6, Para. 2 has played a role in measures taken to combat the Eurozone crisis: 'Where a Member State is in difficulties or is seriously threatened with severe difficulties caused by natural disasters or exceptional occurrences beyond its control, the Council, on a proposal from the Commission, may grant, under certain conditions, Union financial assistance to the Member State concerned.'

[45] It must, though, be remembered that as signatories to the ECHR, EU Member States are obliged to adhere to its provisions on declaration of an emergency.

that bring it close to the characteristic effects of a declaration of emergency or state of exception. Typically, states did not react to 9/11 and the terrorist attacks in Europe with a declaration of emergency and subsequent time-limited emergency measures but with rather far-reaching amendments to normal legislation; in the aftermath of 9/11, packages of anti-terrorist legislation were adopted not only in the United States but in such European countries as, for instance, the UK and Germany too.[46] However, 9/11 only accelerated a long-term post-Second World War development. In the United States, the concept of national security has been invoked to warrant expanding presidential powers ever since the Truman Presidency and the start of the Cold War.[47] Security or national security has become the main justification for a 'permanent state of exception'. EU constitutional law must be analysed in this general cultural framework where a clear-cut concept of emergency or state of exception has increasingly yielded to a diffuse, expansionist and boundary-breaking concept of security.

'Security' is a tricky concept, hard to pinpoint in an unambiguous definition. The most promising way is to approach it through the concept of risk – for many sociological observers a key concept for analysing modern society[48] – and to define 'security' negatively, as connoting *combating risks.* Emergencies are temporarily and territorially limited and located risks that have already realized, with identifiable appearances and sources. 'Security' may also cover risks that have already occurred, but the emphasis is elsewhere: in risk prevention. Security calls for continuous detection and assessment of risks and security threats. Hence its inherent expansionism: ever new risks can be perceived and brought under the umbrella of 'security', labelled as security threats and seen as necessitating security measures. Expansionism is conspicuous in the development of the EU security dimension too, say from the modest start of anti-terrorist cooperation in Trevi to the Internal Security Strategy for the European Union, approved by the European Council in March 2010.[49]

The Strategy is explicit in its support for a comprehensive concept of internal security which reaches far beyond the traditional core fields of policing, crime prevention and maintenance of public safety. In its introductory section, the Strategy declares that '[t]he concept of internal

[46] However, the UK derogated from Art. 5 ECHR and Art. 9 ICCPR (detention without trial).

[47] K. L. Scheppele (2004) employs the term 'national security state'.

[48] See, e.g., U. Beck (1992).

[49] The significance assigned to the Strategy is manifested by the fact that it was published as a brochure, ISS (2010).

security must be understood as a wide and comprehensive concept which straddles multiple sectors in order to address ... major threats ... which have a direct impact on the lives, safety and well-being of citizens, including natural and man-made disasters such as forest fires, earthquakes, floods and storms'.[50] The Strategy identifies the following security threats, 'main challenges for the internal security of the EU': terrorism; serious and organized crime; cybercrime; cross-border crime; violence itself, such as youth violence or hooligan violence at sports events; as well as natural and man-made disasters, such as forest fires, earthquakes, floods and storms, droughts, energy shortages and major information and communication technology breakdowns.[51] A comprehensive concept of security entails that 'internal security must be seen as encompassing a wide range of measures with both horizontal and vertical dimensions'. In the horizontal dimension, 'to reach an adequate level of internal security in a complex global environment requires the involvement of law-enforcement and border-management authorities, with the support of judicial cooperation, civil protection agencies and also of the political, economic, financial, social and private sectors, including non-governmental organizations'. In the vertical dimension, the Strategy emphasizes that EU security policies and initiatives must be seen in the context of international cooperation, regional cooperation between Member States and harmonization of Member State national, regional and local policies.[52]

Related to its diffuse and expansionist character, 'security' possesses an intrinsic boundary-breaking tendency. It tends to blur not only the distinctions between exceptional and normal times, and extraordinary measures and normal legislation, but other divisions of established constitutional doctrine as well: such as external and internal security, war and crime, and soldiering and policing. 'Surface-level' EU constitutional law has still stuck to the dichotomy between external and internal security, the former – the previous first pillar – still regulated by the TEU and still dominated by intergovernmentalism. But as responses to 9/11 clearly proved, the dichotomy is difficult to maintain in practice, and AFSJ strategy documents make incursions into domains falling under Title V TEU. The Internal Security Strategy includes a section on the 'external

[50] *Ibid.*, pp. 14–15.

[51] *Ibid.*, p. 8. The Solidarity Clause of Art. 222 TFEU, which pertains to pending emergencies, also possesses an open-ended structure. Solidarity obligations actualize 'if a Member State is the object of a terrorist attack or the victim of a natural or man-made disaster'.

[52] *Ibid.*, p. 21.

dimension of internal security', premised on the claim that 'a concept of internal security cannot exist without an external dimension, since internal security increasingly depends to a large extent on external security'.[53]

The Strategy also highlights a further typical feature of 'security': an accent on *prevention*. The Strategy calls for prevention and anticipation, a 'proactive, intelligence-led approach'. It underlines that 'a comprehensive approach must be taken that is geared to constant detection and prevention of the threats and risks facing the EU in the various areas of internal security, and the main issues of concern to the public'.[54] The Strategy stresses the need for 'guidelines for hazard and risk-mapping methods, assessments and analyses' as well as an 'overview of the natural and man-made risks that the EU may face in the future'. Such a strategy of prevention and anticipation implies the need for continuous flows of information about potential risks. Accordingly, data processing and exchange of information have formed an essential aspect of the EU security dimension. Europe-wide information systems have abounded, and EU agencies, such as Europol and Eurojust, as well as diverse networks of security professionals, have, to a significant extent, been sites for information sharing. The Hague Programme, adopted by the European Council in 2004, established the principle of availability which was to epitomize 'an innovative approach to the cross-border exchange of law-enforcement information'. This principle 'means that, throughout the Union, a law enforcement officer in one Member State who needs information in order to perform his duties can obtain this from another Member State and that the law enforcement agency in the other Member State which holds this information will make it available for the stated purpose, taking into account the requirement of ongoing investigations in that State' (Para. 2.1). The Internal Security Strategy, in turn, indicates developing a comprehensive model for information exchange as one of its strategic guidelines.[55]

The crucial role of information sharing and data processing is not confined to law enforcement, but covers the whole field of security, defined in terms of risk management. Risks are something quantifiable, something which can be calculated and assessed, and calculation and assessment

[53] *Ibid.*, pp. 29–30. [54] *Ibid.*, pp. 22–3.

[55] It also praises the European Passenger Names Record (PNR) for ensuring 'a high level of data protection, for the purpose of preventing, detecting, investigating and prosecuting terrorist offences and serious crime, based on an impact assessment'. *Ibid.*, p. 24.

are impossible without information. Here we encounter a distinct feature of the modern mode of governance which Michel Foucault discussed under the label of *dispositif de securité* and where the main object of power does not consist of individuals, as it does for disciplinary mechanisms, but populations.[56] Individuals may constitute risks, and preventive measures may be taken against them; yet individuals appear as risks not so much in their irreducible individual capacity but as members of a population.

Since 9/11 terrorism has topped EU lists of security threats. However, in 2001 terrorism was not a novel concern: as our historical exposé has shown, anti-terrorism cooperation was already a main impetus to the Trevi framework in the 1970s. Terrorism exemplifies many of the typical features of the concept of security which pervades EU legislation, as well as programmatic documents and practical activities. Terrorism is hard to capture in an unequivocal definition. Within the EU, terrorism has not found a fixed location in relation to criminality. As the Framework Decision on Combating Terrorism makes clear, terrorism has been considered a criminal offence or, rather, a series of criminal offences. But it seems not to be reducible to criminality but goes beyond it. In anticipation of the declaration of the Union value basis in the Lisbon Treaty (Art. 2 TEU), Recital (1) of the Preamble to the Framework Decision proclaims that 'the European Union is founded on the universal values of human dignity, liberty, equality and solidarity, respect for human rights and fundamental freedoms', and 'based on the principle of democracy and the principle of the rule of law'. Recital (2) identifies terrorism as 'one of the most serious violations of those principles'. In EU legislation and programmes, terrorism is at times assimilated with 'other' serious crimes, at times dealt with as a security threat separate from crime. The EU maintained a distance from the 'War on Terrorism' rhetoric of the Bush administration, but it has not taken a firm position in favour of treating terrorism as a crime either. It is as if defining terrorism 'merely' as a crime would downplay the enormity of the violation of the universalist values and principles invoked in the Recitals of the Framework Decision on Combating Terrorism.

Be that as it may, terrorism proves how conceptual diffuseness and breaking down traditional constitutional distinctions go hand in hand: war and crime, external and internal security or soldiering and policing are hard to keep separate in combating terrorism. The fight against

[56] M. Foucault (2009).

terrorism corroborates the connection between security, prevention and information too. Potential terrorists must be identified and terrorist plots unearthed before their realization. Hence the never-satiated need for registering individuals and intercepting their communications. Terrorism is a de-localized and de-individualized security threat: it does not possess fixed headquarters but operates through networks for which territorial boundaries pose no obstacles. Terrorists, in turn, are seen not as individual persons, but as replaceable cogs in an anonymous machine; the identity of a suicide-bomber is not important, and Al-Qaeda is not in need of even Osama bin Laden. The difference between perceptions of criminal offenders and terrorists is conspicuous.[57]

Freedom, security and justice

EU Treaty law puts (internal) security into the context of the Area of Freedom, Security and Justice. An analysis of the conceptual cluster of 'freedom', 'security' and 'justice' rounds up our discussion of the notion of security which informs security-related EU constitutional law. How do 'freedom' and 'justice' relate to 'security'?[58]

Much has been written about the 'securitization' of the AFSJ, the subjection of freedom and justice to security and their definition through their relation to the latter. And, indeed, a tendency to securitization is easy to perceive, although it is not perhaps as unequivocal as some critical discussants are prone to claim. To begin with freedom, its subordination to security is discernible, first, in its depiction as the source of the security problems which the AFSJ is expected to address. In this quality, 'freedom' is defined, first of all, as freedom of movement within the EU; abolishing internal border controls calls for complementary, flanking security measures. Art. 2 TEU-Amsterdam introduced the AFSJ objective in the following terms: 'to maintain and develop the Union as an area of freedom, security and justice, in which the free movement of persons is assured

57 Similar points are made in O. Lepsius (2004).

58 The concept of area is not without significance either, but a brief comment will suffice here. As Jörg Monar has argued, 'area' has not only a geographic connotation but also alludes to a particular way of conceiving of a policy domain. Before the introduction of the AFSJ, the term 'area' had been used in such notions as 'European higher education area' and 'European social area' to designate 'broad frameworks for common action that go beyond mere intergovernmental cooperation but fall short of fully fledged "common policies" with all the characteristics of the classic Community method, allowing instead the use of a wide variety of methods of governance in this domain'. Monar sees a similar rationale behind the choice of the term 'area' for the AFSJ. J. Monar (2010), p. 556.

in conjunction with appropriate measures with respect to external border controls, asylum, immigration and the prevention and combating of crime'. Lisbon retained this connection between freedom and security, entailing an implicit reduction of freedom to free movement (Art. 3(2) TEU).[59]

Seeing the threats addressed by security arising from freedom is not the only way of perceiving the latter through the lens of the former. In the first two AFSJ programmes, adopted by the European Council in Tampere in 1999 and in The Hague in 2004, the policy measures envisaged were divided along the sub-areas of freedom, security and justice. What fell under 'freedom' was common policy in the field of asylum, migration and borders, with clear emphasis on security-related measures. In essence, the Hague Programme section *Strengthening freedom* was primarily about strengthening security; about building up 'Fortress Europe', as critics have put it.[60]

Yet, from the very introduction of the AFSJ, an ambiguity in the definition of 'freedom' can be observed. The programmatic documents define 'freedom' primarily as free movement within the EU, but they intimate that 'freedom' can be assigned wider contents too. In the Tampere Conclusions, the challenge of the Amsterdam Treaty was seen in ensuring 'that freedom, which *includes* the right to move freely throughout the Union, can be employed in conditions of security and justice accessible to all' (Para. 2; italics added). A wider notion of freedom was also implicit in the characterization of security measures as responding to 'the threat serious crime poses to people's freedom and legal rights' (Para. 6).

Fundamental rights are an obvious point of reference for elaborating a more comprehensive notion of freedom, reaching beyond mere freedom of movement and abandoning the rationale of the economic constitution. All the AFSJ programmes have at least hinted at a link between the freedom dimension of the AFSJ and fundamental rights, although they have been rather indecisive as regards the significance of this link for policy measures. An Annex to the Tampere Conclusions defined the composition

[59] The Lisbon Treaty also kept intact the amendment to the Preamble to the TEU which had been agreed on in Amsterdam and in which the Member States declare their resolution 'to facilitate the free movement of persons, while ensuring the safety and security of their peoples, by establishing an area of freedom, security and justice'.

[60] J. Monar (2010), pp. 558–9, speaks of 'a whole range of objectives in the fields of asylum, immigration and border controls that are mostly aimed at the restrictive management of migration challenges and ensuring border security, objectives which most EU citizens – and certainly third-country nationals – would very likely not normally associate with freedom'.

and working methods of the Convention which was set up to draft the EU Charter of Fundamental Rights. In turn, the Hague Programme put improving 'the common capability of the Union and its Member States to guarantee fundamental rights' high on the list of objectives included in the introductory section. In the section on 'General orientations', it called for full respect for 'fundamental rights, as guaranteed by the European Convention on Human Rights and the Charter of Fundamental Rights in Part II of the Constitutional Treaty and the explanatory notes, as well as the Geneva Convention on Refugees'. It was recalled that 'incorporating the Charter into the Constitutional Treaty and accession to the European Convention for the protection of human rights and fundamental freedoms will place the Union, including its institutions, under a legal obligation to ensure that in all its areas of activity, fundamental rights are not only respected but also actively promoted'. Furthermore, the Hague Programme reaffirmed the 'firm commitment to oppose any form of racism, antisemitism and xenophobia', expressed by the European Council in December 2003, and welcomed 'the Commission's communication on the extension of the mandate of the European Monitoring Centre on Racism and Xenophobia towards a Human Rights Agency' (Para. II.2).

At least at a justificatory level, the post-Lisbon Stockholm Programme has taken the most far-reaching steps in the direction of detaching 'freedom' from its narrow free movement connotation and defining it by reference to fundamental rights and citizenship. Promoting citizenship and fundamental rights heads the list of political priorities in the introductory section of the Programme: 'European citizenship must become a tangible reality', and 'the area of freedom, security and justice must, above all, be a single area in which fundamental rights and freedoms are protected'. Accordingly, the freedom-related section of the Programme bears the title 'Promoting citizens' rights: a Europe of rights'. Top priority is accorded to rapid EU accession to the European Convention on Human Rights, which 'will reinforce the obligation of the Union, including its institutions, to ensure that in all its areas of activity, fundamental rights and freedoms are actively promoted'. This will facilitate the continuing development in step of the case law of the ECJ and the European Court of Human Rights, 'reinforcing the creation of a uniform European fundamental and human rights system based on the European Convention and those set out in the Charter of Fundamental Rights of the European Union'. The programme invites Union institutions and Member States to ensure that throughout the legislative process, legal initiatives will be consistent with fundamental rights and freedoms. For this purpose, Union institutions are called on to make full use of the European Union Agency for Fundamental Rights (Para. 2.1). The measures envisaged pertain not only to full exercise of the right to free movement but also to respect for diversity and protection of the most vulnerable; rights of the individual in criminal proceedings; protection of citizens' rights in the information society; participation in the democratic life of the Union; and entitlement to protection in the information society (Paras. 2.2–7). Migration, asylum and borders are no longer subsumed under the freedom-related section, but external borders and visa policy are dealt with as a sub-section ('Access to Europe in a globalised world') in the security section ('Europe that protects'), while migration and asylum have been dedicated a section of their own ('A Europe of responsibility, solidarity and partnership in migration and asylum matters'). This rearrangement and renaming testifies to an effort to moderate the security emphasis of previous AFSJ programmes.

The Stockholm Programme as a whole can be seen as a response to criticism of the AFSJ, where main concerns have included 'securitization' of the area and lack of democratic and judicial accountability. This goes a long way towards accounting for the attempt to define the freedom aspect through fundamental rights and citizenship, and to sever its umbilical cord to the economic constitution and concomitant cross-border security concerns. Still, the AFSJ Title of the TFEU includes no reference to the EU Charter, nor are there any mutual references between the AFSJ Title and the citizenship provisions of the TFEU.[61]

To conclude, a high degree of ambiguity permeates the discussion of freedom in the AFSJ programmes. This is not merely manifested by the alternation of a narrower, free movement-related understanding and a wider, fundamental rights and citizen-related notion, but also, and perhaps even more significantly, by the definition of the relationship of freedom to security. Three alternatives are conceivable among which the programmes do not make a clear choice. Firstly, freedom can be seen as a source of security problems, as is the case when 'freedom' is primarily defined as free movement of persons. Secondly, it can be understood as an object of protection, as is the case when terrorism and criminality are seen as threatening exercise of citizenship or fundamental rights or basic Union values, at present enshrined in Art. 2 TEU. And, thirdly, freedom in terms of fundamental rights can be defined as a side-constraint which

61 J. Monar (2010), pp. 579–80, speaks here of missed opportunities.

security measures must heed. In Tampere, clear emphasis was on the first alternative: free movement as a source of security problems. The subsequent programmes entailed a shift in the direction of the second and third alternatives without, however, clearly distinguishing between the two.[62] The ambivalence in defining the freedom element and specifying its relation to security may be seen as a token of a basic tension within the constitutional theory of the security constitution: the tension between security and fundamental rights, which will be discussed in more detail in the following section.

Finally, we have the concept of justice. How is 'justice' defined and what is its relation to 'security'? Justice has not been discussed as a substantive value or principle but, rather, as a procedural and institutional question. In all three AFSJ programmes, it has quite consistently been understood in terms of judicial cooperation in cases with a cross-border dimension, under the continuing existence of national judicial systems with their territorially delineated jurisdictions. The Tampere Conclusions proclaimed that in a 'genuine European Area of Justice individuals and businesses should not be prevented or discouraged from exercising their rights by the incompatibility or complexity of legal and administrative systems in the Member States' (Para. 28). Mutual recognition, already introduced in Tampere, is defined in the Stockholm Programme as the cornerstone of judicial cooperation in both civil and criminal matters. Legislative harmonization is invoked as a means to achieve a European Area of Justice too, but secondary to the principle of mutual recognition.

Especially in judicial cooperation in criminal matters, the policy field of justice maintains a close link with security. Measures which according to Art. 67(3) TFEU aim to ensure a high level of security include 'coordination and cooperation between police and judicial authorities and other competent authorities, as well as . . . the mutual recognition of judgments in criminal matters and, if necessary, the approximation of criminal laws'. The Tampere Conclusions made explicit the connection between justice and the security concerns raised by freedom:

> The enjoyment of freedom requires a genuine area of justice, where people can approach courts and authorities in any Member State as easily as in their own. Criminals must find no ways of exploiting differences in the judicial systems

[62] It is evident, though, that 'respect for fundamental rights' alludes to the negative, side-constraint effect of fundamental rights on security measures. What 'active promotion' includes is not as clear.

of Member States. Judgements and decisions should be respected and enforced throughout the Union, while safeguarding the basic legal certainty of people and economic operators. Better compatibility and more convergence between the legal systems of Member States must be achieved. (Para. 5)

Statements like this lend credence to the claim that 'security' is the uniting element in the conceptual cluster of freedom, security and justice.[63] Yet conceding this, as well as the primacy accorded to the fight against terrorism and other security concerns particularly after 9/11, we should register the – at least programmatic – efforts to conceive of freedom with reference to fundamental rights and citizenship and to acknowledge the importance of respecting fundamental rights in security measures. Moreover, 'justice' includes a private law aspect, which is not reducible to security but must be linked to access to justice and, hence, to fundamental rights. Indeed, considerations of access to justice balance the security emphasis, as is conspicuous in the above citation from the Tampere Conclusions.

Security and fundamental rights

The intricate process of constitutionalization, the ever-resurfacing state-sovereigntist concerns, as well as consequent intergovernmental features, lingering reliance on international law instruments and a complicated system of opt-outs and opt-ins, reflect the exceptionally high tension between the transnational, European and the national, Member State level within the security dimension. Let us now turn to the other major tension labelling the security dimension: the tension between security and fundamental rights.

Security possesses both an individual and a social dimension: risks and security threats can be approached from the perspective of both individuals and collectives. The individual and social dimensions do not, of course, exist independently from each other: the security of an individual is socially conditioned, and collectives are composed of individuals (although not reducible to them). Yet, especially in constitutional doctrine, the distinction between individual and collective or social security is important. In constitutional analysis, security can be treated as either

[63] For instance, J. Monar (2010), p. 562, argues that security 'is part of the rationale of the justice concept of the AFSJ and at the same time an essential condition of its concept of freedom'.

an *individual right* or as a *collective good*. Rights must be protected, collective goods produced through public policies. If security is guaranteed as a fundamental right, it is an individual right, in line with other fundamental liberty rights. By contrast, in its collective aspect security relates to a factual state of society, brought about through policy measures. The liberal *Rechtsstaat* tradition, in particular, with its emphasis on the restrictive constitutional function, places collective security – public order and safety (*Allgemeine Ordnung und Sicherheit*), as the term goes – outside the normative sphere of fundamental rights. Security is an extra-constitutional collective good, and one of the central tasks of the constitution is to discipline the exercise of power by police and other security authorities expected to procure the collective good of security. Fundamental rights are supposed to function as side-constraints to security measures and to protect individuals against the security threat posed by uncontrolled security power.

The doctrine of balancing, one of the great global successes of twentieth-century constitutional theory and practice, already signifies a retreat from the liberal *Rechtsstaat* view. As we know, much of the balancing talk has been about liberty and security; about justifying restrictions to liberty in the name of guaranteeing security. Here we encounter one of the paradoxes of constitutional doctrine, evoked at the outset of this chapter: extra-constitutional collective security interests, which individual fundamental rights are supposed to curtail, (re-)enter constitutional doctrine as grounds for limiting those very rights. As Jeremy Waldron, among others, has pointed out, many problems afflict the idea of balancing, both in general and in the particular context of freedom and security.[64] Yet balancing belongs to the standard package of contemporary constitutional doctrine and is implicit in the limitation clauses of Arts. 5–11 ECHR, for instance. What is important for our present discussion is that the idea of balancing does not necessarily entail effacing the distinction between individual fundamental rights and security as a collective good. It still makes sense to discuss within the balancing paradigm, for instance, whether the personal freedom or physical integrity of a suspect or detainee may be restricted in order to enhance the collective security of society.

In recent decades, a tendency to blur in a problematic manner the distinction between individual fundamental rights and collective goods, such as security, has made itself noticeable. The Finnish example is

[64] J. Waldron (2003).

instructive of a more general trend. In Finnish constitutional argumentation at the turn of this century, security as a collective good was no longer treated as an extra-constitutional societal interest which could justify restrictions on fundamental rights; collective security itself was transformed into a fundamental right. This reading of the Constitution was achieved through three argumentative moves.

Firstly, the right to security, explicitly enshrined in the Constitution, was detached from rights to personal liberty and integrity, confirmed in the same provision, and assigned independent legal status. This already points to elevating security as a collective good to a fundamental right; it is difficult to see what independent legal meaning, not included in the rights to liberty and integrity, could be attributed to an individual right to personal security. The second step in the argument consisted of an appeal to the doctrine of horizontal effect (*Drittwirkung*) of fundamental rights; fundamental rights pertain not only to vertical relations between public authorities and private individuals but also to horizontal relations among the latter. Finally, reference was made to the constitutional provision which establishes a general obligation for the state to ensure the realization of fundamental and human rights; this corresponds to the German *Schutzpflicht* (duty of protection) doctrine. Taken together, these arguments – the independent nature of the right to security, the horizontal effect of fundamental rights and the *Schutzpflicht* of the state – entail the obligation of the state to guarantee realization of the right to security in horizontal relations between private individuals. Security as a collective good has been converted into a fundamental right with a rank equal to that of individual liberty rights. By the same token, balancing between liberty and security is redefined as balancing between diverse fundamental rights. This move obliterates from constitutional doctrine the Dworkinian distinction between policies aiming at collective goods and principles focusing on individual rights, with the concomitant *prima facie* primacy of the latter.[65]

Such an understanding of security allows for fundamental rights justification for, say, ever-new police powers: these powers can always be argued to be necessary for fulfilling the obligation of the state to guarantee the fundamental right to security. If and when these powers encroach on individual fundamental rights, such as rights to personal integrity, privacy and confidentiality of correspondence, their constitutional acceptability is claimed to depend on weighing fundamental rights principles of equal

[65] R. Dworkin (1978).

rank. What according to the liberal *Rechtsstaat* view was to be restricted through the system of fundamental rights has been absorbed into the system as one of its constituent elements. The influence of German doctrine on Finnish development was conspicuous. Indeed, a similar development was already discernible in Germany in the 1980s, when the German Constitutional Court, supported by such academics as Robert Alexy,[66] elaborated its doctrines of fundamental rights as general legal principles, the *Drittwirkung* of these rights and principles and the *Schutzpflicht* of the state. Critics, such as Ingeborg Maus and Oliver Lepsius, have pointed to the ensuing danger of weakening the protection of individual liberty rights. Lepsius has drawn attention to the tendency to understand even liberty as a general state of society, rather than in terms of individual liberty rights. Hence balancing tends to be perceived as a comparative weighing up of two kinds of collective good![67]

Evidently, in EU law and complementary programmatic documents 'security' has primarily been employed in its collective sense. In ECJ case law, balancing has been resorted to but without invoking collective security as a fundamental right; balancing has occurred between extra-constitutional security interests and individual fundamental rights. To my knowledge, no attempt has been made either by EU institutions or academic writers to interpret the right to security of person, enshrined in Art. 6 CFREU, in terms of a collective good.[68] As Jörg Monar has noted, the provisions of the AFSJ Title of the TFEU do not establish justiciable rights for citizens but provide for furnishing them public goods; European citizens are not conceived of as (active) rights-holders but as (passive) recipients of public goods. On Monar's reading, the wording of Art. 3(2)

66 See R. Alexy (2002).

67 I. Maus (1989) and O. Lepsius (2004). However, in the 2000s the German Constitutional Court seems to have retreated from treating balancing as involving diverse collective goods pulling in diverse directions. In a series of decisions, most notably in the celebrated *Luftsicherheitsgesetz* ruling, the Court has declined to accord an alleged collective right to security a privileged position with regard to individual rights, O. Lepsius (2006). During the 2000s, the Finnish Constitutional Law Committee has also modified its position, most probably due to academic critique.

68 See, however, *Digital Rights Ireland*, Para. 42, where the Court props up its assessment of the fight against international terrorism and serious crime as an objective of general interest in the sense of the limitation clause in Art. 52(1) CFREU with the observation that Art. 6 CFREU lays down the right of any person not only to liberty, but also to security. Joined Cases C-293/12 and C-594/12 *Digital Rights Ireland and Seitlinger and Others*, judgment of 8 April 2014 (not yet reported).

TEU is symptomatic enough: 'The Union shall offer its citizens an area of freedom, security and justice . . . '[69]

In programmatic contexts, both citizenship and rights vocabulary has been employed. The Tampere Conclusions, the first comprehensive AFSJ programme adopted by the European Council, declared that 'people have the *right* to expect the Union to address the threat to their freedom and legal rights posed by serious crime' (Para. 6, italics added),[70] and the Internal Security Strategy of 2007 even uses the term 'basic right': 'People in Europe expect to live in security and to enjoy their freedoms: security is in itself a basic right.'[71] AFSJ programmes and strategies even hint at the protective duty of the Union. This message is conspicuous in the Preamble to the Anti-Terrorism Framework Decision, where terrorism is characterized as the most serious violation of the universal values on which the Union is founded and which include respect for human rights and fundamental freedoms.

The expansion and constitutionalization of the security dimension has largely coincided with the development of Union fundamental rights law. Maastricht both introduced the security-related pillars and confirmed the status of fundamental rights as principles of Community law. In turn, post-Amsterdam privileging of security issues overlaps the drafting and acceptance of the EU Charter, and, finally, the acknowledgement of its constitutional rank in Lisbon. Still, until Lisbon the effectiveness of fundamental rights constraints on EU security measures was hampered by the limited competence of the ECJ within the third pillar.

In constitutional adjudication, Union security measures have been weighed against fundamental rights not only by the ECJ but by national constitutional courts as well. The pluralism of fundamental rights law in Europe, discussed above in Chapter 3, creates an interface for the two basic tensions we have identified in the constitutional theory of the security dimension: between, on the one hand, European and national

69 J. Monar (2010), p. 579.

70 The Hague Programme, adopted in the aftermath of the terrorist attacks in New York and Madrid, stated that 'the citizens of Europe *rightly expect* the European Union, while guaranteeing respect for fundamental freedoms and rights, to take a more effective, joint approach to cross-border problems such as terrorism, organized crime, irregular migratory flows and smuggling of human beings as well as the prevention thereof' (italics added).

71 ISS (2010), p. 19.

competences and, on the other hand, security and fundamental rights. Member States have been keen to ensure that Union security measures meet the criteria of national fundamental rights law too. Implementation of the EAW Framework Decision raised fundamental rights concerns in several Member States. These concerns were related to extradition of own nationals; the principle of legality; respect for *ne bis in idem* and other procedural rights of defendants; as well as confidence in fundamental rights protection in other Member States which the principle of mutual recognition presupposes. Indeed, during implementation of the EAW Framework Decision, several constitutional courts profited from the opportunity to reconfirm their reservations on the primacy of EU law. Even in applying national provisions implementing the Framework Decision, national constitutional courts have tried to defend the autonomy of their fundamental rights law.

On a referral by the Belgian Constitutional Court (*Cour d'arbitrage*), the ECJ examined the EAW Framework Decision from the perspective of Union constitutional law and found no violation of the fundamental rights principles of legality or equality.[72] AFSJ issues have also figured prominently in ECJ post-Lisbon case law invoking the CFREU with its newly acquired constitutional status. In addition to balancing security and fundamental rights, the case law has touched on the respective jurisdiction of EU and national fundamental rights law, and, through the principle of mutual recognition, the horizontal relationship between fundamental rights protection in different Member States. Here the security dimension has contributed to clarifying issues of larger significance within the juridical constitution.

In *Melloni*, the main legal issue was whether a Member State could refuse to execute a European arrest warrant 'in order to avoid an adverse effect on the right to a fair trial and the rights of the defence guaranteed by its constitution'. As explained in Chapter 3, the Court invoked the primacy, unity and effectiveness of EU law, and rejected a reading of Art. 53 CFREU[73] which would authorize Member States 'to apply the standard

[72] Case C-303/05 *Advocaten voor de Wereld* [2007] I-03633. The issue of legality related to the definition of crimes in the context of which the warrant may be issued and that of equality to the possibility of different practices in different Member States. For an analysis of the ECJ decision see, e.g., A. Hinarejos (2008).

[73] 'Nothing in this Charter shall be interpreted as restricting or adversely affecting human rights and fundamental freedoms as recognised, in their respective fields of application, by Union law and international law and by international agreements to which the Union or all the Member States are party, including the European

of protection of fundamental rights guaranteed by its constitution when that standard is higher than that deriving from the Charter and, where necessary, to give it priority over the application of provisions of EU law'.[74] *Melloni* might be labelled a special case, due to the fact that the EAW Framework Decision includes explicit provisions on the Member State right to refuse a European arrest warrant and that these were expressly designed to heed fair trial concerns. However, the Court formulated its reading of Art. 53 CFREU in general terms, with the clear intention of articulating a principle with general applicability. Daniel Sarmiento has portrayed reference to the primacy, unity and effectiveness of EU law as an exceptional remedy; a last-resort safety measure for extraordinary situations.[75] Yet the way *Melloni* defines the primacy of the principle of primacy with regard to the Member State right to enforce higher national standards appears to deprive Art. 53 CFREU of much of its relevance. Situations addressed by this article are by definition situations of overlapping jurisdiction where the principle of primacy is relevant.

If *Melloni* is important in specifying the relationship between Union and national fundamental rights law from the perspective of EU constitutional law, *NS*,[76] which deals with asylum law, addresses the horizontal relationship between fundamental rights protection in different Member States. In its judgment, the Court first stated that the discretionary power which the Dublin II Regulation on the Common European Asylum System[77] leaves to Member States forms an integral part of this System. When a Member State exercises this power and decides whether or not to examine an application which is not its responsibility under the Regulation, it implements Union law and, consequently, EU fundamental rights law applies (Paras. 65–8).[78] The Court further held that Member States have a duty not to rely on an interpretation of EU secondary legislation which would contradict EU fundamental rights or other general principles of EU law (Para. 77). The Common European Asylum System is built on

Convention for the Protection of Human Rights and Fundamental Freedoms, and by the Member States' constitutions.'

74 Case C-399/11 *Melloni*, judgment of 26 February 2013 (not yet reported), Para. 56.

75 D. Sarmiento (2013b), p. 1295.

76 Joined Cases C-411/10 and C-493/10 *NS and Others*, 21 December 2011 (not yet reported).

77 Regulation No. 343/2003 of 18 February 2013 establishing the criteria and mechanisms for determining the Member State responsible for examining an asylum application lodged in one of the Member States by a third-country national, [2003] OJ L50/1.

78 Here the Court referred to Art. 6 TEU and Art. 51 CFREU, as well as the doctrine defining the applicability of fundamental rights law in national courts. See above, Chapter 3.

the principle of *mutual confidence*. The underlying assumption is that participating States observe fundamental rights and that the Member States can have confidence in each other in this regard (Para. 78).

However, the assumption that asylum seekers are treated in all Member States in compliance with the requirements of the CFREU, the Geneva Convention and the ECHR is rebuttable. The system 'may, in practice, experience major operational problems in a given Member State, meaning that there is a substantial risk that asylum seekers may, when transferred to that Member State, be treated in a manner incompatible with their fundamental rights' (Paras. 80–1). Still, not any infringement of a fundamental right by the Member State responsible suffices to prevent the transfer of an asylum seeker. Only 'if there are substantial grounds for believing that there are systemic flaws in the asylum procedure and reception conditions for asylum applicants in the Member State responsible, resulting in inhuman or degrading treatment, within the meaning of Article 4 of the Charter, of asylum seekers transferred to the territory of that Member State, the transfer would be incompatible with that provision' (Para. 86). If such grounds exist, EU fundamental rights law obliges a Member State not to transfer the asylum seeker to the Member State responsible.[79]

Thus, according to *NS*, EU fundamental rights law imposes on Member States, including their courts, an obligation to monitor compliance with that law in other Member States. Yet the basic, though rebuttable, assumption guiding Member State action is that other Member States comply with the relevant fundamental rights; hence the term 'horizontal

[79] The Court formulated its central conclusion as follows: 'It follows from the foregoing that in situations such as that at issue in the cases in the main proceedings, to ensure compliance by the European Union and its Member States with their obligations concerning the protection of the fundamental rights of asylum seekers, the Member States, including the national courts, may not transfer an asylum seeker to the "Member State responsible" within the meaning of Regulation No 343/2003, where they cannot be unaware that systemic deficiencies in the asylum procedure and in the reception conditions of asylum seekers in that Member State amount to substantial grounds for believing that the asylum seeker would face a real risk of being subjected to inhuman or degrading treatment within the meaning of Article 4 of the Charter' (Para. 94). In Para. 106, the Court put the same conclusion in slightly different words: 'Article 4 of the Charter of Fundamental Rights of the European Union must be interpreted as meaning that the Member States, including the national courts, may not transfer an asylum seeker to the "Member State responsible" within the meaning of Regulation No 343/2003 where they cannot be unaware that systemic deficiencies in the asylum procedure and in the reception conditions of asylum seekers in that Member State amount to substantial grounds for believing that the asylum seeker would face a real risk of being subjected to inhuman or degrading treatment within the meaning of that provision.'

Solange', used by Iris Canor.[80] However, it is important to note that EU law is the applicable law with regard both to the Member State considering the transfer of an asylum seeker and to the Member State responsible. We are dealing with the application and observance of EU fundamental rights law in two Member States and not a direct horizontal relation between national fundamental rights laws. The term 'horizontal *Solange*' is justified in the sense that a Member State's authorities are monitoring the fundamental rights record of another Member State. But, actually, these authorities are exercising 'vertical' EU fundamental rights review.

It would be audacious to derive from *NS* a general doctrine of horizontal *Solange* and a general obligation of Member States to watch over each other's observance of EU fundamental rights. Horizontal *Solange* would be especially relevant for AFSJ legislation based on mutual recognition and the underlying principle of mutual confidence. In its ruling on the EAW, the German Constitutional Court took a position reminiscent of horizontal *Solange*. The Court ruled that 'putting into effect a strict principle of mutual recognition, and the extensive statement of mutual confidence among the states that is connected with it, cannot restrict the constitutional guarantee of fundamental rights'. Accordingly, extradition decisions must always be based on case-by-case weighing.[81] Still, here the standard would be national German but not Union fundamental rights law. In its long dialogue with the German Constitutional Court, the ECJ has never accepted the fundamental rights qualification to the primacy of EU law which the German Court has repeatedly asserted. But nor does ECJ case law provide clear support even for a horizontal *Solange* where the normative yardstick would be provided by EU fundamental rights law. As regards, for instance, the European arrest warrant, the ECJ has not invoked a general doctrine but relied on the explicit provisions of the Framework Decision on mandatory or optional non-execution of such a warrant.[82] However, in the absence of such provisions, a horizontal *Solange*-type argument might be possible.

Kadi, issued in 2008, remains the most pivotal ECJ ruling on the constraints that EU fundamental rights impose on security measures. *Kadi* possesses many legally significant aspects, one of them being the relationship of

[80] I. Canor (2013). [81] BVerfG, 2 BvR 2236/4, 18 July 2008.

[82] See Case C-396/11 *Radu*, judgment of 29 January 2013 (not yet reported). See also Case C-306/09 *IB* [2010] ECR I-10341; and Case C-399/11 *Melloni*, judgment of 26 February 2013 (not yet reported).

EU law with international law. As explained in Chapter 2, *Kadi* reasserted the autonomy of EU law: the fact that the Union measures under scrutiny implemented UN Security Council decisions did not affect the jurisdiction of the Court to assess them by Union fundamental rights law. The Court argued that 'the obligations imposed by an international agreement cannot have the effect of prejudicing the constitutional principles of the EC Treaty, which include the principle that all Community acts must respect fundamental rights, that respect constituting a condition of their lawfulness which it is for the Court to review in the framework of the complete system of legal remedies established by the Treaty' (Para. 285). According to the Court, the Treaty provision on the validity of pre-Membership international obligations (now Art. 351 TFEU) 'may in no circumstances permit any challenge to the principles that form part of the very foundations of the Community legal order, one of which is the protection of fundamental rights, including the review by the Community judicature of the lawfulness of Community measures as regards their consistency with those fundamental rights' (Para. 304). Furthermore, 'the review by the Court of the validity of any Community measure in the light of fundamental rights must be considered to be the expression, in a community based on the rule of law, of a constitutional guarantee stemming from the EC Treaty as an autonomous legal system which is not to be prejudiced by an international agreement' (Para. 316).[83]

In *Kadi*, the Court also took a position on the extent to which security considerations justify restricting EU fundamental rights. It rejected the view that 'restrictive measures such as those imposed by the contested

[83] The Court reconfirmed its position in *Kadi II*, a case where the Commission, the Council and some Member States required setting aside *Kadi*, claiming for instance that an error of law had been committed when the contested regulation had not been afforded immunity from jurisdiction. The Court referred to its post-*Kadi* case law and stated that there had been no change in the factors justifying the position taken in *Kadi*, factors which 'bound up with the constitutional guarantee which is exercised, in a Union based on the rule of law ... by judicial review of the lawfulness of all European Union measures, including those which, as in the present case, implement an international law measure, in the light of the fundamental rights guaranteed by the European Union'. The Court re-invoked its previous position that 'without the primacy of a Security Council resolution at the international level thereby being called into question, the requirement that the European Union institutions should pay due regard to the institutions of the United Nations must not result in there being no review of the lawfulness of such European Union measures, in the light of the fundamental rights which are an integral part of the general principles of European Union law'. Joined Cases C-584/10 P, C-593/10 P and C-595/10 P *Commission and Others v Kadi* (*Kadi II*), judgment of 18 July 2013 (not yet reported), Paras. 66–7.

regulation escape all review by the Community judicature once it has been claimed that the act laying them down concerns national security and terrorism'. With reference to ECtHR case law,[84] the Court held it to be 'the task of the Community judicature to apply, in the course of the judicial review it carries out, techniques which accommodate, on the one hand, legitimate security concerns about the nature and sources of information taken into account in the adoption of the act concerned and, on the other, the need to accord the individual a sufficient measure of procedural justice' (Paras. 343–4). Unfortunately, the Court was not more specific as to what the techniques for accommodating security and fundamental rights concerns are.

Kadi belongs to the pre-Lisbon era when the Charter had not yet been acknowledged as enjoying constitutional status and the Court refrained from invoking it. In contrast, *Digital Rights Ireland* examined the compatibility of the Data Retention Directive[85] with the right to respect for private and family life, guaranteed in Art. 7 of the Charter, and the right to protection of personal data, guaranteed in Art. 8, and assessed whether the Directive met the conditions that the Charter lays down for limiting Charter rights and freedoms. In contrast to the European Convention on Human Rights, the Charter includes a general limitation clause. Limitations must be provided for by law and respect the essence of rights and freedoms. They must also adhere to the principle of proportionality, so that they 'may be made only if they are necessary and genuinely meet objectives of general interest recognised by the Union or the need to protect the rights and freedoms of others' (Art. 52(1) CFREU).

In *Digital Rights Ireland*, the Court applied the three-phase reasoning, analogous to that employed when assessing restrictions on free movement (see Chapter 5), which it has adopted in fundamental rights review. In the first phase, the existence of a restriction is considered, in the second phase a position is taken on justification of an identified restriction and in the third phase the restriction is subjected to a proportionality test. The Court found that retention of data relating to a person's private life and communications in itself constituted interference with the Charter right to respect for private and family life and that access of competent national authorities to the data constituted a further interference.

84 The reference was to the judgment of the European Court of Human Rights in *Chahal v United Kingdom* of 15 November 1996, *Reports of Judgments and Decisions* 1996-V, Para. 131.

85 Joined Cases C-293/12 and C-594/12 *Digital Rights Ireland and Seitlinger and Others*, judgment of 8 April 2014 (not yet reported).

Because the Directive provided for processing personal data it also constituted interference with the fundamental right to protection of personal data (Paras. 34–6). The Court noted that the material objective of the Directive is to contribute to the fight against serious crime and, ultimately, to public security, and stated, referring to *Kadi* and *Tsakouridis*,[86] that the fight against terrorism and serious crime constitutes an 'objective of general interest' for the purposes of the limitation clause in Art. 52(1) CFREU (Paras. 41–2). In the proportionality appraisal, the Court found that retention of data covered by the Directive may be considered to be appropriate for attaining the objective of the Directive. However, the Directive did not confine the restrictions on Charter rights to what is strictly necessary, as required by Art. 52(1). The Court pointed out that the Directive applies to all means of electronic communication and covers all subscribers and registered users, and, consequently, 'entails an interference with the fundamental rights of practically the entire European population'. No differentiation, limitation or exception is made in the light of the objective of combating serious crime. Application of the Directive does not require any evidence that persons at issue might have a link with serious crime or that data are related to a threat to public security. Furthermore, the Directive does not set out an objective criterion by which limits on access by the authorities to data and their use for preventing, detecting or prosecuting offences could be determined, nor does it contain substantive or procedural conditions for such access and use. The Court specifically stressed that

> access by the competent national authorities to the data retained is not made dependent on a prior review carried out by a court or by an independent administrative body whose decision seeks to limit access to the data and their use to what is strictly necessary for the purpose of attaining the objective pursued and which intervenes following a reasoned request of those authorities submitted within the framework of procedures of prevention, detection or criminal prosecutions. (Paras. 56–62)

Digital Rights Ireland (2014) may prove to be a milestone in asserting fundamental rights as a restriction on security-motivated measures; and not only in the EU, but even more generally.

Constitution or anti-constitution?

As we have seen, 'security' is a diffuse, expansionist and border-breaking concept. It is no wonder that it is difficult to mark the exact boundaries

[86] Case C-145/09 *Land Baden-Württemberg v Panagiotis Tsakouridis* [2010] ECR I-11979.

of the security constitution. In this chapter I have identified the security dimension with internal security, addressed at the Treaty level, first, by the third-pillar provisions of the Maastricht Treaty and, finally, after Lisbon, by the AFSJ of the TFEU. But one of the boundaries which the concept of security informing European constitutional law and strategy documents tends to break is that separating internal from external security. Hence, my choice to focus on internal security and exclude Common Foreign and Security Policy from the discussion might be questioned. Or, to take another example: should we, at the level of Treaty law, include in the security constitution the whole AFSJ or just those fields where the security emphasis is prominent? I do not deny the relevance of such questions. But, what perhaps is most important is to note the fuzziness of the boundaries of the security constitution, at the poles of both constitutional law and constitutional object. Indeed, related to the diffuse, expansionist and border-breaking character of 'security', the security constitution does not possess clear-cut contours either.

Another distinctive feature is the combination of transnationalism and intergovernmentalism which characterizes institutional and procedural aspects of the security constitution. A central criterion of the constitutionalization of the security dimension consists of its advancing institutional and procedural transnationalization. Starting from the pre-Maastricht situation where the security dimension was not addressed at Treaty level at all, and ending up with 'communitarization' of the AFSJ in Lisbon, transnationalization has made considerable headway. The powers of the three main transnational institutions – the Commission, the European Parliament and the ECJ – now reach to all AFSJ fields, and the establishment of EU security agencies, such as Europol, Eurojust, Frontex and EASO, has complemented the institutional aspect of the security constitution. But intergovernmentalism has proven to be an ineradicable trait in this constitutional dimension. The Commission has obtained the power of initiative, but a diluted form of Member State initiative still exists too. A quarter of Member States have a power of initiative parallel to that of the Commission in police cooperation and judicial cooperation in criminal matters. In turn, the special legislative procedure called for in several AFSJ provisions includes unanimity in the Council but mere consultation of, or consent by, the European Parliament. Furthermore, EU security agencies do not have operational law-enforcement competences, nor do they wield public power in Member States. Their main function is to support Member State authorities and to provide a site for administrative and professional cooperation, as well as for information sharing and data processing. And, finally, as regards the justice aspect of the AFSJ, mutual recognition as the main option is an intergovernmental alternative to transnational legislative harmonization. All this lends credence to Jörg Monar's point that cooperation rather than integration remains the prevailing principle. This sets the AFSJ aside from domains falling under, say, the microeconomic constitution.[87]

The reason for lingering intergovernmentalism and the continuing dominance of the principle of cooperation should be evident by now. The security constitution touches on, and is prone to collide with, traditional core attributes of state sovereignty. These attributes are related to the Weberian characteristics of the modern state as possessor of a monopoly on legitimate violence. Often enough, they are protected by basic constitutional principles which, according to the constitutional doctrine of Member States, pose insurmountable hurdles to additional transfers of sovereignty rights. Transnational legislative and operational competence in criminal law, policing and anti-terrorist measures also touches on individual fundamental rights, and here too collisions are possible with basic constitutional principles of Member States, even constitutional identity as defined by national constitutional actors. In this respect, the saga of the EAW Framework Decision and the constitutional assessment of its legislative implementation in Member States is instructive enough.

Sovereign power is the main attribute in the traditional three-element concept of the state, espoused, for instance, by the German late constitutionalist school of Carl Friedrich von Gerber, Paul Laband and Georg Jellinek, the other two being population and territory. Member States have been quite jealous in guarding their control over the latter two elements too. Transnationalization has, though, progressed further in the domain of migration, asylum and borders than in criminal law and law enforcement. Yet Member States have retained their power to determine volumes of migration from third countries to their territory, as well as the geographical demarcation of their borders.

State-sovereigntist concerns are more pronounced in some Member States than others, and national constitutional doctrines of core constitutional principles defining national constitutional identity and enjoying protection against transnational intrusion vary as well. This is a central backdrop to a further peculiarity of the security constitution: its mix of coherence and fragmentation. The concept of security creates the necessary coherence which in general justifies talking of a European security constitution. Moreover, the Lisbon Treaty has increased unity in Treaty

[87] J. Monar (2010), pp. 573 ff.

law by assembling AFSJ provisions under the same Title of the TFEU and by harmonizing the legislative instruments and procedures available. Furthermore, the security dimension as a whole displays characteristic operational modes. However, signs of fragmentation are conspicuous too. Ever since its pre-Maastricht origins under the auspices of international law, the security dimension has been the model example of variable geometry. The Schengen system has never – either before or after incorporation of the Schengen *acquis* into the EU legal framework – covered all Member States, and the opt-outs of some Member States have been complemented by the opt-ins of some non-member Schengen associates. The Amsterdam Treaty introduced the objective of establishing the AFSJ and led to replacing conventions as a legal instrument with framework decisions. But as a counterweight, through its provisions on closer (enhanced) cooperation, it (re-)constitutionalized variable geometry within the AFSJ. And as was proved by the Prüm Convention, signed in 2005 by seven Member States,[88] neither did Amsterdam spell the end of resort to international treaties as a means to push security cooperation further in spite of the sovereigntist hesitations of some Member States. The Lisbon Treaty only reaffirmed and even added to the existing fragmentation with its complicated system of opt-outs and opt-ins, as well as provisions on emergency brakes and enhanced cooperation. If the AFSJ has managed to obtain substantive coherence as a policy area, in geographical terms no unitary area of freedom, security and justice exists.

The emphasis on cooperation instead of integration – to use Monar's terms – points to constitutionally relevant specificities in the modes of operation under the security constitution. Cooperation is the prevalent mode of operation of the executive: of administrations, civil servants and professionals. A major part of AFSJ Treaty provisions deals with such cooperation, and, as we have seen, in many cases Treaty provisions have only added a formal constitutional blessing to developments already achieved. The AFSJ is the promised land of networks connecting security officials and professionals, and even AFSJ agencies, some of them – like Europol and Eurojust – provided for in the Treaty, tend to boil down to such networks. Associated with administrative and professional cooperation,

[88] Convention on the stepping up of cross-border cooperation, particularly in combating terrorism, cross-border crime and illegal migration. Subsequently, the Convention was incorporated in the Union legal framework through a third-pillar Council decision. Council Decision 2008/615/JHA of 23 June 2008 on the stepping up of cross-border cooperation, particularly in combating terrorism and cross-border crime, [2008] OJ L210/12.

information exchange and data processing, necessary for identifying and assessing security risks, are vital for the operational modus of the AFSJ, raising constitutional concerns especially in respect of data protection and the right to privacy. It remains to be seen what wider significance *Digital Rights Ireland* will have for the security constitution.

Since its pre-Maastricht beginnings in Trevi and Schengen, the security dimension has been accompanied by allegations of lack of transparency and democratic and judicial accountability. Constitutionalization since Maastricht has not been able to quash this criticism. The post-Lisbon Stockholm Programme bears witness to its continuing pertinence. The European Council refers to 'the increased role that the European Parliament and National Parliaments will play following the entry into force of the Lisbon Treaty and to the greater opportunity Art. 11 TEU provides for citizens and associations to make known and publicly exchange their views in all areas of Union action', and expresses its confidence that 'this will reinforce the open and democratic character of the Union for the benefit of its people'. As regards the AFSJ specifically, reference is made to the co-decision procedure (the ordinary legislative procedure), which grants 'full involvement' of the European Parliament, while the role of the National Parliaments in the legislative procedure is invoked as well. The European Council also points to the enlarged jurisdiction of the ECJ (Para. 1).

Yet it is doubtful whether the Lisbon Treaty or the assurances of the Stockholm Programme will be able to efface concerns about transparency, democracy and accountability. The emphasis on the executive instead of the legislative, the confidential nature of data processed in the security dimension and the scarcity of decisions with direct legal relevance and within the reach of legal remedies pose formidable obstacles to realizing these values even at the state level. In the AFSJ of the EU, with its primacy of administrative and professional cooperation at the expense of legislative integration, the obstacles are considerably higher still. Democratic legitimacy and the rule of law, including judicial review of executive action, belong to the major promises made by modern constitutions, characterizing constitutionalism in its thick normative sense. In these respects, the security constitution of the EU does not fare well, although some undeniable progress has been made on the road from pre-Maastricht to post-Lisbon.

Let us wrap up this exploration of the peculiarities of the security constitution with some comments on the position of the individual. A democratic *Rechtsstaat*, as envisaged by basic modern constitutional principles, such as fundamental rights, the rule of law and democracy, is premised on a conception of individuals as autonomous and responsible persons. European constitutionalization has been a process not only of transnationalization but also of individualization, of connecting transnational institutions directly with European individuals. In this respect, constitutionalization and its expansion to new dimensions have entailed step-by-step building up of European citizenship. The economic constitution, where it all began, treats individuals as economic actors in the marketplace and endows them with market citizenship; juridical constitutionalization, proceeding through such celebrated ECJ rulings as *Van Gend en Loos* and *Costa v Enel*, added to citizenship a judicial layer, while political constitutionalization generated political citizenship. Even the embryonic social constitution, the constitutional underdog in the EU context, gives rise to at least a thin social citizenship.

Here the security constitution amounts to an exception. Although both Art. 3(2) TEU and the AFSJ programmes have flirted with citizenship terminology, the security dimension does not furnish European citizens with new rights that would further enhance their citizenship. In the mirror of the security constitution, individuals are passive recipients of collective security goods rather than active citizens or bearers of rights. Individuals enter the focus of security measures primarily as security risks whose characteristics, propensities and actions must be surveyed and recorded. As objects of surveillance and data processing individuals are treated as replaceable members of a group – a population, as Foucault would put it – rather than as autonomous and responsible, both unique and equal persons, as conceiving of them as bearers of rights and citizens of a democratic polity would presuppose. In this sense, the security dimension is a domain of *de-individualization*, rather than individualization![89]

The security dimension comes up with new divisions and classifications of individuals which do not return to individuals their unique personhood but do counteract the principle of equality. As Samuli Hurri has argued, the ECJ's *ordre public* rulings in the 1970s gave birth to a 'European individual', with a juridical locus in the grey zone between the law of nationals and the law of aliens.[90] With the development of common policies on visas and migration, asylum and borders, new categories of individuals with a legal status different from full-blown citizens and, often enough, objects of diversified systems of information and surveillance have abounded: third-country nationals and illegal immigrants, refugees

[89] See also O. Lepsius (2004). [90] S. Hurri (2014).

and asylum seekers, to name some of the most obvious ones. The security constitution appears to have not only de-individualizing but also *un-equalizing* consequences.

'Security' has largely replaced 'emergency' and 'state of exception' as the principal argumentative device in the domain of the security constitution. European Treaty law hardly mentions emergencies. In institutional practice, though, emergency talk has retained at least part of its justificatory significance, as has recently been proven by the framing and handling of the Eurozone crisis.[91] At the national level, the security dimension is perhaps the primary battlefield between constitutive and restrictive constitutional functions. Within the EU too, the security constitution poses grave fundamental rights problems, which are further aggravated by its de-individualizing and un-equalizing tendencies.

Even without the constitutional black or grey hole of a state of exception, the security constitution displays conspicuous features of an anti-constitution. This is, if you wish, the ultimate paradox of the European security constitution.

[91] On reliance on emergency language in the USA, especially during the George W. Bush administration, see S. Levinson and J. M. Balkin (2010), where the term 'policy of government through emergency' is introduced.

Epilogue

Towards a general theory of the European constitution

This book has applied a relational approach to European constitutionalism. 'Constitution' itself has been understood as a relational concept, connoting the constitutional relation between constitutional law and constitutional object. A relational approach leads to treating the European constitution as a multidimensional and multitemporal process of constitutionalization. At both poles of the constitutional relation, the European constitution displays differentiation, uncommon at the state level. In accordance with the differentiation of constitutional objects, diverse constitutional dimensions can be discerned: a juridical, political, economic, social and security constitution. The juridical and political constitutions are *framing* constitutions, while the economic, social and security constitutions represent *sectoral* constitutionalization. The preceding chapters have corroborated not only the multidimensionality but also the multitemporality of the European constitution. The diverse constitutional dimensions have emerged at different points in time, with the (micro)economic and the juridical constitutions possessing a temporal lead, and developed at a different pace, partly following a distinct constitutional logic but ultimately prompted by extra-constitutional economic, political or ideological factors.

The EU is a transnational polity and legal system which does not share the universal claim to political and juridical authority raised by state constitutions. As the principle of conferral makes clear, European competences must be expressly granted by the Treaties as the 'constitutional charter' of the EU; that is, ultimately by the Member States as *Herren der Verträge*. This is the backdrop to the provisions on policy competences which have provided the Treaty basis for sectoral constitutionalization.

Policy objectives and competences have multiplied since the conclusion of the Treaty of Rome, but this has not eradicated the fundamental *policy orientation*. Because the Founding Treaties presuppose complementary legislative and other measures, they have been called framework treaties – *traités cadre*. But if they are compared with state constitutions, the framework label more befits the latter: state constitutions typically only establish general legislative competence and leave the choice of objectives and policy fields to ordinary, majoritarian law-making. Diverging from state constitutions, the Treaties constitutionalize sectoral policy areas and objectives. By the same token, they constitutionalize disagreements on the background assumptions of sectoral policies. The significance of sectoral constitutionalization also largely accounts for the laggard process of legal cultural sedimentation. In sectoral constitutionalization, European constitutionalism has not been able to draw on Member State constitutional traditions, and the contestedness of the theoretical underpinnings has delayed development of a distinct constitutional culture, impregnating the *Vorverständnis* of European constitutional actors. In constitutional law too, European law is still an emergent legal system in the cultural respect.

Multidimensionality entails another important aspect of relationality: interrelations among constitutional dimensions. Here the distinction between framing and sectoral constitutions has proved crucial. We have seen how the sectoral constitutions have enjoyed substantive or *functional primacy*, and how economic constitutionalization has influenced developments within other sectoral dimensions as well. The original impetus for social constitutionalization arose from the needs of economic constitutionalization, such as facilitating realization of free movement of workers; subsequently, the submission of healthcare and social security to constitutional free movement and competition law has narrowed the institutional and financial leeway in the social dimension; and the Eurozone crisis has demonstrated in a very tangible manner the limits of the protection that social rights can offer against austerity measures. In turn, reacting to the consequences of free movement and the opening of internal borders has been a major rationale behind constitutionalization in the security dimension. Functional primacy has taken diverse guises, but the major expressions are threefold: firstly, the primary constitutional dimension needs support from, and launches developmental processes in, other dimensions; secondly, consequences of the primary constitution call for reactions in the other dimensions; and, thirdly, the primary constitution enjoys *prima facie* prevalence in inter-dimensional conflicts, in, for instance, conflicts between different types of rights – say, economic and social rights. But while sectoral constitutionalization possesses functional primacy, the juridical and political constitutions hold what can be termed *constitutive primacy*. Sectoral constitutionalization would not have been able to take off without the legal, decisional and institutional infrastructure provided by the framing constitutions. In their framing capacity, the juridical and political constitutions also channel the restrictive effects of fundamental rights into sectoral constitutions. Moreover, resolution of conflicts between constitutional dimensions – for example, between different types of rights – falls to the framing juridical constitution. Thus, the ECJ as the European constitutional court is responsible for weighing and balancing rights stemming from diverse constitutions.

We have also learned how important interaction between transnational and national levels is for European constitutionalism. In many respects, European constitutionalism relies on backing from national constitutionalism. This holds not only for the vital legitimating function in the political dimension but for other constitutional dimensions as well. Realization of the European juridical constitution depends on the hinge position of national courts; the European economic constitution presupposes national fundamental rights which guarantee the legal presuppositions for market activities; the European social constitution is premised on the existence of national welfare regimes; and the European security constitution has retained maintaining law and order and safeguarding internal security as a national responsibility. But relations between European and national constitutionalism are not marked only by complementariness and intertwinement; potential for conflict exists as well, as the post-Maastricht debate on constitutional pluralism has pointed out. The debate has been important and instructive but has still focused merely on one constitutional dimension – the juridical one – and one type of relation between European and national constitutionalism.

Examination of sectoral constitutionalization has shown how contested is constitutional theory in the various dimensions. Within the microeconomic constitution, the main frontline separates advocates of market liberalization from those who accept the possibility and need for national or European public regulation; within the macroeconomic constitution, Monetarists have been confident of EMU becoming an optimal currency area while Economists have stressed the necessity of common economic policies as a precondition for common monetary policy; within the social constitution, the primacy of national welfare regimes collides with the prevalence of the economic constitution, and national solidaristic justice confronts European access justice; and, finally, within the security constitution, security and fundamental rights considerations clash with each other, as does transnationalism with state sovereigntism and intergovernmentalism. Given such instability, is it in general warranted to speak of a general theory of the European constitution? In effect, this book as a whole is an attempt to provide elements for such a theory where sectoral constitutionalization and disagreements over its foundations would also find their place. The blueprint for a general theory of the European constitution which emerges from the discussions in this book is a reconstruction, and as a reconstruction it is bound to be controversial as well.

Reflecting the policy orientation of European law and polity, sectoral constitutionalization enjoys functional primacy and accounts for most of the distinctive features of European constitutionalism. Still, a general theory of the European constitution must dwell more on the juridical and political constitutions than the sectoral ones. The juridical and political constitutions do not merely frame the sectoral constitutions and provide the latter with the necessary legal and institutional means. They are not only framing but *summarizing* constitutions too. Sectoral constitutionalization possesses both a substantive and a formal aspect. The juridical and political constitutions stand in a recursive relation to sectoral constitutionalization. They create the possibility for sectoral constitutionalization, but sectoral developments, in turn, influence juridical and political constitutionalization. Sectoral constitutionalization may require new legal instruments and doctrines or new institutions and procedures. It may also impact the relations between the transnational and the national within the juridical and political constitutions or the principles which govern interrelations among Union or Member State institutions. The framing constitutions gather together – summarize – the juridical and political implications of sectoral constitutionalization. These implications affect underpinning constitutional theories too: the legal theory of the juridical constitution and the political theory of the political constitution.

European integration started as economic integration, and sectoral constitutionalization started as economic constitutionalization. Economic and juridical constitutionalization proceeded hand in hand; indeed, the first steps in juridical constitutionalization coincided with the formal aspect of economic constitutionalization. The objective of economic and juridical constitutionalization was to ensure that European law, aiming at establishing the common market, was implemented in Member States effectively and uniformly. For a novel transnational legal system, such as the European one, the constitutional positioning function plays a key role. Since *Van Gend en Loos* and *Costa v Enel*, direct effect and supremacy have defined the relationship between European and Member State law. The gradual expansion of these principles, impelled by the needs of sectoral constitutionalization, recapitulates much of the process of juridical constitutionalization. A clear focus in juridical constitutionalization lay in positioning European law in respect of Member State law. However, defending the principles of direct effect and primacy required a declaration of autonomy from international law as well. As an autonomous legal system, EU law was not – so the ECJ argued – bound by the international law premise which left defining the internal effects of international norms to the constitutional decision of the states.

The microeconomic orientation accounts for the key position of the rule of law and courts as its guarantors in pre-Maastricht constitutionalization; for the characterization of European integration as legal integration and the Community as a *Rechtsgemeinschaft*. In turn, post-Maastricht macroeconomic constitutionalization has relativized the significance of law and courts. Macroeconomic objectives and policies succumb with difficulty to legal regulation, and courts are not suited to reviewing decisions which adhere to economic rather than legal rationality. The Eurozone crisis has demonstrated the limitations of both European and national constitutional review – both *ultra vires* and fundamental rights review – in the macroeconomic field. The social and security constitutions have also impacted the juridical constitution. Constitutionalization in the social dimension involves such juridical innovations as the Community Charter of the Fundamental Social Rights of Workers (1989), and the Maastricht Social Protocol and the adjacent Agreement on social policy, which established a particular legislative regime, lasting until incorporation of the provisions of the Agreement in the Treaty of Amsterdam. The Eurozone crisis witnessed recourse to intergovernmental agreements as instruments of crisis management and their sanctification by the constitutional legislator through the amendment to Art. 136 TFEU. In the security dimension, where state-sovereigntist concerns are particularly enhanced, agreements under international law have played an important role both as precursors to European legislation and as instruments of European security policy. Maastricht introduced third-pillar conventions, which, however, were superseded by framework decisions, a third-pillar novelty adopted in Amsterdam but abolished in Lisbon.

The policy orientation of European law is manifest in its principle of order; that is, the principle which is supposed to bring about the order of the European legal order. European law has never aspired to a Kelsenian formal order where legal instruments would have been unambiguously arranged into a hierarchical pyramid, with higher-level norms both validating lower-order ones and defeating them in situations of conflict. The order that European law has aimed at has been of a teleological nature: substantive coherence brought about by policies. In the Dworkinian distinction between policies and morally laden principles – principles *sensu stricto* – the emphasis in European law has been on the former side. Progress of the fundamental rights dimension and confirmation of the universalist value basis of the Union in Lisbon have partly altered the situation, enhanced the position of principles (*sensu stricto*) and complicated identification of the principle of order in European law. However, paradoxically enough, even the injection of morally related principles through fundamental rights law was originally motivated by policy considerations. Reviewing Member State implementing measures in the light of national fundamental rights was seen to endanger the uniform application of European law and achieving the common market objective. To ward off this danger, expressly spelled out in, for instance, *Hauer* (1979),[1] the ECJ introduced fundamental rights as general principles of European law.

Reinforcing the principle dimension and moderating the policy orientation have had important consequences for the way European law addresses the task of determining its limits. Initially, the constitutional restrictive function fell on the substantive limitation of European law's claim to authority. Fundamental rights brought the European juridical and political constitutions closer to modern state constitutionalism where positivized fundamental rights and the concomitant review mechanisms bear the main responsibility for the self-limitation of law. Fundamental rights review is an addition to the tasks of the ECJ as a constitutional court. Especially since adoption of the EU Charter, the ECJ has displayed signs of fundamental rights activism – such as *Digital Rights*

[1] 'The question of a possible infringement of fundamental rights by a measure of the Community institutions can only be judged in the light of Community law itself. The introduction of special criteria for assessment stemming from the legislation or constitutional law of a particular Member State would, by damaging the substantive unity and efficacy of Community law, lead inevitably to the destruction of the unity of the Common Market and the jeopardizing of the cohesion of the Community.' Case C-44/79 *Liselotte Hauer v Land Rheinland-Pfalz* [1979] ECR 3727, Para. 3.

Ireland in 2014 – which may alter the general impression of the ECJ as a bastion of policy orientation.[2]

The novel importance of fundamental rights has engendered a novel tension between policy and principle orientation in the European constitution: a tension which may manifest in, say, clashes before the ECJ between policy-motivated economic rights and principle-motivated fundamental rights. *Van Gend en Loos* and *Costa v Enel* already articulated another basic tension around which much of the controversy over the legal theory of juridical constitutionalization has gravitated: a tension between *independence* and *integration*. European law was said to be both independent from and integrated into Member State law. Consequently, even from the European perspective, European and Member State law can be seen either as two distinct, although interacting, legal orders or as one integrated legal order. What, however, is important to notice is that the European juridical constitution has not raised the federalist claim of integrating Member State law into European law. The two models relate to how European law requires that national courts conceive of its relationship to national law. In the integrated model, Member State authorities are supposed to treat European law as part of national law and not vice versa.

Different theoretical standpoints lead to different doctrinal positions on the relationship between direct effect and supremacy. Thus, for instance, those who, in the footsteps of Pierre Pescatore, regard direct effect as an infant disease embrace the integrated model. By contrast, those who consider the doctrine of direct effect to be necessary for identifying European norms which can enjoy supremacy over national law adopt the distinct legal orders view. Furthermore, the divergent theoretical positions affect the very definition of direct effect and primacy/supremacy. As Michael Dougan has shown, ECJ case law seems to provide support for both the integrated and the distinct legal orders models.[3] So does Treaty law too: the provision on direct applicability of regulations points to the integrated view, while the provision which presupposes transposition of directives into national law hints at two distinct legal orders. The continuing debate implies that independence and integration should be conceived of in accordance with, not an either–or, but as a both–and logic. To pose independence and integration as mutually exclusive alternatives

[2] Joined Cases C-293/12 and C-594/12 *Digital Rights Ireland and Seitlinger and Others*, judgment of 8 April 2014 (not yet reported).

[3] M. Dougan (2007).

smacks of a Kelsenian aspiration to a hierarchical organizing of law. But European law does not meet the Kelsenian criteria of a hierarchical order either in its internal relations or in its relations with Member State law; to the contrary, by derogating from national conflict-of-norms standards, it tends to confuse even the Kelsenian clarity that Member State national law may previously have possessed. The tension between independence and integration is there to stay, and will influence the doctrine and theory of the juridical constitution even in the future.

European law is enforced by Member State courts which inevitably tend to approach and interpret it through national legal culture. This manifests the perspectivism of legal orders and threatens to reproduce the legal diversity which European law is expected to overcome. The European juridical constitution includes devices for combating not only 'surface-level' diversity but even legal cultural diversity, such as the preliminary ruling procedure and the interpretive principles introduced by the ECJ. Still, the uniformity in Member State law enforcement which European integration requires would ultimately be impossible to attain without sufficient affinities among national legal cultures: the existence of a common legal 'deep culture'. The importance of legal cultural interlegality for the implementation of European law is yet another reason why Kelsen's pure theory of law cannot be a serious candidate for the legal theory of the European juridical constitution.

The legal perspectivism of the legal orders occupying European legal space poses the issue of not only legal diversity but legal pluralism as well. 'Legal pluralism' connotes a constellation where more than one legal system claims authority within the same legal space. The substantively limited claim to authority of European law confronts the universality and exclusivity of national legal sovereignty. No higher-order guarantee exists for the compatibility of overlapping claims to authority. Indeed, Member State constitutional courts have never accepted the primacy of European law without conditions. They have been particularly keen on preserving *Kompetenz-Kompetenz*: *ultra vires* jurisdiction with regard to European law respecting its functionally limited scope. They have also been concerned about the level and scope of European and national fundamental rights review, as well as protection of national constitutional identity. The overhanging possibility of constitutional conflicts manifests the inevitable perspectivism labelling European constitutional space. The ECJ approaches conflict-sensitive issues from the point of view of European law and national constitutional actors, such as national constitutional courts, from the point of view of national constitutional law. However, this intractable perspectivism does not prevent European or national constitutional actors from heeding the perspectivism of their interlocutors and striving for normative and jurisdictional harmony. Often enough, ECJ constitutional jurisprudence responds to or anticipates speech acts of national constitutional courts, which also participate in European constitutional discourse. For their part, national constitutional courts also search for a way to prevent open conflict with the ECJ. This 'embedded openness' is facilitated by a shared legal deep culture which bridges the boundaries of legal orders and involves resources for cross-border dialogue. Legal and constitutional pluralism entails an ever-present risk of clashes of authority between European and Member State law. But although conflicts are possible, they are not necessary, contrary to what disciples of Kelsen have been inclined to conclude in the debate on constitutional pluralism.

The ECJ occupies a crucial position in the European legal system. The Court has not only supervised and enforced the European constitution and thereby exercised functions analogous to a state constitutional court: constitutional review of legislation, including fundamental rights review, and resolution of inter-institutional disagreements or disagreements between the Union and its Member States. It has also played an important role in the development of the European constitution, and promoted both juridical and sectoral constitutionalization. Its impact has, though, varied from dimension to dimension; the impact has been especially significant within the microeconomic and social fields but less so in the macroeconomic and security dimensions. Through the doctrines of direct effect and primacy, the Court has extended its judicial review, including constitutional review, to Member State legislation. Arguably, the weight of ECJ constitutional speech acts has considerably exceeded the bearing that the jurisprudence of state constitutional courts usually has in national constitutional discourse.

The exceptional role of the Court is at least partly due to the cumbersome procedure for Treaty amendments which require unanimity among Member States and ratification by all of them in accordance with the national constitution. Indeed, economic and juridical constitutionalization made significant progress for almost thirty years without any major intervention by the European constitutional legislator. The adoption of the Single European Act in 1986 opened an intensive period of Treaty revisions which, however, seems to have ended in 2009 with Lisbon. In certain respects, Treaty revisions aimed at curbing the Court's judicial activism, which had led to enlargement of Union competences through the doctrine of implied powers, and a liberal reading of the flexibility clause and the general competence for harmonizing measures promoting the common (internal) market. Revisions have strengthened the import of Treaty law in comparison with judicial constitution-making, but have not been able to deprive ECJ jurisprudence of its pertinence in implementing, elaborating and – from time to time – even complementing constitutional law, in particular in the microeconomic and social dimensions. In effect, the centrality of the ECJ cannot be explained merely by the complexity of political constitution-making. The ECJ is the site for the judicial interplay of European and Member State law, as well as European and national constitutionalism. Through the preliminary ruling procedure, the ECJ attempts to impose its constitutional readings and innovations on Member State courts and watches over the supremacy of European law. The emphasis in the judicial review it exercises as a constitutional court has lain on Member State rather than European law, although here the situation may be changing. The ECJ is also the European interlocutor in the pluralist dialogue with Member State constitutional courts.

National courts are the pivotal interface between European and national legal systems. The European juridical constitution regards national courts as 'ordinary courts within the European Union legal order'. It has adopted an integrated view where national courts, when acting within the scope of European law, are incorporated into the European legal system. National courts are the major addressees of the ECJ's judicial speech acts. If national courts had not accepted the constitutional innovations of the ECJ, starting from direct effect and primacy, these would never have achieved their purpose. Neither would the second-order principles of efficiency and uniformity have been realized, had national courts not, by and large, followed ECJ interpretations of European law and, in unprecedented issues requiring clarification, consulted the ECJ in the preliminary ruling procedure.

However, national courts find themselves in an ambivalent position. National legal culture may well – and probably most often does – prioritize the two distinct legal systems model and consider national courts as part of the national system even when implementing European law. In any event, the European juridical constitution also recognizes that, at least outside the scope of EU law, national courts act as 'ordinary courts within the Member State legal order'. Even if national courts and their judges assume the role which the European juridical constitution has designed for them and acknowledge the interpretive authority of the ECJ, their dual role has implications not only for the national but for the European legal order as well. The perspectivism of legal orders imposes limits on the receptiveness of national courts to European law. The *Vorverständnis* of national judges is imbued by their national legal culture, and it would be simplistic to assume that this *Vorverständnis* could just be switched off in EU law-related cases.

Alongside the juridical constitution, the political constitution also stands in both a framing and summarizing relation to sectoral constitutionalization, and, alongside the legal theory of the juridical constitution, the political theory of the political constitution also possesses particular significance for elaborating a general theory of the European constitution. The European juridical and political constitutions are closely intertwined; an abundance of Luhmannian structural couplings can be noted in their interrelations. For instance, provisions on Union institutions exercising legislative functions and on legislative procedure have a dual domicile in both the juridical and political constitutions. The same holds for fundamental rights which can be examined as elements of both of them.

Still, the political constitution possesses a constitutional object of its own – the European polity – and accomplishes tasks which differ from those of the juridical constitution. Its development has been influenced by relatively autonomous factors and considerations, and it has been less sensitive to the functional primacy of sectoral constitutionalization than the juridical constitution. Of course, such aims of political constitutionalization as organizational efficacy or legitimacy cannot be isolated from the impacts of sectoral constitutionalization. Organizational efficacy serves the policy objectives which govern sectoral constitutionalization, while sectoral constitutionalization has produced legitimacy needs to which political constitutionalization has attempted to respond. Yet it would be to overstretch the case to try to explain political constitutionalization merely through internal constitutional logic. Political constitutionalization, especially when driven through Treaty revisions, involves 'high' politics and high-profile clashes of interest, and the logic of politics is different from constitutional logic.

For decades, the theory underlying the institutional organization of the European polity has puzzled political scientists. The reason for embarrassment is evident: the European polity does not adhere to the familiar principles guiding the institutional organization of a democratic *Rechtsstaat* or – as American scholars would put it – a constitutional democracy. Neither separation of powers nor the principles of parliamentary democracy are applicable. Since 1979, the European Parliament has been directly elected, but neither its powers nor its capacity to channel democratic input legitimacy matches Member State parliaments. The European Parliament participates in law-making but it is not the sole legislative institution; it has but limited fiscal, taxation and spending powers; and its powers of oversight and censure over institutions with executive functions are modest in comparison with national parliaments. Successive Treaty revisions have strengthened the formal position of the European Parliament in both legislation and supervision of the Commission, but the simultaneous decline in electoral turnout testifies that the citizenry of the European polity does not possess a sufficiently robust common political identity; no European demos exists which could act as the subject of European democracy. In turn, the principle of separation of powers only applies to the independent European judiciary. By contrast, no identifiable European legislature or executive exists, but legislative and executive functions are distributed among diverse institutions.

Giandomenico Majone has suggested that rather than modern democratic states, the EU resembles pre-modern *mixed government* where each institution was set up to defend divergent interests.[4] As an external description this parallel might be warranted, but it hardly offers backing for reconstructing the normative premises of the European political constitution. Mixed government and the idea of institutions as embodiments of diverse interests might be argued to find correspondence in the constitutional principle of *institutional balance*. Still, it is doubtful whether institutional balance can be elevated to a central principle which would have governed political constitutionalization and which could make the peculiar institutional organization of the EU intelligible. Often enough 'institutional balance' does not signify much more than an acknowledgement that Union institutions reflect different organizational and legitimacy principles without clearly prioritizing any of these. At times, it is used in a mainly negative sense, intimating that EU institutions are not subject to principles familiar from state constitutions, such as separation of powers. A third connotation, perhaps most in line with the idea of mixed government and with its roots in the ECJ's *Meroni* judgment of 1958,[5] simply implies that each institution has to act in accordance with

[4] G. Majone (2009), pp. 46–51.

[5] Case C-9/56 *Meroni v High Authority* [1958] ECR 11. The judgment dealt with the ECSC and not with the EEC.

the powers conferred on it by the Treaties, whatever these powers might be at the actual moment. None of these connotations of 'institutional balance' appears to add much to the political theory of the European political constitution.[6]

Time and again we have observed the contested and ambivalent nature of the theoretical premises of European constitutionalization. Here the political constitution is no exception; rather the contrary. Diverse organizing and legitimizing principles sit uneasily with each other. Transnationalism and direct democratic legitimacy confront intergovernmentalism and the two-stage legitimation mechanism, while non-majoritarian transnational institutions require a legitimacy basis of their own.

The institutional organization of the European polity has always been a mix of transnationalism and intergovernmentalism. Under the Treaty of Rome, transnationalism was represented by the Commission – the successor to the High Authority of the European Coal and Steel Community – and the ECJ, while the intergovernmentalist element was provided by the Council of Ministers, the position of which was strengthened from what it was under the Treaty on the ECSC. Initially, the European Parliament (the Assembly) was composed of representatives of the national parliaments, but direct elections since 1979 secured its place on the transnational side. Many of the Founding Fathers of European integration, most notably Robert Schuman and Jean Monnet, envisaged a continuous expansion and deepening of integration through a development which neofunctionalist political theorists have conceived of in terms of spillover effects. Not only would economic integration expand but it would lead to political integration as well; in the institutional respect, this quasi-automatic developmental logic would entail gradual enhancement of transnational aspects.[7] Yet European political constitutionalization has by no means followed the path of straightforward transnationalization. During the first three decades, the Commission and the ECJ could promote economic integration and constitutionalization largely without needing the support of the intergovernmentalist element. Paradoxically enough, the partial paralysis of intergovernmental decision-making had intergovernmental roots: the Luxembourg Compromise in 1966, which ended the empty-chair crisis and postponed introduction of qualitative majority

6 See on the principle of institutional balance P. Craig (2011) and J. Monar (2011).

7 See, e.g., G. Majone (2009), pp. 42–4 and 143–4.

voting (QMV) in the Council of Ministers.[8] In 1974 intergovernmentalism received a strong injection through establishment of the European Council, composed of Member State heads of state and government. The European Council, though, worked for nearly two decades in the constitutional margins, until its position was formalized in the Maastricht Treaty. Only in Lisbon was it included among the Union institutions. The European Council brought 'high' politics inside the European polity but, by the same token, contributed to softening conflicts of interests and ideology among Member States. Under institutional transnationalism, institutions escape Member State control. The Luxembourg Compromise has never been formally annulled, but Treaty revisions have widened the reach of QMV and invoking vital Member State interests has become less and less frequent. Thus, blurring a clear-cut separation of transnationalism and intergovernmentalism, the intergovernmental Council of Ministers has taken steps in the transnational direction. The Eurozone crisis introduced reverse majority voting in European economic surveillance and weakened the position of the Council with regard to the Commission. As a counterweight, intergovernmentalism both within and outside the Union framework played a vital role in designing and managing rescue measures and mechanisms.

The main transnational institutions in the present EU are the European Parliament, the Commission, the ECJ and the ECB. Yet these are not wholly free from intergovernmental traits either. Members of the European Parliament are elected from national constituencies, and although they are organized cross-nationally into groups along party political lines, national loyalties still play a role. These might, though, be weakening, and the Parliament has shown signs of asserting a transnational, European profile towards intergovernmental institutions. Member States nominate candidates for European judges and Advocates General, but of all European institutions the courts have been able to develop perhaps the most marked transnational European identity and a corresponding European law perspective on European law. Alongside the Court, the ECB has tried to live up to the role of an independent transnational expert body. However, Governors of the central banks of Eurozone states are members of the ECB Governing Council, and the President and other members of the Executive Board are appointed by the European Council. This opens up a possibility of Member State allegiances still having an influence.

[8] See on the empty-chair crisis and the Luxembourg Compromise L. van Middelaar (2013), pp. 54 ff.

The Commission is the most hybrid institution of all. As discussed in Chapter 6, the Treaties portray the Commission primarily as a transnational expert body. Still, the Member States nominate the Commissioners, and the powers of the European Parliament in appointing, supervising and censuring the Commission have been strengthened. Traits of intergovernmentalism and parliamentarism intermingle with the expert role.

In the spillover logic of European integration, foreseen by Jean Monnet, the Commission's role was central, as was evident in the so-called *Community method* to which the Treaty of Rome by and large adhered. Under the Community method, the Commission not only possesses an exclusive legislative initiative but also sets the policy agenda and supervises Member State compliance, assisted by the ECJ. The establishment of the European Council, though initially outside the formal organization of the Community, dealt a blow to the agenda-setting role of the Commission. In the Maastricht Treaty, the European Council was entrusted with the task to 'provide the Union with the necessary impetus for its development and . . . define the general political guidelines thereof' (now Art. 15(1) TEU). In addition, in the first pillar of Common Foreign and Security Policy (CFSP) and the third pillar of Justice and Home Affairs the Community method was abandoned, the Commission was granted but a minor role and intergovernmental features were prominent. Subsequent Treaty revisions have expanded the Commission legislative and policy initiative in the Area of Freedom, Security and Justice (AFSJ), the High Representative of the Union for Foreign Affairs and Security Policy has been integrated into the Commission as one of its Vice-Presidents and the jurisdiction of the ECJ has, with certain exceptions, been extended to the AFSJ. Still, intergovernmentalism dominates the CFSP and impregnates the AFSJ too. Furthermore, in Economic and Monetary Union the Commission has a strong transnational rival in the ECB. Maastricht extended the scope of European integration to new fields, but did not strengthen the position of the Commission as the institutional embodiment of transnationalism, as Monnet's functionalist logic would have suggested. The Commission has tried to defend the Community method, but with only limited success.[9]

[9] See, e.g., Commission White Paper on European governance, COM/2001/0428 final. The Commission argues that the Community method 'provides a means to arbitrate between different interests by passing them through two successive filters: the general interest at the level of the Commission; and democratic representation, European and national, at the level of the Council and European Parliament, together the Union's legislature'. The Commission defines the Community method through three features. Firstly, 'the European Commission alone makes legislative and policy proposals. Its independence

To conclude, political constitutionalization displays no clear preference for either transnationalism or intergovernmentalism. Nor can transnationalism and intergovernmentalism be unambiguously distinguished or identified with particular institutions; rather, they are features which institutions possess to varying degrees and which also affect each other. The term 'intergovernmentalism' might even be considered misleading as it easily brings to mind international organizations functioning under international law. The EU as a whole is a transnational polity, which has left its imprint on Union intergovernmentalism as well. The Union of Member States has been compared to a club which has a distinct collective identity; this influences the behaviour of Member State representatives in such intergovernmental institutions as the Council of Ministers, even the European Council. They are representatives of a Member State, but belong to an institution of a transnational polity and represent this polity and defend its policy vis-à-vis their state and constituency.[10] In order to emphasize divergence from international organizations, some political scientists have preferred the term 'intensive transgovernmentalism' to 'intergovernmentalism'.[11]

Unsettled relations between transnationalism and intergovernmentalism connect to unsettled relations between different legitimacy principles. In the early decades, legitimacy for the European Communities as *funktionale Zweckverbände*[12] was primarily expected to ensue from the results of policy-oriented, functionalist integration, combined with the expert legitimacy of the Commission and the ECJ as embodiments of transnationalism. Member State parliaments and constituencies had injected the nascent European polity with foundational democratic input legitimacy through national procedures of Treaty ratification. The framers of the Treaty did not consider continuous input legitimacy for European institutions and policies to be really an issue. The intergovernmental Council did exercise legislative powers but, under the Community method, was dependent on Commission initiatives. The role of the Assembly (the European Parliament) was merely consultative. Democratic

strengthens its ability to execute policy, act as the guardian of the Treaty and represent the Community in international negotiations.' Secondly, 'legislative and budgetary acts are adopted by the Council of Ministers (representing Member States) and the European Parliament (representing citizens). The use of qualified majority voting in the Council is an essential element in ensuring the effectiveness of this method. Execution of policy is entrusted to the Commission and national authorities.' And thirdly, 'the European Court of Justice guarantees respect for the rule of law'.

10 L. van Middelaar (2013). 11 See G. Majone (2009), p. 163. 12 H. P. Ipsen (1972).

input legitimacy was put on the agenda through 'integration by stealth',[13] facilitated by a liberal reading of Community powers by the Commission and the Court, as well as confinement of Member State legislative sovereignty through economic and juridical constitutionalization. Reactions were twofold, giving rise to a new, persistent tension in the theoretical underpinnings of the European political constitution: a tension between direct and indirect democratic legitimation, clearly reflected in the Maastricht Treaty. The transnationalist camp, with its main home sites in the Commission and European-minded academia, launched the debate on the European democratic deficit and sought to remedy it by Europe-wide democratic procedures, more or less analogous to those of a national democratic *Rechtsstaat*: strengthening the legislative and oversight functions of the European Parliament; adding parliamentary elements to the relationship between the Commission and the Parliament; and developing European citizenship. Intergovernmentalism, embraced by many, if not most, Member States, advocated two primary strategies. Firstly, 'integration by stealth' would be tethered by accentuating the principle of conferral; introducing the principles of subsidiarity and proportionality; and formulating Union competences more precisely in the Treaties. Secondly, Member State oversight would be reinforced and national parliaments would also be involved in European issues, either directly or indirectly, through briefing and supervising national representatives in the European institutions. The latter strategy expresses the complementariness of European and national constitutionalism: through the two-stage legitimation mechanism, European constitutionalism benefits from national democratic input legitimacy.

Now as before, the main obstacle on the transnational way to secure democratic input legitimacy is the lack of sociological and cultural prerequisites for a European demos. Eastern enlargement has only raised the hurdle, and the Lisbon provisions on democratic principles openly acknowledge the importance of two-stage legitimation: Art. 10(2) TEU evokes the democratic accountability of Member State representatives in the European Council and the Council of Ministers, and Art. 12 codifies the role of national parliaments in the Union. However, as we saw in Chapter 6, the Eurozone crisis has complicated the functioning of the two-stage mechanism by confronting Member State citizens directly with the consequences of European policies, in both assisting and beneficiary states. At the same time, the crisis has led to questioning of the legitimacy

[13] The expression is used by G. Majone (2009).

basis of non-majoritarian institutions such as the ECB and the Commission. Independent expert bodies are held to be engaged in non-political public functions which require applying expert knowledge on juridical laws or scientific regularities. They are not conceived to be in need of democratic input legitimacy; to the contrary, attempts to provide such legitimacy would threaten their independence and derail them from rigorous and disinterested employment of their specialized expertise. Independent courts are expected to protect individual rights and the rule of law; independent competition authorities are expected to guarantee economic freedom and a liberal market economy; and independent central banks are expected to secure monetary stability, thus contributing to economic prosperity. The more the Commission or the ECB departs from the expert role and acquires politician or stakeholder features, the shakier becomes reliance on expert and output legitimacy. If transnational institutions engage in policies with redistributive consequences, the need for democratic legitimation is obvious. The dilemma is that neither direct nor indirect legitimation appears to be able to respond to the need. This is a major argument for maintaining core welfare fields under Member State sovereignty.

The sociological and cultural hurdles which hamper developing Europe-wide democracy do not annul the character of the Union as a transnational polity where political constitutionalization affects not only institutions but individuals as well. The institutional organization displays strong intergovernmental traits, but these differ from a standard international organization and should be inserted into an overall transnational context. And although the democratic connection remains weak – at least when compared to Member State national polities – direct links between the individual and institutional pole of the European polity exist which should be conceptualized as *European citizenship*. 'European citizenship' is both a doctrinal and theoretical concept. As a doctrinal concept it refers to the Treaty provisions on European citizenship, now in Arts. 20–4 TFEU, complemented by ECJ citizenship jurisprudence. As a theoretical concept, 'European citizenship' connotes more generally the position of individuals in the European polity, especially the European rights which individuals can invoke at national or transnational level. The multidimensional and multitemporal process of European constitutionalization has gradually enriched citizenship rights. Economic constitutionalization has entailed market rights and market citizenship; juridical constitutionalization has entailed judicial rights and judicial citizenship; social constitutionalization has entailed limited social rights and social citizenship; and political constitutionalization has entailed political citizenship comprising, most importantly, European electoral rights and, finally, full-blown European fundamental rights. Neither in the Treaties nor in ECJ jurisprudence have fundamental rights been related to European citizenship. Hence, as a doctrinal concept, 'European citizenship' does not comprise fundamental rights. In contrast, they are an essential element of 'European citizenship' as a concept of the political theory of political constitutionalization.

In both doctrinal and theoretical respects, European citizenship must be discussed in its interaction with national citizenship; again, it is essential to note the complementariness of transnational and national constitutionalism. The EU as a polity is built on two-channel democratic legitimation – direct and indirect – and, correspondingly, individuals are involved in their capacity as both European and Member State citizens. Furthermore, even when participating in European constitutional practices, European citizens rely on public autonomy – fundamental political rights – granted to them as Member State citizens.[14] In turn, European citizenry as the intermediary between the institutional and individual pole of the polity must be examined through the interrelations between national and transnational demoi and public spheres. Evidently, the political theory of the European political constitution presupposes a civic, instead of a nationalist, understanding of demos. However, the problem, unresolved at the European level, is that a civic demos cannot emerge from scratch, without an initial, even if weak, common identity and sense of belongingness among the citizenry.

As the emphasis on the principle of conferral attests, Maastricht did not deprive the EU of its primary policy orientation. New policy fields have been added to Union objectives and competences, but the political and legal claim of authority is still substantively circumscribed, and the designation of a *funktionaler Zweckverband* has not lost all its justification. However, this designation is increasingly difficult to accommodate with other developments launched in Maastricht: such as elaborating European citizenship and fundamental rights law, defining a universalist value basis for the Union, and attempting to create for it a distinct identity as a foreign and security policy actor on the world scene.

The expansion of European policy objectives and competences beyond economic integration has entailed *variable geometry* as an apparently lasting feature of the European political and juridical constitution. The roots

[14] See on European individuals' dual citizenship, J. Habermas (2013).

of variable geometry lie in the same sovereigntist sensibilities which explain lingering intergovernmentalism and recourse to international law instruments in such delicate fields as external and internal security. Sensibilities are more pronounced in some Member States than others, and ways have been sought to allow Member States which are willing to proceed further in integration to do so. Manifestations of variable geometry can be found in all the sectoral constitutional dimensions, except for the microeconomic one. Moreover, the Lisbon Protocol on the partial opt-out of the UK and Poland from Union fundamental rights review has brought variable geometry to a core area of the juridical and political constitution. Opt-out protocols attached to the Founding Treaties amount to a constitutional form for variable geometry, which was already resorted to in Maastricht in establishing EMU and the special social policy regime.[15] The Maastricht Treaty also explicitly authorized closer cooperation between two or more Member States in third-pillar issues. Together with the special social policy regime, this was the embryo of what subsequently came to be called enhanced cooperation. Since Amsterdam, the Treaties have included general provisions on closer or enhanced cooperation. In Lisbon, variable geometry in the macroeconomic field was reinforced by provisions which facilitate a differentiated legislative framework for the Eurozone. The provisions were in ample use during the Eurozone crisis. Explicit Treaty possibilities for variable geometry have not put an end to recourse to international law agreements as an alternative to primary or secondary legislation, in particular in the macroeconomic and security fields. As argued in Chapter 6, this is not unproblematic from the point of view of constitutional doctrine. What in any event is evident is that in the post-Maastricht era the principle of the unity of the Union has increasingly yielded to differentiated integration.

Constitutions raise a claim of autonomy, which involves an assertion of *constitutional identity*. The constitutional identity of a democratic *Rechtsstaat* includes both particularist and transcultural elements. One of the reservations which Member State constitutional courts have attached to their acceptance of the supremacy of European law concerns preservation of national constitutional identity. In *Kadi*, the ECJ subjected the primacy of international law over European law to a similar identity proviso. Furthermore, post-Lisbon fundamental rights jurisprudence hints at

[15] Denmark and the United Kingdom were granted an opt-out from EMU, and the Social Policy Protocol left the United Kingdom outside the special regime.

an avowal of an inviolable constitutional kernel of European law in the direction of Member States too. As may be recalled from Chapter 3, the Court has argued that Art. 53 CFREU allows Member State authorities to apply higher national fundamental rights standards only in so far as 'the primacy, unity and effectiveness of EU law are not thereby compromised'.

Union constitutional identity shares the general relationality and evolving character of European constitutionalism. Moreover, it expresses the tension between the policy orientation of a *funktionaler Zweckverband* and the universalist pretensions of a putative transnational constitutional democracy. Constitutional identity may acquire different emphases when invoked vis-à-vis international and Member State law. Allan Rosas and Lorna Armati have interpreted *Kadi* as confirming 'a tendency discernible in earlier case law according to which the EU constitutional order consists of some core principles which may prevail over provisions of the Treaties and thus of written primary law'.[16] The authors refer to the ECJ's claim that rights and duties arising from international agreements concluded before accession 'may in no circumstances permit any challenge to the principles that form part of the very foundations of the Community legal order, one of which is the protection of fundamental rights, including the review by the Community judicature of the lawfulness of Community measures as regards their consistency with those fundamental rights' (Para. 304). This implies that foundational principles, such as protection of fundamental rights, override the Treaty provision stipulating that the Treaties do not affect rights and duties created by pre-accession international agreements. But *Kadi* should be read not only as a sign of an internal hierarchy in EU constitutional law, but also as an affirmation of EU constitutional identity vis-à-vis the supremacy of international law.[17]

It is dubious whether fundamental rights principles were part of Community constitutional identity at the time when the ECJ, in *Van Gend en Loos* and *Costa v Enel*, raised the claim of European law's autonomy from both international and Member State law. But constitutional identity is not only a relational phenomenon but a dynamic phenomenon too. Subsequent development of EU fundamental rights law supports *Kadi*'s reading of the foundational principles of the Union and the conclusion which

16 A. Rosas and L. Armati (2012), p. 54.

17 Interestingly enough, in its *Lisbon* judgment (Para. 340) the Court compared the EU's assertion of Union foundational principles on international law with its own defence of German constitutional identity.

Rosas and Armati have drawn from *Kadi*. These authors leave open what else, in addition to protection of fundamental rights, the constitutional identity of the Union might include.[18] In relation to Member State law, direct effect and primacy, together with the justificatory second-order principles of efficacy and uniformity, could well be seen as an essential part of Union constitutional identity. Hence, the ECJ's affirmation in *Melloni*[19] of the primacy which the principle of primacy of European law enjoys over the Member State right to apply higher national fundamental rights standards can be understood as the Court defending Union constitutional identity against Member State measures.[20] In relation to international law, the Union has invoked the newly added principle elements of its putative constitutional identity, while primacy, efficacy and uniformity recall the initial policy orientation which has not lost its pertinence for identity definition either.

The general theory of the European constitution, incorporating main elements of the legal theory of the juridical and political theory of the political constitution, is as contested and replete with tensions as are the foundations of the diverse constitutional dimensions. Disagreements start from the very use of constitutional language and the choice of the disciplinary conceptual framework. In the Prologue, four disciplinary alternatives were presented: an international, administrative, federal and transnational law portrayal of the European polity and its legal system. Now, as we are approaching the end of our recapitulation of European constitutionalism, does the transnational option still appear justified?

Perspectivism of legal disciplines

I shall try to respond to the question indirectly, by pointing to the weaknesses of the alternative options. The international law depiction still has proponents, especially among international lawyers and EU scholars with an international law background. The critical edge of their contributions is usually directed at constitutional conceptualization. One of the

18 D. Sarmiento (2013a) defines the constitutional core and legal identity of the EU through the three normative ideals of Democracy, Rights and Solidarity, to which Arts. 2–4 TEU in particular give expression.

19 Case C-399/11 *Melloni*, judgment of 26 February 2013 (not yet reported).

20 D. Sarmiento (2013b), p. 1295, argues that 'in line with its national counterparts, Luxembourg has powerful reasons to impose its own counter-limits, whose purpose is, in the last instance and in line with previous case law, to guarantee the autonomy of EU law'.

recurring arguments is that Member States, including their constitutional courts, still tend to treat the Union and its legal system as creatures of international law.[21] However, when discussing the constitutional theory of the EU from an EU law perspective, Member State views cannot provide decisive evidence; the perspectivism of legal orders can well produce diverse conceptualizations. Nor does the foundational argument – reference to the Founding Treaties as international treaties concluded under international law – settle the issue. Nothing prevents an international treaty from acquiring features which correspond to the status of constitutional law as higher law or accomplishing constitutional functions. This was already clear to Kelsen,[22] although his views of both constitutional law as higher law and constitutional functions differ from those embraced in this book. Even as international treaties the Founding Treaties diverge from international law standards in the specific procedure where Member State infringements are dealt with. Member States are not allowed to derogate from their Treaty obligations in retaliation for (alleged) breaches by other Member States, as would be the rule under international law. In addition, the principles the ECJ has established for interpreting not only secondary Union law but the Treaties as well display clear differences from the tenets of the Vienna Convention on the Law of Treaties.

The international law account can invoke the international law origin of many central principles and concepts of what I call the European juridical constitution, starting from direct effect, primacy and *effet utile* (effectiveness). But again, international law origins are no guarantee for the continuing relevance of international law; it is possible that principles and concepts are transplanted into a new doctrinal and theoretical environment and obtain normative contents which distance them from the international law setting. Direct effect bears a resemblance to the practice of states which have adopted the monist model in relations between international and national law, and to the international law doctrine of self-executing treaty rules. Still, international law leaves the choice between monism and dualism to states, while direct effect is a principle of European and not national constitutional law. Furthermore, as a result of gradual loosening, the threshold criteria for the direct effect of European law are much more liberal than the international law definition of self-executing treaty rules would allow.[23]

21 B. de Witte (2011b), p. 41. 22 H. Kelsen (1920), p. 194.

23 Bruno de Witte – one of the main advocates of the international law approach – concedes both points concerning the difference of direct effect in European and

Even the principle of primacy, as pronounced by the ECJ, sits awkwardly in an international law framework. Primacy of international agreements is part of established international law doctrine, but here 'primacy' alludes to international relations: parties to a treaty cannot invoke municipal law as a justification for treaty infringement.[24] But the European law principle is about internal and not international primacy. It surely seems overstretched to invoke *pacta sunt servanda*[25] as an international law justification for the claim of European law to internal primacy and to contend that internal primacy is implicit in (other) international treaties as well. It is true, though, that the efficacy of the EU law principle of primacy – and direct effect too – depends on its acceptance by national courts and that national constitutional courts have expressed reservations in terms of *Kompetenz-Kompetenz*, protection of fundamental rights and the inviolability of national constitutional identity. Yet these facts do not deprive the European law principle of primacy of its distinct character.[26] Reconstruction of the constitutional theory of European law and polity proceeds from the perspective of, not national, but European law.

Addressing private parties directly, providing them with justiciable rights and endowing them with legal subjectivity may not have been unprecedented in international treaty law, but, arguably, European law has gone much further in its individual orientation than is usual under international law. Although increasing exceptions can be evoked, the basic assumption in international law doctrine still adheres to the black box model which confines international law to inter-state relations and leaves relations involving private parties to the legislative sovereignty of states. In monist countries national courts apply international law, but here too the self-understanding of EU law departs from precedents of national enforcement of international law. EU law asserts that national courts are an integral part of the Union legal system and that, when enforcing EU law, they act as EU courts. Moreover, intertwinement of the ECJ and national courts through the preliminary ruling procedure

international law doctrine but does not let this concession affect his overall international law characterization of European law. B. de Witte (2011a), pp. 347 and 361.

24 The Vienna Convention on the Law of Treaties explicitly lays down that 'a party may not invoke the provisions of its internal law as justification for its failure to perform a treaty' (Art. 27).

25 The Vienna Convention on the Law of Treaties includes a provision on *pacta sunt servanda* as well: 'Every treaty in force is binding upon the parties to it and must be performed by them in good faith' (Art. 26).

26 B. de Witte (2011a), p. 361.

provides the ECJ with a unique means to watch over and influence how national courts interpret European law.

If EU law is subsumed under an international law framework, then, by the same token, the EU is subsumed under the international law concept of international organizations. Undoubtedly, the EU shares some of the features which international lawyers consider characteristic of international organizations, such as functionally limited powers and the principle of conferral. However, EU powers do not fit in with the standard template of international organizations. This holds especially for the exclusive powers of the Union, but also for shared powers in so far as their exercise pre-empts Member States from exerting their legislative sovereignty. As a rule, international organizations do not claim legal authority within the legal space of a state and with regard to private parties; even if organizations have rule-making powers, their exercise does not lead to normative pluralism, not to speak of systemic pluralism. Furthermore, in standard cases they are not detached from Member State control the way the EU is. Finally, the objectives of the EU do not mesh with the idea of a global common good orientation of international organizations.

Since *Van Gend en Loos*, the ECJ has asserted the distinctiveness of European law with regard to international law. Yet Bruno de Witte argues that the Court has not explicitly rejected the international law character of EU law and the Community/Union but left open whether distinctiveness from or within international law is at issue. Even the relationship between the international legal order under the United Nations and the Community legal order, which the ECJ discusses in *Kadi*, might still be a relationship under the broad umbrella of international law.[27] Apparently, the ECJ has not explicitly pronounced on the applicability of the concept of international organization to the Community/Union either. By contrast, in the drafting process of a regime on the responsibility of international organizations, the Commission emphasized the specialty of the European Union and the European Community as testimony to the diversity among international organizations. In particular, it considered the European Community 'an international organization with special features as envisaged in the founding treaties'[28] and pointed to

[27] B. de Witte (2011b), pp. 38–41.

[28] UN Doc. A/CN.4/556, 12 May 2005, at 5. See also UN Doc. A/CN.4/593, 31 March 2008, 4: the 'Commission expresses some concerns as to the feasibility of subsuming all international organizations under the terms of this one draft in the light of the highly diverse nature of international organizations, of which the European Community is itself an example'. See also J. Klabbers (forthcoming).

'significant differences between traditional international organizations ... and organizations such as the European Union'.[29] Here the Commission does not decline the applicability of the concept of international organization but is content with stressing the particular features of the Community/Union.

It may be that the ECJ has been attentive to Member State sensibilities and refrained from explicitly renouncing the international law framework. But since in *Costa v Enel* it deleted the last three words of the characterization of European law in *Van Gend en Loos* as 'a new legal order of international law', the Court has not explicitly pronounced in favour of the international law portrayal either. On the other hand, it has not only developed doctrines which are difficult to accommodate with international law but from time to time explicitly brushed aside Member State objections grounded in international law. Of course, all deviations from standard international law doctrine can be explained away as testifying to the vast potential and flexibility of international law or its creative and innovative development.[30] And if the EU does not conform to the established concept of an international organization, perhaps the concept needs overhaul to facilitate the re-entry of the EU.[31] However, taken together these are not very convincing strategies but raise the question of the very point of disciplinary divisions and conceptual grids in law. Should they not aid us in orienting ourselves in our new lawscape? This they can hardly accomplish if they lose too much of their analytical rigour and are transformed into elastic conceptual balloons, always inflatable with new contents.

The tenacity of the international law approach may at least be partly due to the perceived lack of credible alternatives; especially if the *sui generis* proposal is barred as a declaration of theoretical impotence. Thus, de Witte does not display much patience with the federal option, which he shuts out with reference to the uncontested prevalence of federal law over state law and the equally uncontested *Kompetenz-Kompetenz* of a federal constitution, which allocates powers between federal and state levels.[32] De Witte's observations are pertinent if we include the Member State perspective in the legal characterization of the EU. Yet the EU constitution has pretensions which do resemble those of a federal

[29] UN Doc. A/CN.4/637, 14 February 2011, p. 7. See also J. Klabbers (forthcoming).

[30] Cf. B. de Witte (2011b). [31] J. Klabbers (forthcoming).

[32] B. de Witte (2011a) and (2011b), pp. 45–7.

constitution: both supremacy over Member State law and *Kompetenz-Kompetenz* over its own powers. Besides, if the supremacy of federal law over state law and *Kompetenz-Kompetenz* of the federal constitution are understood in a Kelsenian sense so that state law derives its validity from the federal constitution, a corresponding claim has most likely never been raised in European constitutional discourse; not even by scholars embracing the integrationist legal theory of the juridical constitution.

The EU as a polity is as difficult to compress into a federal mould as the European legal system, at least without considerably stretching established categories. According to the standard understanding, federations are composite entities, consisting of a federal level – often called the federal state – and federated entities – often called states. States are component units of the federation and as such 'absorbed' by the federation; they do not have any independent existence beyond the federation. They may have extensive legislative and other powers but they exercise those powers as component units of the federation. In accordance with the black box model, the federation as a whole claims universal and exclusive sovereignty within its territory and in its external relations. As a rule federations are unitary actors in the international arena, although the federal constitution may accord federated entities restricted treaty-making powers as well.[33] As to their origins, federations come in two main groups: integrative and devolutionary.[34] But whatever the origin of a federation, a federal constitution stipulates allocation of competences between the federal and federated levels.

It should be evident that the European Union is not a federation in this standard sense. The Union is not a composite entity with Member States as its component units, nor are Member States 'absorbed' by the Union but exist independently from it. Member States do not owe their powers to the Union constitution, but the basic position is the universality and exclusivity of their internal and external sovereignty. An overall federalist portrayal of the EU is possible only by way of conceptual dilution. If 'federalism' is used to connote a vaguely defined federal principle, the EU

33 This is the case in, for example, Bosnia and Herzegovina. According to Art. III(2a) of the Constitution, 'the Entities shall have the right to establish special parallel relationships with neighboring states consistent with the sovereignty and territorial integrity of Bosnia and Herzegovina'. Art. III(2c) provides that 'each Entity may also enter into agreements with states and international organizations with the consent of the Parliamentary Assembly' and that 'the Parliamentary Assembly may provide by law that certain types of agreements do not require such consent'.

34 See K. Lenaerts (1998).

may well meet the criteria. If federalism is, for instance, reduced to the basic tenet that 'power will be divided between a central authority and the component entities of a nation-state or an international organization so as to make each of them responsible for the exercise of their own powers'[35] and a more appropriate expression is substituted for 'component entities', then, certainly, the Union can be seen as an example of federalism.

Robert Schütze has defended the federalist approach by replacing European 'deductivism' with American 'inductivism'. In his appraisal, American federalism occupies a position between the national and the international, while European deductivism has squeezed federalism back to the compartment of nation states. American inductivism, harking back to James Madison, facilitates distinguishing analytically between three dimensions in federalism: foundational, institutional and substantive. The first of these relates to the origin and character of the federation; the second to the composition of its government; and the third to the scope and nature of the federal government.[36] Schütze's analytic-inductive emphasis is welcome and hints at avoiding easy either–or conclusions. But his very starting point, where European deductivism and American inductivism seem to shake hands, makes federalist discussion in the context of the Union problematic. The EU is not a 'compound polity' where Member States would be constituent elements, as states are constituent elements of the United States of America or the Federal Republic of Germany. Nor does Schütze succeed in his efforts to avoid state-like attributes and expressions evoking state connotations when describing the American inductive understanding of federalism. American federalism meshes well with the traditional black box model and shares crucial state-like traits with European 'deductivist' federalism. The methodology may be different in Madison's 'inductivism' and the 'deductivism' of German *Begriffsjurisprudenz*. And, indeed, applying to the EU 'lump' concepts with their origins in state-related disciplines of international or constitutional law, including federal constitutional law, may require analytical unpacking in order to adjust them to a new transnational setting. US federalism may stand between the 'national' and the 'international', as Schütze defines the terms, but federal constitutionalism still remains a sub-species of state constitutionalism. Schütze overstates his case when accentuating the distinctiveness of US federalism in order to prove the federalist credentials of the EU.

[35] *Ibid.*, p. 748. [36] R. Schütze (2009), pp. 14 ff.

It is wholly warranted to insist on core elements in both international law and federal concepts – elements which are related to the state orientation of both sets of concepts – without falling guilty of the *Begriffsjurisprudenz* sin of conceptual deductivism. Conceptual frameworks are there to orient us in our ever more rapidly altering lawscape and to render it intelligible for us. Flexibility is needed more than ever, but if all conceptual firmness is abandoned and all conceptual contents are taken to be up for grabs, the orienting and heuristic function of conceptual tools is lost as well. Rejecting international law and federalist options does not necessarily imply a theoryless *sui generis* portrayal of European law and polity: a conceptual white flag as it were. European law and constitutionalism can be approached as an epitome – and, evidently, the most advanced epitome – of transnational law and constitutionalism.

The federal law approach acknowledges the constitutional dimension of the EU and its legal system, but does not do justice to the complex interaction between Union and Member State level constitutionalism. While the federal portrayal risks subjecting national to Union constitutionalism, the administrative law account is prone to commit the reverse error and subsume Union under national constitutionalism. The Union is contended to possess no constitutional potential of its own; it represents administrative, regulatory governance, and the democratic and constitutional legitimacy it is able to display is derived from Member State constitutionalism. The key normative principle connecting European regulatory governance to Member State constitutionalism is the administrative law concept of *delegation*. The Treaties are of a framework character – *traités cadre* – and resemble national framework laws establishing regulatory agencies, which enjoy broad autonomy and even possess normative and (quasi-)judicial functions. Member States are principals which through the Treaties have delegated regulatory powers to the Union as their agent. Oversight of the Union by national executives, constitutional courts and, increasingly, parliaments too, corresponds to the oversight that a principal, such as a national legislature or executive, exercises over an agent in administrative law delegation. Complemented by procedural devices of administrative law, aiming at reason giving and accountability, national oversight mediates national democratic and constitutional legitimacy to the EU. Thus, in the account of Peter Lindseth, the administrative law principle of delegation connects Union regulatory governance to *polyarchic* Member State constitutionalism.[37]

Lindseth employs a thick normative concept of constitutionalism. Under such a concept, much of the constitutional analysis of this book would have remained unwritten. But even when adopting such a demanding notion of constitutionalism, the conclusions that Lindseth draws from his often perceptive observations are open to criticism. He is right in pointing out that the Union too needs 'democratic and constitutional legitimacy' but does not alone possess the normative and cultural resources this requires. But admitting this, one should not wholly ignore Union attempts to build up direct democratic legitimacy through the European Parliament and European citizenship or substantive constitutional legitimacy through fundamental rights law. However, Lindseth's main error lies in neglecting the interplay between the European and national levels. The contribution of national constitutionalism to the 'democratic and constitutional legitimacy' of the Union is not an argument for denying European constitutionalism; instead, it calls for examining European constitutionalism in its interrelations with its national counterpart. European constitutionalism serves diverse constitutional functions and in some of these, perhaps most notably in the legitimating one, it is in an important way dependent on support from national constitutionalism. And as is evident from the Lisbon provisions on democratic principles, European constitutional law does not make any secret of this either.

Lindseth has adopted a Member State perspective. His analysis of how Member States attempt to manage the tension between 'regulatory autonomy and derivative legitimacy' is also instructive for a constitutional account which assumes the European perspective and examines European constitutionalism in its interaction with the national level. Still, even from a Member State perspective Lindseth's administrative law summarization of his analysis may be questionable. Just as the European constitutional perspective should heed Member State perspectivism, reconstruction of the Member State perspective remains deficient if it ignores European perspectivism, as expressed, first of all, in the rulings of the ECJ. Secondly, in his choice of disciplinary perspective, Lindseth taps into American administrative law doctrine and theory, from where the central concepts of delegation, regulatory function and agency are drawn. It is not at all certain that the administrative law notion of delegation corresponds to the way Member State law conceptualizes transfer of powers

[37] P. Lindseth (2010).

to the Union. In Art. 23, the German Basic Law, for instance, speaks of *transfer of sovereign powers*, which clearly transcends mere administrative law delegation. Indeed, it comes close to the vocabulary employed by the ECJ, which ever since *Van Gend en Loos* and *Costa v Enel* has referred to Member States *limiting their sovereign rights*.[38] Thirdly, widening of Union powers, including fundamental rights review, makes it increasingly artificial to reduce them to regulatory governance, susceptible to (American) administrative law conceptualization.

This book is not only an attempt to reconstruct the theoretical bases of European constitutionalization; it is also meant to be a modest contribution to the discourse on the theory of transnational law and constitutionalism.[39] Transnational law breaks out from the black box model of territorially delineated state legal systems, complemented by the black box of international law focusing on inter-state relations. Transnational law raises functionally defined claims of authority within the legal space which in the black box model is reserved for state law and contests the universal and exclusive claim of the latter. This creates the constellation of legal pluralism in its normative and systemic versions: pluralism of legal orders and pluralism of legal systems. European constitutional pluralism is an offshoot of the more general phenomenon of legal pluralism which results from the intrusion of transnational law into the legal space of state law, which in the black box model is only opened towards international law through the constitutional choice between monism and dualism and towards the legal orders of other states through conflict-of-laws rules of private international law.

Instances of transnational law may have their background in international law from which they, however, have detached in some crucial respects. This is the case with not only EU law but also with, say, the ECHR or WTO law. The distinctive features of transnational law, escaping from the straitjacket of the black box model, can be attached to either norm formation or norm application. Transnational norm-giving assumes other forms than bi- or multilateral treaties between states. In turn, norm application that involves establishing dispute-solving or sanctioning bodies outside the control of nation states suggests the emergence of transnational law. But, of course, no impermeable boundary exists between norm

[38] In effect, P. Lindseth (2010), p. 23, criticizes the term 'conferral of powers', used in the TEU, for obscuring the principle of delegation!

[39] I have discussed the theory of transnational law in greater detail in K. Tuori (2014).

formation and norm application, despite the ingrained thought habits of (us) Continental European lawyers. Through its case law, a court-like body established by an international treaty elaborates on and complements the treaty rules it is supposed to apply. Provisions of treaties applied by international courts and other monitoring bodies are usually formulated in very general terms, and for an obvious reason too. Political consensus among states is the easier to reach the vaguer the provisions under negotiation are; hence, their specification is left to legal experts responsible for monitoring adherence to the treaty.

Instances of transnational law, such as EU law, the ECHR and WTO law, display a similar pattern: they all have their background in international law but have subsequently severed their international law moorings and, by the same token, largely elude the control of the signatory states. Yet they still bear traces of their origin, as can be seen, for instance, from the dual nature of the Founding Treaties of the EU. From the internal perspective of EU law, assumed by the ECJ, they are embodiments of constitutional law, with legal effects analogous to those of state constitutions. But they have also retained their character of international treaties, as have Member States their position of *Herren der Verträge*.[40] The hybrid nature of our examples relates them to recent fragmentation debate among international lawyers. Indeed, from an international law perspective they appear as instances of fragmentation which, in the view of some observers, worryingly threatens the cogency of international law. Particular court-like bodies that do not defer to the precedents of the International Court of Justice shake its status as the guarantor of the unity of international law. The qualified approach of some special courts, including the European Court of Human Rights, to the Vienna Convention on the Law of Treaties has also been conceived as jeopardizing the coherence of international law.[41]

But whether we conceive of the ongoing process as fragmentation of international law or as the dawn of transnational law, the growing plethora of legal orders and systems does not mesh with the dichotomy of municipal and international law. The municipal legal order has lost its monopoly over determining legal relations involving private individuals. Even in dualist states, transnational norms are directly effective,

[40] The position of Member States as 'Masters of the Treaties' is one which the German Constitutional Court (BVerfGE) does not tire of repeating. See, e.g., Para. 231 of the BVerfGE *Lisbon* ruling (2 BvE 2/08, 30 June 2009). In turn, the ECJ has characterized the Treaties in constitutional terms ever since *Les Verts* (Case C-294/83 [1986] ECR 1339).

[41] See Report of the Study Group of the ICL (2004). See also M. Koskenniemi and P. Leino (2002) and M. Scheinin (2006).

bypassing a transformative act by the national legislator. This is the case in Finland, for instance. The Constitution sets out that international treaties and other international law obligations must be incorporated into the national legal order before they can have internal legal effects. Nonetheless, this constitutional requirement cannot block the direct effect of, for instance, EU law provisions, preliminary rulings of the ECJ, or precedents of the European Court of Human Rights. Here no prior decision by the national legislator is needed.

The deficiency of the black box model is even more conspicuous in examining instances of transnational law which altogether lack a background in international treaty law and which have – if we are to lend credence to Niklas Luhmann's disciples in autopoietic systems theory – emerged from autonomous operation of denationalized social subsystems. The examples most often invoked are the *lex mercatoria* of international trade, the *lex sportiva* of international sports and the *lex digitalis* of the Internet. Their legal orders have been subsumed by neither municipal nor international law, while disputes are settled and sanctions imposed by designated transnational bodies.[42]

EU law is only one, although the most developed, instance of transnational law. Nor are conflicts of authority a specificity of EU law's relation to Member State legal systems, but can – and are almost bound to – arise in other areas too, where the substantively limited claims of transnational law confront the universal and exclusive pretensions of national law, particularly those endowed with the prestige of constitutional law. Fundamental rights monitoring touches upon the constitutional foundations of the national legal order. In Europe, overlaps between national and transnational fundamental rights regimes entail potential clashes of authority in the relations of national constitutional courts not only with the ECJ but with the European Court of Human Rights as well. According to Art. 35(1) ECHR, the way to the Human Rights Court is open only after national remedies have been exhausted. This implies a hierarchical superiority of the transnational Strasbourg court over national courts, including constitutional ones. But constitutional courts are hesitant to acknowledge the interpretive authority of the Human Rights Court without qualification. Arguably, the reserve which the German Constitutional Court has displayed again expresses a more general attitude among its counterparts in other Signatory States.[43]

42 For succinct presentations of these transnational legal systems, see B. Zangl and M. Zürn (2004).

43 See on the *Görgülü* saga M. Hartwig (2005) and B. Peters (2012).

Introduction of the EU's own fundamental rights regime, where final jurisdiction lies with the ECJ, has led to an overlap with the claim to authority of the Human Rights Court, which holds itself competent to review EU law-related legal acts of the Signatory States. As explained in Chapter 3, the Strasbourg Court has assumed towards EU law a posture analogous to that of the German Constitutional Court: its *Bosphorus* ruling reads like a variant of the *Solange* doctrine. The Court announces the suspension – but mere suspension! – of its ultimate authority with regard to application of the Convention to EU law-related legal acts of the Member States. Suspension is conditional on EU institutions providing equivalent protection, and the Court reserves to itself the right to revoke its authority.[44] If the EU accedes to the Convention, as is laid down in Art. 6(2) TEU-Lisbon, doctrines on respective responsibilities in human rights monitoring will obviously be in need of reformulation for both the ECHR and the EU.

International law too has had an acknowledged compartment in the black box model. As *Kadi* attests in the relations between EU law and UN law, transnational law may contest the authority not only of state law but also of (general) international law. A typical developmental path of instances of transnational law has been their gradual disconnection from their original anchorage in international law. The International Court of Justice (ICJ), with its general jurisdiction, has been the traditional guarantor of the unity of international law. A central backdrop to debates on fragmentation of international law consists of tribunals with a more restricted jurisdiction contesting the binding effect of ICJ precedents.[45] At least in some cases, this can be interpreted as testifying to movement of a regime of international law towards an instance of transnational law. Authority contests between general international law, enforced by the ICJ, and transnational or international courts or tribunals with a restricted jurisdiction bear resemblance to the almost inevitable frictions which occur when the substantively limited claims of transnational law confront the universal pretentions of state law.[46]

Overlaps in the fundamental rights monitoring of the EU and the Human Rights Court prove that the substantive scopes of two instances

[44] *Bosphorus v Ireland* (App. no. 45036/98) ECHR 2005-VI, Paras. 155–6. Of the quite extensive literature, see in particular S. Douglas-Scott (2006).

[45] M. Koskenniemi and P. Leino (2002).

[46] R. Y. Jennings (1995); Y. Shany (2003); B. Simma (2009). See also special issue, 'The proliferation of international tribunals: Piecing together the puzzle', *NYU Journal of International Law and Politics* 31(4) (1999).

of transnational law can collide as well, producing clashes of authority which transcend the mere border conflicts allowed for by the black box model. Another example is the refusal of the ECJ to accept WTO law's claim of direct effect within EU and, indirectly, Member State law.[47] In turn, in the fragmentation discussion in international law, a favourite illustration is the contest between the WTO and the international environmental law regime concerning jurisdiction over the whale trade.[48]

The alternative approaches of radical and dialogical pluralism (see Chapter 3) are available for discussing not only the pluralist relations between EU and Member State constitutional law, but even other examples of conflicts of authority involving instances of transnational law. Radical pluralists of the Kelsenian, Koskenniemian or Luhmannian persuasion see no peaceful way out of the conflicts between rival claims of authority. It may be recalled how contemporary Kelsenians have transferred the premises of the pure theory of law from 'simple' legal diversity to the pluralist constellation created by the rise of transnational law. According to the Kelsenian view, each of the conflicting legal orders, including such an instance of transnational law as EU law, is subjected to its specific *Grundnorm*, which establishes its normativity and crowns its hierarchical structure of authority (validity). Contests of authority are bound to receive different solutions in legal systems deferring to different *Grundnorms*. No neutral ground exists where legal orders subordinated to diverse *Grundnorms* could meet, but the solution to the contested issue, say *Kompetenz-Kompetenz* with regard to EU law, depends on the referential legal order; that is, the legal order from the perspective of which it is approached. Now, so Kelsenian radical pluralists argue, institutional legal actors such as judges or legislators are bound to adopt the perspective (the *Grundnorm*) of the legal order under which the institution they serve has been established and its powers defined, and whose norms they are expected to apply and uphold. Following this line of argument, it is inevitable that Member State constitutional courts assess EU law's claims to authority in light of the national constitution, whereas the ECJ treats EU law as an independent legal order and employs the constitutional criteria of that order. Kelsenian premises do not admit of any (legal) principle which could bridge the gulf between the perspectives of self-contained legal orders; what we have here is the black box model revisited and complemented with boxes for transnational law.

47 See Case C-377/02 *Léon Van Parys NV* [2005] ECR I-1465.
48 M. Koskenniemi and P. Leino (2002); M. Koskenniemi (2007).

Kelsenians and 'crits' might seem to be odd bedfellows. However, Koskenniemi cites with approval Kelsen's statement of the twin features of solipsism and imperialism, characterizing especially those state legal orders which subscribe to the monist doctrine in relations between municipal and international law. At the end of the day, this avowal of affinity is perhaps not so surprising, considering that 'solipsism' and 'imperialism' are apt descriptions of Koskenniemi's portrayal of the antagonistic relations among international law regimes as well.[49] This kinship in no way effaces the vast distance separating Kelsen's internal and Koskenniemi's external legal theoretical point of view. For Koskenniemi, conflicts of jurisdiction between rival legal regimes are irresolvable, not because of divergent *Grundnorms*, but because of divergent institutional biases and the irreconcilability of the strategic interests which the institutional actors of different regimes are pursuing: say, the ECJ and national constitutional courts. Koskenniemi's legal strategism cannot – and is not even interested in doing so – come to terms with dialogical inter-regime relations. From Koskenniemi's external perspective, legal actors are moved by their particular interests and strategic aims; their primary objective is not to reach a consensus with their interlocutors in the illocutionary dimension of legal discourse, but to pursue their extra-discursive, perlocutionary aims. This produces a rather cynical picture of our global, transnationalized legal landscape: a picture of conflicts and battles over jurisdiction – the right to state the law. Koskenniemi recognizes merely one side of the coin. But there is a reverse side to that coin too.

Autopoietic systems theorists applying and elaborating Luhmann's ideas reject Koskenniemi's interpretation of the intractability of inter-regime conflicts. Gunther Teubner and Andreas Fischer-Lescano argue that ultimately inter-regime conflicts do not derive from policy divergences and strategic interests of institutional actors but originate in the self-contained, autopoietic character of the global social sub-systems which have given rise to transnational law. Nothing can be done to the very source of the problem: the evolutionary accomplishment of (global) social differentiation. Teubner's and Fischer-Lescano's favourite citation from the Master is the following: 'The sin of differentiation cannot be undone. Paradise is lost.'[50] At most, we are entitled to hope that some of the consequences of transnational legal fragmentation can be

[49] M. Koskenniemi (2007).

[50] A. Fischer-Lescano and G. Teubner (2004), p. 1007. The citation is from N. Luhmann (2004), p. 344.

managed, through, for instance, conflict rules of a new type, focusing on the functional location of legal issues; mutual observation of systems of transnational law; and a striving for compatibility of the respective claims and criteria of validity. Yet instances of transnational law are tied to the particular rationality of the respective global social system – economy, health, sports, and so on – and each instance produces its own functionally oriented conflict rules and reactions to problems of compatibility. The source of the problem remains, and no guarantee exists for the congruence of the separate treatment of inter-regime disputes in each legal subsystem.[51]

Radical pluralists shut their eyes to phenomena attesting to cross-boundary interlegality in constellations of normative or systemic pluralism. Dialogical pluralists aid us in complementing the one-sided view of the present global lawscape which radical pluralists are able offer us. Indeed, in recent debates many scholars have examined forms of peaceful contact and adjustment between pluralist legal orders or systems.[52] If these scholars are right in their observations, as I think they are, pluralist relations between transnational and national or international law, or among instances of transnational law, are not marked merely by conflicting claims of authority and an unremitting contest over jurisdiction; they also manifest overlap, interpenetration and dialogue. My proposal to conceive of the inevitable perspectivism of law in legal cultural terms alludes to the common 'deep cultural' foundations – the 'universal code of legality' – which make such dialogue possible. Diverse legal systems may use diverging dialects and idiosyncratic idioms but they all talk law and, hence, are able to communicate with each other. The alternatives of conflict- and dialogue-oriented approaches are available for examining, not only European constitutional pluralism, but the new legal pluralism produced by the rise of transnational law in general.

In addition to the perspectivism of legal orders and legal roles, *perspectivism of legal disciplines* is the third major epitome of perspectivism in present-day law. International, federal, administrative and transnational law provide distinct disciplinary approaches to European law and polity

51 A. Fischer-Lescano and G. Teubner (2004). Teubner's later account of transnational constitutionalism is more open to inter-regime interaction, but, as critics have noted, at the price of compromising on the conceptual rigour of Luhmannian autopoietical systems theory. G. Teubner (2012); J. Priban (2012).

52 Of the already quite extensive literature see, e.g., N. Walker (2008), N. Krisch (2010) and P. S. Berman (2012).

and thus manifest the perspectivism of legal disciplines. In discussing this version of legal perspectivism too, both a conflictual and dialogical emphasis is possible. An external sociological observer is prone to explain the variation in the accounts of different legal disciplines by strategic disciplinary interests, by the stakes involved in the legal power game. A similar view, focusing on the perlocutionary aspect of legal discourse, is cherished by Koskenniemi's critical legal scholarship. In his depiction of legal power games, Pierre Bourdieu emphasizes that the autonomy of the legal field is only relative in character. Players have supporters in other social fields, such as business and politics, and the power relations prevailing in these fields affect the score in the legal field. The respective strength of economy and politics cannot but influence the respective power position of, say, private and public law.[53]

Bourdieu's scheme could easily be transferred to an analysis of the disciplinary contest over the legal characterization of the EU and its law. The contest can be depicted as a battle over legal language and concepts as the vocabulary of this language: what, exactly, are the legal concepts which should be applied to the EU and its legal system? The stakes are high. At issue is, first, the power to define the EU in legal terms. Are the Treaties 'ordinary treaties' of international law or have they acquired constitutional features and cut off their international law roots? Is the EU just an international organization among others, established by sovereign states, or has it developed into a federal or transnational polity? A Bourdieuan legal sociologist or a Critical Legal Scholar assumes that because of their professional and institutional interests and biases, international lawyers stick to the vocabulary of their discipline, and stress the international law quality of the Treaties and the international organization quality of the EU. Correspondingly, constitutional lawyers of a federal or transnational stamp compose their accounts of European law and polity in constitutional terms, defending the institutional and academic status of their disciplines.

The stakes in the academic contest are still raised by the value-laden and persuasive character of constitutional and international law concepts. In the context of the EU, these concepts convey messages of the preferable direction of not only European law but European integration in general. Scholarly speech acts insert themselves in two registers: the academic one and another, more general and politically coloured one. International law vocabulary implies retaining European integration under strict Member

[53] P. Bourdieu (1987).

State control. Here the administrative law account joins forces with international law, while federal or transnational constitutionalism tends to accord integration a more autonomous dynamic. The wider, political, context of the argument draws attention to the role of external supporters, engaged in their own power games in their social fields. Scholars may sometimes find surprising, and even unwelcome, fans at the European or national level among Eurosceptic or Euro-enthusiastic politicians and bureaucrats.

Again, an account focusing on the strategic, perlocutionary aims of the discussants has its justification. But, again, it catches but one side of the coin. The participants in EU law discourse make normative claims too, and the illocutionary edge of their speech acts is affected by their legal cultural, including disciplinary, *Vorverständnis*. A distinct disciplinary perspective entails employing particular concepts, principles, theories and methods, at least in some respects distinct from those used in other disciplines. Disciplinary perspectivism is likely to affect one's view of the pluralist relations among legal orders and systems. Arguably, Koskenniemi's legal strategism is associated with his disciplinary identity as an international lawyer. International law is intimately linked with politics. This makes it particularly conflictual by nature and confers a more obviously strategic label upon its argumentation than is usual in other fields of law. In international law, court procedures are still quite underdeveloped, and as a rule the jurisdiction of courts or other dispute-resolving bodies depends on the consent of the parties. These distinct features probably impregnate the *Vorverständnis* of international lawyers and leave an imprint on their legal theoretical views.

But as is the case when examining the perspectivism of legal orders or legal roles, the effects of the perspectivism of legal disciplines should not be exaggerated either. Again, exclusive perspectivism with its solipsist generalizations overstates its case. Representatives of diverse disciplines adopt divergent perspectives on law but usually they get each other's point and are able to engage in joint legal argument. Private and public lawyers or international and constitutional lawyers offer different conceptualizations of, say, EU regulatory private law or the Founding Treaties. Still, they usually acknowledge that the interlocutor too is talking law and that there might be something to be learned from the other discipline. Discipline-specific idioms exist, but the fundamentals of legal language – basic concepts as the vocabulary of law and basic patterns of legal argumentation as its grammar – are shared across disciplinary boundaries.

Adopting the perspective of transnational constitutionalism need not and should not imply isolation from international, federal or administrative law discourse. To the contrary, transnational constitutionalism should heed the conceptual, normative and methodological proposals by international law and federal or 'polyarchic' state constitutionalism, and, after critical examination and paying due attention to the problem of translation, be ready to welcome them in its disciplinary arsenal. In effect, the preceding chapters offer examples of concepts or principles originating from international law or federal constitutionalism. For the doctrine and theory of transnational law and constitutionalism, dialogical cross-boundary relations are a necessity: as a newcomer, transnational law and constitutionalism cannot but be, to a certain extent, parasitic on more established legal fields and disciplines. Furthermore, international law retains its significance for a constitutional analysis adopting the perspective of EU law also for the reason that international law instruments are from time to time used as a means of European policies: as precursors of, or alternatives to, Union legislation.

Final comment

In my analysis of the particularity and theoretical bases of European constitutionalism, I have tried to be alert to the perspectivism of my enterprise: the combined perspectivism of European law; a European constitutional theorist socialized in continental, Finnish legal culture; and the nascent discipline of transnational law and constitutionalism. Albeit primarily engaged in a second-order theoretical discourse, my enterprise probably has normative implications for first-order European constitutional discourse as well. Whether it will be acknowledged as a constitutional speech act in this discourse is not for me to decide.

Bibliography

Ackerman, B. (1993) *We the People, Volume I: Foundations* (Cambridge, Mass.: Harvard University Press)

Agamben, G. (2005) *State of Exception* (University of Chicago Press)

Akkermans, B. and E. Ramaekers (2010) 'Article 345 TFEU (ex Article 295 EC), its meanings and interpretations', *European Law Journal*, 16: 292–314

Alexy, R. (2002) *A Theory of Constitutional Rights* (Oxford University Press)

Alter, K. J. (2001) *Establishing the Supremacy of European Law. The Making of an International Rule of Law in Europe* (Oxford University Press)

Amtenbrink, F. and J. de Haan (2003) 'Economic governance in the European Union: Fiscal policy discipline versus flexibility', *Common Market Law Review*, 40: 1057–1106

Armstrong, K. A. (2010) *Governing Social Inclusion: Europeanization through Policy Coordination* (Oxford University Press)

Austin, J. L. (1984) *How to Do Things with Words* (Oxford: Clarendon Press)

Avbelj, M. (2011) 'Supremacy or primacy of EU law: (Why) does it matter? *European Law Journal*, 17: 744–63

Avbelj, M. and J. Komárek (2012) *Constitutional Pluralism in the European Union and Beyond* (Oxford: Hart Publishing)

Azoulai, L. (2008) 'The Court of Justice and social market economy: The emergence of an ideal and the conditions for its realization', *Common Market Law Review*, 35: 1335–55

Baquero Cruz, J. (2002) *Between Competition and Free Movement: The Economic Constitutional Law of the European Union* (Oxford University Press)

(2008) 'The legacy of the Maastricht-Urteil and the pluralist movement', *European Law Journal*, 14: 389–422

(2011) 'The case law of the European Court of Justice on the mobility of patients: An assessment' in J. W. Gronden, E. Szyszczak, U. Neergaard and M. Krajewski (eds.), *Health Care and EU Law* (The Hague: TMC Asser Press), 79–102

Barnard, C. (2011) 'EC "Social" policy: From employment law to labour market reform' in P. Craig and G. de Búrca (eds.), *The Evolution of EU Law*, 2nd edn (Oxford University Press), 641–86

Beck, U. (1992) *Risk Society: Towards a New Modernity* (London: Sage)

Belke, A. (2010) *Driven by the Markets? ECB Sovereign Bond Purchases and the Securities Markets Programme* (Essen: Ruhr Economic Papers)

Bellamy, R. (2007) *Political Constitutionalism: A Republican Defence of the Constitutionality of Democracy* (Cambridge University Press)

Benjamin, W. (2004) 'Critique of violence' in M. Bullock and M. W. Jennings (eds.), *Selected Writings, Volume I: 1913–1926* (Cambridge, Mass.: Harvard University Press), 236–52

Berman, P. S. (2012) *Global Legal Pluralism: A Jurisprudence of Law Beyond Borders* (Cambridge University Press)

Besselink, L. (2010) 'National and constitutional identity before and after Lisbon', *Utrecht Law Review*, 6: 1–49

Böhm, F. (1928) 'Das Problem der privaten Macht', *Die Justiz*, 3: 324–45

(1933) *Wettbewerb und Monopolkampf. Eine Untersuchung zur Frage des Wirtschaftlichen Kampfrechts und zur Frage der Rechtlichen Struktur der Geltenden Wirtschaftordnung* (Berlin: Carl Heymanns Verlag)

(1953) 'Geleitwort' in H. Sinzheimer, *Jüdische Klassiker der Deutschen Rechtwissenschaft* (Frankfurt am Main: Vittorio Klosterman), xvi–xxviii

(1966) 'Privatrechtsgesellschaft und marktwirtschaft', *ORDO*, 17: 75–151

Bourdieu, P. (1987) 'The force of law: Toward a sociology of the juridical field', *Hastings Law Journal*, 38: 805–53

Busch, K., C. Hermann, K. Hinrichs and T. Schulten (2013) *Euro Crisis, Austerity Policy and the European Social Model: How Crisis Policies in Southern Europe Threaten the EU's Social Dimension* (Berlin: Friedrich-Ebert-Stiftung)

Buzan, H., O. Waever and J. Wilde (1998) *Security: A New Framework for Analysis* (Boulder: Rinner)

Calliess, C. (2011) 'Perspektiven des Euro zwischen Solidarität und Recht: Eine rechtliche Analyse der Griechenlandhilfe und des Rettungsschirms', *Zeitschrift für Europäische Studien*, 14: 213–82

Canor, I. (2013) '*My brother's keeper?* Horizontal *Solange*: "An ever closer *distrust* among the peoples of Europe"', *Common Market Law Review*, 50: 383–421

Cappelletti, M., M. Seccombe and J. Weiler (eds.) (1985) *Integration through Law: Europe and the American Federal Experience* (Berlin, Walter de Gruyter)

Chiti, E., A. J. Menéndez and P. G. Teixeira (2012) *The European Rescue of the European Union* (Oslo: ARENA Centre for European Studies)

Claes, M. (2006) *The National Courts' Mandate in the European Constitution* (Oxford: Hart Publishing)

(2013) 'National identity: Trump card or up for negotiation?' in A. Saiz Arnaiz. and C. Alcoberro Llivina (eds.), *National Constitutional Identity and European Integration* (Cambridge: Intersentia), 109–39

Constantinesco, L. J. (1977) 'La constitution économique de la CEE', *Revue Trimestrelle de Droit Européen*, 13: 244–81

Craig, P. (1992) 'Once upon a time in the West: Direct effect and the federalization of EEC law', *Oxford Journal of Legal Studies*, 12: 453–79

(2011) 'Institutions, power and institutional balance' in P. Craig and G. de Búrca (eds.), *The Evolution of EU Law*, 2nd edn (Oxford University Press), 41–84

(2012) 'The stability, coordination and governance treaty: Principle, politics and pragmatism', *European Law Review*, 37: 231–48

(2013) *The Lisbon Treaty: Law, Politics, and Treaty Reform* (Oxford University Press)

Damjanovic, D. and B. de Witte (2009) 'Welfare integration through EU law: The overall picture in the light of the Lisbon Treaty' in U. Neergaard, R. Nielsen and L. M. Roseberry (eds.), *Integrating Welfare Functions into EU Law* (Copenhagen: Djof Publishing), 581–609

Davies, B. (2012) *Resisting the European Court of Justice: West Germany's Confrontation with European Law, 1949–1979* (Cambridge University Press)

Davies, G. (2006) 'The process and side-effects of harmonization of European welfare states', *Jean Monnet Working Paper*, 02/06

(2011) 'Legislating on patients' rights' in J. W. Gronden, E. Szyszczak, U. Neergaard and M. Krajewski (eds.), *Health Care and EU Law* (The Hague: TMC Asser Press), 191–210

(2013a) 'Freedom of contract and the horizontal effect of free movement law' in D. Leczykiewicz and S. Weatherill (eds.), *The Involvement of EU Law in Private Law Relationships* (Oxford: Hart Publishing), 53–69

(2013b) 'Democracy and legitimacy in the shadow of purposive competence', *European Law Journal*, available online at http://onlinelibrary.wiley.com/doi/10.1111/eulj.12079/pdf

de Grauwe, P. (2011) 'Who cares about the survival of the Eurozone?' *CEPS Commentary*, available at www.ceps.eu

(2013) 'Design failures in the Eurozone: Can they be fixed?', *LSE LEQS Paper*, No. 57

de Grauwe, P. and Ji, Y. (2013) 'More evidence that financial markets imposed excessive austerity in the Eurozone', *CEPS Commentary*, available at www.ceps.eu

Dehousse, R. (1998) *The European Court of Justice: The Politics of Judicial Integration* (Basingstoke: Macmillan)

Derrida, J. (1990) 'Force of law: The "mystical foundation of authority"', *Cardozo Law Review*, 11: 919–1045

de Sousa Santos, B. (2002) *Toward a New Legal Common Sense: Law, Globalization, and Emancipation*, 2nd edn (Toronto: Butterworths)

de Witte, B. (2001) 'Old-fashioned flexibility: International agreements between Member States of the European Union' in G. de Búrca and J. Scott (eds.), *Constitutional Change in the EU: From Uniformity to Flexibility* (Oxford: Hart Publishing), 31–58

(2011a) 'Direct effect, primacy, and the nature of the legal order', in P. Craig and G. de Búrca (eds.), *The Evolution of EU Law*, 5th edn (Oxford University Press), 323–62

(2011b) 'The European Union as an international legal experiment' in G. de Búrca and J. H. H. Weiler (eds.), *The Worlds of European Constitutionalism* (Cambridge University Press), 19–56

Dickson, J. (2011) 'Directives in EU legal systems: Whose norms are they anyway?' *European Law Journal*, 17: 190–212
(2012) 'Towards a theory of European Union legal systems' in J. Dickson and P. Eleftheriadis (eds.), *Philosophical Foundations of European Union Law* (Oxford University Press), 25–53
Dougan, M. (2007) 'When worlds collide! Competing visions of the relationship between direct effect and supremacy', *Common Market Law Review*, 55: 931–63
Douglas-Scott, S. (2004) 'The rule of law in the European Union: Putting security into the "Area of Freedom, Security and Justice"', *European Law Review*, 29: 219–42
(2006) 'A tale of two courts: Luxembourg, Strasbourg and the growing European human rights acquis', *Common Market Law Review*, 43: 629–65
Drexl, J. (2010) 'Competition law as a part of the European constitution' in A. von Bogdandy and J. Bast (eds.), *Principles of European Constitutional Law* (Oxford: Hart Publishing), 659–98
Dworkin, R. (1978) *Taking Rights Seriously* (London: Duckworth)
Editorial comment (2013) '*Ultra vires*: Has the *Bundesverfassungsgericht* shown its teeth?' *Common Market Law Review*, 50: 925–9
Enchelmaier, S. (2007) 'The ECJ's recent case law on the free movement of goods: Movement in all sorts of directions', *Yearbook of European Law*, 26: 115–56
(2010) '*Moped trailers, Mickelson & Roos, Gysbrechts*: The ECJ's case law on goods keeps on moving', *Yearbook of European Law*, 29: 190–223
Esping-Andersen, G. (1990) *The Three Worlds of Welfare Capitalism* (Cambridge: Polity Press)
Eucken, W. (1952) *Grundsätze der Wirtschaftspolitik* (Tübingen: J. C. B. Mohr)
Fabbrini, F. (2013) 'The fiscal compact, the "golden rule", and the paradox of European federalism', *Boston College International and Comparative Law Review*, 36: 1–38
Fichera, M. (2011) *The Implementation of the European Arrest Warrant in the European Union: Law, Policy and Practice* (Cambridge: Intersentia)
Fischer-Lescano, A. and G. Teubner (2004) 'Regime-collisions: The vain search for legal unity in the fragmentation of global law', *Michigan Journal of International Law*, 25: 999–1046
Foucault, M. (2009) *Security, Territory, Population, Lectures at the Collège de France 1977–1978*, M. Senellart (ed.) (Basingstoke: Palgrave Macmillan)
Fuller, L. L. (1969) *The Morality of Law* (New Haven, Conn.: Yale University Press)
Gerber, D. J. (1994) 'Constitutionalizing the economy: German neo-liberalism, competition law and the "new Europe"', *American Journal of Comparative Law*, 25: 25–84
(1998) *Law and Competition in Twentieth Century Europe. Protecting Prometheus* (Oxford University Press)
Giddens, A. (1979) *Central Problems in Social Theory* (London: Macmillan)
Gilbert, M. (2012), *European Integration: A Concise History* (London: Rowman & Littlefield Publishers)
Glenn, H. P. (2005) *On Common Laws* (Oxford University Press)

Grabenwarter, C. (2010) 'National constitutional law relating to the European Union' in A. von Bogdandy and J. Bast (eds.), *Principles of European Constitutional Law* (Oxford: Hart Publishing), 83–129

Gross, O. (1998) 'Once more unto the breach: The systematic failure of applying the European Convention on Human Rights to entrenched emergencies', *Yale Journal of International Law*, 23: 437–501

(2000) 'The normless and exceptionless exception: Carl Schmitt's theory of emergency powers and the "norm-exception" dichotomy', *Cardozo Law Review*, 21: 1825–60

Gross, O. and F. Ni Aolain (2001) 'Emergency, war and international law: Another perspective', *Nordic Journal of International Law*, 70: 29–63

Groussot, X. (2006) *General Principles of Community Law* (Groningen: Europa Law Publishing)

Groussot, X., T. Lock and L. Pech (2011) 'EU accession to the European Convention on Human Rights: A legal assessment of the Draft Accession Agreement of 14th October 2011', *European Issues*, No. 218

Guastaferro, B. (2012) 'Beyond the exceptionalism of constitutional conflicts: The ordinary functions of the identity clause', *Yearbook of European Law*, 31: 263–318

Guild, E. (ed.) (2006) *Constitutional Challenges to the European Arrest Warrant* (London: Wolf Legal Publishers)

Günther, K. (1993) *The Sense of Appropriateness* (Albany, NY: State University of New York Press)

Habermas, J. (1989) *The Structural Transformation of the Public Sphere* (Cambridge, Mass.: MIT Press)

(2013) *The Crisis of the European Union: A Response* (Berlin: Polity Press)

Haeyk, F. A. (1982) *Law, Legislation, and Liberty, Volume I* (London: Routledge & Kegan Paul)

Halberstam, D. (2009) 'Constitutional heterarchy: The centrality of conflict in the European Union and the United States' in J. Dunoff and J. Trachtman (eds.), *Ruling the World? Constitutionalism, International Law, and Global Governance* (Cambridge University Press), 326–55

(2010) 'Local, global and plural constitutionalism: Europe meets the world' in G. de Búrca and J. H. H. Weiler, *The Worlds of European Constitutionalism* (Cambridge University Press), 150–202

(2012) 'Systems pluralism and institutional pluralism in constitutional law: National, supranational, and global governance' in M. Avbelj and J. Komárek (eds.), *Constitutional Pluralism in the European Union and Beyond* (Oxford: Hart Publishing), 85–125

Hänninen, S. (2010) 'Social constitution in historical perspective: Hugo Sinzheimer in the Weimar context' in K. Tuori and S. Sankari (eds.), *The Many Constitutions in Europe* (Aldershot: Ashgate), 219–40

Hartwig, M. (2005) 'Much ado about human rights: The Federal Constitutional Court confronts the European Court of Human Rights', *German Law Review*, 6: 869–94

Heipertz, M. and A. Verdun (2010) *Ruling Europe: The Politics of the Stability and Growth Pact* (Cambridge University Press)

Herlin-Karnell, E. (2012) *The Constitutional Dimension of European Criminal Law* (Oxford: Hart Publishing)

Herzog, R. and L. Gerken (2008) 'Stop the European Court of Justice', *EU Observer*(10 September)

Hinarejos, A. (2008) 'On the legal effect of framework decisions and decisions: Directly applicable, directly effective, self-executing, supreme?' *European Law Journal*, 14, 620–34

Hofmann, H. (2009) 'Legislation, delegation and implementation under the Treaty of Lisbon: Typology meets reality', *European Law Journal*, 15: 482–505

Hurri, S. (2014) *Birth of the European Individual: Law, Security, Economy* (Abingdon: Routledge)

IMF (2013) 'Greece: Ex post evaluation of exceptional access under the 2010 stand-by arrangement', Country Report No. 13/156, 5 June

Ipsen, H. P. (1972) *Europäisches Gemeinschaftsrecht* (Tübingen: J. C. B. Mohr)

Isiksel, N. T. (2010) 'Fundamental rights in the EU after *Kadi* and *Al Barakaat*', *European Law Journal*, 16: 551–77

ISS, European Council (2010) *Internal Security Strategy for the European Union: Towards a European Security Model* (Luxembourg: Publications Office of the European Union)

Issing, O. (2008) *The Birth of the Euro* (Cambridge University Press)

Itzcovich, G. (2012) 'Legal order, legal pluralism, fundamental principles. Europe and its law in three concepts', *European Law Journal*, 18: 358–84

James, H. (2012) *Making the European Monetary Union* (London: Belknap Press)

Jennings, R. Y. (1995) 'The proliferation of adjudicatory bodies: Dangers and possible answers, implications of the proliferation of international adjudicatory bodies for dispute resolution', *ASIL Bulletin: Educational Resources on International Law*, 2–7

Joerges, C. (1996) 'The market without the state? States without a market? Two essays on the law of the European economy', *European University Institute Working Paper*, Law 1996/02

(2004) 'What is left of the European economic constitution?', *European University Institute Working Paper*, Law 2004/13

Joerges, C. and F. Rödl (2004) 'The "Soziale Marktwirtschaft" as a model for social Europe?' in L. Magnusson and B. Stråth (eds.), *A European Social Citizenship? Preconditions for Future Policies from a Historical Perspective* (Brussels: PIE-Peter Lang), 125–58

Käseberg, T. and A. van Laer (2013) 'Competition law and industrial policy: Conflict, adaptation and complementarity' in K. K. Patel and H. Schweitzer (eds.), *The Historical Foundations of EU Competition Law* (Oxford University Press), 162–90

Kelsen, H. (1920) *Allgemeine Staatslehre* (Berlin: Springer)

(1989) *Pure Theory of Law* (Gloucester, Mass.: Peter Smith)

Klabbers, J. (forthcoming) '*Sui generis*? The EU as an international organization' in D. Patterson (ed.), *A Companion to EU Law and International Law* (Wiley)
Koh, H. H. (1990) *The National Security Constitution: Sharing Power after the Iran-Contra Affair* (New Haven, Conn.: Yale University Press)
Komárek, J. (2007a) 'European constitutionalism and the European Arrest Warrant: In search of the limits of the "contrapunctual principles"', *Common Market Law Review*, 44: 9–40
(2007b) 'In the court(s) we trust? On the need for hierarchy and differentiation in the preliminary ruling procedure', *European Law Review*, 32: 467–91
Konstadinides, T. (2012) 'Drawing the line between circumvention and gap-filling: An exploration of the conceptual limits of the treaty's flexibility clause', *Yearbook of European Law*, 31: 227–62
Koskenniemi, M. (2007) 'International Law: Constitutionalism, managerialism and the ethos of legal education', *European Journal of Legal Studies*, 1, 1–18
Koskenniemi, M. and P. Leino (2002) 'Fragmentation of international law? Postmodern anxieties', *Leiden Journal of International Law*, 15: 553–79
Koukiadaki, A. and L. Kretsos (2012) 'Opening Pandora's box: The sovereign debt crisis and labour market regulation in Greece', *Industrial Law Journal*, 41: 276–304
Krisch, N. (2010) *Beyond Constitutionalism. The Pluralist Structure of Postnational Law* (Oxford University Press)
Kumm, M. (2005) 'The jurisprudence of constitutional conflict: Constitutional supremacy in Europe before and after the Constitutional Treaty', *European Law Journal*, 11: 262–307
(2012) 'The moral point of constitutional pluralism defining the domain of legitimate institutional civil disobedience and conscientious objection' in J. Dickson and P. Eleftheriadis (eds.), *Philosophical Foundations of European Union Law* (Oxford University Press), 216–46
Lenaerts, K. (1998) 'Federalism: Essential concepts in evolution: The case of the European Union', *Fordham International Law Journal*, 21: 746–98
Lenaerts, K. and T. Corthaut (2006) 'Of birds and hedges: The role of the primacy in invoking norms of EU law', *European Law Review*, 31: 287–315
Lenaerts, K. and M. Desomer (2005) 'Towards a hierarchy of legal acts in the European Union? Simplification of legal instruments and procedures', *European Law Journal*, 11: 744–65
Lepsius, O. (2004) 'Liberty, security and terrorism', *German Law Journal*, 5: 436–60
(2006) 'Human dignity and the downing of aircraft: The German Federal Constitutional Court strikes down a prominent anti-terrorism provision in the new Air-transport Security Act', *German Law Journal*, 7: 761–76
Levinson, S. and J. M. Balkin (2010) 'Constitutional dictatorship: Its dangers and its design', *Minnesota Law Review*, 94: 1789–1866
Lindseth, P. (2010) *Power and Legitimacy: Reconciling Europe and the Nation-State* (Oxford University Press)
Lock, T. (2012) 'End of an epic? The Draft Agreement on the EU's accession to the ECHR', *Yearbook of European Law*, 31: 162–97

Lord, C. (2012) *On the Legitimacy of Monetary Union* (Stockholm: Swedish Institute for European Policy Studies)

Luczak, J.-M. (2009) *Die Europäische Wirtschaftsverfassung als Legitimationselement europäischer Integration: Ein Beitrag zur Wirtschaftsverfassungsrechtlichen Analyse des EG-Vertrages unter Einbeziehung der Änderungen des Unionrechts durch den Vertrag von Lissabon* (Berlin: Duncker & Humblot)

Luhmann, N. (2004) *Law as a Social System* (Oxford University Press)

MacCormick, D. N. (1995) 'The Maastricht-Urteil: Sovereignty now', *European Law Journal*, 1: 359–66

(1998) 'Risking constitutional collision in Europe?' *Oxford Journal of Legal Studies*, 18: 517–32

(1999) *Questioning Sovereignty: Law, State and Nation in the European Commonwealth* (Oxford University Press)

(2008) *Institutions of Law* (Oxford University Press)

MacCormick, D. N. and O. Weinberger (1986) *An Institutional Theory of Law* (Dordrecht: D. Reidel Publishing Company)

Majone, G. (2009) *Dilemmas of European Integration: the Ambiguities and Pitfalls of Integration by Stealth* (Oxford University Press)

(2014) *Rethinking the Union of Europe Post-Crisis: Has Integration Gone Too Far?* (Cambridge University Press)

Marsh, D. (2011) *The Euro: The Battle for the New Global Currency* (London: Yale University Press)

Martines, F. (2014) 'Direct effect of international agreements of the European Union', *European Journal of International Law*, 21: 129–47

Martinsen, D. (2005a) 'The Europeanization of welfare: The domestic impact of intra-European social security', *Journal of Common Market Studies*, 43: 1027–54

(2005b) 'Towards an international health market with the European Court', *West European Politics*, 28: 1035–56

Maus, I. (1989) 'Die Trennung von Recht und Moral als Begrenzung des Rechts', *Rechtstheorie*, 20: 191–210

Mazzone, J. (2005) 'The security constitution', *UCLA Law Review*, 53: 29–151

Menéndez, A. (2009) 'European citizenship after *Martinez Sala* and *Baumbast*: Has European law become more human but less social?' *ARENA Working Paper*, No. 11

Mestmäcker, E.-J. (2003) *Wirtschaft und Verfassung in der Europäischen Union: Beiträge zur Recht, Theorie und Politik der europäischen Integration* (Baden-Baden: Nomos)

(2013) 'Towards a concept of a workable European competition law: Revisiting the formative period' in K. K. Patel and H. Schweitzer (eds.), *The Historical Foundations of EU Competition Law* (Oxford University Press), 191–206

Michaels, R. (2005) 'The re-state-ment of non-state law: The state, choice of law, and the challenge from global legal pluralism', *Wayne Law Review*, 51: 1209–59

Micklitz, H.-W. (2005) *The Politics of Judicial Co-operation in the EU: Sunday Trading, Equal Treatment and Good Faith* (Cambridge University Press)

(2011a) 'Introduction' in Micklitz (ed.), *The Many Concepts of Social Justice in European Private Law* (London: Edward Elgar Publishing)

(2011b) 'Universal services: Nucleus for a social European private law' in M. Cremona (ed.), *Market Integration and Public Services in the European Union* (Oxford University Press), 63–102

Monar, J. (2001) 'The dynamics of justice and home affairs: Laboratories, driving factors and costs', *Journal of Common Market Studies*, 39: 747–64

(2010) 'The Area of Freedom, Security and Justice' in A. von Bogdandy and J. Bast (eds.), *Principles of European Constitutional Law*, 2nd edn (Oxford: Hart Publishing), 551–85

(2011) 'The European Union's institutional balance of power after the Treaty of Lisbon' in *The European Union after the Treaty of Lisbon: Visions of Leading Policy-Makers, Academics and Journalists* (Luxembourg: Publications Office of the European Union), 60–89

Monti, G. (2013) 'EU competition law from Rome to Lisbon: Social market economy' in C. Heide-Jørgensen, C. Bergqvist, U. Neergaard and S. T. Poulsen (eds.), *Aims and Values in Competition Law* (Copenhagen: Djøf Publishing), 13–52

Myrdal, S. and M. Rhinard (2010) *The European Union's Solidarity Clause: Empty Letter or Effective Tool?* (Stockholm: Swedish Institute of Internal Affairs)

Nebbia, P. (2008) 'The double life of effectiveness', *Cambridge Yearbook of European Legal Studies*, 10: 287

Neumann, F. L. (1978) 'Über die Voraussetzungen und den Rechtsbegriff einer Wirtschaftsverfassung' in A. Söllner (ed.), *Wirtschaft, Staat, Demokratie* (Frankfurt am Main: Suhrkamp), 76–102

Niemann, A. and P. C. Schmitter (2009) 'Neofunctionalism' in A. Wiener and T. Diez (eds.), *European Integration Theory*, 2nd edn (Oxford University Press), 45–66

Nörr, K. W. (1994) '"Economic constitution": On the roots of a legal concept', *Journal of Law and Religion*, 11: 343–54

Nozick, R. (1975) *Anarchy, State, and Utopia* (Oxford: Blackwell)

Oliver, P. and W. H. Roth (2004) 'The internal market and the four freedoms', *Common Market Law Review*, 41: 407–41

Pace, L. F. and K. Seidel (2013) 'The drafting and the role of Regulation 17: A hard-fought compromise' in K. K. Patel and H. Schweitzer (eds.), *The Historical Foundations of EU Competition Law* (Oxford University Press), 54–88

Patel, K. K. and H. Schweitzer (2013a) 'Introduction' in K. K. Patel and H. Schweitzer (eds.), *The Historical Foundations of EU Competition Law* (Oxford University Press), 1–18

(2013b) 'EU competition law in historical context: Continuity and change' in K. K. Patel and H. Schweitzer (eds.), *The Historical Foundations of EU Competition Law* (Oxford University Press), 207–30

Payandeh, M. (2011) 'Constitutional review of EU law after *Honeywell*: Contextualizing the relationship between the German Constitutional Court and the EU Court of Justice, *Common Market Law Review*, 48: 9–38

Pech, L. (2010) '"A Union founded on the rule of law": Meaning and reality of the rule of law as a constitutional principle of EU law', *European Constitutional Law Review*, 6: 359–96

Peers, S. (2007) *EU Justice and Home Affairs Law*, 2nd edn (Oxford University Press)

Pernice, I. (2001) 'Der Beitrag Walter Hallsteins zur Zukunft Europas: Begründung und Konsolidierung der Europäischen Gemeinschaft als Rechtsgemeinschaft', *Walter Hallstein Institute Paper*, 9/01

(2009) 'The Treaty of Lisbon: Multilevel constitutionalism in action', *Columbia Journal of European Law*, 15: 349–407

Pescatore, P. (1983) 'The doctrine of direct effect: An infant disease of community law', *European Law Review*, 8: 155–77

Peters, B. (2012) 'Germany's dialogue with Strasbourg: Extrapolating the *Bundesverfassungsgericht*'s relationship with the European Court of Human Rights', *German Law Journal*, 13: 757–72

Poiares Maduro, M. (1998) *We the Court: The European Court of Justice and European Economic Constitution* (Oxford: Hart Publishing)

(2000) 'Europe's social self: "The sickness unto death"' in J. Shaw (ed.), *Social Law and Policy in Evolving European Union* (Oxford: Hart Publishing), 325–49

(2003) 'Europe and the constitution: What if this is as good as it gets?' in J. H. H. Weiler and M. Wind (eds.), *European Constitutionalism Beyond the State* (Cambridge University Press), 74–102

(2006) 'Contrapunctual law: Europe's constitutional pluralism in action' in N. Walker (ed.), *Sovereignty in Transition* (Oxford: Hart Publishing), 501–37

Prechal, S. (2006) *Directives in EC Law*, 2nd edn (Oxford University Press)

(2007) 'Direct effect, indirect effect, supremacy and the evolving constitution of the European Union' in C. Barnard (ed.), *The Fundamentals of EU Law Revisited: Assessing the Impact of the Constitution Debate* (Oxford University Press), 35–69

Priban, J. (2012) 'Constitutionalism as a fear of the political? A comparative analysis of Teubner's *Constitutional Fragments* and Thornhill's *A Sociology of Constitutions*', *Journal of Law and Society*, 39: 441–71

Ramírez Pérez, S. M. and S. van der Scheur (2013) 'The evolution of the law on Art. 81 and Art. 82: Ordoliberalism and its Keynesian challenge' in K. K. Patel and H. Schweitzer (eds.), *The Historical Foundations of EU Competition Law* (Oxford University Press), 19–53

Rasmussen, M. (2012) 'Establishing a constitutional practice of European law: The history of the legal service of the European executive 1952–65', *Contemporary European History*, 21: 375–97

Raz, J. (1979) *The Authority of Law: Essays in Law and Morality* (Oxford University Press)

Reich, N. (1992) 'Competition between legal orders: A new paradigm of EC law', *Common Market Law Review*, 29: 861–96

(2010) 'The public/private divide in European law' in H. W. Micklitz and F. Cafaggi (eds.), *European Private Law after the Common Frame of Reference* (Cheltenham: Edward Elgar Publishing), 56–89

Rideau, J. (2013) 'The case law of the Polish, Hungarian and Czech constitutional courts on national identity and the "German model"' in A. Saiz Arnaiz and C. Alcoberro Llivina (eds.), *National Constitutional Identity and European Integration* (Cambridge: Intersentia), 243–61

Rödl, F. (2010) 'The labour constitution' in A. von Bogdandy and J. Bast (eds.), *Principles of European Constitutional Law* (Oxford: Hart Publishing), 623–58

Rosas, A. and L. Armati (2012) *EU Constitutional Law: An Introduction*, 2nd edn (Oxford: Hart Publishing)

Rousseva, E. and M. Marquis (2012) 'Hell freezes over: A climate change for assessing exclusionary conduct under article 102 TFEU',*Journal of European Competition Law & Practice*, 4: 32–50

Sadurski, W. (2008) '"Solange, chapter 3": Constitutional courts in Eastern Europe – Democracy – European Union', *European Law Journal*, 14: 1–35

Sankari, S. (2013) *European Court of Justice Legal Reasoning in Context* (Groningen: Europe Law Publishing)

Sarmiento, D. (2013a) 'The EU's constitutional core' in A. Saiz Arnaiz and C. Alcoberro Llivina (eds.), *National Constitutional Identity and European Integration* (Cambridge: Intersentia), 177–204

(2013b) 'Who's afraid of the Charter? The Court of Justice, national courts and the new framework of fundamental rights protection in Europe', *Common Market Law Review*, 50: 1267–1304

Sauter, W. (1998) 'The economic constitution of the European Union', *Columbia Journal of European Law*, 4: 27–68

Sauter, W. and H. Schepel (2009) *State and Market in EU Law* (Cambridge University Press)

Scharpf, F. W. (1999) *Governing in Europe: Effective and Democratic?* (Oxford University Press)

(2010) 'The asymmetry of European integration, or why the EU cannot be a "social market economy"', *Socio-Economic Review*, 8: 211–50

(2012) *Legitimacy Intermediation in the Multilevel European Polity and its Collapse in the Euro Crisis* (Cologne: Max Planck Institute for the Study of Societies)

Scheinin, M. (2006) 'Human rights treaties and the Vienna Convention on the Law of Treaties: Conflicts or harmony?' in Venice Commission (ed.), *The Status of International Treaties on Human Rights* (Strasbourg: Council of Europe Publishing), 43–55

Schepel, H. (2012) 'Constitutionalizing the market, marketing the constitution, and to tell the difference: On the horizontal application of the free movement provisions in EU law', *European Law Journal*, 18: 177–200

Scheppele, K. L. (2004) 'Law in a time of emergency: States of exception and the temptations of 9/11', *Journal of Constitutional Law*, 6: 1–75

Schilling, T. (1996) 'The autonomy of the community legal order: An analysis of possible foundations', *Harvard International Law Journal*, 37: 389–410

Schmitt C., (1924) 'Die Diktatur des Reichspräsidenten nach Art. 48 der Reichsverfassung', *Veröffentlichungen der Vereinigung der Deutschen Staatsrechtslehrer*, 1: 63–104

(1958) 'Weiterentwicklung des totalen Staats in Deutschland' in Schmitt, *Verfassungsrechtliche Aufsätze* (Berlin: Duncker & Humblot)
(1985) *Politische Theologie* (Berlin: Duncker & Humblot)
(1996) *The Concept of the Political* (University of Chicago Press)
(2004) *Political Theology*, trans. G. Schwab (University of Chicago Press)
(2008) *Constitutional Theory*, trans. and ed. J. Seitzer (Durham, NC: Duke University Press)
Schuknecht, L., P. Moutout, P. Rother and J. Stark (2011) *The Stability and Growth Pact: Crisis and Reform* (Frankfurt: European Central Bank)
Schütze, R. (2006) 'Supremacy without pre-emption? The very slowly emergent Doctrine of Community Pre-emption', *Common Market Law Review*, 43: 1023–48
(2009) *From Dual to Cooperative Federalism: The Changing Structure of European Law* (Oxford University Press)
Schweitzer, H. (2007) 'Competition law and public policy: Reconsidering an uneasy relationship. The example of Art. 81', *European University Institute Working Paper*, Law 2007/30
Searle, J. (1988) *Speech Acts* (Cambridge University Press)
Shany, Y. (2003) *The Competing Jurisdictions of International Courts and Tribunals* (Oxford University Press)
Shuibhne, N. (2013) *The Coherence of EU Free Movement Law: Constitutional Responsibility and the Court of Justice* (Oxford University Press)
Simma, B. (2009) 'Universality of international law from the perspective of a practitioner', *European Journal of International Law*, 20: 265–97
Skinner, Q. (1978) *The Foundations of Modern Political Thought, Volume II: The Age of Reformation* (Cambridge University Press)
(2002) *Visions of Politics, Volume I: Regarding Method* (Cambridge University Press)
Slaughter, A.-M., A. Stone Sweet and J. H. H. Weiler (eds.) (1998) *The European Court and National Courts: Doctrine and Jurisprudence* (Oxford: Hart Publishing)
Snell, J. (2003) 'Who's got the power? Free movement and allocation of competences in EC law', *Yearbook of European Law*, 22: 323–52
(2010) 'The notion of market access: A concept or a slogan?', *Common Market Law Review*, 47: 437–72
(2014) 'The internal market and the philosophies of market integration' in C. Barnard and S. Peers (eds.), *European Union Law* (Oxford University Press), 300–24
Spaak Report (1956) 'Rapport des chefs de délégation au Ministres des Affaires Entrangères', 21 April, available at www.unizar.es/euroconstitucion/library/historic%20documents/Rome/preparation/Spaak%20report%20fr.pdf
Spaventa, E. (2004) 'From Gebhard to Carpenter: Towards a (non-)economic constitution', *Common Market Law Review*, 41: 743–73
(2009) 'Federalisation versus centralisation: Tensions in fundamental rights discourse in the EU' in M. Dougan and S. Currie (eds.), *50 Years of the European Treaties: Looking Back and Thinking Forward* (Oxford: Hart Publishing), 343–64
Stone Sweet, A. (2004) *The Judicial Construction of Europe* (Oxford University Press)

Streeck, W. (1995) 'Neo-voluntarism: A new European social policy regime', *European Law Journal*, 1: 31–59

Streit, M. E. and W. Müssler (1995) 'The economic constitution of the European Community: From "Rome" to "Maastricht"', *European Law Journal*, 1: 5–30

Streit, M. E. and M. Wohlgemuth (2000) 'The market economy and the state: Hayekian and ordoliberal conceptions' in P. Koslowski (ed.), *The Theory of Capitalism in the German Economic Tradition: Historism, Ordo-Liberalism, Critical Theory, Solidarism* (Berlin: Springer), 224–71

Teubner, G. (2012) *Constitutional Fragments: Societal Constitutionalism and Globalization* (Oxford University Press)

Thym, D. (2012) 'Attack or retreat? Evolving themes and strategies of the judicial dialogue between the German Constitutional Court and the European Court of Justice' in M. Claes, M. de Visser, P. Popelier and C. van de Heyning (eds.), *Constitutional Conversations in Europe* (Cambridge: Intersentia), 235–49

Tridimas, T. (2006) *The General Principles of EU Law*, 2nd edn (Oxford University Press)

Tuori, K. (2002) *Critical Legal Positivism* (Aldershot: Ashgate)

(2011) *Ratio and Voluntas* (Aldershot: Ashgate)

(2014) 'Transnational law: On legal hybrids and perspectivism', in M. Maduro, K. Tuori and S. Sankari (eds.), *Transnational Law: Rethinking European Law and Legal Thinking* (Cambridge University Press), 11–57

Tuori, K. (Kaarlo) and K. (Klaus) Tuori (2014) *The Eurozone Crisis: A Constitutional Analysis* (Cambridge University Press)

Twining, W. (2000) *Globalization and Legal Theory* (Evanston, Ill.: Northwest University Press)

Usher, J. A. (2007) 'The evolution of the free movement of capital', *Fordham International Law Journal*, 31: 1533–70

van Middelaar, L. (2013) *The Passage to Europe: How a Continent Became a Union* (New Haven, Conn.: Yale University Press)

Vauchet, A. (2010) 'The transnational politics of judicialization. *Van Gend en Loos* and the making of the EU polity', *European Law Journal* 16: 1–28

Venice Commission (2010) Report on constitutional provisions on amendments of the constitution, Study No. 469/2008, 19 January (CDL-AD(2010)001)

von Bogdandy, A. and S. Schill (2011) 'Overcoming absolute primacy: Respect for national identity under the Lisbon Treaty', *Common Market Law Review*, 48: 1417–53

von der Groeben, H. (1961) 'Policy on competition in the EEC', *Bulletin of the European Economic Community*, Supplement

von Savigny, F. C. (1981) *System des Heutigen Römischen Rechts* (Aalen: Scientia)

Waever, O. (1995) 'Securitization and desecuritization' in R. D. Lipschutz (ed.), *On Security* (New York: Columbia University Press), 46–86

Waldron, J. (2003) 'Security and liberty: The image of balance', *Journal of Political Philosophy*, 11: 191–210

Walker, N. (2002) 'The idea of constitutional pluralism', *Modern Law Review*, 65: 317–59

(2003) 'Postnational constitutionalism and the problems of translation' in J. H. H. Weiler and M. Wind (eds.), *European Constitutionalism Beyond the State* (Cambridge University Press), 27–54

(2006a) 'Late sovereignty in the European Union' in Walker (ed.), *Sovereignty in Transition* (Oxford: Hart Publishing), 3–32

(2008) 'Beyond boundary disputes and basic grids: Mapping the global disorder of normative orders', *International Journal of Constitutional Law*, 6: 373–96

Walker, N. (ed.) (2006b) *Sovereignty in Transition* (Oxford: Hart Publishing)

Weatherill, S. (2011) 'The limits of legislative harmonization ten years after *Tobacco Advertising*: How the Court's case law has become a "drafting guide"', *German Law Journal*, 12: 827–64

Wegmann, M. (2002) *Früher Neoliberalismus und Europäische Integration* (Baden-Baden: Nomos)

(2008) *Der Einfluss des Neoliberalismus auf das Europäische Wettbewerbsrecht 1946–1965. Von den Wirtschaftswissenschaften zur Politik* (Baden-Baden: Nomos)

Weiler, J. H. H. (1981) 'The community system: The dual character of supranationalism', *Yearbook of European Law*, 1: 267–306

(1999) *The Constitution of Europe* (Cambridge University Press)

Weiler, J. H. H. and M. Wind (eds.) (2003) *European Constitutionalism Beyond the State* (Cambridge University Press)

Werner Committee (1970) 'Report to the Council and the Commission on the realization by stages of economic and monetary union in the Community (Werner Report)', 8 October, available at ec.europa.eu/economy_finance/emu_history/documentation/chapter5/19701008en72realisationbystage.pdf

Wintgens, L. (2012) *Legisprudence: Practical Reason in Legislation* (Farnham: Ashgate)

Zahle, H. (1995) 'The polycentricity of the law or the importance of legal pluralism for legal dogmatics' in H. Petersen and H Zahle (eds.), *Legal Polycentricity: Consequences of Pluralism in Law* (Aldershot: Ashgate), 185–200

Zangl, B. and M. Zürn (eds.) (2004) *Verrechtlichung: Baustein für Global Governance* (Bonn: Dietz)

Index

accession negotiations, EU autonomy concerning, 99–102
access justice
  complementary *vs* conflicting concepts of, 265–8
  social policy and, 231
administrative law, European constitution and, 3–4, 347–9
Advocates General
  European constitutional discourse and, 116–17
  legal scholarship and, 117–18
age discrimination, ECJ case law on, 261n.67
Agreement on the European Economic Area, 53–9
Åkerberg Fransson case, 93–4, 95–6
Albany case, 237–43
Alexy, Robert, 114, 303–4
allocative justice, 265–8
Amsterdam Treaty
  AFSJ and, 315–16
  freedom and justice in security provisions of, 296–301
  Schengen Convention and, 275–6
  security constitutionalization and, 278–84
anti-discrimination law
  internal market law and welfare services and, 237–43
  mobile workers and citizens and, 243–8
  primacy of national welfare state and, 232–4
  regulatory private law and, 257–65
anti-trust law, competition law and, 161–4
Anwendungsvorrang. See disapplication
area concept, security constitutionalization and, 296n.58
Area of Freedom, Security and Justice (AFSJ), 49–50, 108–12
  Amsterdam Treaty and powers of, 278–84
  citizenship issues and, 316–18
  Community method and, 333–40
  emergency situations in, 291n.44
  European constitutional discourse and, 118–20
  internal security issues and, 269–73, 296–301
  Lisbon Treaty provisions concerning, 284–8
  Stockholm Programme response to, 296–301
  transnationalization and, 312–18
asylum policies
  AFSJ provisions concerning, 278–84
  European Asylum Support Office, 282
  freedom and justice and, 296–301
  fundamental rights *vs* security in, 304–12
  Schengen Agreement and, 275–6
asymmetric internal and external shocks, fiscal policy and, 183–7
Australia, federalism in, 164–9
autonomy
  direct effect of European law and, 60–8
  in European law, 53–9, 321–3
  institutional autonomy, 53–9
  legal diversity and principle, 83–6
  normative autonomy, 53–9
  positioning function and, 28–37
  strengthening of European economic governance impact on, 192–5
autopoietical systems theory
  perspectivism and, 78–81
  radical pluralism and, 102–7
  transnational law and, 351, 353–5

balance of payments, Member States' policies and, 174–8
balancing doctrine, security constitutionalization and, 301–12
banking union proposals, 195–9
  international agreements and, 202n.50
Baquero Cruz, Julio, 164n.90
Basic Law (Germany), 90–6
Baumbast and R v Secretary of State for the Home Department, 245–6
Belgian Constitutional Court, EAW Framework Decision and, 306
Bellamy, Richard, 24
Benjamin, Walter, 290
black box model
  international law and, 342–3, 349–58
  legal diversity and, 81–6
  legal pluralism and, 86–8
  radical pluralism and, 102–7
  transnational law and, 349–58
Bloch, Ernst, 108
Böhm, Franz, 128–31, 132–4, 135–6, 161–4, 167–8, 213–14
border controls. *See also* cross-border transactions
  Amsterdam Treaty on free movement of persons and, 278–84
  freedom and justice and, 296–301
  Frontex border system, 282
  security constitutions and, 275–6
Bosman case, free movement law and, 143–4
Bosphorus doctrine, 349–58
  European Court of Human Rights and, 99–102
Bourdieu, Pierre, 356
Brentjens case, 241n.25
Bretton Woods system, 176
Brigade Rosse, 274–5
Brown v Board of Education, 121
BRT v Sabam, 140–1
budgetary planning
  democratic input legitimacy and, 217–26
  independent budget office proposals and, 220n.78
  strengthening of European economic governance concerning, 192–5
budget deficits, strengthening of European economic governance and, 192–5

capital movement, right to, security constitutionalization and, 274n.5
cartels
  competition law and, 157–64
  economic constitutionalization and regulation of, 138–40
Cassis de Dijon formula, 33–4, 83–6
  free movement law and, 141–50, 234–7
  microeconomic constitutionalization and, 209–17
  mutual recognition principle and, 153–5
central bank independence
  European monetary policy and, 178–83
  prohibition of financing and, 181
centralized socialist planning, competition law and, 150–2
centralized theory
  microeconomic constitution and, 172
  public interventionism and, 155–7
Charter of the Fundamental Rights of the European Union (CFREU), 92, 93–5, 118–20
  asylum seekers and, 306–8
  ECJ rulings on fundamental rights and, 324–5
  economic *vs* fundamental rights in, 168n.94
  Equality Title in, 257–65
  European Convention on Human Rights and, 99–102
  freedom and justice in security policies and, 296–301
  labour law and, 257–65
  law on universal services and, 264–5
  rule of law in, 211–14
  security of the person in, 304–12
  social constitutionalization and, 227–32
  social rights and, 251–6
  states of exception and, 291–2
Chicago School, competition law and, 161–4
child pornography, security provisions in Amsterdam Treaty and, 282
citizenship. *See also* European citizenship
  constitutional functions and, 28–37
  direct input legitimacy and, 217–26
  economic rights and, 167–8
  European constitutionalism and, 108–12
  free movement law and, 143–4
  security *vs* fundamental rights and, 304–12, 316–18
  transnational constitutionalism and, 37–44
  transnationalism and intergovernmentalism and, 333–40
codificatory constitutions, 28–37
coherence
  in European legal system, 45–53
  in security constitutionalization, 289–96
  security constitutionalization and, 312–18
Cohn-Bendit case, 63n.38

collective good, security as, 301–12
colonial legal regimes
  black box model and, 85n.7
  legal pluralism and, 86–8
Commercial Solvents case, 140
Commissioner for Economic and Monetary Affairs, 209–17
Commission v Council, 177–8, 210
Committee on Operational Cooperation on Internal Security (COSI), 277n.11
common currency, macroeconomic constitutionalization and introduction of, 178–83
Common European Asylum System, 306–8
Common Foreign and Security Policy (CFSP), 282–4
  Community method and, 333–40
  internal security issues and, 269–73
common good, principle of, security constitutionalization and, 269–73
common market
  competition law and, 157–64
  economic constitutionalization and establishment of, 136–8, 152, 164–9
  exchange-rate stability and, 174–8
  free movement law and, 141–50
  social constitutionalization and, 227–32
  social security issues and, 243–8
Common Market Law Review, 117–18
Community Charter of Fundamental Social Rights of Workers, 251–6, 321–3
  regulatory private law and, 257–65
Community law. *See* European Community law
Community method, 333–40
community of law, European Union and concept of, 211–14
competences in policy
  coordination of social security services and, 243–8
  economic constitutionalization and, 148–50
  economic policy and division of, 183–7
  EU legislative harmonization and, 172–3
  European economic constitutionalization and division of, 164–9
  in European legal system, 45–53
  European monetary policy, 178–83
  of European Union, 58–9
  implied powers doctrine and enlargement of, 327–8
  macroeconomic policies and transfer of, 178
  pre-emption doctrine and, 202–6
  primacy principle and, 65–8
  security provisions in Lisbon Treaty and, 284–8
  ultra vires review of, 90, 92–6
Competition Authority
  economic constitutions and, 209–17
  macroeconomic constitutionalization and, 217–26
  ordoliberal economic constitutionalism and, 131–6
  political dimensions of economic constitutions and, 169–73
competition economics, economic constitutionalism and, 128–31, 134–6
competition law
  economic activities included in, 148–50
  economic constitutionalization and, 138–40, 146–8, 164–9
  economic freedom *vs* individual rights in, 164–9
  internal market law and welfare services and, 237–43
  legitimacy and, 169–73
  publicization of, 145–6
  on public undertakings, universal services and, 263–4
  social constitutionalization, 234–7
  transnational constitutionalism and, 166
  underlying controversies in, 150–64
  welfare services for mobile workers and citizens and, 243–8
competition model, public interventionism and, 155–7
competition theory
  democratic input legitimacy and, 221–6
  exchange-rate stability and, 174–8
  political dimensions of economic constitutionalization and, 169–73
complementarity, transnational constitutionalism and, 38–41
comprehensive powers, principle of, pre-emption doctrine and, 202–6
conditionality of financial assistance
  Eurozone crisis and, 187–92
  pre-emption doctrine and, 202–6
Conference of European Community Affairs Committees (COSAC), 37–44
conferral, principle of
  constitutional relationality and, 21–8
  EU institutional competence and, 92–6
  European economic constitutionalization and, 164–9
  European legal system and, 45–53
  EU transnational polity, 320–1

conferral, principle of (*cont.*)
  rule of law and, 214–16
  Solange doctrine and, 90–6
  transnationalism and intergovernmentalism and, 333–40
conflict
  constitutional relationality and, 21–8
  economic *vs* fundamental rights and, 168–9
  legal pluralism and, 102–7
consistent interpretation, principle of, 63–5
Consten and Grundig case, 140
  competition law and, 146–8
constituent power, 108–12
constitutional conflicts
  legal pluralism and, 326–7
  radical pluralism and, 102–7
  transnational constitutionalism and, 37–44
constitutional culture, constitutional theory and, 15–17
constitutional identity, autonomy and assertion of, 333–40
constitutionalism
  anti-constitutional elements in security constitutionalization and, 312–18
  constitutional culture and, 15–17
  defined, 1–9
  doctrinal research *vs*, 5–9
constitutionalization
  European constitution in context of, 108–12
  relationality and, 21–8
  speech act theory and, 122–4
constitutional law
  as higher law, 10–14
  ordoliberal constitutional theory and, 132–4
constitutional moment
  concept of, 32n.6
  for constituent power, 108–12
'constitutional mutation', Eurozone crisis and, 108–12
constitutional object
  constitutional functions and, 28–37
  relationality and, 21–8
  speech acts and, 120–4
Constitutional Treaty
  constitutional theory following failure of, 108–12
  failure of, 4–5
  Founding Treaties and, 21–8
  freedom and justice provisions in, 296–301
  legal scholarship and, 117–18
  national courts' positioning and, 88–9
  parasitic legitimacy and failure of, 35–7
  primacy principle and, 65–8
constitutive function, 28–37
  constitutional object and, 28–37
  security constitutionalization and, 269–73
constitutive primacy, 320–1
constructivist approach, security constitutionalization and, 289–96
consumer law, regulatory private law and, 257–65
content-based legitimacy, constitutional functions and, 28–37
Continental Can case, competition law and, 146–8
contractual freedom, economic freedom and, 167–8
Convention on the Implementation of the Schengen Agreement, 275–6
convergence criteria
  EMU eligibility and, 183–7
  Eurozone crisis and, 187–92
  Eurozone regime and, 199–209
  Member State fiscal and monetary policy and, 178–83
  rule of law and, 209–17
cooperation procedures
  in Amsterdam Treaty security provisions, 278–84
  Fiscal Compact and, 206–9
  security constitutionalization and, 276–8, 315–16
  transnationalization and, 312–18
Copenhagen School of security studies, 289–96
core welfare services
  internal market law and, 237–43
  national welfare state and, 227–32
corporatist ideology, economic constitutionalism and, 128–31
Costa v Enel, 53–9
  constitutional identity and, 333–40
  direct effect of European law and, 60–8, 321–3
  Eurozone regime and, 199–209
  fundamental rights protections and, 96–9, 316–18, 324–5
  international law and, 344
  national law and, 88–9
  primacy principle and, 65–8, 70
Council of Europe, social rights and, 251–6
Council of Foreign Ministers, Common Foreign and Security Policy and, 272–3
Council of Ministers, 108–12
  intergovernmentalism and, 331–3
  qualitative majority voting, 331–3
Counter-Terrorism Group, 282–4
Courage case, 140–1

Court of Justice of the European Union (CJEU), 94n.26, 94n.27. *See also* European Court of Justice (ECJ)
court systems, European constitutional discourse and, 112–20
criminal law
  fundamental rights *vs* security and, 306
  security provisions in Amsterdam Treaty and harmonization of, 280–2
  security provisions in Lisbon Treaty and, 287–8
crisis prevention/crisis management transition, macroeconomic constitutionalization and, 187–92
cross-border transactions. *See also* border controls
  competition law and, 157–64
  denationalization and deterritorialization of welfare services and, 248–51
  economic constitutionalization and, 141–50, 152
  healthcare and, 237–43
  open markets and free competition and, 153
  security constitutionalization and, 273–8
  social justice and, 265–8
cultural diversity
  primacy of national welfare state and, 232–4

Dassonville formula, 33–4
  free movement law and, 141–50, 234–7
  microeconomic constitutionalization and, 209–17
Data Retention Directive, 49–50
Davies, Gareth, 172–3, 248–51
decentralized theory, public interventionism and, 155–7
Decker case, 243–8
'de-constitutionalization', Lisbon Treaty and, 5–9
defendants' rights, security *vs* fundamental rights and, 304–12
Defrenne cases, 260
delegation, administrative law concept of, 345–8
Delors Committee, 177, 186
democratic input legitimacy, 34–5
  European polity and, 329–31
  European Union and, 217–26
  neutrality in economic policy and, 183–7
  political dimensions of economic constitutionalization and, 169–73
  primacy of national welfare state and, 232–4
  security constitutionalization and, 316–18
  strengthening of European economic governance and, 192–5
  technocratic policy and, 41–4
  transnationalism and intergovernmentalism and, 333–40
democratic procedures, origin-based legitimacy and, 28–37
demos
  constituent power and, 108–12
  direct input legitimacy and, 217–26
  European citizenry as, 28–37
  European constitutionalism and, 108–12
  transnationalism and intergovernmentalism and, 333–40
  as transnational network, 38–41
denationalization of welfare services, 248–51
de-politicization, democratic input legitimacy and, 217–26
derogation
  Eurozone regime and, 199–209
  from fundamental rights, security constitutionalization and, 269–73
  internal market law and welfare services and, 237–43
  limitation and, 270n.2
Derrida, Jacques, 290
de Sousa Santos, Boaventura, 80
deterritorialization of welfare services, 248–51
de Witte, Bruno, 61, 63n.38, 206–9, 344–5
dialogical pluralism, 102–7
  transnational law and, 353–5
Dickson, J., 67n.46
Digital Rights Ireland case, 49–50, 311, 324–5
dimension-specific constitutional theory, 5–9
direct applicability
  competition law and, 157–64
  direct effect of European law and, 62–3
  economic constitutionalization and, 136–8, 140–1
  macroeconomic policies and, 178
direct effect. *See also* horizontal direct effect; indirect horizontal effect
  competition law and, 157–64
  denial of, for WTO law, 59
  ECJ jurisprudence on economic rights and, 164–9, 327–8
  economic constitutionalization and, 136–40
  European law and, 60–8, 321–3

direct effect (*cont.*)
  extension in European law of, 65–7
  free movement law and, 148–50
  integrated model and, 65–8
  juridical constitution, 28–37
  legal certainty and, 70
  narrow *vs* broad concepts of, 68
  perspectivism and, 340–58
  primacy and, 65–8, 70
  regulatory private law and, 257–65
  social constitutionalization and absence of, 227–32
  state liability and, 68–9n.49
  supremacy principle and, 325–6
Directive 2011/85, 192–5
directives
  direct effect of European law and, 62–3
  horizontal direct effect and, 63
  indirect horizontal effect and, 63–5
  integrated model and, 65–8
  strengthening of European economic governance and, 192–5
  transposition of, 70–1
Directorate-General, 209–17
dirigiste economic theory
  French embrace of, 174–8
  in Nazi Germany, 135–6
  ordoliberalism and, 150–2
disapplication, primacy principle and, 69–71
discursiveness
  European constitutionalism and, 17–18
  speech acts and, 120–4
doctrinal scholar perspective, European constitutional discourse and, 112–20
dominance, abuse of
  competition law and, 146–8, 157–64
  ECJ jurisprudence concerning, 140
double hermeneutics, European constitutionalism and, 5
Dougan, Michael, 68, 325–6
Dred Scott decision, 121
Drexl, Josef, 159–60, 163–4
drug trafficking
  security provisions in Amsterdam Treaty and, 282
  Trevi framework for security and, 275–6
dualist model, primacy principle and, 65–8
Dublin II Regulation on the Common European Asylum System, 306–8
Dworkin, Ronald, 15–16, 46
  economic *vs* fundamental rights and, 168–9
  European constitutionalism and theories of, 114
  on European legal order, 324–5
  on security *vs* fundamental rights, 302–3
Economic and Monetary Union (EMU)
  Community method and, 333–40
  establishment of, 174–8
  Eurozone crisis and, 187–92
  Eurozone regime and, 199–209
  microeconomic constitutionalization and, 321–3
  rule of law and, 209–17
  social policy and, 227–32, 251–6
  transnationalism and intergovernmentalism and, 333–40
  underlying economic assumptions in, 183–7
economic constitutionalization. *See also* macroeconomic constitutionalization; microeconomic constitutionalization
  democratic input legitimacy and, 221–6
  European economic constitution and national constitutions, 164–9
  Eurozone regime and, 199–209
  framing of, 9–10
  free movement law and, 141–50
  functional primacy, 320–1
  historical evolution of, 108–12, 127–36
  individual rights and, 316–18
  internal market law and welfare services and, 237–43
  market citizenship and, 108–12
  mutual recognition and, 83–6
  neutrality of, 164–9
  political dimensions of, 169–73
  process of constitutionalization, 136–50
  relationality and, 21–8
  sectoral dimensions, 319–20
  security constitutionalization and, 273–8
  social constitutionalization and, 227–32
  underlying controversies, 150–64
  in Weimar Republic, 128–31
economic freedom
  competition law and, 157–64
  democratic input legitimacy and, 221–6
  direct effect and, 148–50
  economic constitutionalism and, 132–4
  security constitutionalization and, 273–8
  social policy of Member States and, 234–7
economic integration
  constitutional relationality and, 21–8
  democratic legitimacy and, 169–73
  European integration as, 321–3
  microeconomic constitution and, 127–36
  monetary policy and, 183–7
  pacemaker constitution and, 108–12
  social constitutionalization and, 227–32

welfare services for mobile workers and citizens and, 243–8
economic law, ordoliberal theory of, 131–6
economic policy, macroeconomic constitutionalization and, 183–7
economic rights, ECJ jurisprudence concerning, 164–9
economic service principle, internal market law and welfare services and, 237–43
Economist approach
microeconomic constitutionalization and, 321–3
monetary union and, 183–7
EEC Treaty, European legal autonomy and, 53–9
effective competition structure concept, competition law and, 146–8
efficacy, principle of
community law and, 57–8
economic constitutionalization and, 136–8
elections
democratic input legitimacy and, 217–26
direct input legitimacy and, 217–26
embedded openness, of constitutional orders, 102–7, 326–7
empty-chairs crisis, 331–3
economic constitutionalization and, 136–8
energy supply crises, states of exception and, 291n.44
enhanced cooperation procedures, Fiscal Compact and, 206–9
erga omnes doctrine, 99–102
Erhard, Ludwig, 135–6
ESMA ruling, 195–9
Esping-Andersen, Gosta, 233, 248
ETA movement, 274–5
Eucken, Walter, 128–31, 135–6, 174–5
EU Counter-Terrorism Coordinator, 282–4
EU law. *See* European law; European Union
Euro Group, 194–5, 200
Eurojust, 287, 315–16
establishment of, 282
Europarechtsfreundlichkeit principle, 94, 104
European Anti-Fraud Office (OLAF), 282
European Arrest Warrant (EAW), 88–9, 280–4
fundamental rights *vs* security and, 304–12
transnationalization and, 280–4, 304–18
European Asylum Support Office (EASO), 282
European Central Bank (ECB), 178–83
changing role of, 195–9
democratic input legitimacy and, 221–6
Eurozone crisis and, 187–92
macroeconomic constitutionalization and, 209–26
rule of law and, 216–17
transnationalism of, 331–3
European citizenship
introduction of, 243–8
transnationalism and intergovernmentalism and, 333–40
European Coal and Steel Community (ECSC), 41–4, 331–3
competition law and, 146–8, 150–2
pacemaker constitution and, 108–12
European Commission
AFSJ and role of, 278–84
Community method and, 333–40
competition law and, 118–20, 146–8, 157–64
competition policy, free movement law and, 146–8
core welfare services and policies of, 237–43
denationalization and deterritorialization of welfare services and, 248–51
economic constitutionalization and, 138–41
European Council and, 192–5
Eurozone crisis and, 187–92, 221–6
excessive deficit procedures and, 181–2
implementation of microeconomic constitution and, 169–73
macroeconomic constitutionalization and, 217–26
rule of law and, 216–17
Schengen Convention and, 276–8
security constitutionalization and, 284–8
transnationalization and, 312–18, 331–3
European Committee of Social Rights, 256n.57
European Community law
autonomy of European law and, 57
core welfare services and, 237–43
economic constitutionalization and, 136–40, 148–50, 164–9
European legal system and, 49–50
exclusion of fundamental rights in, 90
fundamental rights and, 92
international law and, 53–9
positioning of international law and, 59–60
rule of law and, 211–14
social constitutionalization and, 227–32
Solange doctrine and, 90–6
state liability for breaches under, 64n.41

European constitutionalism
  constituent power and, 108–12
  direct effect *vs* primacy in, 65–8
  Eurozone crisis and mutation of, 187–92
  Eurozone regime and, 199–209
  general theory of, 319–40
  juridical and political dimensions of, 9–10
  legal theory concerning, 108–12
  national constitutions and economic constitution of, 164–9
  primacy of national welfare state and, 232–4
  as social constitution, 227–32
  theoretical bases of, 1–9
  transnational law and, 349–58
European Convention on Human Rights (ECHR), 48–9, 99–102, 296–301
  asylum seekers and, 306–8
  security constitutionalization and, 269–73
  states of exception and, 291–2
  transnational law and, 349–58
European Council, 91–2
  AFSJ and role of, 278–84, 296–301
  Common Foreign and Security Policy and, 272–3
  Community method and, 333–40
  Decision 2011/99, 190–2
  European Commission and, 192–5
  European constitutional discourse and, 118–20
  security constitutionalization and, 280–2, 284–8, 296–301
  Stability and Growth Pact and, 182–3
  strengthening of European economic governance and, 192–5
  Tampere Conclusions and, 304–12
  terrorism policies of, 282–4
  transnational polity of, 91–2, 108–12
European Court of Human Rights (ECtHR), 99–102
  fundamental rights *vs* security in, 309–11
  security constitutionalization and, 296–301
  transnational law and, 349–58
European Court of Justice (ECJ)
  asylum procedures, 308n.79
  autonomy of European law and rulings of, 53–9, 321–3
  Community method and, 333–40
  competition law and jurisprudence of, 146–8, 157–69
  conferral principle and, 214–16
  denationalization and deterritorialization of welfare services and, 248–51
  derogation in free movement of workers and, 274–5
  direct effect of European law and, 60–8, 138–40, 164–9
  economic constitutionalism and jurisprudence of, 127–8, 136–8, 140–1, 148–50, 209–17
  enhanced cooperation in jurisprudence of, 206–9
  on EU institutional competence, 92–6
  EU institutional organization and, 91–2, 108–12
  European constitutional discourse and, 1–9, 34–5, 112–20
  European Court of Human Rights and, 99–102
  European legal system and, 108–12, 327–8
  excessive deficit sanctions regime, 177–8
  financial stability in jurisprudence of, 195–9
  Founding Treaties and, 10–14
  free movement law jurisprudence and, 141–50, 152–3, 164–9, 210–11
  fundamental rights cases and, 90–6, 251–6, 304–12, 324–5
  German Constitutional Court and, 88–9
  host country and home country models of public interventionism and, 155–7
  implementation of microeconomic constitution and, 169–73
  intergovernmentalism and, 331–3
  internal market law and welfare services and, 237–43
  on international agreements, 59
  international law *vs* European law in jurisprudence of, 340–58
  juridical constitutionalization and, 34–5
  jurisdiction and competence conflicts, 50–3
  Kadi and *Kadi II* cases and, 310n.83
  law-making powers, 45–53
  legal discourse on landmark cases of, 120–4
  legal diversity in jurisprudence of, 83–6
  legal scholarship and, 117–18
  legislative harmonization and, 172–3
  Lisbon Treaty security provisions and, 284–8
  microeconomic constitution and, 21–8, 217–26
  multidimensionality of, 320–1
  national courts and, 102–7, 118–20, 326–7
  positioning of international law in European law hierarchy by, 59–60
  pre-emption doctrine and, 72–4, 202–6

primacy principle and, 65–8, 138–40
principle of conferral and, 92–6
on regulations, 62–3
regulatory private law and, 257–65
rule of law and, 216–17
Schengen Convention and, 276–8
security provisions in Amsterdam Treaty and, 280–2
social policy of Member States and, 234–7
state liability cases and, 69–71
transnationalization and, 312–18
transnational law and, 349–58
trigger model and, 65–8
welfare services for mobile workers and citizens and, 243–8
European courts, fiscal and economic policy and, 209–17
European Currency Unit (ECU), 177n.8
European economic governance
Commission White Paper on, 333–4n.9
conferral principle and, 214–16
democratic input legitimacy and, 221–6
Eurozone crisis and, 187–92
Eurozone regime and, 199–209
strengthening of, 192–5
European Financial Stability Mechanism (EFSM), 187–92
Eurozone regime and, 199–209
pre-emption doctrine and, 202–6
principle of conferral and, 214–16
European law
autonomy of, 53–9, 321–3
constitutional discourse and, 112–20
definitions, 1n.1
direct effect in, 65–7
economic and juridical constitutionalization and, 321–3
European constitution in context of, 1–9
European legal system and, 45–53
Eurozone crisis management and, 187–92
general principles, 74–7
German Constitutional Court review of primacy of, 90–6
international law and positioning of, 59–60
legal diversity and, 102–7
legal pluralism and, 86–8
national law and, 50–3, 88–9
OMT programme and, 195–9
openness principle concerning, 92–6
perspectivism in, 78–81
positioning of, 59–71
pre-emption in supremacy in, 72–4
primacy of, 65–8
transnational law and, 349–58
European legal system
juridical and political constitutions and, 45
structure and characteristics of, 45–53
European majoritarianism, public interventionism and, 155–7
European Monetary System (EMS), 174–8
European Monitoring Centre for Drugs and Drug Addiction (EMCDDA), 282
European Parliament, 91–2, 108–12
AFSJ and role of, 278–84
direct input legitimacy and, 217–26
European Commission powers, 221–6
fundamental rights joint declaration and, 91–2
intergovernmentalism of, 206–9, 331–3
normative constitutionalism and, 41–4
perspectivism and, 78–81
polity building and, 329–31
Schengen Convention and, 276–8
transnational constitutionalism and, 37–44
transnationalization and, 312–18
European Police College (CEPOL), 282
European polity, juridical and political constitutions and, 45
European regulatory private law, 231
European Resolution Fund, 195–9
European Security Strategy, 282–4
European Social Charter of the Council of Europe, 251–6
European Stability Mechanism (ESM)
democratic input legitimacy and, 221–6
establishment of, 187–92
Eurozone regime and, 202–3
pre-emption doctrine and, 202–6
principle of conferral and, 214–16
strengthening of European economic governance and, 192–5
European System of Central Banks (ESCB), 178–83
European Union (EU)
competence of institutions in, 92–6
complementarity and, 38–41
constitutional functions and, 28–37
constitutional relationality and, 21–8
economic constitutionalization and, 164–9
European constitution in context of, 1–9
European legal system and, 50–3
Eurozone crisis management and, 187–92
formal and material constitutions and, 10–14
fundamental rights and, 17n.26

European Union (EU) (*cont.*)
institutional organization, 108–12
internal security issues and, 269–73
legal diversity in legislation of, 83–6
perspectivism in law and, 78–81
polity and constitutional functions in, 28–37
pre-emption doctrine and, 72–4, 202–6
primacy of national welfare state and, 232–4
rule of law and, 209–17
transnational constitutionalism and, 38–41
European Union Agency for Fundamental Rights, 296–301
European Union Counter-Terrorism Strategy, 282–4
European University Institute, 127–8
Europol, 278n.16, 287, 315–16
Eurozone crisis
crisis prevention/crisis management transition and, 187–92
democratic input legitimacy and, 217–26
economic constitution and, 108–12
European Central Bank and, 195–9
international law and agreements concerning, 108–12
limitations of European and national constitutionalization and, 321–3
macroeconomic constitutionalization and, 174–8
national welfare state and, 232–4
polycentricity of legal sources and, 81–6
principle of legality and, 216–17
reverse majority voting and, 331–3
social policy in wake of, 251–6
states of exception and, 291n.44
Eurozone regime
constitutional basis for, 199–209
transnationalism and intergovernmentalism and, 333–40
excessive deficit procedures
Eurozone regime and, 199–209
Maastricht Treaty provisions for, 181–2, 186
pre-emption doctrine and, 202–6
rule of law and, 209–17
strengthening of European economic governance and, 192–5
excessive imbalances procedure, 192–5
Exchange Rate Mechanism (ERM), 177n.8
exchange-rate stability
EMU eligibility and, 183–7
European monetary policy and, 178–83
Member States and, 174–8
exclusion, primacy of European law and, 69–70
exclusive perspectivism
interlegality and, 85–6
legal pluralism and, 86–8, 102–7
principles of, 78–81
existential threat, security constitutionalization and concept of, 289–96
expert bodies
democratic input legitimacy and, 221–6
legitimacy of, 333–40
macroeconomic constitutionalization legitimacy and, 217–26
rule of law and role of, 209–17

federalism
EU polity and, 345–8
European economic constitutions and, 164–9
pre-emption doctrine and, 72–4
primacy of national welfare state and, 232–4
FIDE association of European law scholars, 117–18
field pre-emption, 72–4
financial markets
banking union proposals and, 195–9
discipline imposed on Member States by, 186
Eurozone crisis and, 187–92
financial stability mechanisms
democratic input legitimacy and, 221–6
European Central Bank and, 195–9
Eurozone crisis and, 187–92
Member State coordination and, 206–9
Finland, financial liability issues for, 192–5
Finnish Constitution, 31, 218–19n.76
security *vs* liberty in, 302–3
Fiscal Compact, 192–5
national constitutions and, 206–9
pre-emption doctrine and, 202–6
fiscal policy
democratic input legitimacy and sovereignty in, 217–26
ECB and, 195–9
Eurozone crisis and, 187–92
Eurozone regime and, 199–209
monetary stability and, 183–7
primacy of national welfare state and, 232–4
social policy and, 227–32
strengthening of European economic governance concerning, 192–5
Fischer-Lescano, Andreas, 80, 354–5
flexibility clause (Treaty of Rome)
ECJ jurisprudence and, 327–8

economic constitutionalization and, 148–50
European legal system and, 45–53
football hooliganism, Trevi framework for security and, 275–6
formal constitution
concept of, 10–14
European law and, 108–12
formal sanctions
democratic input legitimacy and, 221–6
Eurozone crisis management and, 192–5
Foto-Frost ruling, 58–9
Foucault, Michel, 295, 317
Founding Treaties. *See also* treaty law; specific treaties
as constitutional charter, 108–12
constitutional dimensions, 21–8
constitutional functions and, 28–37
EC (EU) constitutional charter and, 10–14
EU institutional competence and, 92–6
European constitutional discourse and, 112–20
European legal system and, 50–3
European monetary policy and, 178–83
internal security issues and, 269–73
international law autonomy and, 53–9
national constitutions and, 206–9
perspectivism and, 340–58
strengthening of European economic governance and, 192–5
transnational law and, 349–58
fragmentation, security constitutionalization and, 312–18
Framework Agreement on the European Financial Stability Facility (EFSF), 187–92
Framework Decision on Combating Terrorism, 282–4, 294–6, 304–12
Framework Decision on the European Arrest Warrant, 88–9, 280–4, 304–18
framework decisions, security provisions in Amsterdam Treaty and, 278–84
framing constitutions
constitutional functions and, 28–37
juridical and political constitutions as, 319–20
multidimensionality, 320–1
relationality and, 21–8
France
constitutionalism in, 108–12
Constitutional Treaty failure in, 4–5
European monetary policy and, 178–83
Monetarist approach embraced by, 183–7
Frankovich case, 64–5
freedom, security constitutionalization and, 296–301
free movement law
Amsterdam Treaty on free movement of persons, 278–84
ECJ jurisprudence and, 141–50, 210–11
economic activities included in, 148–50
economic constitutionalization and, 138–40
economic freedom *vs* individual rights in, 152, 164–9
home country model of, 172
internal market law and welfare services and, 237–43
ratione personae and, 145–6
security constitutionalization and, 273–8
social constitutionalization and, 234–7
transnational constitutionalism and, 166
underlying controversy in, 157–64
welfare services for mobile workers and citizens and, 243–8
free movement of goods, economic constitutionalization and, 141–50
Freiburg group, economic constitutionalism and, 130–1
Frontex border system, 282
functional primacy, sectoral constitutions, 21–8, 320–1
fundamental rights law
access justice and, 265–8
constitutional identity and, 333–40
constitutional theory and, 15–17, 28–37
economic rights and, 164–9
European legal system and, 45–53, 324–5
freedom and justice in security constitutions and, 296–301
German Constitutional Court review of, 90–6
legal pluralism and, 88–94, 102–7
primacy principle and, 96–9
security constitutionalization and, 269–73, 301–12, 321–3
social constitutionalization and, 227–32
Solange doctrine and, 90–6
state of exception and, 289–96
transnational law and, 349–58
'funktionaler Zweckverband', transnationalism and intergovernmentalism and, 333–40

GB-Inno-BM case, 146
Gebhard v Consiglio dell'Ordine degli Avvocati e Procuratori di Milano, 235n.13
Geltungsvorrang. See invalidation
general constitutional theory
constitutional pluralism and, 5–9
EU constitutional law and, 10–14

Geneva Convention, asylum seekers and, 306–8
German Constitutional Court, 48–9
  direct input legitimacy and rulings of, 217–26
  ECB Outright Monetary Transactions programme, 116–17, 118–20
  European Central Bank and, 195–9
  European constitutional discourse and, 117–18
  on fiscal and social policy, 227–32
  fiscal and social policy and rulings by, 232–4
  identity review by, 96–9
  legal pluralism and, 102–7
  national law and, 88–9
  primacy of EU law and rulings of, 90–6
  security *vs* fundamental rights in, 303–4
  transnational law and, 349–58
  ultra vires jurisdiction of, 92–6
Germany
  European monetary policy and, 178–83
  financial liability issues for, 192–5
  monetary union and, 183–7
  reunification of, 108–12
Gesamtentscheidung (comprehensive decision), 132–4, 135–6
  competition law and, 150–2, 161–4
  economic constitutionalization and, 136–8, 164–73
  fundamental rights and, 166–7
  implementation of microeconomic constitution and, 169–73
Gewerbeordnung liberalization, 166–7
GlaxoSmithKline case, 159n.76
Görgülü case, European Convention on Human Rights and, 101–2
gouvernement des juges (des experts), 172
government debt
  Eurozone crisis and, 187–92
  Maastricht Treaty provisions concerning, 181, 185
  strengthening of European economic governance and, 192–5
Greek debt crisis, 187–92
  strengthening of European economic governance and, 192–5
Grundnorms
  constitutional law and, 10–14
  legal diversity and, 82–3
  normative autonomy and, 53–9
  perspectivism and, 78–81
  radical pluralism and, 353–5
Grundsätze der Wirtschaftspolitik (Eucken), 174–5
Grzelczyk case, 249
Günther, Klaus, 113

Habermas, Jürgen, 42
Hague Programme (2004), 281, 297, 305n.70
Halberstam, Daniel, 106
Hallstein, Walter, 170, 213
harmonized model
  microeconomic constitution and, 172
  regulatory framework and, 153–5
Hart, H. L. A., 82
Hauer v Land Rheinland-Pfalz, 168–9, 324
Hayek, Friedrich, 130, 134–5, 266
healthcare
  access justice and, 265–8
  denationalization and deterritorialization of, 248–51
  internal market law and, 237–43
  for mobile workers and citizens, 243–8
heterarchical model, radical and dialogical pluralism and, 102–7
hierarchy of legal norms, European legal system and, 45–53
higher law, constitutional law as, 10–14
High Representative of the Union for Foreign Affairs and Security Policy, 285, 333
Hoffmann-La Roche v Commission, 148n.54
Holmes, Oliver Wendell, 136n.25
home country model
  free movement law and, 172
  regulatory framework and, 153–5
Honeywell case, 94–5
horizontal direct effect. *See also* indirect horizontal effect
  European law and, 63
  security constitutionalization and, 302–3, 308–9
'horizontal *Solange*', security *vs* fundamental rights and, 308–9
host country model
  microeconomic constitution and, 172
  regulatory framework and, 153–5
Hurri, Samuli, 274, 317
hybrid space
  of legal pluralism, 86–8
  political dimensions of economic constitutionalization and, 169–73
  radical pluralism and, 102–7
  transnational law and, 349–58

identity review
  in German Constitutional Court, 90–6
  legal pluralism and, 96–9, 102–7
illocution
  European constitutional discourse and, 112–20
  legal discourse and, 120–4
  perspectivism and, 78–81
  speech acts, 120

immigration
Amsterdam Treaty on free movement of persons, 278–84
freedom and justice and issues of, 296–301
state of emergency provisions and, 291n.44
impediment-based competition, economic constitutionalism and, 132–4
imperative reasons principle, social policy of Member States and, 234–7
implicit social theory of law, 35–7
implied powers doctrine, ECJ jurisprudence and, 327–8
independence, primacy principle and, 65–8
indirect horizontal effect, 63–5
individual rights
derogation of free movement and, 273–8
direct effect of European law and, 60–8
European constitutional law and, 50–3
evolution of individualization and, 108–12
security constitutionalization and, 272–3, 301–12, 316–18
transnational constitutionalism and, 37–44
inflation rate, EMU eligibility and, 183–7
information sharing, security constitutionalization and, 294–6
infrastructure services, internal market law and, 237–43
institutional autonomy, 53–9
European transnationalization and intergovernmentalism and, 331–3
institutional balance principle, European polity and, 329–31
institutional interlocking, transnational constitutionalism and, 37–44
instrumentality, economic *vs* fundamental rights and, 168–9
insurance-based healthcare and social security systems, denationalization and deterritorialization of, 248–51
integrated model
Community method and, 333–40
European legal diversity and, 83–6
primacy principle and, 65–8
rule of law and, 213–14
integration by stealth, transnationalism and intergovernmentalism and, 333–40
Interacting Legal Systems model, 67n.46
Intercreditor Agreement, 187–92
inter-dimensional relationality, European constitution and, 9–10
intergovernmental institutions
European constitutional discourse and, 112–20
European constitutionalism and, 108–12
European polity and, 331–3
Eurozone crisis and, 187–92
financial assistance and, 206–9
institutional interlocking and, 37–44
security constitutionalization and, 312–18
security provisions in Amsterdam Treaty and, 278–84
security provisions in Lisbon Treaty and, 287–8
interlegality
legal diversity and, 85–6
legal pluralism and, 102–7
perspectivism and, 78–81
transnational constitutionalism and, 37–44
interlocutionary speech acts, European constitutional discourse and, 120–4
internal markets
competition law and, 157–64
national welfare policy and, 234–7
security constitutionalization and, 275–6
welfare services and, 237–43
internal security
Amsterdam Treaty and development of, 278–84
as EU objective, 278
Internal Security Strategy for the European Union, 292–4, 304–12
international agreements
ECJ jurisprudence concerning, 59, 140
principle of conferral and, 214–16
stability mechanisms and, 202–3
International Court of Justice, transnational law and, 349–58
Internationale Handelsgesellschaft case, 57–8, 66n.44
Solange doctrine and, 90–6
international institutions of power
perspectivism concerning, 343
Solange doctrine and, 90–6
international law
European constitutionalism and, 108–12
federalism and, 345–8
internal effects of, 60–8
legal autonomy of Member States and, 53–9
legal diversity and, 82–3
perspectivism and, 340–58
perspectivism on, 340–58
primacy principle and, 65–8

international law (*cont.*)
security constitutionalization and, 272–3, 275–6
transnational law and, 349–58
International Monetary Fund (IMF), Eurozone crisis and, 189
interpretive autonomy, 53–9
legal pluralism and, 102–7
ultra vires review and, 92–6
inter-state commerce, constitutional principles and, 164–9
invalidation, primacy principle and, 69–71
invocabilité, French legal principle of, 68
Irish Republican Army (IRA), 274–5
Italian constitutional court, national law and, 88–9

Jellinek, Georg, 314
judicial system
Amsterdam Treaty on cooperation of, 278–84
European constitutional discourse and, 112–20
juridical constitution and, 108–12
security provisions in Lisbon Treaty on cooperation of, 287
juridical constitutionalization
autonomy and, 60–8
constitutional functions and, 28–37
content-based legitimacy of, 34–5
direct applicability and direct effect and, 141n.36
ECJ jurisdiction and, 50–3, 327–8
economic constitutionalization and, 136–8, 148–50
European constitutional theory and, 321–3
European legal system and, 45–53
Eurozone regime and, 199–209
framing of, 9–10, 45–77, 319–20
fundamental rights and, 92
judicial citizenship and, 108–12
legal diversity and, 83–6
Member State law and, 88–9
multidimensionality of, 320–1
perspectivism and, 340–58
political constitution and, 45
qualified monism and, 59
relationality and, 21–8
theoretical divergence concerning, 65–8
Treaties' provisions on, 50–3
welfare services for mobile workers and citizens and, 243–8
justice
complementary *vs* conflicting concepts of, 265–8
security constitutionalization and, 296–301
justification for restriction, free movement law and, 141–50

K.4 Committee, 277n.11
Kadi case, 49–50
constitutional identity in, 338–40
Eurozone regime and, 202
legal autonomy of European law and, 57
positioning of international law in European law hierarchy and, 59–60
security *vs* fundamental rights in, 309–11
transnational law in, 352
Kadi II case, 310n.83
Kantian philosophy, perspectivism and, 78–81
Keck formula, 33–4
free movement law and, 141–50
Kelsen, Hans
cultural levels of law and theory of, 85–6
European constitutionalism and theories of, 114
legal diversity and theory of, 81–6
legal order in theory of, 324–6
normative autonomy and, 53–9
perspectivism and theory of, 78–81
pure theory of law of, 10–14, 45–53
radical pluralism and, 102–7, 353–5
supremacy *vs* primacy and, 69–71
Keynesian economics, competition law and, 160–1
Kohll case, 247–8
Kokott AG, 191, 202–3n.51
Kompetenz-Kompetenz ruling, 58–9
European constitutional discourse and, 118–20
legal pluralism and, 326–7
primacy principle and, 342
radical pluralism and, 102–7, 353–5
ultra vires review and, 90, 92–6
Koskenniemi, Martti, 79–80
radical pluralism and, 102–7, 353–5
Kücükdeveci case, 94n.26
Kumm, Mattias, 106n.44

Laband, Paul, 314
labour law
free movement of workers and, 273–8
primacy of national welfare state and, 232–4, 237
regulatory private law and, 257–65
labour mobility, macroeconomic constitutionalization and, 251–6
Laval case, 27–8, 146n.50
economic *vs* fundamental rights and, 168–9

social justice and, 265–8
social policy of Member States and, 234–7, 251–6
legal actors
constitutional speech acts and, 120–4
European constitutional discourse and, 112–20
in Kelsenian theory, 83–6
perspectivism of, 78–81
legal certainty, primacy *vs* direct effect and, 70
legal culture
European constitutional discourse and, 112–20
European law and, 326
interlegality and, 85–6
perspectivism and, 78–81
legal disciplines, perspectivism and, 78–81, 355–8
legal diversity
perspectivism and, 81–6
radical and dialogical pluralism and, 102–7
legality, principle of, principle of conferral and, 214–16
legal order
in European law, 324–5
legal diversity and, 81–6
perspectivism and, 78–81
pluralism of, 86–8
legal perspectivism. *See* perspectivism
legal pluralism
basic principles of, 86–8
conflict *vs* dialogue and, 102–7
European constitution and, 3–4, 5–9
European Convention on Human Rights and, 99–102
European fundamental rights and, 88–102
European law and, 326–7
exclusive perspectivism and, 102–7
identity and, 96–9
legal diversity and, 81–6
radical pluralism and, 102–7
security *vs* fundamental rights and, 304–12
ultra vires review of EU institutional competence and, 93–4
legal positivism, polycentricity and doctrine of, 81–6
legal practices
constitutional theory and, 15–17
European constitutional discourse and, 112–20
legal roles, perspectivism and, 78–81
legal scholarship
doctrinal research *vs*, 5–9
European constitutional discourse and, 112–20
perspectivism in, 78–81
legal sources, polycentricity and doctrine of, 81–6
legal theory, economic constitutionalism and, 134–6
legislative acts
pre-emption doctrine and, 202–6
regulatory private law and, 261n.67
legislative competences, economic constitutionalization and, 136–40, 148–50
legisprudence (*Gesetzgebungslehre*), 114
legitimacy principles
constitutional functions and, 28–37
of macroeconomic constitutionalization, 217–26
political dimensions of economic constitutionalization and, 169–73
security constitutionalization and, 316–18
transnationalism and intergovernmentalism and, 333–40
Leitbild social security coordination, 243–8
Lepsius, Oliver, 303–4
Les Verts v Parliament ruling, 11–12, 55
rule of law and, 211
lex digitalis, 351
lex loci laboris, welfare services and, 248–51
lex mercatoria, 351
lex posteriori principle
positioning of European law and, 70–1
primacy principle and, 65–8
lex specialis, positioning of European law and, 70–1
lex sportiva, 351
Limburg principles, 255
limitation
constitutional relationality and, 21–8
derogation and, 270n.2
security constitutionalization and, 269–73
Lindseth, Peter, 3–4, 43, 348–9
Lisbon case, 93–4, 117–18
constitutional identity and, 339n.17
democratic input legitimacy and, 218
fiscal *vs* social policy in, 230
Lisbon Treaty
absence of primacy principle in, 65–8
competition law and, 157–64
core welfare services and sovereignty in provisions of, 237–43
'de-constitutionalization' and, 5–9
democratic input legitimacy and, 217–26

Lisbon Treaty (*cont.*)
elimination of federalist connotations in, 5
European Council establishment and, 331–3
European legal system and, 45–53
Eurozone regime in, 199–209
free movement provisions in, 297n.59
fundamental rights law and, 92
law on universal services in, 264–5
Member State constitutionalism and, 41–4
Member State identity in, 96–9
national courts' positioning and, 88–9
parasitic legitimacy and, 35–7
pre-emption doctrine and, 72–4, 202–6
Protocol on shared competences, 72–4, 202–6
security constitutionalization and, 282, 284–8, 315–16
security *vs* fundamental rights and, 304–12
social constitutionalization and, 227–32
terrorism provisions in, 294–6
transnational constitutionalism and, 37–44
Loan Facility Agreement, 187–92
Lochner v New York, 121, 136n.25
locus standi proceedings, European Union courts, 50–3
locutionary speech, 120
lois fondamentales, EU constitutional law and, 10–14
long-term interest rate, EMU eligibility and, 183–7
Luftsicherheitsgesetz ruling, 304n.67
Luhmann, Niklas, 9, 351
constitutional relationality, 21–8
European constitutionalism and theories of, 114
perspectivism and theory of, 78–81
radical pluralism and, 102–7
on state constitutions, 45
transnational law and, 353–5
Luisi and Carbone case, 247
'lump concepts', constitutional theory and, 11
Luxembourg Compromise, 136–8, 331–3

Maastricht case (German Constitutional Court), 38
direct input legitimacy and, 217–26
European constitutional discourse and, 117–18
Maastricht Treaty
Community Charter of Fundamental Social Rights of Workers and, 251–6
Community method and, 333–40
competences in, 48–9
competition law and, 161–4
Economic and Monetary Union provisions, 21–8
EMU and, 174–8
European Central Bank role and, 195–9
European Council establishment and, 331–3
Eurozone crisis and, 187–92
Eurozone regime and, 199–209
free movement law and, 143–4
fundamental rights and, 92
fundamental rights law and, 15–17
macroeconomic constitutionalization and, 174–83
Member State identity and, 96–9
open markets and free competition in, 153
political constitutionalization and, 34–5, 108–12
regulatory private law and, 257–65
rule of law in, 211–14
Schengen Convention and, 276–8
security constitutionalization and, 275–6
security *vs* fundamental rights and, 304–12
shared liability for government debt and, 181
Social Policy Protocol and Agreement, 21–8, 321–3
strengthening of European economic governance and, 192–5
transnationalism and intergovernmentalism and, 333–40
MacCormick, Neil, 22, 38, 102
macroeconomic constitutionalization
banking union proposals and, 195–9
crisis prevention/crisis management transition and, 187–92
Eurozone regime and, 199–209
framing of, 9–10
historical evolution of, 108–12, 174–8
legitimacy concerns for, 217–26
Maastricht principles and, 178–83
mutation of, 174–226
primacy of national welfare state and, 232–4
rule of law and, 209–17
social policy and, 227–32, 234–7, 251–6
Stability and Growth Pact and, 182–3
underlying economic assumptions in, 183–7
Majone, Giandomenico, 330–1
mandatory requirements doctrine, 235n.12

Mangold case, 65, 94–5
market access, free movement law and, 144–5
market economies
competition law and, 150–2, 153
economic constitutionalism and, 128–31, 134–6, 164–9
juridical constitutionalization and, 34–5
microeconomic constitutionalization and, 321–3
public interventionism and, 152
social policy and, 227–32, 251–6
substantive legitimacy and, 169–73
market justice, 265–8
Marleasing case, 64
materia constitutionis, European constitutionalization and, 21–2, 164–9
material constitution
concept of, 10–14
relationality and, 21–8
Maus, Ingeborg, 304
Melloni case, 99, 306–8
constitutional identity and, 340
Member State Ministers of Justice and Home Affairs, 275–8, 282–4
Community method and, 333–40
security *vs* fundamental rights and, 304–12
Member States, law and constitutions of. *See also* national constitutions and legislation
Amsterdam Treaty on free movement of persons and, 278–84
citizenship and, 37–44
Community method and, 333–40
competition law and, 146–8
complementarity and, 38–41
constitutional discourse and, 28–37, 112–20
convergence criteria and, 199–209
democratic input legitimacy and, 41–4, 217–26
demos and, 108–12
denationalization and deterritorialization of welfare services and, 248–51
derogations on security-related issues by, 273–8
direct applicability principle and, 62–3
ECB Outright Monetary Transactions programme and, 116–17
ECJ jurisdiction over legislation and, 50–3, 327–8
economic and juridical constitutionalization and, 321–3
economic constitutionalization and, 136–8, 164–9
European Commission and, 118–20
European Convention on Human Rights and, 99–102
European law primacy over, 60–8, 325–6
Eurozone crisis and, 187–92
federalism and, 345–8
financial markets' impact on, 186
fiscal and economic policy sovereignty and, 178–83
Fiscal Compact and cooperation of, 206–9
Founding Treaties and, 10–14
framing of, 9–10
free movement law and, 141–50
fundamental rights law and, 92, 304–12
horizontal direct effect and, 63, 308–9
identity and, 96–9
intergovernmental agreements and, 206–9
intergovernmentalism and, 333–40
interlegality and, 85–6
internal market law and welfare services and, 237–43
juridical and political constitutions and, 45
labour law and, 257–65
law on universal services and, 263–4
legal autonomy and, 53–9
legal diversity and, 83–6, 102–7, 174–8
legal practices and, 15–17
macroeconomic constitutionalization and, 209–17, 251–6
monetary and economic policy and, 174–8
monetary policy and, 178–83
perspectivism and, 78–81, 340–58
political dimensions of economic constitutionalization and, 169–73
positioning of, 88–9
pre-emption doctrine and, 72–4, 202–6
primacy of national welfare state and, 232–4
primacy principle and, 65–8
public interventionism and, 155–7
regulatory private law and, 257–65
rule of law and Union relations with, 214–16
security constitutionalization and, 272–3, 284–8, 304–12
social policy and, 171–2, 227–32, 251–6
state liability for breaches, European law obligations, 63–5
strengthening of European economic governance and, 192–5
supremacy principle and, 70–1, 72–4
TEEC legal system and, 140n.34
transfer of sovereign rights by, 92–6

Member States (*cont.*)
transnationalism and, 37–44, 312–18, 333–40, 349–58
transnationalization and, 312–18
Trevi framework for security and, 275–6
Memoranda of Understanding (MoU)
Eurozone crisis and, 187–92
strengthening of European economic governance and, 192–5
strict conditionality conditions in, 251–6
merger control, competition law and, 146–8, 157–64
Merger Regulation, economic constitutionalization and, 148–50
Mestmäcker, Ernst-Joachim, 151, 159–60
meta-language
European constitutionalism and, 5
second-order discourse and, 5–9
Micklitz, Hans-W., 231, 265
access justice theory of, 265–8
microeconomic constitutionalization
banking union proposals and, 195–9
competition law and, 157–64
European Commission and, 118–20
framing of, 9–10
free movement law and, 141–50
historical evolution of, 108–12, 127–36
Member State legal diversity and, 174–8
origin-based legitimacy and, 28–37
overview of, 127–73
political dimensions of, 169–73
relationality and, 21–8
rule of law and, 209–17
sectoral issues in, 321–3
security constitutionalization and, 273–8
social policy and, 227–32, 234–7
underlying controversies concerning, 150–64
mixed government model, European polity and, 329–31
mobile workers
denationalization and deterritorialization of welfare services and, 248–51
derogations on security-related issues and, 273–8
social justice for, 265–8
welfare services for, 239
Moldovan Constitution, 165–6
Monar, Jörg, 304–5
Monetarist approach
economic policy and, 183–7
monetary policy
democratic input legitimacy and, 217–26
ECB role in, 195–9
economic policy and, 183–7
Eurozone crisis and, 187–92
Maastricht principles for common European policy, 178–83
macroeconomic constitutionalization and, 174–8
strengthening of European economic governance and, 192–5
monist model
direct effect of European law and, 61
legal diversity and, 82–3
primacy principle and, 65–8
monitoring procedures, Eurozone crisis management and, 192–5
Monnet, Jean, 41–2, 331–3
Mont Pelerin Society, 130, 134–5
moral hazard
banking union proposals and, 198–9
fiscal policy in Maastricht model and, 183–7
government spending and borrowing and, 181
Müller-Armack, Alfred, 171
multidimensionality
constitutional dimensions and, 320–1
in European constitutional discourse, 118–20
multilateral surveillance
Eurozone crisis and, 187–92
Eurozone regime and, 199–209
Maastricht Treaty provisions for, 181–3
pre-emption doctrine and, 202–6
strengthening of European economic governance and, 192–5
municipal law
European Convention on Human Rights and, 99–102
positioning of, 88–9
transnational law and, 349–58
transposition of directives and, 70–1
Müssler, Werner, 161–2
mutual positioning
fundamental rights pluralism and, 99–102
transnational constitutionalism and, 37–44
mutual recognition principle
freedom and justice in security constitutionalization and, 296–301
free movement law and, 141–50, 235n.12
fundamental rights *vs* security and, 304–12
legal diversity and, 83–6
market regulation and, 153–5
security provisions in Amsterdam Treaty and, 280–2
security provisions in Lisbon Treaty and, 284–8
transnationalization and, 312–18

national central banks
  European Central Bank and, 195–9
  European monetary policy and, 178–83
  Eurozone crisis and, 187–92
national constitutions and legislation, 37–44. *See also* Member States, law and constitutions of
  democratic legitimacy and, 41–4, 217–26
  denationalization and deterritorialization of welfare services and, 248–51
  direct effect and, 68–9n.49
  economic constitutionalization and, 136–8
  European constitutional discourse and, 118–20
  European economic constitution and, 164–9
  European legal system and, 45–53
  Eurozone crisis and, 321–3
  Fiscal Compact and, 206–9
  free movement law and, 141–50
  fundamental rights law and, 92
  German Constitutional Court review of primacy of, 90–6
  identity of, 96–9
  indirect horizontal effect and, 63–5
  individual rights and, 60–8
  interpretive autonomy of, 92–6
  legal diversity and, 83–6
  ordoliberal economic constitutionalism and, 131–6
  positioning function of, 88–9
  primacy of national welfare state and, 232–4
  primacy principle and, 65–8
  social constitutionalization and, 227–32
  strengthening of European economic governance and, 192–5
  supremacy principle and, 69–71
  transnationalization and, 312–18
  transposition of directives and, 70–1
national courts
  democratic input legitimacy and, 221–6
  duty of application in, 69n.51
  European constitutional discourse and, 112–20, 328–9
  European Court of Justice and, 102–7
  fiscal and economic policy and, 209–17
  institutional interlocking and, 37–44
  interpretive autonomy of, 92–6
  security *vs* fundamental rights in, 304–12
National Health Service (NHS) systems
  denationalization and deterritorialization of welfare services and, 248–51
  internal market law and, 237–43
nationalistic ideology, democratic input legitimacy and, 217–26
national parliaments
  intergovernmental financial agreements and, 206–9
  transnational constitutionalism and, 37–44
national private law systems, economic constitutionalization and, 167n.91
national welfare policy
  denationalization and deterritorialization of, 248–51
  internal market law and, 237–43
  microeconomic constitutionalization and, 234–7
  mobile workers and citizens, 243–8
  regulatory private law and, 257–65
  social justice and, 265–8
national welfare state
  European constitutionalism and, 227–32
  primacy of, 232–4
ne bis in idem principle, 93–4, 95–6
  Schengen Convention and, 275–6
  security *vs* fundamental rights and, 304–12
negative externalities, fiscal policy in Maastricht model and, 183–7
negative integration
  social policy of Member States and, 234–7
  welfare services for mobile workers and citizens and, 243–8
neofunctionalism, European constitutionalization, 112n.7
neoliberal movement
  competition law and, 161–4
  economic constitutionalism and, 130n.10
  economic integration and, 151n.58
Netherlands, Constitutional Treaty failure in, 4–5
Neumann, Franz L., 129n.6
neutrality principle, macroeconomic constitutionalization and, 183–7, 251–6
New Austrian School, 135n.23
no-bailout clause
  European Central Bank and, 195–9
  Eurozone crisis management and, 190–2
  in Maastricht Treaty, 181, 185
non-economic services of general interest, internal market law and, 242
non-state actors, free movement law and, 145–6
normative autonomy, 53–9
normative legal principles
  autonomy of European law and, 53–9
  constitutional culture and, 15–17

normative legal principles (*cont.*)
European constitutional discourse and, 112–20
first-order discourse and, 5–9
legal diversity and, 83–6
perspectivism and, 78–81
pluralism of, 86–8
state legal orders and, 45–53
supremacy and, 65–8
Nörr, Knut Wolfgang, 129–30
Norwegian Constitution of 1814, 31–3
Nozick, Robert, 266
NS and Others case, 307–9

object language, European constitutionalism and, 5
obligatory deposits, Eurozone crisis management and, 192–5
obstacle pre-emption, 72–4
Omega Spielhallen- und Automatenaufstellungs-GmbH case, 27–8, 168–9
'One Big Legal System' model, 67n.46
Ordnungspolitik
democratic input legitimacy and, 221–6
implementation of microeconomic constitution and, 169–73
monetary union and, 183–7
ordoliberal economic constitutionalism and, 131–6
ordoliberalism
banking union proposals and, 199
competition law and, 150–2, 157–69
democratic input legitimacy and, 221–6
economic constitutions and, 127–36
European Central Bank activities and, 195–9
European monetary policy and, 178–83
free movement law and, 152, 164–9
macroeconomic policy and, 174–8
market economies and, 153
monetary policy and, 183–7
political dimensions of economic constitutions and, 169–73
rule of law and, 213–14
ordre public, 317
security constitutionalization and, 273–8
organized crime, Trevi framework for security and, 275–6
organizing function, constitutional object and, 28–37
origin-based legitimacy, constitutional functions and, 28–37
output legitimacy, democratic input legitimacy and, 221–6
Outright Monetary Transactions (OMT) programme, 116–17, 118–20, 195–9
democratic input legitimacy and, 221–6

pacemaker constitution, evolution of, 108–12
parasitic legitimacy, 35–7
Paris Treaty on the European Coal and Steel Community, 41, 51, 109, 273
Part of Member States' Legal Systems Model, 67n.46
Patient Rights Directive (2011) (European Commission), 243–51
Pech, Laurent, 213–14
performance-based competition, economic constitutionalism and, 132–4
perlocutionary speech acts, 120
discourse analysis and, 120–4
perspectivism of legal disciplines and, 355–8
perspectivism, 78–107
European constitutionalism and, 17–18
European law and, 326–7
legal culture and, 102–7
of legal disciplines, 355–8
legal diversity and, 81–6
in legal theory, 78–81
Pescatore, Pierre, 68, 325
Philip Morris case, 148
Poiares Maduro, Miguel
on economic constitutionalization, 152
on legal autonomy, 57
on legal pluralism, 102–7
political dimensions of economic constitutionalization and, 169–73
on public interventionism, 155–7
on social policy and constitutional theory, 227–32
police operations
Amsterdam Treaty on cooperation of, 278–84
security provisions in Lisbon Treaty on cooperation of, 287
security *vs* fundamental rights in, 303–4
Trevi framework for security and, 275–6
Police Working Group on Terrorism, 282–4
policy orientation
constitutional law and legitimacy of, 34–5
legal practices and, 15–17, 324–5
macroeconomic constitutionalization and, 174–8
political constitutionalization
citizenship and, 108–12
constitutional functions and, 28–37

European constitutional theory and, 321–3
framing of, 9–10, 319–20, 329
fundamental rights and, 92
intergovernmentalism and, 333–40
juridical constitution and, 45
relationality and, 21–8
speech acts and, 120–4
technocratic policy and, 41–4
transnationalization and, 331–40
welfare services for mobile workers and citizens and, 243–8
political dimensions of economic constitutions, 169–73
neutrality in economic policy and, 183–7
polity building
constitutional functions and, 28–37
European institutional organization and, 329–31
speech acts and, 120–4
polycentricity, legal diversity and, 81–6
positioning function
constitutional object and, 28–37
European law and, 59–60, 70–1
international law and, 59–60
mutual positioning and, 37–44
national courts' role in, 88–9
Poucet and Pistre case, 239
pouvoir constituant, constitutional theory and, 13–14, 108–12
power, security constitutionalization and role of, 294–6
precedence, in European law, 69–71
Prechel, Sacha, 68
pre-emption doctrine
Eurozone regime and, 202–6
as supremacy sub-principle, 72–4
prevention, security constitutionalization and, 294
price stability
European Central Bank activities and, 195–9
European monetary policy and, 178–83
neutrality in economic policy and, 183–7
open market economy and, 174–8
primacy, principle of
direct effect and, 65–8, 70
disapplication and invalidation and, 69–71
ECJ jurisprudence and, 327–8
economic constitutionalization and, 136–40
European law and, 65–8
exclusion and substitution aspects of, 70n.53
free movement law and, 141–50
identity and, 96–9
international law and, 340–58
juridical constitution, 28–37
legal certainty and, 70
national courts and, 113
supremacy principle *vs*, 69–71
private law
Eurozone crisis and, 187–92
integration with public law, 132–4
national private law systems, 167n.91
regulatory private law, 231, 257–65
rule of law and, 213–14
private parties, economic constitutionalization and, 136–8
privatization, of free movement law, 145–6
proportionality test
economic *vs* fundamental rights and, 168–9
European legal system and, 45–53
free movement law and, 141–50
fundamental rights *vs* security, 311
public interventionism and, 155–7
security provisions in Amsterdam Treaty and, 280–2
social policy of Member States and, 234–7
protection, duty of, security constitutionalization and, 302–3
Prüm Convention, 315
public finances criteria
EMU eligibility and, 183–7
European Central Bank and, 195–9
financial markets and, 186
public interventionism
banking union proposals and, 199
centralized/decentralized variants, 155–7
economic constitutionalism and, 152, 164–9
microeconomic constitutionalization and, 321–3
public law
integration with private law, 132–4
publicization of competition law, 145–6
public order, security constitutionalization and, 301–12
public security, security constitutionalization and, 273–8
Pupino ruling, security provisions in Amsterdam Treaty and, 278–84

qualitative majority voting (QMV), 331–3

radical pluralism
conflictual approach and, 102–7
transnational law and, 353–5

ratione personae, free movement law and, 145–6
Rechtsgemeinschaft principle, rule of law and, 211–14, 321–3
Rechtsstaat state model
competition law and, 161–4
constitutional identity and, 333–40
European legal system and, 45–53
European polity and, 329–31
in ordoliberal theory, 131–6
political dimensions of economic constitutions and, 169–73
polity and constitutional functions in, 28–37
restrictive function in, 269–73
rule of law and, 211–14
security constitutionalization and, 301–12
redistribution
democratic input legitimacy and, 217–26
Maastricht Treaty fiscal policy and, 183–7
primacy of national welfare state and, 232–4
social constitutionalization and, 227–32
referential legal order
legal diversity and, 83–6
legal pluralism and, 102–7
regime change, economic constitutions and, 164–9
Regulation 17/62, 139–41, 159–60
Regulation 407/2010, 205
Regulation 1175/2011, 194–5
Regulation 1408/71, 244–50
regulations
direct effect of European law and, 62–3
ECJ jurisprudence concerning, 140–1
Eurozone regime and, 199–209
integrated model and, 65–8
market forces and, 152–3
strengthening of European economic governance and, 192–5
regulatory competition, free movement law and, 141–50
regulatory private law, social justice and, 265–8
relationality, 21–44
constitutional dimensions, 9–10, 21–8
European constitutionalism and, 17–18
rent-seeking behaviour
competition law and, 150–2
economic constitutionalism and, 131–6
rescue packages
ECB role in, 195–9
Eurozone crisis and, 187–92
Eurozone regime and, 199–209
principle of conferral and, 214–16
strengthening of European economic governance and, 192–5
residence-based social security services, 248–51
restrictive function
constitutional object and, 28–37
economic constitutionalization and, 164–9
European legal system and, 45–53, 324–5
free movement law and, 141–50, 234–7
state constitutions, 269–73
result-based legitimacy, 34–5
reversed majority voting, 192–5, 331–3
revolutionary constitutionalism, constituent power and, 108–12
right to establishment, security constitutionalization and, 274n.5
risk assessment, security constitutionalization and, 292–4
Rödl, Florian, 227, 229
Röpke, Wilhelm, 130
Rote Armee, 274–5
rule of law
European Union and, 209–17
security constitutionalization and, 316–18
state of exception and, 289–96
rule pre-emption, 72–4

safety, security constitutionalization and, 301–12
Säger ruling, 144n.44, 144n.45, 236n.15
Sarmiento, Daniel, 307
Savigny, Carl Friedrich, 21–2
Scharpf, Fritz, 34–5, 219
Schengen Agreement, 275–6, 312–18
Schengen Information System, 282
Schilling, Theodor, 54
Schmidberger case, 27–8, 168–9
Schmitt, Carl, 13–14, 122–4, 289–91
ordoliberal economic constitutionalism and, 131–6
Schuman, Robert, 331
Schütze, Robert, 346
Schweitzer, Heike, 159–60
secondary legislation
economic constitutionalization and, 136–8
Eurozone regime and, 199–209
integrated model and, 65–8
intergovernmental financial agreements and, 206–9
international law and, 59–60
primacy principle and, 65–8
social constitutionalization and, 227–32
welfare services for mobile workers and citizens and, 243–8

second-order discourse
economic constitutionalization and, 136–8
European constitutionalism and, 5–9, 112–20
sectoral constitutions
complementarity and, 38–41
constitutional functions and, 28–37
ECJ jurisdiction and, 50–3, 327–8
economic, social, and security dimensions, 18, 319–20
in European constitutional discourse, 118–20
framing of, 9–10
multidimensionality, 320–1
relationality and, 21–8
Securities Market Programme (ECB), 195–9
security constitutionalization
Amsterdam Treaty and evolution of, 278–84
anti-constitutional elements in, 312–18
framing of, 9–10
freedom, security and justice and, 296–301
functional primacy, 320–1
fundamental rights and, 301–12, 321–3
historical evolution of, 108–12, 273–8
insecurity of, 269–318
Lisbon Treaty and, 284–8
paradoxes within, 269–73
relationality and, 21–8
restrictive functions of, 269–73
risk assessment and, 292–4
sectoral dimensions, 319–20
states of emergency and, 269–73, 289–96
security of the person concept, 304–12
self-executing treaty rules, 62–3
economic constitutionalization and, 136–8
self-regulation, market forces and, 152–3
separation of powers, state of exception and, 289–96
September 11, 2001 attacks
anti-terrorist legislation following, 291–2
security constitution and, 108–12, 282–4
Services Directive (2006) (European Commission), 243–8
services of general economic interest principle
core welfare services and, 237–43
law on universal services and, 264–5
sex trafficking, security provisions in Amsterdam Treaty and, 282
shared competence
democratic legitimacy and, 217–26
Lisbon Protocol on, 72–4, 202–6
shared liability for government debt, no-bailout clause in Maastricht Treaty and, 181
Signatory States, 99–102
Simmenthal case, 69n.51
sincere cooperation, duty of, 63–5
pre-emption doctrine and, 202–6
single currency, economic convergence criteria and, 183–7
Single European Act (SEA)
competition law and, 161–4
ECJ jurisprudence and, 327–8
economic and monetary union and, 174–8
economic constitutionalization and, 136–8
European legal system and, 45–53
law on universal services and, 264–5
social policy of Member States and, 234–7
ultra vires jurisdiction and, 92–6
single resolution mechanism (SRM), banking union proposals and, 195–9
single supervisory mechanism (SSM), banking union proposals and, 195–9
Sinzheimer, Hugo, 128–31
six-pack regulations, 192–5
Eurozone regime and, 199–209
pre-emption doctrine and, 202–6
Skinner, Quentin, 122
Snell, Jukka, 154–5, 172
social constitutionalization
complementary *vs* conflicting concepts of justice and, 265–8
consequences of macroeconomic constitutionalization and, 251–6
denationalization and deterritorialization of welfare services and, 248–51
economic constitutionalization and, 321–3
European constitution as, 227–32
framing of, 9–10, 227–68
free movement law and, 234–7
functional primacy, 320–1
primacy of national welfare state and, 232–4
regulatory private law and, 257–65
relationality and, 21–8
sectoral dimensions, 319–20
social citizenship and, 108–12
welfare services for mobile workers and citizens and, 243–8
socialist states, economic constitutions and, 164–9
social justice, 265–8

social market economy
political dimensions of economic constitutionalization and, 169–73
social constitutionalization and, 227–32
social policy
constitutional functions and, 21–8
economic constitutionalization and, 167–8
integration of public and private law and, 132–4
Maastricht Treaty fiscal policy and, 183–7
Member State sovereignty and, 171–2
for mobile workers and citizens, 243–8
security constitutionalization and, 301–12
social constitutionalization and, 227–32
social justice and, 265–8
Social Protocol, regulatory private law and, 257–65
social security services
denationalization and deterritorialization of, 248–51
internal market law and, 237–43
for mobile workers and European citizens, 243–8
soft law
fiscal and economic policy and, 209–17
healthcare for mobile workers and citizens and, 243–8
macroeconomic policy and, 174–8
strengthening of European economic governance and, 192–5
Solange doctrine
European Court of Human Rights and, 99–102
fundamental rights law and, 90–6
security *vs* fundamental rights and, 308–9
transnational law and, 349–58
ultra vires review of EU institutional competence, 92–6
solidaristic social justice, 265–8
Solidarity Clause
EU anti-terrorism strategies and, 282–4
state of exception and, 291–2
solidarity principle
denationalization and deterritorialization of welfare services and, 248–51
internal market law and welfare services and, 237–43
primacy of national welfare state and, 232–4
social rights and, 251–6
Sonderweg doctrine, economic constitutionalization and, 140–1
sovereignty
AFSJ provisions and issues of, 278–84
black box model and, 81–6
democratic input legitimacy and, 217–26
denationalization and deterritorialization of welfare services and, 248–51
direct effect of European law and, 60–8
European Central Bank and national fiscal sovereignty, 195–9
Eurozone crisis and, 187–92
Eurozone regime and issues of, 199–209
fiscal policy responsibility and, 183–7
internal market law and welfare services and, 237–43
of Member State fiscal and economic policy, 178–83
Member State social policy and, 171–2
pre-emption doctrine and, 202–6
security constitutionalization and, 272–3, 276–8, 284–8
security provisions in Lisbon Treaty and, 287–8
social constitutionalization and, 227–32
Solange doctrine and, 90–6
Solidarity Clause provisions concerning, 284–8
state of exception and, 289–96
strengthening of European economic governance and, 192–5
transnational constitutionalism and, 37–44
transnationalization and, 312–18
Spaak Report, 153n.64, 159, 161, 174–5
speech act theory
ECJ jurisprudence and, 327–8
elements of, 120
European constitutional discourse and, 112–20
legal discourse and, 120–4
macroeconomic constitutionalization and, 174–8
national courts and, 328–9
perspectives on constitutional discourse and, 120–4
social policy and, 243–8
state of exception and, 289–96
Stability and Growth Pact (SGP)
development of, 179–81
Eurozone crisis and, 187–92
Eurozone regime and, 199–209
excessive deficit sanctions and, 177–8
fiscal policy and, 183–7
macroeconomic constitutionalization and, 182–3
pre-emption doctrine and, 202–6
strengthening of European economic governance and, 192–5

state constitutions
  European economic constitutions and, 164–9
  federalism and, 345–8
  free movement law and, 141–50
  fundamental rights and, 165–6
  German legal scholarship concerning, 108n.1
  legal orders, substantive coherence and, 45–53
  legal pluralism and, 86–8
  legal practices and, 15–17
  legitimacy of, 34–5
  Lisbon Treaty security provisions and, 284–8
  macroeconomic policies and, 178
  market justice and, 265–8
  neutrality in economic policy and, 183–7
  as normative entity, 108–12
  in ordoliberal theory, 131–6
  political dimensions of economic constitutions and, 169–73
  primacy of national welfare state and, 232–4
  relationality and, 21–8
  restrictive functions of, 269–73
  security provisions in Amsterdam Treaty and, 280–2
  security *vs* fundamental rights in, 302–3
  strengthening of European economic governance and, 192–5
state liability
  Eurozone crisis and, 192–5
  supremacy principle and, 69–71
state of exception, security constitutionalization and, 289–96
states of emergency
  risk assessment and, 292–4
  security constitutionalization and, 269–73, 289–96
Stauder v Stadt Uhm, 91
Stockholm Programme (2010), 280–2, 296–301, 316–18
Strasbourg jurisprudence
  European Convention on Human Rights and, 99–102
  transnational law and, 349–58
Streit, Manfred E., 161–2
strict conditionality of financial assistance
  Eurozone crisis management and, 190
  social services cuts and, 251–6
  strengthening of European economic governance and, 192–5
Stufenbau (legal norms)
  constitutional law and, 10–14
  European legal systems and, 45–53
  legal diversity and, 82–6
  supremacy *vs* primacy and, 70–1
subsidiarity, principle of
  European legal system and, 45–53
  pre-emption doctrine and, 72–4
  rule of law and, 214–16
substantive coherence, European legal system, 45–53
substantive constitutionalization, doctrine *vs* theory, 108–12
substantive legitimacy
  constitutional functions and, 28–37
  political dimensions of economic constitutionalization and, 169–73
  principle-oriented constitutionalism and, 34–5
substitution, primacy of European law and, 69–70
sui generis approach, international law and, 344–5
summarizing constitutions, European constitutional theory and, 321–3
supplementary pension schemes, internal market law and, 237–43
supremacy principle
  competition law and, 157–64
  direct effect and, 325–6
  economic constitutionalization and, 136–8
  European law and, 10–14, 50–3, 69–71, 321–3
  integration and, 65–8
  pre-emption as sub-principle of, 72–4
  pre-emption doctrine and, 202–6
surface-level doctrine
  European economic constitutions and national constitutions and, 164–9
  legal diversity and, 326
  security constitutions and, 269–73
  social constitutionalization and, 227–32
Swedish Constitution, 31
symbolic legitimacy, constitutional functions and, 28–37
systemic pluralism, 86–8
system legitimacy, constitutional law, 34–5

Tampere Conclusions, 280–2, 296–301
  security *vs* fundamental rights and, 304–12
taxation
  European economic governance and, 192–5
  Eurozone crisis and, 187–92
  internal market law and welfare services and, 237–43
  macroeconomic constitutionalization and, 183–7

taxation (*cont.*)
national welfare state and, 232–4
primacy of national welfare state and right of, 232–4
welfare services financing through, 248–51
technocratic policy, transnational constitutionalism and, 41–4
TeliaSonera, 158n.72
territorial criteria, in black box model, 86–8
terrorism
derogation in free movement of workers and, 274–5
security constitutionalization and, 294–6
security provisions in Amsterdam Treaty and, 282–4
Trevi framework for security and, 275–6
Tesauro, AG, 152
Teubner, Gunther, 23–4, 80, 354–5
TFEU
AFSJ provisions in, 284–8
anti-discrimination law and, 257–65
conferral principle and, 214–16
constitutional discourse and, 118–20
direct effect of European law and, 60–8
directives provisions, 62–3
economic constitutionalization and, 136–40, 148–50
enhanced cooperation in, 206–9
European Central Bank activities and, 195–9
European legal system and, 50–3
Eurozone crisis and modifications to, 187–92
on Eurozone regime, 199–209
excessive deficit procedures and, 181–2
free movement law and, 141–50
indirect horizontal effect and, 63–5
internal market law and welfare services and, 237–43
internal security issues and, 269–73
legislative harmonization in, 172–3
Member States' monetary policy and, 174–8
monetary policy in, 178–83
positioning of European law and, 59–60
pre-emption doctrine and, 72–4, 202–6
primacy principle and, 65–8
security *vs* fundamental rights and, 304–12
social policy and, 227–32, 243–8
Solidarity Clause in, 282–8
strengthening of European economic governance and, 192–5
Thomas Pringle v Government of Ireland, 187–95, 202–3, 206–9
social rights and, 251–6
speech act theory and, 209–17
three-pillar EU structure, security constitutionalization and, 276–8
T-Mobile Netherlands case, 157n.70
Tobacco Advertising case, 48–9, 150n.57, 172–3
trade unionism, social policy of Member States and, 237
transcendentalism, perspectivism and, 78–81
transnational law and constitutions, 37–44
competition law and, 150–2, 157–64
complementarity and, 38–41
constitutional functions and, 28–37
economic constitutionalization and, 164–9
European constitutional discourse and, 118–20, 349–58
European Convention on Human Rights and, 99–102
European institutional organization and, 331–3
evolution of, 108–12
framing of, 9–10
free movement law and competition law and, 166
fundamental rights pluralism and, 99–102
legal diversity and, 85–6
legal pluralism and, 86–8
market justice and, 265–8
open markets and free competition and, 153
perspectivism and, 78–81, 355–8
primacy of national welfare state and, 232–4
public interventionism and, 155–7
security constitutionalization and, 269–73, 276–8, 312–18
security provisions in Amsterdam Treaty and, 278–84
social policy and, 227–32
transparency, security constitutionalization and, 316–18
treaty law. *See also* Founding Treaties; specific treaties
democratic input legitimacy and, 221–6
direct applicability and, 325–6
direct effect of European law and, 65–7
ECJ jurisprudence and, 327–8
economic constitutionalization and, 148–50, 164–9
EU anti-terrorism strategies and, 282–4
European Central Bank and, 197n.41
fiscal and economic policy and, 209–17

free movement law and, 141–50
legal cultures and, 102–7
national welfare regimes and, 237–43
social constitutionalization and, 227–32
social rights component in, 251–6
transnational constitutionalism and, 37–44
Treaty of Amsterdam
Area of Freedom, Security and Justice and, 49–50
core welfare services and sovereignty in provisions of, 241–2
intergovernmental agreements and, 206–9
law on universal services in, 264–5
regulatory private law and, 257–65
security constitution and, 108–12
social policy agreements in, 321–3
Treaty of Paris, pacemaker constitution and, 108–12
Treaty of Rome
Community method and, 333–40
competition law and, 150–2, 157–64
consumer law in, 262–3
economic constitutionalization and, 136–40, 152, 164–9
economic integration and, 127–8
establishment of EMU and, 174–8
European legal system and, 45–53
Eurozone crisis and, 187–92
evolution of security constitution and, 273–8
fundamental rights and, 90
juridical constitutionalization and, 34–5
legal autonomy and, 53–9
macroeconomic constitutionalization and, 174–8
microeconomic constitutionalization and, 21–8
pacemaker constitution and, 108–12
regulatory private law and, 257–65
social constitutionalization and, 227–32
social security issues and, 243–8
technocratic policy and, 41–4
transnationalism and, 331–3
welfare services for mobile workers and citizens and, 243–8
Treaty on Stability, Coordination and Governance (TSCG), 187–95
Eurozone regime and, 199–209
pre-emption doctrine and, 202–6
Treaty on the ESM, 187–92
Treaty on the European Economic Community (TEEC), 1n.1
competition law and, 146–8, 150–2, 157–64
direct effect of European law and, 60–8
directives, provisions in, 63n.37
economic constitutionalization and, 136–40, 148–50
free movement law and, 141–50
legal autonomy of, 53–9, 140–1
legislative harmonization in, 172–3
macroeconomic policies and, 174–8
regulatory private law and, 257–65
social policies and, 243–8
Treaty on the European Union (TEU), 16–17n.25
AFSJ provisions and, 278–84
citizenship issues and, 316–18
complementarity and transnational constitutionalism and, 38–41
constitutional identities and, 102–7
enhanced cooperation in, 206–9
European Commission powers, 221–6
European Convention on Human Rights and, 99–102
internal security issues and, 269–73
legal autonomy of European law and, 53–9
legal tradition and culture in, 85–6
list of objectives in, 109n.3
Member State constitutionalism and, 41–4
Member State identity in, 96–9
pre-emption doctrine and, 72–4
principle of conferral and, 214–16
rule of law in, 211–14
security provisions in, 284–8
security *vs* fundamental rights and, 304–12
social constitutionalization and, 227–32
social rights in, 251–6
transnationalism and intergovernmentalism and, 333–40
Trevi framework, security constitutionalization and, 275–6
trigger model
direct effect and primacy, 65–8
exclusion and substitution aspects of, 70n.53
Tsakouridis case, 49–50, 311
Twining, William, 82, 87
two-pack regulations, 192–5, 255n.54, 256n.56
Eurozone regime and, 199–209
pre-emption doctrine and, 202–6

ultima ratio review
of EU institutional competence, 92–6
Eurozone crisis and, 321–3
ultra vires review
conferral principle and, 214–16
democratic input legitimacy and, 221–6

ultima ratio review (*cont.*)
economic constitutionalism and, 148–50
European legal system and, 45–53
German Constitutional Court and, 90, 92–6
primacy principle and, 65–8
rule of law and, 216–17
unanimity requirement
ECJ jurisprudence and, 327–8
security provisions in Amsterdam Treaty and, 280n.17
uniformity, principle of
community law and, 57–8
economic constitutionalization and, 136–8
Union Courts, competences and procedures, 50–3
Union Fundamental Rights Agency, 49–50
Union of Member States, 333–40
United Kingdom
derogation policy of, 199–209
labour law and, 257–65
material constitution in, 10–14
United Kingdom v Parliament and Council, 197–8
United States
constitutionalism in, 108–12
EU anti-terrorism cooperation with, 282–4
federalism in, 164–9, 345–8
legal discourse in, 120–4
national security concepts in, 291–2
pre-emption doctrine in, 72–4, 202–6
universality, legal pluralism and, 86–8
universal services, law on, regulatory private law and, 257–65
UN Security Council, Resolutions 1373 and 1390, 282–4
US Constitution, 269

validation
speech acts and, 120–4
supremacy *vs* primacy and, 70–1
Van Duyn case, 62–3
Van Gend en Loos case, 52n.15, 53–9
constitutional identity and, 333–40
direct effect of European law and, 60–8, 70, 321–3
Eurozone regime and, 199–209
fundamental rights protections and, 96–9, 316–18, 324–5
international law and, 344
juridical constitutionalization and, 136–8
national law and, 88–9
Van Rompuy Working Group, 198
variable geometry principle
security constitutions and, 275–6
transnationalism and intergovernmentalism and, 333–40
Verfassungslehre (Schmitt), 13–14, 132–4
competition law and, 128–31, 132–4, 135–6, 161–4
Vienna Convention on the Law of Treaties, 341
Viking case, 27–8, 146n.50
economic *vs* fundamental rights and, 168–9
social justice and, 265–8
social policy of Member States and, 234–7, 251–6
Von Colson case, 63–5
von der Groeben, Hans, 138–40, 169–73
von Gerber, Carl Friedrich, 314
Vorverständnis of legal actors
European constitutional discourse and, 112–20
judicial roles and, 113
legal diversity and, 81–6
national courts and, 328–9
perspectivism and, 78–81, 102–7, 355–8
state of exception and, 289–96

wage flexibility, macroeconomic constitutionalization and, 251–6
Waldron, Jeremy, 302
Walker, Neil, 4–5
Walrave and Koch case, 145–6
Walter Lippmann Colloquium, 130n.10
Watts v Bedford Primary Care Trust and Secretary of State for Health, 237–8n.18
Weber, Max, 272–3
Wegmann, Milene, 130n.10
Weiler, Joseph, 3
Weimar Republic, 122–4
economic constitutionalism and, 128–31
Schmitt's constitutional theory and, 13–14, 122–4
Weinberger, Ota, 22
welfare policy
denationalization and deterritorialization of, 248–51
European constitutionalism and, 227–32
internal market law and, 237–43
Maastricht Treaty fiscal policy and, 183–7
macroeconomic constitutionalization and, 251–6
mobile workers and citizens, 243–8
'welfare tourism', welfare services for mobile workers and citizens and, 243–8

Werner Group, 177–8, 182
Wettbewerb und Monopolkampf (Böhm), 132–4, 167–8
Wirtschaftsverfassung (postwar German economic policy), 135–6
workers' rights, welfare services for mobile workers and citizens, 243–8
World Trade Organization (WTO)
  ECJ denial of law by, 59
  transnational law and, 349–58

www.ingramcontent.com/pod-product-compliance
Lightning Source LLC
LaVergne TN
LVHW011531200926
848484LV00001B/223

* 9 7 8 1 1 0 7 0 8 7 0 9 5 *